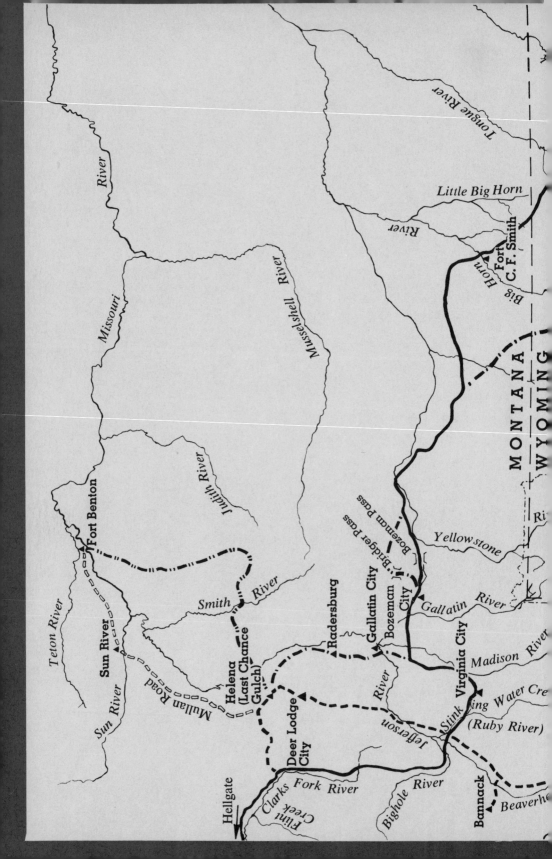

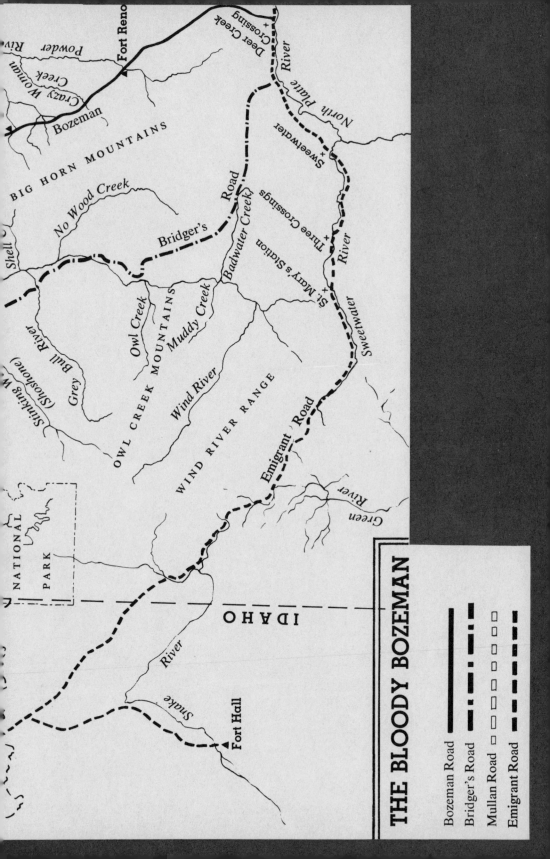

THE BLOODY BOZEMAN

Bozeman Road
Bridger's Road
Mullan Road
Emigrant Road

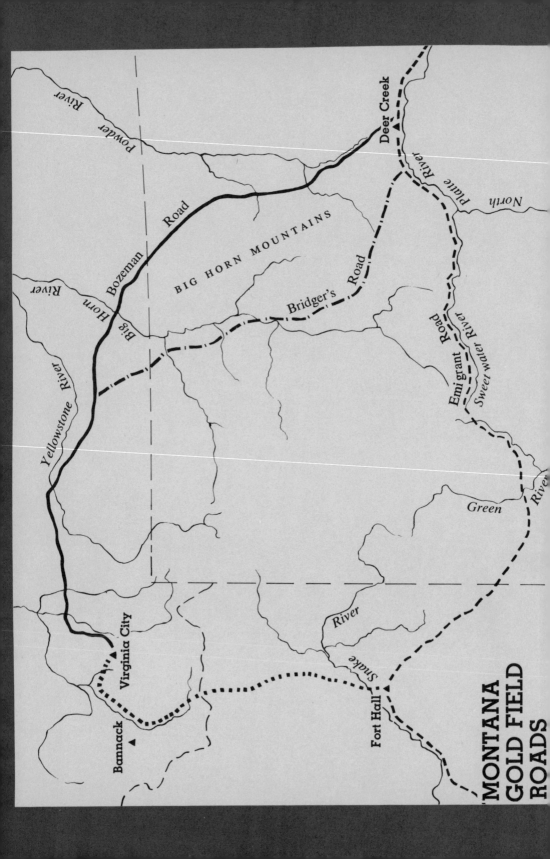

THE BLOODY BOZEMAN

BOOKS BY DOROTHY M. JOHNSON

Beulah Bunny Tells All
The Hanging Tree
A Man Called Horse (*original title* Indian Country)
The Bloody Bozeman

For Young Readers

Famous Lawmen of the Old West
Greece: Wonderland of the Past and Present
Farewell to Troy
Some Went West
Flame on the Frontier
Warrior for a Lost Nation
Western Badmen
Montana
Witch Princess

BOOKS IN THE AMERICAN TRAILS SERIES

DOOMED ROAD OF EMPIRE
The Spanish Trail of Conquest
  by Hodding Carter

THE GREAT NORTH TRAIL
America's Route of the Ages
  by Dan Cushman

THE DEVIL'S BACKBONE
The Story of the Natchez Trace
  by Jonathan Daniels

THE OLD POST ROAD
The Story of the Boston Post Road
  by Stewart H. Holbrook

WESTWARD VISION
The Story of the Oregon Trail
  by David Lavender

THE GOLDEN ROAD
The Story of California's Spanish Mission Trail
  by Felix Riesenberg, Jr.

THE GATHERING OF ZION
The Story of the Mormon Trail
  by Wallace Stegner

THE CALIFORNIA TRAIL
An Epic with Many Heroes
  by George R. Stewart

THE EL DORADO TRAIL
The Story of the Gold Rush Routes across Mexico
  by Ferol Egan

THE BLOODY BOZEMAN
The Perilous Trail to Montana's Gold
  by Dorothy M. Johnson

IN PREPARATION

THE SANTA FE TRAIL *by William Brandon*

THE SISKIYOU TRAIL *by Richard Dillon*

THE LONG TRAIL *by Gardner Soule*

THE GREAT PHILADELPHIA WAGON
  ROAD *by Parke Rouse*

THE TRANS-CANADA CANOE
  TRAIL *by David Lavender*

Dorothy M. Johnson

THE BLOODY

The Perilous

BOZEMAN

Trail to Montana's Gold

McGRAW-HILL BOOK COMPANY

New York   Toronto

Library of Congress Catalog Card Number: 70-163845

FIRST EDITION

07-032576-6

To Peter and Suzann Stickney
Good friends, good neighbors

Contents

CONTENTS

CONTENTS

CONTENTS

Acknowledgments

Great credit is due to those who have saved the letters and journals of pioneers and have made them available for research in libraries. The late Nellie Kirkaldie Gray, daughter of Franklin Kirkaldie, kept the letters her father wrote to her mother during their five years of separation. Mrs. Gray's daughter-in-law, Mrs. Irene Askew Gray of Bozeman, presented them to the Montana Historical Society. Copies are also in the Library of Montana State University, Bozeman.

Don Fletcher, Bozeman, and Fred L. Gibson, Livingston, gave the letters of Ellen Gordon Fletcher to the Montana State University Library. Mrs. Bert Gibson, Clyde Park, daughter of M. A. Switzer, made his reminiscences available to libraries. The touching story of Mrs. Busick, written by one of her daughters, Mrs. Elizabeth E. O'Neil, came from Miss Laverne O'Neil, Seattle.

John Comfort, Virginia City, let me make notes from copies of the Vigilantes' fragmentary remaining records. His great-uncle, John Lott, was the Vigilantes' treasurer. William A. Bertsche, Jr., of Great Falls, lent me the original journals kept by members of the Wilbur Fisk Sanders family.

Miss Cyrile Van Duser, Missoula, introduced me to the site of old Fort Phil Kearny several years ago. Miss Lillian Hornick, Missoula, was my good companion on another trip to some of Wyoming's historical sites in 1969, and Mrs. Elsa Spear Byron, dedicated history buff of Sheridan, Wyoming, showed me battlegrounds and routes. Mrs. Helen M. Peterson, publisher of the *Hardin* (Montana) *Tribune-Herald*, took me to the now quiet meadow where the Hayfield Fight occurred and to Fort Smith, the modern town named for Fort C. F. Smith.

Norman Weinstein, Helena, introduced me to Robbers Roost, where road agents took their ease while waiting for the next gold-bearing traveler to come along. Mrs. Zena Hoff, Virginia City, has brought the violent years of Alder Gulch to life for me many times as we walked with the ghosts of villains and Vigilantes.

Fred Burnell and Peter Stickney, U.S. Forest Service, and Dr.

ACKNOWLEDGMENTS

William M. Fry, all of Missoula, helped me over rough spots on the Bozeman Trail with old and new maps, and Mr. Burnell made the maps for this book.

Ford Bovey, Virginia City, and Dean Robert Van Horne, University of Montana, cleared up for me the method of weighing gold. Other especially kind people at the University were Dr. Carling Malouf, Larry Barsness (author of *Gold Camp*), and Dale Johnson.

Many dedicated librarians searched out old documents and rare books. Particularly helpful were Miss Minnie Paugh, Montana State University, Bozeman; Mrs. Harriett Meloy, Montana Historical Society, Helena; Dr. Gene M. Gressley, University of Wyoming, Laramie; Mrs. Alys Freeze, Denver Public Library; and Judith Austin, Idaho State Historical Society.

My thanks are due to Dr. Merrill Burlingame, professor emeritus at Montana State University, for manuscript material; Mrs. Robert James, Grant, Montana; Dr. Robert Athearn, University of Colorado, Boulder; Dr. Daniel O. Magnussen, Stout State University, Menomonie, Wisconsin; Thomas Edward White, Fort Laramie National Historic Site, Wyoming; Clifford D. Coover, Shelby, Montana; Don Anderson, Madison, Wisconsin (who made available a manuscript about Nelson Story); and A. B. Guthrie, Jr., of Missoula.

DOROTHY M. JOHNSON
Missoula, Montana

1862

□□□□□□□□□□

□□□□□□□□□□

Before the Bozeman Trail

The Bozeman Trail was the road to the gold in Montana. It led only to Montana, up from the great transcontinental Emigrant Trail, and it was blazed only after gold was known surely to be there for the taking. The Bozeman Trail, the Bozeman Cutoff, the Montana Road—it went by all these names—shortened the route to the rich new gold fields by some 400 weary, plodding miles. On the Bozeman Road, wagon trains no longer had to cross the backbone of the continent twice.

But the long way was safer, as safety went in those parts in the 1860s. The enraged Sioux Indians fought the palefaces for every mile of the bloody Bozeman as long as it lasted—only six years. John Bozeman and John Jacobs marked the trail in 1863, the Army established three forts on it in 1866, and in 1868 the U.S. government gave up and abandoned the beleaguered forts. The Indians had won that war.

The new road was not for the handful of hardy frontiersmen and professional prospectors who were in present Montana already. They had drifted up from California or the diggings in Colorado Territory, a few had come down from Canada, and some had used the Missouri River for their road, fighting the current up to the inland port of Fort Benton.

The Bozeman Trail was for a kind of man who was new in wilderness Montana, the man who came hopefully out from the States to better his condition. He was a farmer eking out a living somewhere in the Middle West or fleeing the catastrophes of the War of the Rebellion. Or he was a lawyer or a doctor or a storekeeper, doing better than eking but wanting to do better still. He went west to find prosperity. He plodded beside his ox team to put behind him the sickening sights and smells of barns and houses burned by the Yanks or the Rebs or to escape being drafted.

This new man was not a born adventurer, but in his stubborn, sometimes cautious way he was a gambler. He knew or soon learned that hostile Indians barred the trail through the Powder

River country of present Wyoming. He gambled his life to better his condition, but he didn't really believe that *his* hair might make fringes for a Sioux or Cheyenne war shirt or that *his* mutilated body might be clawed out of a shallow grave by wolves. He preferred not to face the fact that, if he should be captured, he might scream prayers for the mercy of death for hours before that mercy came.

There was gold in the northern Rockies, in a tumbled spread of mountains cut with deep canyons and perilous rivers. E. D. Pierce, lately come from California, found gold in October of 1861 where Oro Fino Creek flows into the Clearwater. He talked the suspicious Nez Percé Indians into letting him and his friends pan the gravel. Gold seekers were highly excitable; no more than a whispered rumor was needed to bring them slogging through that country with all their worldly goods roped on the back of a pack horse. Thousands of them swarmed into present Idaho in '62. There was gold on the Salmon River. There was gold in the Boise Basin. The prospectors whooped and hollered and built sluices of boards they whipsawed with great labor or bought at great cost.

And a few of them wandered eastward across the Continental Divide into what is now Montana. There were rumors of placers near Deer Lodge. There were rumors that you probably couldn't get to the Pierce and Florence mines in present Idaho anyway from wherever you happened to be, inching your way from Denver or Salt Lake, where you had picked up information from someone who seemed to know.

The northern Rockies were tough to travel in. If one side of your wagon tipped too much as you traversed a steep side slope, you stopped and changed wheels, with much labor and appropriate language. You took the big hind wheel off the uphill side, took off the smaller front wheel from the downhill side, and switched them. With the two big wheels downhill on the slope, you had a better chance to escape upsetting the whole vehicle and damaging wagon, freight, and passengers. If the passengers had good sense, they walked. When you got off that side slope, you changed wheels again. And at some places, in some seasons, no amount of struggle could get you through, so you went to some other place that was more accessible, because gold is where you find it.

One wagon train coming up from Denver City reached a grasshopper-infested area along a stream on the evening of July 27,

1862. They gave it an obvious, appropriate name, Grasshopper Creek.[1]

The movers camped there for the night, and the next day the men went prospecting for gold. They always did, everywhere they went. That very day three men found gold in placer diggings so rich that the event made history. This was what they were looking for, free gold in the dirt and gravel of a stream bed, gold that a man could wash out with crude equipment—with no more than his gold pan if that was all he had. No investment of imported capital was required, although quartz mining came later to Grasshopper Creek. Placer mining was a poor man's dream.

Later major gold discoveries in Montana are well documented, even down to where the discoverers came from originally and who said what when the shining glory showed in the pan, but this one is shadowy. It usually gets no more mention than "John White and party found a rich placer on July 28."

The "party" consisted of Charlie Reville and William Still, whose names everybody soon forgot. John White was better remembered because he was murdered eighteen months later.

Word of the Grasshopper diggings spread fast. More people came. Between fifty and seventy-five miners were at work by September 8 when a ten-wagon train of supplies intended for the Deer Lodge area pulled in. Here was a market, so the train unloaded. The new, temporary camp might have starved without that freight, because everybody was too busy to worry yet about supplies for the winter. Later that month, however, twenty-five men from Grasshopper Creek, with nine ox teams and six mule teams, stopped digging long enough to go down to Salt Lake, more than 300 miles, for more supplies. It was hard for any man to turn his back on all that pay dirt! An estimated $700,000 in gold was taken out of the Grasshopper diggings before winter freezing stopped operations.

It was time to build some cabins, or at least to throw together some wakiups of brush and poles. Nobody expected to be comfortable, but nobody cared to freeze, and freezing was easy in that high country. A saloon was built, and a story about one of the customers indicates what the term "pay dirt" meant. This man walked in with a lot of mud on his boots, and someone said, "I'll bet he's carrying around a lot of gold on his shoes." Just for fun, the boys scraped off the mud and washed $5 worth of gold out of it.

The camp became known as Bannack City, named for the Bannock Indians. Nobody worried about how to spell either one.

The uneasy temporary population of Bannack City that winter included at least thirty-six women. Some of these ladies had been wandering for a long time with their menfolks, and this gold camp was no more dismal or uncomfortable than the others they had lived in.

Years later, when they had become Pioneer Settlers, no longer homeless wanderers, some of them argued about who were the very first women to get there. Perhaps the first were Smith Ball's wife and sister; perhaps, Wilson Waddams' wife and his daughter Sarah, who was in her teens. Sarah was really an old settler when she died at ninety-three.

The miners built what they had to build. One structure was an eight-sided log fort for protection from the Indians. The Bannocks and Snakes were sometimes troublesome and demanding because they were suspicious of these invading whites, but they were a lot more friendly than the tribes farther east in Montana.

The miners cooperated to dig ditches, because you can't placer without water, and your claim may be far from a stream. But Bannack, in its beginnings, lacked a competent engineer. One ditch that was dug with great toil turned out to be useless because it went uphill.

They lived harshly and precariously at the Grasshopper diggings. When they did build cabins, the floors were dirt and the roofs leaked. A child might have to hold an open umbrella over Mama while she made bread. This was less for Mama's comfort than to keep the dirt on top of the roof from dripping into the dough.

What that rough camp was like in its first winter is told in a letter that Mrs. Emily R. Meredith, age twenty-six, wrote home to America the following spring, April 30, 1863. She and her husband had arrived there by accident. At the Snake River, near present Blackfoot, Idaho, they were warned in early September that the snow was too deep to permit them to reach the Salmon River mines. There was, however, a shadow of hope for a living at the mines "at Deer Lodge."

Deer Lodge, now a town in western Montana, was then a vaguely defined area where a changing group of white men were working at one thing or another—trading with Indians, raising a little grain, prospecting for gold.

The Merediths didn't get to Deer Lodge, either. But they reached Bannack about September 6 and looked around.

"The diggings did not then appear very rich," Mrs. Meredith wrote, "but they paid very good wages, and that was a great mercy to the scores and hundreds of people who arrived there about bankrupt."

The Merediths were too doubtful about their prospects to build a house the first month they were there, but the weather was good, mining could continue, and the gold didn't play out. Prices were high and kept going up—flour, $1.50 a sack back home, was $25 here—but the populace finally realized how really rich the mines were. On one claim, $2,500 was rocked out [2] in three hours. Emily saw the weighing of gold that was washed out of one wheelbarrow full of dirt: two ounces,[3] $36 at current prices for clean gold.

"A person ought to make money pretty fast here to pay them for living in such a place," she wrote. Two-thirds of the people were "infidels and 'secesh.' " She didn't know how many deaths had occurred during the winter, "but that there have not been twice as many is entirely owing to the fact that drunken men do not shoot well."

In Bannack's interracial clash, the Indians were in danger from the whites instead of the other way around. Hoodlums fired into the tepees of a group of Shoshones, Bannocks, and Paiutes who camped there while passing through to hunt. Five Indians and two white men were killed. The arrogant badmen were arrested and tried in one of the catch-as-catch-can court procedures that were the best a new settlement could arrange, and there was talk of hanging them, but they were banished instead. Men who had anything to do with their arrest received vicious, threatening letters.

The Merediths had very little money when they arrived, but Emily's husband made hay that he sold for $12 to $20 a ton. He could have got $100 during the winter but he needed money at once and couldn't wait. He speculated—everybody speculated, with their labor, lives, and money—by sending two yoke of oxen and $100 to Salt Lake to buy flour. He had the oxen and the wagon sold in exchange for flour, which he paid to have freighted back by wagon—and then the price went down to $10 a sack.

He speculated by investing $400 in the building of a good two-room house made of sawed logs. He sold it at cost to move to Gallatin City at the three forks of the Missouri River and try farming. The Gallatin Valley was great for fattening cattle, but sixteen head of his were stolen on the way down, so the Merediths sold their supply of seed after five weeks, gave up the idea of farming, and returned to Bannack in March, 1863.

They paid $15 a month rent for one room with a dirt floor. Meredith could get work driving a team, mining, or digging ditches at $4 a day, but he hurt his side and was laid up with a racking cough.

With two partners, he bought some grazing land and grazed stock at $1.50 a head for cattle, $2 a head for horses. Because he offered the security of insurance on this stock, he had plenty of business— 200 head by the end of his first month in the business. It wasn't easy money. He and his partners had to take turns staying out there every night to guard the customers' stock. That was how they insured them.

Emily Meredith detested infidels, secessionists, drunks, and other sinners, but she didn't complain about physical discomforts. "If I only had a house with a floor in it and a stove," she wrote, "I should consider myself quite fixed." But she had learned to cook very well in a fireplace, so she didn't really need a stove, and she admitted that in the dirt-floored one room she was living more comfortably than most people in the camp.

CHAPTER 2

The Footloose Ones

What is now western Montana was not quite devoid of white inhabitants in 1862 when the crowds began to come to Bannack. There were some aging mountain men and Indian traders, left over from the days of beaver trapping, who had taken Indian wives and raised families of half-blood children. They often lived like Indians, because that was a pretty good way to live and they were used to it. When a man had a snug elk-skin lodge for his home, and a wife or two to look after it, he could move whenever he took a notion, or go visit his old friends and his wife's relations. But some of them had permanent log houses that became the nuclei of settlements.

And there were young adventurers who had drifted around the West, trying their hand at one thing or another, competent fellows and self-reliant, who could live off the country (while wishing for bread and coffee and sugar), speak one or more Indian languages, raise some grain, whipsaw lumber, do blacksmithing, butcher a beef or a buffalo, and build a noose to hang a horse thief after they tried him fair and square.

They were of a later generation than the beaver trappers, the mountain men. There was a long-established road across the continent from the Missouri River leading to California and Oregon and Salt Lake City—the Oregon Trail, or the Overland Trail, or, as some called it, the Emigrant Road. These young adventurers had followed it westward, and they could go home again. Sometimes they thought they might. Some of them actually started.

They were strong, tough, flexible. They could adapt to almost any situation. They were not driven by anything. They were unencumbered by families or by ambition. They didn't have to make good, although they dreamed of getting rich. The fastest way to get rich was to find gold. And so, wherever they went, and whatever else they did, they pecked away at the gravel in stream beds and swirled it with water in a pan and looked for a show of colors.[4] And they dreamed.

Two of these fiddle-footed fellows were the Stuart brothers, James and Granville. James died when he was only forty-one but Granville lived to be eighty-four and became the very prototype of Montana pioneers. A cowboy who married one of his half-Indian daughters said of him, "Granville Stuart *was* the history of Montana."

James and Granville had been roaming around in California for five years when, in 1857, they decided to go back across the Plains, horseback, to see their folks in Iowa. They didn't get to Iowa.

Nine other footloose drifters decided to go along. They weren't doing anything that they couldn't stop. They weren't leaving anything behind that mattered. They rode out from Yreka, California, on June 14, 1857, each riding a horse or a mule, leading a pack animal for each two men's scanty belongings. They were pretty well armed, each man had blankets and a change of underwear, and they had grub for almost two months. What more could anyone want?

They lived off the country, made good time, and enjoyed the trip for a month. Then Granville took sick, on Malad Creek, 240 miles north of Salt Lake City—strangely enough, he had been very sick at the same place five years before, when he was going to California. This time he was so very ill with mountain fever [5] that his companions knew he couldn't travel for a long time, if he ever got well enough to travel at all. His brother James and a cousin, Rezin (Reese) Anderson, stayed there with him. The others, after waiting for ten days, went on to the States.

The sick man and his two relatives stayed at the camp of Jake Meeks, a trader who was spending the summer at a place on the Overland Trail sixty miles north of the site where Corinne, Utah, later developed. Granville's illness delayed the three men so long that they gave up the idea of going back to Iowa. They didn't dare try; as Granville wrote later, "The Mormons had all the roads leading to the States or California patrolled by Mormon troops, and arrested and carried into Salt Lake City all persons found going either way. And most of those so taken were never heard of again, for the feeling against all Gentiles was very bitter, because of the near approach of the United States army, under General A. S. Johnston."

The Stuarts and Anderson were in a bad spot. Meeks told them, "I'm going to winter in the Beaverhead. Why not come along up there?" They had never heard of the Beaverhead, but nobody (barring possibly a few Indians) would dispute their passage to it, so they went. And helped make history.

They crossed the Continental Divide, from west to east, at Monida Pass in October, 1857. They were in Oregon—not that the name mattered much. Later the place where they wintered would be in Washington, then in Idaho, then in Montana. At the time, designations of smaller areas were more important.

The Beaverhead was beautiful country, with tall bunch grass that waved in the wind like a field of grain. Game was plentiful—antelope, elk, bighorn sheep, black-tailed deer—and that was a good thing, because after their civilized grub gave out they lived on meat alone.

A dozen or more white men lived within a radius of twenty-five miles, most of them with Indian wives and half-blood families. The Stuarts and Anderson were very comfortable in an elk-skin tepee, part of a group of ten persons including the Indian wives of two of the men. They did some trading with the Indians, occasionally visited neighbors a few miles away, and grouched about the monotony of meat straight, especially toward spring, when the game was very lean. Wanting vegetables to vary the diet, they found that thistle roots, chopped out of the frozen ground with an axe, improved deer and antelope soup considerably.

One of their neighbors there, and later when they moved again, was a squaw man named John M. Jacobs, described as "a red-bearded Italian." He had long been a wanderer in the mountains. In 1863 he was to help John M. Bozeman mark the rough road that became known as the Bozeman Trail. Sometimes it was called the Bozeman-Jacobs Trail, but Jacobs, who helped make history, was destined for obscurity.

In the spring of 1858, the Stuarts, Anderson, and a man named Ross moved over to the Deer Lodge Valley to see about a rumor. A Red River half-breed named Benetsee was said to have found gold there in 1852.

The Stuarts weren't making history yet. They were just living, and wandering, and working up to a rage every time the Blackfeet stole some of their horses. They wandered back to Mormon country, quieter now, traded horses, traded cattle, and in the spring of 1861 they were back in the Deer Lodge, irked by the horse-stealing propensities of Indians of various tribes.

What life was like for white men in 1861 in eastern Washington Territory—which became Idaho and then Montana—is made vivid in Granville Stuart's *Forty Years on the Frontier,* based on the journals that he and his brother James took turns keeping. They settled down, more or less, in the Deer Lodge Valley at a place that became known as American Fork and later as Gold Creek.

They had a few white men as neighbors. They had many visitors, both white and Indian. A good Indian was one who didn't steal their horses. To such, and there were many, the Stuarts extended hospitality if they came a few at a time, and even credit for trade goods. For furs the brothers exchanged what the Indians wanted: calico, combs, red cloth for women's leggings, vermilion paint, beads, knives, powder, lead, percussion caps.

Gossip about the neighbors enlivened their days. For example, one Indian wife, Mrs. Dempsey, was busy chopping wood when Charles Allen came along half drunk and began to order her around. She swung with the axe but missed. He grabbed her by the hair. In no time his face looked as if he had tangled with a wildcat

—which he had. She grabbed a stick of wood and blacked both his eyes and knocked out a tooth.

"Mrs. Dempsey is known in these parts to be a lady of uncertain temper," commented Granville, "but 'more power to her elbow,' say we all, for who could put up with the gang of drunken loafers that hang around Dempsey's without losing their temper."

The Stuarts raised some cattle and grain, kept a few horses, planted a garden (almost everything froze), and had high hopes of gold from the ground they constantly prospected. And they had a great treasure: five books. Some Indians had brought word that a white man in the Bitterroot Valley had a trunk full of them. The Stuart brothers wrapped up their blankets and some dried meat, saddled their horses, and set off for those books, 150 miles away, with three dangerous rivers to ford.

On arrival, they found that the owner of the books had gone somewhere else, and the man who had them (in the tepee where he lived) had no authority to sell them. The Stuarts made a good case for their need of reading matter and promised to take all the blame if the owner objected to the sale. They talked the possessor into selling them five books at $5 each—half the money they possessed —and went happily back to their ranch.

It was hard to choose among the books, but they decided on illustrated editions of Shakespeare and Byron, a Bible in French, Headley's *Napoleon and His Marshals*, and Adam Smith's *Wealth of Nations*. When Granville was an old man, he still had all but the last-named, which had disintegrated from handling.

The Stuarts did not use liquor, and this abstemiousness saved them both money and trouble. James was a great one for poker, but by no means the luckiest player in the community. He resolved to give up gambling, but he noted his losses thereafter with dismal regularity. On the other hand, once he came back from a six-day trip with winnings of $425.

There wasn't a great deal of amusement aside from cards and an occasional shooting match at a target. When Granville got a new Maynard rifle, with brass cartridges that he could reload and use over, he felt competent to beat anybody, but an old Indian named Pushigan shot so much better that the brothers lost all the money they had with them and the horses they were riding as well.

That year James received from the East some things he had sent for: a few medical books, some surgical instruments, and a supply of drugs. James was educated far beyond the average of frontiersmen. Back home in Iowa, he had finished a year of high school, had "read medicine" under the tutelage of a physician, and attended a course or two of medical lectures. His brother Granville described him as one of the best-read physicians and surgeons in Montana—even later, when several of them drifted in—but James practiced only among his friends and not for pay.

In July, James came back, disgusted, from a thirty-eight-day horseback journey up to Fort Benton to buy supplies. Fort Benton was the head of navigation on the Missouri River. In the summer of 1859 the steamboat *Chippewa* had reached that point; the following year the *Chippewa* and the *Key West* both arrived July 2. So in 1861 it was reasonable to expect a couple of steamboats. But James waited around for an interminable time before the news came that the *Chippewa* wasn't going anywhere any more.

Four hundred miles downstream, a fool deckhand had gone down to the hold with a lighted candle to steal alcohol out of a barrel. The alcohol caught fire, and when the fire reached twenty-five kegs of gunpowder, the boat blew up. Packages of damaged merchandise were found three miles away. No steamboats at all reached Fort Benton in 1861.

On the way to Benton, with a companion, James had no tea, coffee, sugar, or bread, nothing but poor buffalo bull meat. His mouth watered for civilized grub. But he went back to Gold Creek on the same dull ration of tough meat and cold water, and he was justifiably mad.

When some freight wagons went by, that was newsworthy. They came from Salt Lake City, 500 miles away. Flour and other staples could be brought in from Fort Walla Walla, only 425 miles to the west, but the road through the mountains was so nearly impassable that Walla Walla might as well have been in the Sandwich Islands.

Not until July 15, 1861, did the little settlement at American Fork learn that there was a war going on—and had been for three months. A worn scrap of newspaper came to the community, passed from one man to another, and Granville wrote: "Bad news from the states. The North and South are fighting." Thereafter, the Stuart journals and American Fork ignored the war, being unable to find out anything about it anyway.

So the good life went for the sturdy, adventurous, self-sufficient pioneers in western Montana in 1861. It was never the same after that, for the following year brought more white men—even a few white women!—and John White "and party" made the rich discovery at Grasshopper Creek—richer placer diggings than the hardworking, hopeful Stuarts ever found.

CHAPTER 3

The Year Things Changed

For James and Granville Stuart and their neighbors around American Fork, the year 1862 began with a real wingding, a grand ball at John Grant's place, eight miles from the Stuarts'. All the ladies were at least half Indian, dressed to kill in bright calico with scarlet leggings, beaded moccasins, plaid blankets, and all the ornaments they could fasten on. Their children, too, were duded up in bead-trimmed buckskin ornamented with fringes and embroidery of dyed porcupine quills.

The Stuarts, like the other men, trimmed their hair and beards, shook some of the wrinkles out of their best flannel shirts, and made themselves fine in fringed and beaded buckskin suits.

The party lasted for three days, although it wasn't planned that way. The guests danced all night to the music of two fiddles and then couldn't go home because of a howling blizzard. So after breakfast on New Year's Day they all went to bed in their clothes, on buffalo robes spread on the floor of the several rooms in Johnny Grant's house. His wife and some other women roused and prepared dinner, served at two o'clock in the afternoon, and then everybody danced some more until nine in the evening, when they stopped for supper.

The blizzard was still going on, so they danced until it stopped, around daylight on January 3. After another breakfast—it was a good thing the Grant ménage had plenty of grub—men, women, and children rode home on horseback. The weather was bitter cold and snow was fourteen inches deep, but everybody made it.

Two weeks later Granville wrote:

All the women in this part of the country have been at John Grant's, having I suppose an Indian Dorcas Society something after the manner of their white sisters, and like them it has broken up in a row. All the women have left for home. That is, they have joined their own people, leaving a goodly number of widowers.

The next thing on the agenda was for the widowers to hunt up missing wives and pay a horse or some good blankets to their fathers-in-law to get the women back.

There was much coming and going, even in winter, and all travelers stopped with the Stuarts. Bannocks chased Flatheads, who had stolen some horses, and brought back the horses and two scalps. In February, the journal noted that two Flatheads had found a Snake Indian camped, so they killed him and took his lodge, eight horses, and one of his three wives. The other two got away. One of the Flatheads brought the captive woman to the Stuart place, where James and a man named Powell ransomed her so she wouldn't be made a slave by the Flathead women. "This woman is fair with red cheeks and brown hair and eyes and is evidently half white," James noted.

On February 27 the journal relates, "Thos. Adams took unto himself a wife last night. The bride is Louise, Lone-penny's step-daughter, a Flathead damsel."

A few days later James brought his ransomed captive Snake woman home from the Powells', because Powell's wife didn't want her around, and anyway the Stuarts had no cook, so "it seems to fall to my lot to take her and take care of her at least until we can turn her over to some of her own people, should she wish to go.

"I might do worse," James commented. "She is neat and rather good-looking and seems to be of a good disposition. So, I find myself a married man. Granville says 'Marrying is rapidly becoming an epidemic in our little village.'" Such was romance in the Rockies! James didn't even mention his new helpmate's name.

Adams' wife left him, by mutual agreement, after less than a week of informal wedded bliss. He must have had and lost another Flathead wife before her, however, because on October 28 the journal noted:

Indian village moved today. Everybody trading for Indian horses. . . . Thomas Adams captured his little boy from the Indians. The boy's mother left Adams; going back to her tribe and Adams had not seen the child before, but when he found him with the village he took him. The little fellow cannot speak English and is weeping bitterly for his Indian relatives.

Two days later:

Adams's little boy wept all night and we persuaded him to let the child join his Indian mother. He has finally consented and handed the boy over to a couple of Flatheads, who will join the village tomorrow. The child is once more happy.

On May 2, James wrote:

Granville was married today to Aubony, a Snake Indian girl, a sister of Fred Burr's wife. She has been living with Burr's family, is a fairly good cook, of an amiable disposition, and with few relatives.

This lack of family was an advantage to the bridegroom, who would be expected to entertain his wife's relatives *ad nauseam*. Aubony, also called Ellen, bore nine children to Granville and also brought up two sons of James.

The Stuarts' little community was amused by news from the settlement over at Hell Gate (precursor of present Missoula), where the citizens were putting on airs and had a justice of the peace. Montana's first court trial had just been held there.

Tin Cup Joe sued "Baron" O'Keefe for killing a horse. Harsh words were exchanged in court. O'Keefe yelled that the judge was a squaw man whose only business was to populate the country with half-breeds. Then almost everybody got into the fight, which was declared a draw. The jury, which had quietly sneaked out, came back with a verdict that O'Keefe owed Tin Cup Joe $40 damages, but the boys at American Fork, hashing it over later, agreed that they wouldn't care to be the ones who had to make the fiery Baron pay the judgment.

There was war news, but not about the War of the Rebellion way back in America. These were local wars, Gros Ventres versus Piegans, some Nez Percés versus some Bannocks.

In this year of 1862 the Stuarts went into placer mining seriously. Using 1000 feet of whipsawed lumber at 10¢ a foot, they set the first sluices [6] in Montana. Everybody around was washing dirt, but nobody was getting rich at $3 from a hundred pans. Still, it looked promising. Two men working together panned out $10 one day, $9 the next; another made about $3.50 in three hours.

The Stuarts, with their sluices, in one cleanup found $12, most of it in one nugget, the first ever found in Montana. Granville kept it all his life. But another cleanup brought only $4.25 for two days' work. Exasperating business, gold mining—nobody was getting enough to shout for joy, but it was too good to quit. They felt they just hadn't struck the right spot yet. Granville remarked once that it is better to be lucky in mining than to have the wisdom of Solomon.

At the beginning of summer a party of sixteen eager miners, forerunners of many more, arrived at American Fork from Colorado. They were acquaintances of Thomas Stuart, brother of James and Granville, but Thomas didn't come until later.

In this party was John Merin Bozeman, age twenty-five, who had left his home, his wife, and three small daughters in Georgia two years before. He never saw them again. John was like his father, William; *he* left a wife and *five* children behind when he joined the California rush in '49. He was never heard from again.

More people came swarming in, most of them bound for somewhere else, preferably the mines farther west, in the Salmon River country. But they mostly didn't go on. Some had come up the Missouri from St. Louis; four steamboats made it to Fort Benton in June. The bunch from Colorado, called Pikes Peakers, found good prospects near Gold Creek and called their place Pikes Peak Gulch.

The finest thing that happened was the arrival, among other emigrants, of the Burchett family, B. B. Burchett, his wife, and "two very handsome daughters, one a blonde and the other a brunette, and two little tow-headed boys."

The Stuarts suddenly realized what they had been missing. "It looks like home," one of them wrote in their journal, "to see little blonde children playing about and to see white women. Miss Sallie Burchett is sixteen years old and a very beautiful girl. Every man in camp has shaved and changed his shirt since this family arrived. We are all trying to appear like civilized men."

The community faced up to incoming civilization in another way: sprawling Missoula County, Washington Territory, held an election on July 16. Thirty men voted. Granville Stuart was elected one of two county commissioners, and James was elected sheriff: but they didn't take office until some time later.

That was an exciting summer. Another white lady arrived: handsome, seventeen-year-old Mrs. J. B. Caven, with her husband, known as Buz. He was welcome, too, for he was a fine violin player. Now there was elevating society in the community. The journal noted:

> We purchased a good violin sometime ago, so we have the Cavens over often and enjoy the society of an intellectual white woman and good music. Certainly we are approaching civilization or rather civilization is coming to us. All the men are shaving nowadays and most of them indulge in an occasional haircut. The blue flannel shirt with a black necktie has taken the place of the elaborately beaded buckskin one. The white men wear shoes instead of moccasins and most of us have selected some other day than Sunday for wash day.

James was not yet officially sheriff; he hadn't taken the oath or made bond. But that didn't keep him from setting out with a companion for Fort Benton on July 25 after a horse thief. They overtook the fellow next day and were home with him on the twenty-eighth. They called a miners' court, which tried him and found him guilty. But he was young and contrite; they couldn't bear to inflict the normal penalty, hanging. He was sentenced to restore all the stolen property he had with him and to leave within twelve hours. But he was destitute, so the court—that is, the whole camp—took up a collection of $15 and some provisions and sent him on his way.

On the same day when the contrite horse thief was hustled out of camp by a lot of miners who weren't so hard-boiled as they thought they were, John White "and party" hit pay dirt down south on Grasshopper Creek. Three days later, John M. Jacobs arrived at American Fork from Soda Springs in Idaho with a train of forty wagons, heading over the mountains to Fort Walla Walla. He didn't bring news of the Grasshopper gold strike. He must have been past there when it occurred. Strangely enough, the Stuart journal doesn't mention when this news arrived, although on August 10 there was "a general stampede over the mountains to Powell's new discovery." Powell was a neighbor; he may have gone to Grasshopper and sent back word.

The Stuarts' cousin, Rezin Anderson, arrived unexpectedly on August 15 from the States, with news and letters from home, and the men stayed up all night talking, but the journal doesn't mention what news he brought of the war back there. He had been with the

Stuarts before, had gone down the Missouri in a Mackinaw boat in the spring of 1861, and they thought he had joined the Army.

Late in August, two miners from the gold fields west of the mountains arrived in American Fork looking for stolen horses. And sure enough, there were the horses, ridden in a few days before by three fellows, card sharps, who came with six good horses and precious little else.

When the two miners, Bull and Fox, asked for help in arresting the horse thieves, the local citizens were glad to comply, because a horse thief was the lowest form of life known. Steal a man's horse and set him afoot, and he could well die in the wilderness. James Stuart had not yet taken the oath or made bond as sheriff, so it was simply as an enraged citizen that he took part in the proceedings that followed.

Fox and Bull caught the youngest of the three villains—a young man named C. W. Spillman, whose appearance impressed everyone favorably—and tied him up while they went for the other two. These were found running a monte game in a saloon. William Arnett, who acted like a real tough, was dealing, with a Colt's Navy revolver across his knee. Ordered to throw up his hands, he grabbed his gun, but Bull shot and killed him instantly. B. F. Jermagin begged, "Don't shoot, don't shoot, I give up!" The posse tied him and young Spillman up until morning.

They began the day by burying Arnett with the cards still clenched in his left hand and the revolver in his right. Then they held a short, no-nonsense trial. Jermagin claimed that the others had picked him up along the trail and he had no idea where they got those horses. Spillman admitted that this was true. So Jermagin was acquitted and warned to leave within six hours. He didn't need that much time to get out.

Then and for several years thereafter only two kinds of punishment were practical and common in the gold camps: death or banishment. There were no jail sentences because there were no jails, and nobody bothered much about petty offenses. Murder, horse stealing, and armed robbery were serious, but even these often went unpunished.

With Arnett buried and Jermagin banished, the miners tried young Spillman. They found him guilty and sentenced him to hang half an hour later. This was a strange young man. He didn't even argue. All he wanted was writing material so he could write a letter to his father, begging forgiveness for bringing disgrace on his family. His half hour wasn't up yet when he finished, but he told his captors that he was ready to go. They hanged him at 2:22 P.M., August 26, 1862. This was the first execution in Montana.

Nobody even thought of hanging Bull for shooting Arnett. Of course not. Arnett had it coming because he was a horse thief. Justice was as simple as that. But the Stuarts were deeply moved by the death of Spillman. James wrote that he "walked to his death with a step as firm and countenance as unchanged as if he had been the nearest spectator instead of the principal actor in the tragedy. It was evident that he was not a hardened criminal and there was no reckless bravado in his calmness. It was the firmness of a brave man, who saw that death was inevitable, and nerved himself to meet it." Spillman's last letter was not mailed to his father. It was thought kinder to let him wonder for the rest of his life what had become of his son.

Granville wrote many years later that he had always regretted that Spillman did not plead for his life, because probably the death penalty would have been commuted to banishment. He felt Spillman had got himself into a perilous situation and made no effort to get himself out, so what happened to him was really his own fault.

In September, Granville and F. H. Woody, a business partner of the Stuarts, started to Hell Gate to try to organize the government of sprawling Missoula County, Washington Territory. Granville was a county commissioner and Woody was county auditor. James now became sheriff by taking the oath and making bond.

Visitors came and went, including Captain James L. Fisk, who had just brought an expedition of 125 people across the Plains from Minnesota. This was a government-sponsored, well-guarded, and well-guided wagon train; and Fisk brought more emigrants in 1863, 1864, and 1866, the last time without government sponsorship or money.

Most of the newcomers who stopped at American Fork, Gold Creek, had never heard of it before but intended to go to the Florence area in present Idaho. Gold is gold, however, and the Stuarts and their neighbors in Pioneer and Pikes Peak Gulches were getting fair returns, so why not stay and look around?

The Fisk train had reached Fort Benton early in September, then followed the new Mullan Road and on the twenty-sixth stopped at American Fork to get some animals shod. The Mullan Wagon Road was another government project. It ran from Fort Walla Walla through the mountains and over the prairie to Fort Benton on the Missouri River. Its major purpose was not to get civilians to the gold fields, but to speed the movement of troops over to the Oregon country to fight the Indians who harassed settlers there. Troops and supplies could now come up the Missouri by steamboat and trudge the rest of the way on the Mullan military road. But anybody could use the road, and for a few years a great many people did. After Fisk got his wagon train to the Deer Lodge Valley, he continued on to Fort Walla Walla by the Mullan Road.

By October of 1862 the Stuarts had heard so much about the boom at the Grasshopper diggings, had talked to so many men who reported that everybody there was making money, that they decided to have a look for themselves. After the look, they judged that it would be smart to move down there and go into business. They hired a man to put up a log building for them there, twenty feet square, for $140. James Stuart and Frank H. Woody opened a store in it with stock from American Fork. Granville drove the cattle down to Bannack and set up in the meat business. Cousin Rezin continued with the money-making blacksmith shop at their old hangout. The Stuarts didn't always stay in Bannack. Sometimes they moved back to American Fork for a while.

Mining went well at the Grasshopper diggings, business was good, and outlawry became a highly profitable career for a bunch of the worst villains who ever set foot in a gold camp. Gone were the days, by the end of 1862, when the scattered pioneers of Montana lived in relative peace and did not worry very much about anything. In Bannack every man went armed. Everyone had reason to be suspicious about the past record and future intentions of almost everyone else.

That winter, back in the States, men who dreamed of bettering their condition prepared to set forth for the new gold fields as soon as grass was high enough to feed their animals in the spring of '63.

And at the Grasshopper diggings, young John Bozeman and old John Jacobs, with their hats on and their boots steaming in front of a sheet-iron stove, smoked their pipes and hashed over an idea:

Find and mark a short wagon route to Bannack from the Oregon Trail, the long Emigrant Road; cut three or four hundred miles off the distance via two mountain passes and Fort Hall, and collect for guide service.

The Yellowstone Expedition

So there was gold on Grasshopper Creek, no doubt about it. And a fair number of people lived there—uncomfortably, of course—during the first winter after discovery; enough people to stake out all the likely-looking claims that first fall and winter.[7]

If there was gold in one place, there must be gold in another. A man could get to a new discovery fast and still be too late. Why should a latecomer wring his hands at Bannack City? He might as well go look for a place of his own.

In the early spring of '63 a group of twenty-three men arranged to look over new country farther east, along the Yellowstone River and its tributaries.

On April 9, fourteen of them rode out of Bannack City, with pack horses carrying their grub and tools, bedding and tents. They went two or three at a time; a large group would have given the wary, watchful miners an idea that they should drop their spades and follow to a new and secret discovery.

The next day the explorers organized, set up some rules, and signed the following compact:

> Having determined to explore a portion of the country drained by the "Yellowstone," for the purpose of discovering gold mines and securing town sites, and believing this object could be better accomplished by forming ourselves into a regularly organized company, we hereby appoint James Stuart captain, agreeing upon our word of honor to obey all orders given or issued by him or any subordinate officer appointed by him. In case of any member refusing to obey an order or orders from said captain, he shall be forcibly expelled from our camp. It is further understood and agreed, that we all do our equal portion of work, the captain being umpire in all cases, sharing equally the benefits of said labor both as to the discovery of gold and securing town sites.

Then they signed it:

James Stuart	Samuel T. Hauser
Cyrus D. Watkins	Henry A. Bell
John Vanderbilt	William Roach
James N. York	A. Sterne Blake
Richard McCafferty	George H. Smith
James Hauxhurst	Henry T. Geery
Drewyer Underwood	Ephraim Bostwick

The fifteenth man, George Ives, caught up the next day—he had been looking for his horse, as somebody was always having to do—but did not sign. All fifteen shared desperate dangers and bloody battle. They set up only one townsite, and they found no gold worth dividing.

The Yellowstone Expedition was about run-of-the-mine in its makeup. Its members ran the gamut of available frontiersmen. Sam Hauser, for instance, became Governor of Montana Territory twenty-two years later. George Ives has a more lurid place in history. In December of the same year he rode with the Stuart group, Ives was hanged for an especially brutal murder, by no means his first.

Now there should have been twenty-three men, not fifteen.

The missing eight had been over at Deer Lodge (or LaBarge City or Cottonwood, different names for the same place) buying horses and supplies. They agreed to meet the Stuart party at the mouth of the Beaverhead River, but they missed that river altogether and went up the Stinking Water.

They never found Stuart's party, but five of the eight men found fame and fabulous, fleeting fortune through a series of strange and perilous coincidences.

The eight who never connected with Stuart were William Fairweather, Henry Edgar (who kept a journal in a memorandum book), Tom Cover, Barney Hughes, Mike Sweeney, Harry Rodgers, Lew Simmons, and George Orr. The first six had prospected together in the Salmon River country in Idaho, arriving at the Grasshopper diggings late in the fall of 1862.

They left Deer Lodge on March 23, and they left George Orr, too. At the last minute he decided to stay there and work. If the others came back broke, he joshed, he would have a grubstake for them.

The other seven rode and camped, lost their horses several times but found them again, hunted and fished, prospected and argued. And every day they hoped to meet the Stuart party. On April 16 they came upon a trail made by shod horses and concluded that they were catching up. For days they kept on that trail. On April 26 they camped where Stuart's party had been only two days before; they found a note that said so.

On May 1 they saw *unshod* pony tracks—therefore Indian horses, an estimated thousand of them, and those Indians had passed since Stuart had. Now the seven seekers were getting worried. And well they might be worried, for the next day they were captured.

CHAPTER 2

The Road-Finders

Two or three weeks after the setting forth of these two groups of gold seekers, with their belongings on pack horses, a smaller party, only three persons, rode off in the same general direction, toward the Yellowstone River, but for another purpose. They were going to mark the way that became known as the Bozeman Trail. They were John M. Bozeman, age twenty-six, John M. Jacobs, a squaw man who had been in the mountains for many years, and Jacobs' half-Indian daughter, age seven or eight. Nobody has ever explained what so young a child was doing on that long and perilous journey. She couldn't yet have learned enough household skills from her Indian mother to be very useful around camp. Maybe she coaxed her indulgent papa until he agreed, "All right, you can come. Mind you don't get in the way."

Nobody has explained in print why Jacobs, the experienced frontiersman, and Bozeman, the young man from Georgia, took it upon themselves to find a shorter route for wagons going along the Oregon Trail to the gold fields. The frontier badly needed easier ways to get from one place to another. But Bozeman and Jacobs were not out to do a good deed. They were not impelled by simple Christian charity. Almost nobody was, and travelers knew better than to expect it. Bozeman and Jacobs had something to sell: a promise of time saved, and their services as guides along the way. Travelers paid money for that kind of thing; and like almost everybody on the frontier, Bozeman and Jacobs simply wanted to make money.

They didn't actually build a road, of course. They simply found a way and marked it. The "road" had to be passable for wagons; it didn't have to be smooth, but the drivers who would use it must be assured that their stock wouldn't play out for lack of grass and water. Some of the water on that route was so bad that the only polite thing that could be said for it was that it was wet.

Jacobs, long-time wanderer in the Rockies, knew how the rivers ran. He must have been the real trail-finder. Bozeman, with only four years of frontier experience, was the promoter. He was going to sell emigrants and freighters the guided tour from the Oregon Trail up to the new gold fields.

Bozeman, Jacobs, and the little girl could travel fairly fast down toward the Oregon Trail, because they were not encumbered by a wagon. But the men had to keep in mind the requirements of loaded, swaying wagons and oxen, mules, and horses.

So that spring of 1863 there were three groups traveling horseback, heading for the Yellowstone, all for substantially the same reason: to make money.

CHAPTER 3

Stuart Meets the Crows

James Stuart kept a journal of the Yellowstone Expedition, not because he was its elected leader but because it was his custom to note each day what had happened, even when he was at home with his brother Granville. Then they took turns.

He noted on Sunday, April 12, "We had a guard last night for the first time; it seems like old times to have to stand guard." They were about fifty miles out from Bannack, and they were frontierwise. They knew how much pride the Crow Indians took in their horse-stealing skill. Besides, that had been a lean winter, and the Indians had lost a lot of horses by starvation. They needed to replenish their herds. (Even when they didn't need to, they stole horses just for fun.)

Each day James noted events—the elk and black-tailed deer sighted and shot for food; distances traveled; country observed; horses that broke their picket ropes and stampeded and had to be searched for; the creeks, their flow estimated in sluice-heads of water, because they had to have water if they were going to placer gold.

But first they had to find the gold. On April 13, Geery and McCafferty raised the color on Granite Creek, but they agreed with James Stuart that it wouldn't be wise to tell the others. If everybody got excited, the expedition would break up right there, before it really got started. No, they would look more thoroughly along that creek when they came back. There might be even better prospects in the far drainage of the Yellowstone River.

Unfortunately, they couldn't go back that way. Three of the fifteen could never go back anywhere. James Stuart always figured, though, that his men would have been the ones to strike it rich if they had gone back, because that creek flowed into Alder Gulch. But they were lucky—twelve of them were lucky—to get out with their lives.

The Stuart party met a few Bannock Indians, didn't trust them for a minute but got along with them pretty well. They ate well, for game was plentiful, deer, elk, and antelope, and Bostwick killed a grizzly that tried to kill him first. That night they had antelope steaks fried in bear's oil. Stuart commented, "High living!" It was, indeed. Most wild meat was lean after the winter, and the men hungered for fat but needed to conserve the bacon they carried. When they butchered game, they threw out what they did not eat. There would be more tomorrow.

They rode on, always looking for good prospects, having a right good time, not always sure where they were. Stuart had brought along a map and notes, as the Lewis and Clark Expedition had described the country almost sixty years before, but on April 22 he commented that those explorers had "played us out; if we had left the notes and map of their route at home and followed the Indian trail, we would have saved four days' travel in coming from Bannack City here."

James Stuart was a dryly humorous journal keeper. On the north bank of the Yellowstone he wrote:

Saw many prairie-dog towns today for the first time on the trip. Such great big fat "critters" running all over town barking bloody murder, and their companions, little diminutive owls, sitting on the largest houses and viewing the hubbub with looks of the greatest gravity and wisdom. It made me feel good to see them enjoying the excitement of strangers going through town.

The Yellowstone country was displeasing in one respect:

If ever I get back to where I can get some good water to drink, I will be happy. All the water in this country reminds me of puddles in a brick-yard; it not only looks bad, but also has a nauseating taste; yet it seems to be healthy enough, for all of the party are in excellent health. I suppose a person would soon become accustomed to it, so that good, clear cold water would not taste right.

On the twenty-seventh, looking for buffalo, he found fresh tracks of twelve horses. "I suppose it is a war-party of natives," he wrote, "and, if so, I expect they will visit us tonight in search of our horses."

Not that night but the next afternoon, thirty Indians rode into camp, firing guns in greeting and yelling "How-d'ye-do" and the name of their people, Apsoroka.[8] White men called them Crows. They wanted to talk.

Stuart couldn't speak Crow, but he could get along in the Snake language, and so could one of the Crows. Besides, all the Indians of the Plains used the swift, graceful, hand-sign talk, and most white men picked up enough of it to be useful.

James Stuart, as chief of the palefaces, sat in solemn council with three Crow leaders. He wrote about it laconically:

They (the interpreter and chiefs) sat down in a circle, and requested the pleasure of my company. I complied with the invitation, and our party stood guard over our horses and baggage, while I smoked and exchanged lies with them. It would take me a week to write all that was said, so I forbear. Meanwhile, the other Indians began disputing with each other about who should have our best horses. I requested the chief to make them come out from among the horses and behave themselves, which he did. At eight P.M. I put on double guard, and at ten P.M. all but the guard retired to rest.

James understated the tension of that day. When his narrative of "The Yellowstone Expedition of 1863" was published in 1876, it carried copious notes by Sam Hauser, who was determined to tell posterity how cool and wise James Stuart remained during that awful time. About this council he wrote:

> For several hours, in fact during the whole time he was smoking and talking with the chiefs, there was a constant struggle and excitement in the camp—the young bucks taking forcible possession of our horses and blankets, and our men by superior strength retaking them, and in many instances handling them without gloves, by throwing them violently to the ground; upon which the Indians would become perfectly frantic with rage, drawing their guns, bows, and knives, pointing to their chief, and making signs that upon a signal from him they intended to take our scalps.

Several times Indians fired their guns (they had a few sawed-off double-barreled shotguns) near the white men's heads or threatened murder with bow and arrow.

Watkins and Bostwick had been in Indian fights before and wanted to get on with this one in earnest. Watkins drew his revolver but an Indian standing behind him threw a buffalo robe over him and held his arms. Sam Hauser, like the others, was worried. He ran to Stuart and told him the shooting was going to start unless something happened to stop it. Stuart told him to keep cool and wait until he himself began the fight or ordered it to start.

"And turning to the chief," Sam Hauser recollected, "he told him, in a peremptory tone, to order his men to come out from among the horses and tents and keep quiet. The chief, who instantly saw that a crisis had come, signaled his men to drop their guns (for both parties were in the attitude of battle), which they did, and quieted down and gathered around the camp fire."

The talk broke up at bedtime, and Stuart quietly gave Hauser some orders to pass along: At daylight they should saddle their riding horses; if the Indians tried to take their packs or pack horses, the whites should kill as many as they could and then mount and head north toward distant Fort Benton. One frightening thing that Stuart had learned in his talk with the leaders was that the main camp of the Crows was across the river, only twenty miles away.

Stuart himself wrote later that the Indians wandered around camp all night, like evil spirits. Every few minutes one of his men would rush out of his tent and prevent an Indian from stealing something. The Crows, he said, "would steal the world-renowned Arabs poor in a single hour."

By the dawn's early light, about three o'clock, after a restless night for everybody, the Crows forcibly traded horses and blankets with the whites. The palefaces didn't have a chance to bridle a single horse. Stuart retained his icy calm. His men tried to imitate him, but they were fuming—didn't he intend to put up any fight at all?

He certainly did. He bided his time—and when his time came, he threw down on the chief, with his rifle muzzle not more than two feet from the old warrior's chest. Every man in his party presented a rifle or a revolver muzzle at the nearest Indian—and every Indian, dropping his robe or blanket, turned out to have a gun pointed at a white man.

"But fortunately," Hauser wrote, "they all looked to their chief, and saw that he was lost if a gun was fired.

> We, too, looked to our captain, and our danger was almost forgotten in admiration. His whole features, face, and person had changed; he seemed and was taller; his usually calm face was all on fire; his quiet, light blue eyes was [sic] now flashing like an eagle's, and seemingly looked directly through the fierce, and for a time, undaunted savage that stood before him. For several seconds it was doubtful whether the old warrior-chief would cower before his white brother, or meet his fate then and there.

Stuart won. The chief signaled, and his warriors unwillingly lowered their weapons. The gold seekers were permitted to leave—with eight Indians accompanying them for a while as a gesture of friendship, which Stuart's men did not appreciate at all. But they all got safely away (for the time being) on April 29.

About sundown they saw two Indians coming, judged that there were more behind them, and tied up the horses to prevent theft. Stuart's party did not move or speak as the two Crows came up. The Indians didn't speak for a while, either, but sat on their horses and took an inventory of the palefaces. Then one of them asked for the chief. Stuart stepped forward.

The Indian dismounted, pulled off his saddle, sat down on it, pulled off his hat—everything had to be done with proper deliberation and dignity—and took out of it a roll of papers. He undid sundry wrappers and then presented a paper signed by the Indian agent at Fort Union, at the mouth of the Yellowstone River. The paper said the bearer was Red Bear, one of the principal chiefs of the Crow nation.

The Stuart party gave them some supper, and Red Bear assured the whites that he was a friend. They had a long talk with him; he asked about Jim Bridger, the old mountain man whom everybody knew, and discussed a rumor that a steam boat had been captured by Indians near Fort Union.

After everybody went to bed (a little jumpy) the guards caught an Indian creeping up to a couple of their horses. Stuart reminded Red Bear that the Crows were supposed to be friends of the party. The chief scolded the would-be thief, everybody calmed down, and in the morning the visiting red men departed.

The night before, Red Bear had insisted on giving Stuart a fine present of a black horse, and Stuart had magnanimously returned the compliment by giving Red Bear a white mare. Stuart discovered before long that Red Bear had got the best of that deal.

On May 1 the Crows proved what everybody agreed on already: that they were the world's most cunning and successful horse thieves. Bostwick and Geery were on night guard when an Indian attracted their attention. While they were crawling along to get a shot at him, his partner made off with Bostwick's roan horse at the other end of the camp—and in bright moonlight, too.

Nothing much happened on May 2, but Stuart noted:

> In the timber along the river, we saw many houses built of dry logs and bark; some are built like lodges, but the most of them are either square or oblong, and among them were many large and strong corrals of dry logs. The Crows evidently winter along here, and, from the sign, they are very numerous.

Indeed they were. On that same day, the seven missing miners who were following ran into a great bunch of Crows and came to the end of their pursuit of Stuart, whose baptism of horror was yet to come.

CHAPTER 4

The Missing Seven Meet Trouble

Along toward morning on May 2 the horses of the seven pursuing travelers became very restless; Henry Edgar and Bill Fairweather were standing guard. Just as morning came, the hills were suddenly alive with Indians. And very neatly the seven palefaces were captured. The Indians had control of everything they owned except their weapons.

They were lucky in one respect: there was no serious problem in communication because Lew Simmons had once lived with the Crows and could speak their language. He sat in powwow with the Crow leaders, Red Bear and Little Crow, while his friends tried to follow out his instructions not to be afraid although they were prisoners. Edgar wandered through the Indian village and counted tepees—180 of them. This was a big camp, for one lodge might house ten or more persons. Edgar wrote that night in his memorandum book:

> We talk the matter over and agree to keep together and if it has to come to the worst to fight while life lasts. All the young ones are around us and the women. What fun! We get plenty to eat; Indians are putting up a great big lodge, medicine lodge at that. Night, what will tomorrow bring forth? I write this—will anyone ever see it? Quite dark and such a noise, dogs and drums!

They lived through the night, with the medicine man drumming and singing the whole time, and their captors even let them have coffee for breakfast.

Simmons came to tell the others that they were wanted in the medicine lodge, and blithe Bill Fairweather, who never gave a damn about anything, called out, "Ten o'clock, court now opens."

The medicine lodge was filled with the seated dignitaries of the village. In the center was a bush—a medicine bush, the white captives figured out—and they were marched around and around it while the Crow warriors silently looked them over. Then they were led to a chief's lodge and told to stay there.

Damp with the sweat of tension, they relaxed enough to laugh about their "cake walk," and Fairweather announced that if they had to go through that nonsense again he was going to pull up the medicine bush and whack the medicine man over the head with it. The others told him not to, but when they were called back to repeat the peculiar ring-around-the-rosy, Bill did exactly what he had threatened. He yanked up the bush and slapped it down on the medicine man's head.

There was utter silence for a moment. Then the palefaces ducked out with the Indians after them. Simmons, the interpreter, stayed inside, horrified. The other six stood three and three, back to back, ready for death but determined on a good fight first. The two chiefs drove the crowd back. And for the time being the captives were safe again. They stayed put, as ordered, in a chief's lodge with a guard around it while one of the chiefs, outside on horseback, made a speech. Simmons joined them and said the chief was talking in their favor.

"He began the talk about noon," Edgar wrote, "and he was still talking when I fell asleep at midnight." The long-windedness of their champion seems less remarkable than the fact that any of the captives, whose fate was at stake, could go to sleep at all.

The next morning, May 4, they heard the verdict. If they went on down the river, the Indians would kill them. If they went back, the Indians would give them horses to speed them on their way. There wasn't much point in arguing. After all, these men were miners, not crusaders; they were in no mood to fight for civil rights.

They did get horses, not their own but poor bony creatures that the Indians didn't want. Except Bill Fairweather, on whom the Indians looked with awe. He had not only tempted fate by hitting the medicine man with the sacred bush, he had also wandered around with a rattlesnake on each arm. For some reason, rattlesnakes never bit Bill Fairweather. To this great medicine man of the whites the Indians carefully returned his own three horses.

The men got their saddles, a hundred pounds of flour, some coffee and sugar, a plug of tobacco, and two robes each (in exchange for their spare clothes and blankets), and were glad to get so much as a farewell present.

At the last minute, Lew Simmons asked for their advice. Should he go with them or stay with the Crows? Harry Edgar advised him to stay if he didn't want to risk his scalp with the white men. He stayed. He had standing with the Indians. He was safer there.

They put some forty-five miles between themselves and the village by traveling at night. They slept all the next day, May 5, and traveled again all night. When they had time to wonder at something more than being alive, they wondered where the Stuart party was. The Indians had told Simmons that Stuart was one day ahead.

Years later, Edgar told a writer for the *Anaconda Standard* that they gave credit for their escape to Lew Simmons, who could talk to their captors, and Bill Fairweather, that reckless fellow whose sheer bravado impressed Indians who made a cult of desperate courage.

They were safe for the time being. All they had to do was go back to Bannack City. On the way they found pay dirt and made history.

CHAPTER 5

Death and the Stuart Party

On May 3, the day when the missing miners waited to learn whether they would live or die, Stuart's party camped three miles below Pompey's Pillar, that landmark named for Sacajawea's baby, Pomp, by Captain William Clark, who had left his name on the rock along with a date, July 25, 1806.

Stuart's expedition was having a grand time. About sundown that same day, the men chased a bunch of buffalo just for the hell of it. "They came in [to a waterhole] on a run," James wrote, "and did not halt until they were all in the hole. Four or five of us went out to give them a scare. We went on the bank above, and within ten feet of them, and gave a yell. Such fun! They run over one another, fell down in heaps, nearly drowned a lot of calves, etc. Just such another stampede a man would probably never witness again in a lifetime. We laughed till we could hardly stand."

Two days later, Stuart's expedition reached the juncture of the

Big Horn River with the Yellowstone and washed a few pans of loose gravel. They found from ten to fifty fine colors of gold in every pan. All of them figured they would find good diggings up the Big Horn.

Here Stuart did some calculating. The party had traveled 401 miles from Bannack City to the mouth of the Big Horn, but they had wasted 75 miles by following Lewis and Clark's notes. So the actual distance was 326 miles, and a good wagon road could be made with little trouble, he remarked.

Where the rivers meet, the party made a rough survey and laid out a townsite, with a ranch of 160 acres for each man. They named it Big Horn City. It never amounted to much. Big Horn (without the "City") is there today, with a population of ten, give or take a couple.

They were getting more cautious about Indians. "Saw fresh Indian sign near camp," Stuart wrote on May 8; "everybody on the lookout; do not intend to let any more of them come into camp; would rather fight than have friends steal everything we have; and it is impossible to let more than two of them come in without their stealing, and all of us on guard at that."

May 9, he commented, "Found the remains of an Indian *buried up a tree*. Suppose it to be a Sioux, and wish they were all up trees."

On May 11, across the Big Horn River and about a mile away, he sighted "three white men, with six horses, three packed and riding three."

Stuart waited until they were three-quarters of a mile away and then hailed them. The strangers did not answer and did not stop. In fact, they moved a little faster.

Stuart sent two men across to invite them to camp and exchange news—but the mysterious strangers had disappeared up a creek bed, apparently running their horses as soon as they got out of sight.

The Stuart pursuers found a frying pan and a deck of cards on their trail. Nobody knew who those three white men were, where they had come from, or where they were going. It was all very peculiar. James was mad. These strangers had acted unmannerly. He wrote:

> I have given orders to have the next small party we meet brought into camp dead or alive, for it is played out letting people pass us

in that way in the mountains without giving an account of themselves.

The three white men who had disappeared so strangely were John Bozeman, John Jacobs, and little Miss Jacobs. They weren't guilty, although they acted that way. They were just good and scared, because they assumed that the visible members of the Stuart party were Indians. They had been chased by Indians just a few days before. And two days after they evaded the Yellowstone Expedition, they had a harder go with Indians.

On May 12, James Stuart wrote:

Saw plenty of fresh Indian signs near camp. Sixteen horses have been here today, and probably more whose tracks we did not see. We will have to look out for squalls, as there is evidently a war party in the neighborhood.

It is eleven years today since I left the home of my boyhood. Who knows how many more it will be before I see it again, if ever?

Then this veteran frontiersman, aged thirty-one, went on night guard with George Smith. A little after eleven o'clock all hell broke loose.

Crow scouts had been prowling around almost every night, on the lookout for horses to steal, but there had been no real trouble since that first confrontation when Stuart glared down the Indians. There was no reason to expect anything more than attempted horse theft now. But rain threatened at bedtime, so the men carried all their flour, the saddles, and most of their other baggage into the three tents that housed all but two of the party. All this stuff, piled inside next to the tent walls, absorbed some of the enemy's fire when trouble came.

Watkins had been moody all day; several times he had called Sam Hauser's attention to the mournful cooing of a dove, remarking that it had made him sad, he kept thinking of his boyhood home and his mother. This was strange, for he was, Hauser recollected, the most reckless of the party and usually didn't seem to think of home, death, or anything else.

In one tent, Drew Underwood and Hauser shared blankets, and under the same canvas slept York and McCafferty. A second tent housed Geery, Bostwick, Ives, and Watkins. In a third were Bell, Vanderbilt, and Blake. The other two men who had expected to sleep that night, Hauxhurst and Roach, didn't put up a tent but spread the canvas over their bed.

The guards, Stuart and Smith, were lying flat, wondering what made the horses so uneasy, when a party of Crows fired a volley into the camp. Stuart was lying between two horses. Both of them fell almost on top of him. Four horses, altogether, were killed in that volley, and five more wounded. In the tents, seven men were wounded.

Under the shooting and the yelling, Sam Hauser heard his bed-mate, Underwood, groan, "I'm shot through and through!"

Hauser thought he was, too, because he had felt the shock of a bullet and blood was trickling down his side. He thrust a hand inside his shirt and realized that he wasn't badly hurt; the ball had flattened when it struck a thick memorandum book in his left shirt pocket and stopped against a rib near his heart.

Smith fired his shotgun but probably missed. Stuart, lodged between the fallen horses, couldn't see to fire at all. He yelled, "Tear down the tents—they're a target," and York rushed out and did so.

Stuart took control as soon as he crawled out from under the bleeding hulks of the horses. Every man who could still shoot was to take his weapons, crawl away from the tents, and lie flat.

All the men who could crawl did crawl—but not one of them could see his hand before his face in the darkness. They could hear the Indians talking, and arrows whirred past them often. They didn't know how many men were living, how many were dead, and they could not even comfort the wounded because the least sound told their attackers where they were.

Hauser crawled through the darkness to Stuart and whispered, "How many of our men are killed?"

The whispered answer was, "Don't know. You're the third man who has reported. You and Underwood crawl toward the river about fifty yards; don't fire until you can punch your guns against them. There will be a general rush on us before morning. Remember, don't shoot until the rush is made and you can touch them with your guns. If you fire sooner, the flash of your guns will direct a hundred shots to you."

And so the commander gave his whispered orders, and the men obeyed, waiting in darkness, in dreadful silence, through the hours until morning.

Before dawn, Stuart came, walking upright, without fear, and frightened Hauser considerably. Hauser whispered, "Why don't you crawl? You'll be killed."

Stuart whispered back, "I'm going to see how the boys are, and get some water for Bell and Bostwick. There's enough of us left to give them a lively rattle in the morning."

Hauser appealed to him once more to get down on the ground, but "I wasn't born to be killed by these red devils," Stuart replied, and calmly walked down to the river and fetched water for the wounded.

When daylight came, the Crows had gone up a ravine where they were out of sight but could keep an eye on the besieged whites. Dim dawn enabled the Stuart party to assess the horror. C. D. Watkins was shot through the head. The ball went in his right temple and came out his left cheekbone. He was unconscious—but he crawled around aimlessly on his forearms and knees.

Bostwick was wounded in five places. One shoulder blade was shattered, his right thigh was broken in three places, and another ball had passed through the flesh of his right thigh. He was conscious and in agony.

H. A. Bell was shot under the bottom rib on his left side, and near the left kidney. That ball came out near the thigh joint.

Underwood was shot once, but the ball made six wounds. He was a fleshy man; the ball passed through his upper left arm and then through both breasts.

H. T. Geery had an arrow wound, not dangerous, in the back of his left shoulder. George Ives had a flesh wound in one hip, and Hauser's wound was only a scratch, thanks to his memorandum book.

So that was the situation they had to face—seven of the fifteen wounded, three severely wounded and likely to die. The others would not, could not leave them.

Over morning coffee, which nobody really relished, they came to their decision. They dared not go back the way they had come. That would take them back in the path of the whole Crow nation.

So they would ride south, to the Oregon Trail. They would go over South Pass and by way of Fort Bridger—a long, weary journey, more than a thousand miles, back to Bannack City, part of it through totally unexplored country inhabited by the hostile Sioux. But going into Sioux country would rid them of the hostile Crows.

They would lighten their packs and thus speed their progress by discarding all but five or six days' grub supply in the hope of covering seventy-five miles in the first twenty-four hours. And they would wait decently until noon or a little later so that Watkins,

Bostwick, and Bell could die. Stuart, that well-read physician, did what he could for the wounded men, but he had not brought his surgical kit—and he would never again need it so badly. Bell refused to let him probe his wounds, believing that he was bound to die, and the others were equally sure of it.

By noon the wounded men were still alive, so they set forth—but not at the mile-devouring speed they had intended.

Before they set out, Hauser, Geery, and Underwood had a quiet, private talk and made a pact.[9] Each man agreed that if he were to be mortally wounded and unable to travel, he would save one shot for himself so as to free the others to go on. On the other hand, if a wounded man had a chance of pulling through, the others would stay by him. They talked this over with the other men, who all subscribed to it. James Stuart would have the deciding vote as to whether a wounded man might recover.

They were desperate and reckless. None of them expected to live through the perils before them. But they wanted someone to get back to a settlement to tell how and where and when the others had died. Jim Stuart cheered them by estimating that half of them might live to tell the tale if they played it cool all the way.

Before riding off, they even challenged the Crows in the hills to a final fight. James Stuart chose the battleground and, using the sign-talk lingua franca of the Plains plus English, told them they were cowards, thieves, and murderers. But the Indians stayed behind their rocks.

At three in the afternoon, the wounded men were still living. Bell even thought he could ride, although Stuart was sure that he would fall dead off his horse in an hour or so. While men were helping the suffering Bell into his saddle, Bostwick made his last decision. He asked for his revolver and demanded that the others go on without him. He would, he said, take some of the red devils with him when he went and save one bullet for himself to avoid torture. Geery handed him the cocked revolver, and Bostwick shot himself through the head. They left him there, as he had intended.[10]

Knowing they were followed by hidden Indians, the others rode five miles. Bell was still alive; he began to hope he had a future. They rested a while—and realized that they would now need the provisions they had thrown away, because there was no hope of traveling as fast as they had intended.

The next day, May 14, they covered twenty miles, but it was not all progress. They changed direction several times to confuse the Crows behind them. They were exhausted when they stopped at about four o'clock in the afternoon. In camp another dreadful thing happened: Geery accidentally shot himself in the chest while trying to pull his rifle toward him across a blanket.

All of them remembered now the harsh vow they had taken. They begged Geery to forget it. He *might* live.

Geery spoke to James Stuart: "Tell them the truth, Jim, that I can't live more than a few hours."

Stuart, with tears running down his cheeks, would not lie but answered evasively, "Never mind, Geery. We'll stay by you. All the Indians in the world couldn't drive us away from you."

Turning his head to the others, Geery said, "See, comrades, Jim knows that I am fatally wounded and must die soon, but he avoids telling me; and the fact that you would all stay by me and die for me has determined me."

He put the muzzle of his pistol against his breast and added, "Remember, I am not committing suicide. I am only shortening my life a few hours to prevent you from foolishly sacrificing yours in defense of mine. God knows I don't want to die. I fear death but have a Christian hope in eternity, but I must die, rather to save than to sacrifice. Remember this place and where I am buried; describe it to my friends some day if any of you live to tell of it."

All the men were weeping now.

Geery said good-by: "God bless you all, comrades; I must die, and in time for you to bury me and escape before dark. Bury me in this coat, and here."

Before he could pull the trigger, Stuart did him one last anguished service. He warned him to point the pistol at his temple, not at his heart.

Now let Sam Hauser tell of the end of Henry Geery:

> Geery replied: "Thanks, Jim; and may God bless you all, and take you safely out of this." As he placed the pistol to his temple the men, with weeping eyes and full hearts, all turned to walk away as they could not bear to see him fire. He pressed the trigger, and only the cap exploded. I never heard one sound half so loud before; it echoed in all directions as if to make him realize what he was doing.
>
> I then appealed to him, saying, "Geery, for God's sake don't; this is a warning." To which he paid no attention nor made any reply

but rather seemed to be soliloquizing, and said, "I don't know what to think of that; it never snapped before." Cocking his pistol again, he engaged a few seconds in mental prayer, and again pulled the trigger that launched him into eternity. The report of the fatal shot was awful. . . .

His comrades cried like children as they dug his grave and buried him, as he had asked, in his soldier overcoat. Then they piled brush on the grave and burned it to conceal the burial place from the Indians so they would not dig him up for his scalp and his clothes. The men moved on about six miles before camping for the night.

They got into hideously rough country where water was hard to reach. They could not get down to the stream and they suffered from thirst, especially Bell, who was still alive. They traveled sometimes through deep snow, soaked with rain and half blind in fog. For days they had no fresh meat, not daring to fire a gun for fear of attracting Indians.

On May 17 Stuart wrote, "It will be a scratch if any of the party are seen any more, but I suppose it is all for the best. Man proposes, and God disposes."

Stuart noted each day the estimated miles covered and the compass course, with a wild guess as to where they were. They crossed two streams on rafts they had to build. The weather was foul. Bell's mare fell down in a steep gully and couldn't get out, so they left her. Two men killed an elk fawn, and the party ate it up at one meal. Their bread supply was so low that they no longer had it at every meal. They killed five buffaloes and dried some seventy-five pounds of meat. Stuart thought, on May 22, that he recognized the Wind River Mountains to the west.

Two days later he wrote, "Our route, since the massacre, has been through a part of the country too mean for Indians to either live or hunt in, and I came through it to keep out of their way. We are traveling for safety, not comfort."

The horses suffered from scanty grass and alkali water.

On May 26 they came to a wide, shallow river. Plenty of Indian signs. And at noon they found wagon tracks!

CHAPTER 6

"I Have Found a Scad!"

The six men who never caught up with James Stuart crossed the Madison River on May 14 and began to relax. Now they felt safe from the Indians. After two days on bread alone with no meat, they shot a mountain sheep, an elk, then more sheep. Now they were simply on a pleasant camping trip, replete with fresh meat, and finding fairly good prospects for gold almost every time they moved camp.

May 26 was the day that changed their world, the same day that Stuart's survivors rejoiced at the sight of wagon tracks.

Bill Fairweather and Henry Edgar guarded the camp and looked after the horses that day while the others went up a nameless creek to prospect. Bill walked across to a bar to find a place to stake the horses; his own saddle horse had a lame leg that required doctoring. When he came back to camp he said, "There's a piece of rimrock sticking out of the bar over there. Get the tools and we'll go and prospect it." He got the pick and shovel, and Henry took the pan. Bill dug and filled the pan.

"Now wash that pan," he advised, "and see if you can get enough to buy some tobacco when we get to town." He moved on to dig and pan some more.

Edgar had half the dirt washed out of the pan and had seen some gold when Bill yelled, "I have found a scad!" [11]

Henry Edgar shouted, "If you have one, I have a hundred!"

Edgar finished panning his dirt. The gold in that one pan weighed out at $2.40. Bill's scad, a nice piece, weighed the same. They had their tobacco money all right. They ran for another gold pan. In a few minutes they had gold worth $12.30.

Their comrades, returning, grouched because the horses weren't taken care of. Edgar, with a grin, showed the glittering contents of his pan to Sweeney. But *he* wasn't going to fall for any smart tricks. "Salted!" he yelled.

"You can pipe Bill and me down and run us through a sluice box," Edgar argued, "and not get a color! The horses can go to the devil—or the Indians."

They talked and roasted venison until late that night. And no happier bunch of men ever went off to dreamland than Bill Fairweather, Henry Edgar, Mike Sweeney, Barney Hughes, Tom Cover, and Harry Rodgers.

The next day was even better. They panned all day long, aiming for a grubstake, and washed out $150 in good clean dust. To cap that grand day, Edgar and Fairweather each shot an antelope for supper.

On May 28 they staked the ground. Each claim was 100 feet. To claim a water right in a written note to leave, they had to call the creek something. Henry Edgar called it "Alder" for the green alders growing along the banks.

They agreed not to divulge a word about the discovery in Bannack while they got their grub supply. They pulled out about noon. Next day Edgar wrote, "All well. Breakfast such as we have, bread and antelope and cold water and good appetites. What better fare could a prince wish?"

May 30 they were in Bannack—and such a supper! Salt Lake eggs, ham, potatoes.

Their lucky strike on Alder Creek was the worst-kept secret in the West. No man of the six breathed a word, but they looked too happy, spent gold too freely for supplies other than tobacco. The day after they reached Bannack, Henry Edgar sat in a saloon, all cleaned up and wearing his store clothes, and heard total strangers tell him earnestly about how the discoverers had brought in a horse load of gold! When they were ready to go back to Alder Creek, seventy miles to the east, a gold rush tagged behind them.

Prospectors were ever a skittish lot. They used to tell a story about one who died and tried to get into heaven, but St. Peter refused him entrance.

"The place is full of prospectors," he complained. "They've dug up the golden streets and almost ruined heaven."

"Let me in," the newcomer coaxed, "and I'll get rid of the rest of them."

St. Peter doubtfully agreed, and soon little groups of men were standing around, whispering excitedly about a rich gold strike in hell. Suddenly there was a rush for the gate, and they poured out—with the newcomer at the tail end of the procession.

"Here, here!" cried the gatekeeper. "Why are *you* leaving?"

The prospector yelled back over his shoulder, "You never can tell—there might be something to it!"

CHAPTER 7

The Survivors Sight Civilization

At noon on May 28, two days after they came upon those wonderful, promising wagon tracks, James Stuart and his men came in sight of the Oregon Trail. Now life stretched out before them. In the afternoon they saw telegraph poles! It was almost like being home again, seeing the great road and the telegraph after running the gantlet for 400 miles through the territory claimed by the Crow nation.

Another mile and they spotted a wagon train far ahead. They shouted and yelled for joy. They were, Stuart commented, "equal to a Chinese camp on a drunk, for noise."

About sundown they came to the place where the wagons had stopped, a settlement called Pacific City. And they scared the wary wagon-train people half out of their wits. The pilgrims thought they were being attacked by these wildly yelling riders and got ready to kill the survivors of the Yellowstone Expedition.

There were four soldiers with the emigrants. The soldiers gave them enough provisions to last a week. They were first-rate fellows, Stuart said, and the emigrants were the best outfitted of any train he had seen in years. His men kept eating until ten o'clock that night. Nobody had any news from the States.

"These emigrants are out and out know-nothings," Stuart wrote. "It seems like old times to be with them. The most of them do not seem to have any more sense than children, and can ask more foolish questions in an hour than could be answered in a week."

The survivors of the Yellowstone Expedition rested and then moved westward, rejoicing as they went. The sorely wounded Bell had survived the desperate jouney. They left him at the last crossing of the Sweetwater. He was going in a spring wagon to the Three Crossings, where there was a surgeon, and would go on to Bannack City later. Now Stuart and his companions kept meeting old friends along the way and at stations where they stopped. Latest news from the Civil War was that the South was winning.

Heading up toward Bannack City on June 9 they had news of that roaring camp; Bannack was still having a man for breakfast now and then.

There was no lack of company now. Stuart found himself guiding a party of angry, wrangling emigrants. He was blithe again, after his frightful experiences; he could laugh up his sleeve at the oddities of human nature.

Not until June 21 did he get a hint of the great news of that year of 1863:

> Jake Meeks passed while we were camped. He has been in Bannack City with four loads of flour, which was dull sale; had to store it until times are better. He also told us that there has been a big stampede from Bannack to some new diggings that have been struck on Stinking Water river.[12] I am afraid it is our place that we found as we went out in April.

It was, almost; if Stuart's expedition had been able to go back the way they went out, they would almost certainly have found Alder Gulch.

They reached Bannack City late in the evening on June 22. Stuart wrote:

> Everybody was glad to see us, and we were glad to see everybody, although our hair and beards had grown so, and we were so dilapidated generally, that scarcely any one knew us at first; and no wonder, for we had ridden sixteen hundred miles, and for the last twelve hundred without tents or even a change of clothes.

He was no richer than before, except in experience, but he was alive. He was not fated to be one of the discoverers of Alder Gulch. But neither was he fated to be killed by Indians.

CHAPTER 8

The Perils of Domesticity

James Stuart was back home at American Fork within a reasonable time after reaching Bannack, but he didn't stay there long. Miners around American Fork were abandoning their diggings and moving down to the new Stinking Water mines—Alder Gulch, that is. Every day people passed on their way to the fabulous new discovery. James Stuart and Rezin Anderson set out July 27 to see for themselves what was going on.

Granville stayed home. He was playing a quiet game of cribbage with a friend that evening when all the women in the settlement rushed in, yelling and arguing, headed by Mrs. Mat Craft, the only white woman in the community. They were all mad and all talking at once—in English, Salish, Blackfeet, Snake, and Bannock.

"Some were weeping, some ready for a fight; a regular Tower of Babel performance," Granville wrote. "We finally learned that all the commotion was caused by Mrs. Craft's having accused Pierrot's squaw of stealing her 'shimmy.' They appealed to me to settle the row; but what could one lone man do in a case of this kind? I was no Solomon."

Just the same, he had to act like one. He understood the Snake language and some Flathead, but not at the rate words were being flung at him, so he called in his wife, Aubony, to interpret the fight. And it turned out that there had been no shimmy theft, really. Mrs. Craft had imported that new fangled garment from the States, and an Indian girl who was visiting Mrs. Pierrot wanted to make one like it. So she had bought material and surreptitiously borrowed the original to use as a pattern. When Mrs. Craft missed it, she was so furious that the girl was afraid to confess and hid it instead.

With the situation clarified and the high-style shimmy returned to its proud owner, the angry ladies calmed down and dried their tears.

CHAPTER 9

Jacobs and Bozeman Meet Hostiles

It was on May 13 that the Stuart survivors with their suffering wounded started down toward the Oregon Trail to go home the long way around. On that day, in another place, the seven captured and then released miners—down to bedrock for provisions but gloriously and unbelievably alive—argued about which way to go. Their decision led them to the richest placer discovery in America.

On the same May 13, Bozeman and Jacobs and the little half-Indian girl had their own desperate encounter with hostiles. Riding along, they came suddenly on some seventy-five Indians, on horseback and loaded for bear. The redskins galloped toward them, yelling.

Two men couldn't fight seventy-five. They were too wise to try. Jacobs, that experienced old frontiersman, managed to drop his gun and bullet pouch into some sagebrush without being caught at it.

The usual stormy session followed. The Indians argued about whether to kill their captives then or later. Meanwhile, they took everything—arms, ammunition, grub, blankets—and divvied it up among themselves, jeering and threatening.

One of them grabbed the little girl and gave her a severe beating with the ramrod out of a rifle, punishment for being caught in the company of white men, even though one of them was her own father.

When the Crows had had their fun and had taken some loot, their attitude toward the captives relaxed a little. The three were not to be slaughtered, after all. They could go on their way—but first, a little matter of trading horses. The three trail blazers gave up their mounts in exchange for miserable Indian ponies and rode off, half naked.

But they sneaked cautiously back after a while, so that Jacobs could recover his gun and ammunition. There were only five balls in the bullet pouch.

Then they rode as fast as their half-dead ponies could take them, not stopping to make any meat. Before they realized it, they were out of buffalo country. Jacobs' five shots didn't bring down much in the way of small game. The three riders were almost starved when they reached the Oregon Trail. But they got there, they were restored, and early in July they were ready to do business with the guided tour of what came to be called the Bozeman Trail.

The Bozeman Trail, by Grace Raymond Hebard and E. A. Brininstool, says John Bozeman recruited his first emigrant train at the Missouri River. Some other sources say he went "to Missouri" to find wagons to guide up his trail. Neither is true. There was no reason to go so far when hundreds of emigrant wagons were traveling along the Oregon Trail through present Wyoming. That trail had been the major overland route for twenty years.

Hebard and Brininstool say:

> Bozeman and John M. Jacobs, in the winter of 1862–1863, left Bannack . . . for the Missouri River, with a determination to find this shorter route for the emigrants and freighters on their way to the Montana goldfields. . . . [They didn't go in the winter; their horses would have starved. They went in the spring of 1863.]
>
> The exhausted but undaunted couple finally reached the Missouri. In the spring of 1863, at the Missouri, Bozeman took command of a wagon train of freighters and emigrants, with a determination to retrace his route on the east side of the Big Horn Mountains.

They did not reach the Missouri or even try. They reached the North Platte, and at Deer Creek Crossing (now Glenrock, Wyoming) they found plenty of travelers who were willing to listen to their promise of a short road to Montana gold at Bannack.

Now it was needed more than ever, because while their backs were turned the missing miners had discovered Alder Gulch, which put the Grasshopper diggings in the shade.

CHAPTER 10

The Way to the Gold Fields

The first comers to the Grasshopper diggings were people accustomed to hardship. They were already in the West—men, some with families, who had left the California gold fields or those in Colorado, looking for something richer. News of the riches at the Grasshopper diggings spread fast, down to Denver and then to the Middle West and the Eastern states.

Those who came in 1863 had a vastly greater distance to travel than the first arrivals. They went along the Oregon Trail. St. Joseph, Missouri, or Omaha, Nebraska, was the jumping-off place for most of them. They crossed Nebraska and Wyoming, along the Platte River most of the way, and came to the far-flung Rocky Mountains. The continent's backbone barred the way to Idaho, but benevolent Nature had arranged an easy place to get over the Great Divide, at the south end of the Wind River range, southwest of the middle of Wyoming.

South Pass was not impressive. Some emigrants went over it without realizing that they had crossed the Continental Divide. But they weren't looking for a scenic route. What they wanted was an easy one. This was easy, all right, but the Oregon Trail had to swing southwest there, and if you were going to what is now Montana you wanted to go *north*west. Then there were more mountains, and a desert, followed by worse mountain country than you had ever dreamed of. Anyway, you were on the wrong side of the Divide, after all. You still had to go over it, eastward this time, at Monida Pass, to reach the Montana gold fields.

John Bozeman's road avoided all those mountains. It did not go over the Divide at all.

Crossing the Plains was a great adventure for anyone, but by 1863 the adventurers were not trail blazers. America had been moving west along the Emigrant Trail for twenty years. Everybody knew, or knew of, someone who had made the journey. Everybody could get advice and warnings aplenty about crossing the Plains.

And there were guidebooks. They had a brisk sale to potential pilgrims who had never before bought a book of any kind. Maybe a man had, for study, a copy of the *New Guide for the Overland Route to California,* by Andrew Child, published in 1852. This would be frayed, ragged, and dirty, because someone took it along to California and brought it back after he was disillusioned there— or, less likely, after he got rich.

This told the traveler that oxen, medium sized and six or seven years old, were preferable to mules for motive power and that he should have four yoke (pairs) in the team for each wagon. One wagon for each three persons was about right, and no more than eight wagons should travel together, because larger parties caused unnecessary delay. This advice about small parties was good in the early 1850s when the book was new, but only a few years later it was dangerously out of date. The Indians were angry by that time, and a big wagon train was needed for defense.

A more recent book was *The Prairie Traveler, A Handbook for Overland Expeditions,* by Captain Randolph B. Marcy, published in 1859. It was used for twenty years, even though by 1863 it was already out of date. Captain Marcy wrote his book because the War Department had suggested that it was needed. He gave brief details about no less than twenty-eight routes to various destinations. But when he wrote, Idaho did not exist. Travelers went to California or Oregon, New Mexico or Texas, Great Salt Lake City or the Cherry Creek diggings, which became Denver in 1860.

This is the kind of information provided on part of the route from Laramie Crossing of the South Platte to Fort Bridger via Bridger's Pass, 520½ miles:

MILES

Laramie Crossing to:

14 Bryan's Crossing.—Road runs on the south side of the Platte. Good grass and water.

12 First Crossing of Pole Creek.—Pole Creek is a rapid stream, sandy bed, 15 feet wide, and two feet deep. Good grass on the creek, and wood three miles off on the bluffs.

37 Second Crossing of Pole Creek.—Road runs along the creek. Good grass and good camps at any point. Good road.

17¼   Third Crossing of Pole Creek.—Good camp. Wood on the bluffs.

20½   Fourth Crossing of Pole Creek.—Creek dry for three miles. Good grass.

20¼   Bluffs covered with dead pines.—Creek is crossed several times. Road runs over a rough, broken country. Good grass.

And so forth. Sometimes there was "poor grass" or "grass not plentiful"; sometimes both grass and water were bad. The pilgrim might have to use sagebrush for fuel. On other routes he would be warned to gather *bois de vache*, wood of cow, translated in polite English as buffalo chips, and to keep it dry, because if it gets wet it's no longer chips and won't burn.

Captain Marcy knew the problems and told his readers what they needed to know, such as the comparative merits of oxen versus mules and where to buy the animals (cheaper on the frontier). He told how to organize a company of emigrants, elect a captain, and divide the camp work fairly. He told what kind of wood a wagon should be built of, how much and what kind of supplies to take, how to make pemmican, what kind of clothing was best suited to hard travel, how to select and use firearms, how to sink a well in a muddy stream bed with a quicksand bottom; how to make camp chairs, build a fire, jerk meat, and track Indians (assuming that the reader really wanted to meet some), and how to deal with them after he caught up with them—or they caught up with him.

Captain Marcy recommended a party of fifty to seventy-five well-armed men. Members of a group that big could take turns herding and guarding the grazing stock; they could sometimes, by a show of strength, intimidate small parties of Indians or, if they had to, fight off larger bands.

Guidebooks went out of date before they could be printed, because conditions changed so fast. Grass at a "good" camping place might be eaten off early in the season so that animals coming through later had to be herded two miles away. The wobbly beginnings of a settlement, where a traveler hoped to buy emergency supplies or have some blacksmithing done, might be only charred ruins by the time he reached it, burned by Indians.

Some guidebooks were altogether too optimistic. In 1859 there were two popular guides for getting to the Denver region, written by men named Byers and Oakes. The pilgrims who followed them went west with the jubilant slogan "Pikes Peak or Bust," and returned in wrath with the motto "Kill Byers and Oakes."

When the great migration of '63 started out, as soon as the prairie grass greened up in the spring, headed for the new gold fields, theirs was a new adventure. The discovery at Grasshopper Creek was too new to have produced any printed guide. Still, if a man managed to get way out there to the Rocky Mountains he would be somewhat seasoned and experienced. He could always ask somebody he met on the road about the problems up ahead. Freighters were always moving along the way, and there were disappointed adventurers heading home. Of course, a freighter who had made money hauling goods from Salt Lake to the gold camps would have a different story from the one told by a ragged fellow on his way back to the States.

If, having passed Fort Laramie, having put behind him all those toilsome miles, a man heard of a road through the Powder River country that avoided the mountain passes altogether (especially if he was a flatlander who knew nothing of mountains), he listened carefully. A *new* road, a road hundreds of miles shorter, sounded good; but no matter where he came from, he had heard that the Sioux and their allies the Cheyennes didn't want white people coming through there. He had to balance the saving of time and effort against the perils of attack by painted savages.

CHAPTER 11

The First Conducted Tour

Oscar Collister was not quite twenty when, in October, 1861, he and three other young telegraphers were sent to the wild West by the Western Union Telegraph Company to man remote stations along the line that was being built from Omaha to Salt Lake City. The California State Telegraph Company was being built eastward to Salt Lake from San Francisco. They connected soon after Collister reached his post.

Collister's assignment was Deer Creek Station on the Oregon

Trail, about one hundred miles west of Fort Laramie and twenty-eight miles east of the site where Casper, Wyoming, later developed. He never did figure out why he was chosen for the dangerous job at Deer Creek. Collister was not the sturdy, brawny type of pioneer: he weighed only 100 pounds and had had a sickly boyhood. But telegraphers were in great demand—so great that recruiting officers were forbidden to enlist them for the Army.

Collister had already been fired from a railroad job because the superintendent believed that confining work would kill him. At Deer Creek he was not confined. His district stretched some forty miles in each direction from his station, and he had to keep the line open. He almost got fired when Ed Creighton, who had built the line, got a look at the frail young operator. But after Collister rode out, found, and repaired a break in the wire twenty-five miles from his station, Creighton decided this was the kind of man he needed.

Breaks were sometimes caused by Indians pulling down the talking wire. A small war party from one Sioux village cut a chunk out of the telegraph line, and each man in the party made a bracelet of the shining wire. But soon after, the village was stricken with a mysterious disease (high fever and rash) that killed several people. The wire, the village medicine man decided, was responsible for their affliction. The Great Spirit was protecting the white man's medicine wire. The medicine man ordered all the pieces of wire buried, and for more than two years that particular band of Sioux let the telegraph line alone.

The Deer Creek settlement consisted of a scattering of log buildings, totaling about fifteen rooms in all, used as storerooms and dwellings for the employees of a French-Canadian trader named Bisonette. There was a stockade used for a corral. Collister had a cabin to himself and at first ate at the cookhouse. The usual menu was wild meat, bread cooked in a skillet, and coffee. The young telegrapher ate more than seemed possible for a man of his size.

Bisonette took a liking to Collister and coached him on the customs of the West. He needed instruction; he had been there only a few days when he won an argument (about a point in Lincoln's inaugural address) with a Pony Express rider named Bond who was known to be a killer. Collister was just lucky. Bond decided to kill him next time he talked back, not now. The occasion did not arise, for the Pony Express ended with the completion of the transcontinental telegraph line and Bond went somewhere else.

Deer Creek was a busy place. It was a stop on Ben Holladay's stage line, and most emigrant trains stopped there under the gracious shade trees to pick up mail, replenish supplies, make repairs, and get the latest telegraphic news about how the war was going back home.

A frequent visitor was the terrifying Joseph Albert Slade, division superintendent for the Overland stage line. Slade was a ruthless killer—that was why Ben Holladay hired him to clean the ruffians off the line—and a dedicated hater. Among the people he hated were "frenchmen"—the French half-breeds employed by Bisonette.[13] One of young Collister's problems was to keep on good terms with both the division superintendent and the trading-post employees. He managed to do it.

Although a good gust of prairie wind might have blown the frail young operator off his feet, he was durable. He was eighty-nine when he told the story of his life for publication in *Annals of Wyoming* in 1930.

He had been at Deer Creek for almost two years when an event occurred that became historically important:

> In the summer of 1863 a man named Bozeman, accompanied by an old time mountaineer and guide, whose name I have forgotten [John M. Jacobs; being forgotten was his destiny], arrived at Deer Creek from Montana, having staked out a trail . . . that would shorten the distance of the then existing route to Montana from points east of the Missouri River.
>
> They established a camp and started in to divert emigrants destined to Montana. They were not long in gathering a sufficient number of wagons to make a good sized party, and started out to establish the new trail, going directly down the old trader's trail to Powder River, then to Lodgepole Creek. Here they awoke one morning to find themselves surrounded by Indians and their route blocked. No hostile demonstrations were made, or calls for a pow-wow to explain. This condition continued for several days. Finally two men volunteered to make a trip back to Deer Creek to report to the military officers and get an escort. They studied the situation for two or three nights, always watching for a chance to escape, before they found an opening that they considered safe. They succeeded in getting out unmolested and came through all right.
>
> Lodgepole Creek was about a hundred and fifty miles from Deer Creek, so these men had no little journey to make in order to report this predicament. The situation was reported to Fort Laramie, and a company of sixty cavalrymen were immediately started for the

scene of the trouble, with orders to take them through to Montana, but the night they crossed the North Platte, a telegram came cancelling the order to escort them to Montana, and instead, instructing that they be escorted back to the old Mormon trail at any point they might choose east of the South Pass. The last order was obeyed and the party was next heard from at South Pass.

In the spring of 1864, young Collister was fed up with Deer Creek. He couldn't cook, so he boarded with men who had Indian wives, and he didn't think much of their cooking. He obtained an honorable release from his job with Western Union Telegraph Company. One evening just before he left for Salt Lake, he had a final visit from an Indian girl called Bright Star, who had called often (with a chaperone) on other occasions and now had had a vision that she wanted to warn him about. His life was in danger; he would be shot in the back with an arrow by an Indian who did not like him. Bright Star had seen Collister (alias Mela Hoska Chischela) and herself together in the happy hunting grounds. She had consulted a medicine man, who told her that Collister must go away over the high mountains because a war between the whites and Indians was on. Two days later he was on his way to Salt Lake, and before he got there the Indian War of 1864–1868 had begun.

At Deer Creek, Bozeman circulated among the wagons, spreading the gospel about his guided tour to the gold fields, and he made a lot of converts. The emigrants were hopeful or they wouldn't have come so far with so much effort and expense. They were suspicious, because they had listened to a lot of lies and rumors. They were flexible: if they were going to "the Beaverhead," to "the Grasshopper diggings," to "Bannack City"—all the same thing—they didn't *have* to go by the old, long route, twice over the Rockies, when they could save so much time on Bozeman's road.

One advantage of the new road, as anybody could see, was its newness. A man wouldn't have to graze his stock miles from camp. The grass hadn't been all used up by the animals with a lot of trains ahead of him. Plenty of grass, the young promoter promised. Plenty of water—with some exceptions, of course. Plenty of wood to burn. Lots of wild game for fresh meat. And with a strong party, they could stand off the Indians if any Indians came. What more could anyone ask?

Bozeman made a fine impression on the pilgrims. He was tall and good-looking, with a tinge of red in his cheeks. He knew how a frontiersman ought to dress, so he wore a fine suit of fringed buckskin.

He and Jacobs had raised a stake somehow after they reached the relative civilization of the main trail, hungry and half naked. They had also recruited a third guide, a French half-blood who was touted as an authority on getting the tour up to the Big Horn River. His name was Rafiel, or perhaps Raphael (nobody bothered about spelling), and his nickname was Boullion, because he was very fond of soup. He was also very fond of whiskey.

CHAPTER 12

Sam Word's Story

One of the wagons that pulled up at Deer Creek was driven by a young lawyer from Missouri, Sam Word, aged twenty-six, who had left a law practice, his wife, and a small son back home while he fared forth for the gold fields to better his condition.

Word had a wagon and three yoke of oxen when he left St. Jo, Missouri, on May 7. Nine days later he reached Marysville, Kansas, in a party that had grown to include four wagons, nine men, two dogs, three ponies, and eleven yoke of oxen. As they moved west, they joined up with more travelers.

Word missed his wife and worried about her and the boy, but he was a sincerely religious man and trusted in the will of God. When he left home, he had told his wife of the places along the Oregon Trail where he could expect to catch up with his mail. Whenever he got a letter, he mentioned it in his journal, and every time he wrote to her he told her to which station she should address the next one.

After a month on the road, he killed the first jackrabbit he had ever seen. It made good, tender eating. The next day, near Ash Hollow, he learned how to hunt antelope. He lay flat on his back and waved his rifle with a handkerchief tied to the end of the barrel. When the animals approached, curious about this phenomenon (as who wouldn't be?), he fired.

He did his first washing on June 13, with a tub and washboard borrowed from one of the families in the wagon train, and had a good bath in the North Platte River. He rejoiced that he probably wouldn't have to do another washing for a month. Emigrants got used to being pretty gamey.

The next day, Sunday, they had preaching in camp. Word decided that the sermon-giver was "a one-horse preacher."

There was plenty of time to visit around among the wagons when they camped to cook and sleep and graze the stock. On Monday Word noted that a woman of sixteen, married just before she left on this journey, was very sick and so was one of the preacher's children. The train was waiting a day or two for the child to die.

"May the Lord save us from such an affliction," wrote sympathetic young Sam Word. "May he spare our little boy that he may be a blessing to us in our old age. Nevertheless his will be done and not mine."

The next day the preacher's child died and burial was the same afternoon. The train moved on, leaving another grave on the Oregon Trail. On June 22 they reached Fort Laramie. When you got that far, you had made progress and you were committed to the undertaking.

Eight days later they camped a few miles west of Deer Creek Station and got the word about the proposed Bozeman cutoff that would run north. Several men in the party were thinking of trying the route that John Bozeman was promoting. Wagons had been gathering for two weeks.

The grass was good, Bozeman assured them. Yes, the route had its dangers, because it went through the heart of the Indian country. But by the old route, Bannack City was 800 miles away. The new one was only about 400 or 450—nobody knew except approximately. They could save a month or six weeks of travel drudgery if they went with Bozeman and Jacobs.

On July 2 they were still waiting, considering, trying to decide. More wagons came in every day, some freight wagons with goods for the miners, a few families, but mostly unencumbered men anxious for a try at the riches in the earth. They kept hearing rumors of new gold discoveries—*The Powder River, that's the place! No, I heard it was the Yellowstone.* The rumors were only rumors, but it all sounded fine. Of course, there *were* Indians up that way. How could a man tell what was best for him to do?

Until he reached this camp, Word had been a loner, driving his wagon and fending for himself. Now he teamed up with George W. Irvin II, who had just broken up with his partner. They divvied up, the partner taking the wagon and the load and Irvin taking the team—a yoke of oxen and a yoke of cows. Irvin would ride his pony, take turns driving, and board with Sam Word.

Still at Deer Creek on Independence Day, they celebrated by eating fresh peaches and drinking some whiskey to feel patriotic. Oscar Collister rode over from the telegraph office with the latest war news: there had been a big fight near Gettysburg, in Pennsylvania, just yesterday. The rebels were said to be repulsed and retreating. This was the first war news travelers had had in a long time.

One bad thing about Bozeman's road was that Sam Word would miss getting any mail if he went that way, but he planned to write to the postmasters at Fort Bridger and Salt Lake City to have his letters forwarded to Bannack City. "Will write home tomorrow," he noted in his journal. "Wish I could see my beloved wife and child tonight. I may never see them again, this is a dangerous road to travel."

On Sunday, July 5, Word wrote, "We start out tomorrow on our perilous trip. Trust that Providence will extend his protecting care over us."

The men who were going with Bozeman held a meeting and elected a captain, James Brady. And on July 6 at about eight o'clock in the morning, forty-six wagons with eighty-nine men, ten women, and several children started on the new route to the gold-rich Beaverhead country. They left the North Platte about eight miles above Deer Creek Station.

The country was rough enough to require unhitching and double-teaming to get the heavy wagons through in some places, but the grass was good and there was water. They traveled ten miles the next day and camped near a spring and a slough. There would be no more water for twenty miles.

A Mexican in the train rode back to Deer Creek and returned with more war news, and Sam Word wrote: "Hooker and Lee have had a big fight—Lee is reported cut to pieces and his army destroyed, losing fifty thousand in killed and wounded and eighteen thousand prisoners. Don't believe a word of it—think if they have fought Lee is victorious."

This was more of the big fight at Gettysburg, a Northern victory. War news delivered from Deer Creek by a Mexican on a horse might well be garbled in transmission. It wasn't General Joseph E. Hooker, it was General George G. Meade; and nobody knew it then, but the "big fight at Gettysburg" was the turning point of the war. It was also the mid-point. If Meade had followed up his victory, the war would have ended long before April 9, 1865.

The days passed, and the miles piled slowly up behind the plodding teams. Grass was good and water was tolerable; there was no wood, but sagebrush and greasewood burned hotly for cooking. On July 8 the travelers could see the beginning of the Wind River Mountains far to the left.

Next day they made twelve or fourteen miles along Dry Creek, which had virtually no water in it, and the guides told them they would cross this creek about a hundred times before reaching its mouth on Powder River.

Next day they had something to think about: the grass had been eaten off by a lot of Indian ponies—three or four thousand, someone guessed. And the water was awful. There was nothing to do about the water, but at each camp the wagons circled to form a corral so the stock, after grazing, could be penned inside and wouldn't stampede if the Indians came.

July 12 was Sunday, and the train moved on, although Word would have preferred to lay up and observe the Sabbath. There was more water now, but it tasted very salty, and the creek bed was white with alkali, which he called saleratus.

Next day the cattle and all the emigrants were sick from the awful water. The cattle had something like the colic; "They are puffed up with wind and breathe hard, groaning considerably. We gave them fat meat, lard and vinegar, which appeared to relieve them." Forcing fat down the throat of an alkalied ox was the standard treatment.

Sam fell off his mule the next day when it shied at a jackrabbit. He was pretty lame afterward. He wrote, "Have just had a bath and a good wash in the river, put on some clean clothes and feel like I could rest well tonight. If I were only at home in a clean bed with my good little wife, I would rest so much better. I hope she is well and enjoying herself. May the Lord watch over her and our little boy."

Everything was going pretty well with the first wagon train up Bozeman's Trail. Sam saw snow on July 16 on the Wind River Mountains. He had never seen snow in July before. He shot a big gray wolf at 215 yards. Next day, with two other men, he traveled fifteen miles to the Big Horn Mountains to prospect for gold but did not raise the color. (He was learning the slang of the gold fields.)

The train camped that night on Willow Creek, a branch of Crazy Woman Fork of Powder River. (Remember Crazy Woman; the Indians certainly kept it in mind. Crazy Woman Fork was an ideal spot for an ambush, and it was the scene of many a bloody battle during the few years that the Bozeman Trail was used.)

The next morning, July 20, the men turned out the stock to graze and everybody was eating noon dinner when James Kirkpatrick, age fifteen, noticed movement on a distant ridge. He called John Bozeman's attention to the matter.

"Indians," said Bozeman. He peered through his telescope and reported, "Not many of 'em have guns."

Someone yelled, "Indians!" and the whole camp went into a panic.

Men shouted, "Bring in the stock!" but nobody did it. Everyone was too busy making sure firearms were loaded. A man named Baker hastily loaded his muzzle-loader, then laid it down. His wife noticed it, loaded it again, and put it down. Baker, justifiably excited about the prospect of fighting Indians, rammed in a third charge. Fortunately he caught on to the condition of his weapon before firing it or he would have blown himself up.

A few men ran, and others leaped on horses and galloped, to bring the herd into the enclosure made by the corraled wagons. And then the Indians came—not curdling the blood with war whoops but acting quite friendly. Bozeman and Jacobs tried to get their frantic tourists calmed down, especially the ten women.

"There's squaws with them Injuns," Bozeman pointed out. "That's a good sign. And they're making signs that they're friendly."

There were some 150 Indians, Cheyenne and Sioux—a lot more of them than there were defenders in the wagon corral. Bozeman and Jacobs and old Soup made ready for a parley, to be conducted with proper dignity, but the emigrants' womenfolks took over. When you have company, you feed them, insisted the ladies. Therefore they would lay out a feast to pacify the visitors.

"Don't you do it!" warned Bozeman. "They'll take it as a sign of weakness. They'll think we're scared."

The emigrant women went right ahead anyway, bustling around to lay out the plates and bring goodies from the food boxes in the wagons. One arrogant young buck scornfully started to ride his horse over the spread-out viands. John Bozeman drew a bead on him, but the old chief prevented calamity. He grabbed the young brave's bridle, chewed him out, and sent him away.

"Another moment," the Kirkpatrick boy said years later, "and the whole pack would have been killed, and we would have had to fight all the Sioux and Cheyennes in Wyoming as we went our way."

The emigrant ladies served their feast (which some of the Indians sullenly refused) while their menfolks followed inquisitive Indians around and snatched back what they stole. Then one of the Indian leaders made a speech. Jacobs and old Soup must have been the interpreters. The old chief politely but firmly issued an ultimatum to the white invaders. His message was frank and clear:

You can't go on in the direction you are going. You are going into our country, where we hunt. This is the only good big hunting ground left for us. Your people have taken the rest or scared the game away.

We won't let our women and children starve. This is where we make meat, and we will keep this land.

Along the great road to the south, white men have driven away all the buffalo and antelope. We won't let you do that here.

If you will turn back to the Platte, we will let you go. We will not hurt you. But if you go on into our hunting country, our people will wipe you out. They have already been warned with signal fires on the mountains.

This statement of position left nothing in doubt. There was no diplomacy or hypocrisy about it. *Go back or we'll kill you.* The emigrants listened grimly, took sidelong, meaningful looks at one another. They glanced toward the mountains and saw the signal smokes.

The emigrants needed to go into executive session with no Indians listening in on their powwow. The three guides and the train

[63]

captain, James Brady, got together for a moment and figured out what to do about privacy for discussion. They gave the word to the old chief:

We have to talk about this. You leave one man here to take our message to you after we talk. The rest of you go away now.

This idea was satisfactory to the Indians. They left—with a telescope and nine horse bridles. Then the emigrants argued. They argued for ten days. Sometimes the train moved back a couple of miles to get better feed for the stock. The continuing debate was interrupted by a couple of interesting events, a bear fight and a wedding.

The bear, identified as a grizzly, showed up in a clump of willows. Bozeman and Jacobs and Soup, wise in the ways of grizzlies, yelled a warning—*nobody* fooled with a grizzly. An Indian who succeeded in killing one was entitled to count *coup* on it and claim the same honor as if he had killed an armed human enemy.

The pilgrims weren't so smart. Fifteen or twenty of them piled into the brush with rifles and pistols, chasing the bear. Somebody yelled, "A man killed!" One woman fainted and the rest all screamed.

One elderly man came staggering out with his whole lower lip torn and hanging loose at one end. Somebody sewed it up with black thread and put a bandage on. Another man had his scalp slashed clear to the skull.

When the bear gave up and died with forty lead balls in him, the mighty hunters butchered him—plenty fat, and big as a cow (someone estimated enthusiastically)—and the camp ate bear meat for supper.

The wedding was less exciting. A young woman who had left her husband down on the Platte was traveling with a fellow named Beaumont, and the good women of the wagon train thought it was scandalous. They grumbled about it until everybody was upset. So Beaumont and his female companion decided to get married.

John Bozeman obligingly performed the ceremony, such as it was. He had no legal right to marry anyone, but, then, the bride had no right to get married again, either. The respectable ladies were satisfied with the arrangements, however; Bozeman, Beaumont, and the bigamous bride had all proved that their intentions were good.[14]

Meanwhile, the debate continued. Move on and fight Indians, or turn back and waste all the effort they had expended since the sixth of the month? They still saw Indians watching on the hills.

The guides recommended waiting for reinforcements and then pushing through. A train of seventy-five freight wagons belonging to the Creighton brothers, Ed and John, was probably on the Bozeman Cutoff now, coming up from Deer Creek.

"You can travel with the wagons in a double line," John Bozeman urged. "We're well armed and we've got plenty of provisions. We can night-guard the oxen—they don't stampede easy, like horses. We'll get you through in first-rate shape."

James Brady, their elected captain, thought so too. He had something to lose (besides his life) if he guessed wrong: four teams of oxen, three spans each, pulling wagons loaded with freight to sell at the gold camp.

But more and more of the men liked the idea of fighting Indians less and less. A few of them had women and children along. All of them could feel their hair stand up for a scalping knife.

Three men volunteered to ride back and scout for Creighton's train or, if it wasn't on the way, to telegraph back to Fort Laramie and ask for a military escort if they couldn't get one at Deer Creek. After all, that's what Fort Laramie was *for*, to protect emigrants.

Lieutenant William Coleman was one of the messengers. The guide Rafiel, or Soup, was another. George Irvin, who had teamed up with Sam Word, was the third. They rode at night, hoping the Indians wouldn't notice.

They didn't meet Creighton's train of freight wagons. They went clear back to Deer Creek Station and dispatched a telegram to Fort Laramie.

Meanwhile the beleaguered wagon train camped, moved a little to get grass, worried, and debated what to do.

"It makes me sick to think of it," Sam Word wrote in his journal. "Lose time and travel three hundred miles for nothing."

But neither did he like to take too many risks. There would be enough trouble on the old Oregon Trail and on the way up to Grasshopper diggings through the Rockies.

George Irvin, Lieutenant Coleman, and Soup were entangled in red tape down at Deer Creek. Major Thomas L. Mackey, commanding officer at Fort Laramie, referred their request to General

Keene in Omaha. General Keene approved. Major Mackey did not. He did as he was told, but he sent a diplomatically phrased objection back to the general on August 3:

> In obedience to your order I have organized an expedition and it marches this morning to the relief of the emigrant train encamped on Powder River. Your order taken in connection with that of Mr. Coleman would seem to imply that I am to send this escort through to Bannock City. This I am inclined to think you will change upon a full understanding of the fact.
>
> I understand that a treaty exists with the Indians reserving the Country North of the Platte to them as a hunting ground, and especially stipulating that no highway should be made through this Country. This route these emigrants have taken runs directly through this reservation. When this train was about ready to leave Deer Creek on this trip they were told by some Indians of the existence of this treaty and warned not to attempt it as they would not be permitted to go through.
>
> Learning these facts I telegraphed Lt. Love commanding at Deer Creek not to let them move in that direction. Several dispatches passed between myself and the leaders of this train, in reference to the matter and they were so urgent in their request to be permitted to go through this route that I finally recalled the order to Lt. Love at the same time telling these men that if they went over this route they did so at their own peril.
>
> Under these circumstances they having been repeatedly warned and finally got into trouble on account of their own willfulness, I think they should be brought back to the old road and not sent through.
>
> The expedition composed of sixty men will leave here to day with Ninety days rations with orders to escort the train through to Bannock City or as far as necessary. Should you see fit to order the train to be brought back to Deer Creek I can reach the command five days hence.
>
> P.S. Since writing the foregoing I have seen the guide employed by the leaders of the train. He tells me that the Indians offered no objection to the train turning back but would not allow them to proceed as their going across there was in violation of their treaty with Gen. Harney. The Indians engaged are the Sioux and Cheyennes.

But it was not any mere treaty that turned back Bozeman's first guided tour, and it was not the Army's refusal to provide an escort.

What decided the emigrants was the Indians' clear and frank state-ment of purpose: *Go back or we'll wipe you out.*

The three-man mission came back into camp bringing a fourth man, one Bovier, who had been very friendly toward Sam Word weeks before on the main trail. He put the blame on Rafiel, old Soup, who wouldn't take the party up to the Big Horn River, not through all them Injuns. Bovier said Rafiel was a coward and ought to be shot. Bovier himself, he assured the emigrants grandly, could have helped them get through, but he had to go back. He worked for the Army and had permission to be away only long enough to guide them back to the Platte. *Hurry* them back to the Platte was probably his real assignment. Guides they already had in plenty.

John Bozeman said they didn't need old Soup anyway. *He* would guide the party all the way. All he insisted on was that eight wag-ons agree to go along with him. Just eight.

But only four wagons pulled out of line to bull through the In-dian menace by taking John Bozeman's road. One of these be-longed to eager young Kirkpatrick and his brother.

Bozeman counted wagons and shook his head. "You better go back with the rest," he advised.

They did; all the wagons went back, with their drivers fuming and cussing about the time lost, the provisions wasted.

Nine men on horseback went on, however, with Bozeman as their leader. One of them was George Irvin, who left his stock for Sam Word to use and look after. The ten riders, with one pack horse, left at midnight, with the other emigrants all turning out to wish them luck. They figured on a ride of 600 or 700 miles through In-dian country.

Their route, Bozeman explained, was from the headwaters of the Powder River and across the Big Horn Mountains into the country between the Big Horns and the Wind River Mountains.

The intrepid horseback party had all their grub on that lone pack horse: fifty pounds of baked bread and crackers, about the same of dried buffalo meat, and plenty of salt. They would depend mainly on the game they could kill.

They traveled only at night, to evade the Indians—and the sec-ond night out the pack horse fell off a precipice into a river.

For twenty-one days they had no food at all except fresh meat without salt—and half-cooked meat, at that, because their kettles had gone with the pack horse. They dared not have much of a cooking fire, in case inquisitive Indians should see the smoke. But there was plenty of game, including buffalo and black bears.

They crossed from the Wind River Valley to the Stinking Water, now named the Shoshone, a tributary of Clark's Fork of the Yellowstone, and into the badlands of northwestern Wyoming. And there they had the worst experience of the whole journey. They traveled for four days—and after the first one they didn't even have half-raw meat without salt. There was no game. Even the birds of the air shunned that area. For a full day and a night neither men nor beasts had a drink of water.

Their horses were exhausted. The men, tired and dejected, lost all hope on the fourth day. They were ready to give up and die. But John Bozeman wasn't. He urged and encouraged and jollied them up on their feet again. To keep the horses staggering along, only half the men rode at any one time. The miserable travelers strung out over a long distance.

Suddenly the horses perked up a little and moved with more enthusiasm. Bozeman called a halt and about midnight got the whole party together. He was not a talkative man, but the news he imparted didn't require many words: "Boys, we have been thirty-two hours without water. The horses have found it. I can smell it myself."

And the others realized that "smelling water" was a fact for men as well as horses. It was a kind of dampness in the nostrils. An hour later they were on the Stinking Water, flat on their bellies, sucking up fresh, cool, plentiful water.

At sunrise after that wonderful, wallowing drink of water, they even got something to eat. John Bozeman killed an eagle. The national emblem wasn't much meat for ten starving men, but it cheered them up. That was their first food after three days.

They found plenty of game after that in the Big Horn Basin, from Stinking Water to Clark's Fork and the Yellowstone—and there were plenty of Indians, too. Several times they came upon abandoned Indian camps, and twice they were so close to Indians that the dogs ran out and barked. Bozeman's party backtracked in a hurry.

But in all that terrible journey they never had an Indian fight, never had a man sick, and never lost one of their ten remaining tired horses.

At dawn one day they stood on a knoll on the top of the Belt

Mountains at a place that Irvin proposed should be named Bozeman Pass. He was always proud afterward that he had that honor, for he thoroughly admired John Bozeman. From Bozeman Pass they looked down at the beautiful Gallatin Valley.

At sunset the next day, at the Three Forks of the Missouri, they suddenly came upon two white men cooking supper over a campfire—ah, the marvelous smell of bacon frying! Bozeman's party sat up all night, cooking and eating bacon. Fifteen or twenty minutes after each meal, their stomachs rebelled, they vomited, and then cooked more bacon.

While they reveled in the feast, they heard the tremendous news of the gold discovery at Alder Gulch. The gold there was supposed to be fabulously rich. Just about everybody had stampeded over from Bannack City, and camps had sprung up, were still growing. In one of them, Nevada City, there had already been a very peculiar killing. One of Sheriff Henry Plummer's deputies, name of Dillingham, had been gunned down right in a crowd of miners by two other deputies, but there was so much quick tussling that a man couldn't be sure just who did it. There was a quick trial of the killers, who were sentenced to hang, but it all came to nothing. Nobody was hanged—after the graves were dug and ready. The new diggings were rich, rich, rich, and the camp was a place of turmoil.

The rescued travelers talked and ate all night, and the next morning all twelve men started for the brand-new diggings, the land of promise, seventy miles away, and its busiest, biggest camp, Virginia City.

The two good Samaritans had just come from there, had intended to stay out a while, panning for new prospects. But they went back with the rest because their unexpected guests had eaten up the entire grub supply. When Irvin told his story twenty-five years later, the only one of his companions that he named was his hero, John Bozeman. He did not even name the two prospectors whose food supply, freely given in disaster, revived the famished men who had completed Bozeman's first conducted tour.

CHAPTER 13

The Long Road, After All

Meanwhile, the wagons had turned back July 31 on the Bozeman Cutoff, with their grumpy owners expecting to reach the old road, the Oregon Trail, somewhere near Willow Springs in three more days if they were lucky. They weren't lucky.

But living was good, if not easy. The streams were full of fish; there were plenty of elk and an occasional buffalo, though no herds of them; and currants, gooseberries, and raspberries were plentiful.

Tempers were short, however. Sam Word fired his driver, Dan— the fellow was too independent, always growling when asked to do anything. And water was scarce. They got some for their stock, by digging holes and letting the water seep in, but not enough.

A small wagon, only two horses drawing it, broke down. They moved the load, divided it among other wagons, and abandoned the broken one.

Word's young cattle got out of hand, ran over another man's wagon, and turned it over. He wrote sourly, "It's loaded with two barrels of whiskey, pity it didn't burst them open, then our guides wouldn't be so drunk while on duty." The guides were old Soup, who had turned out to be a coward; Bovier, on leave from government service to hurry them back to the Platte; and John Jacobs.

Water became scarcer. Men could no longer get enough seep in holes dug in stream beds. They had to carry the alkali-foul water in buckets to the animals and still the stock was thirsty. Everybody was grouchy. Wagons no longer traveled in an orderly line. They didn't corral, either.

On August 9, after ten days instead of three, they reached the Platte, not at Willow Springs but at the Red Buttes, some forty miles above Deer Creek. Human beings and animals alike were frantic with thirst.

At the Red Buttes they found a train of thirty or forty freight wagons camped, en route from St. Joe, Missouri, to Salt Lake. Some of them would probably go on to Bannack. Bannack was still the destination of the wagons that had toiled part way up John Bozeman's trail and then toiled back again. Bannack, the Grasshopper diggings—not the new, swarming camps along Alder Gulch. News of that great discovery had not, apparently, filtered down to the Oregon Trail. Sam Word didn't mention it in his journal. Maybe he didn't believe it any more than he believed what he had heard about the big fight at Gettysburg. He did comment in camp at the Red Buttes:

> We have been unlucky indeed, have lost considerable over a month and gained nothing, except we've seen the country and had some exciting adventures. I don't know that I regret it much, though I preferred not losing any time. I have however learned many things by the months of experience. I came out in part for the purpose of seeing the country and having some adventures.

He was an honest journal keeper. To better one's condition was the high-sounding reason that every solid citizen gave. Not all of them admitted that the far wolf-howl of adventure had helped to lure them on.

The route they had tried, John Bozeman's road, certainly was much shorter than any other if you wanted to reach the headwaters of the Missouri (the Continental Divide), Word decided. And he was sure there would be a road through there some day, as he was sure of another thing: "The government ought to give immigrants [sic] all the assistance they wish in their efforts to develop the country."

Heaven knows the government was trying on the Oregon Trail, and it tried on the new cutoff three years later.

On the eleventh of August, Word and the other wagons pulled out to go on west. He kept running into men he knew and getting word of other acquaintances who were on the road. Everybody seemed to be going west—or moving east after going west.

On August 12 they camped at a military post and telegraph station on the Sweetwater River, close enough to famous Independence Rock so that he rode over for a good look. He even knew some of the men whose names were carved there.

Word telegraphed home that he was well and asked for an answer to be sent to the next stop. His young oxen were tiring, so he traded them, paying $35 to boot, for an older yoke of heavier cattle. The telegram he sent cost $40, and he began to worry a little about running short of money. There would still be expenses, for bridge and ferry tolls, for repairs, replenishing supplies, for emergencies.

Two days later, at the telegraph station at the Three Crossings of the Stillwater, he rejoiced in the answer to his telegram. Everyone was well and little Willie was growing. Little Willie's adventuresome papa could not expect to hear from home again until he reached Salt Lake. That was the longer way to Bannack.

On August 17 they reached South Pass Station, where Lander's Cutoff left the road to Salt Lake. Most of the train took the cutoff, rougher but shorter.

On August 18 Word went over South Pass, that admirable place where Nature took pity on the men to come when she heaped the Rocky Mountains. At South Pass, she made it easy to get over the Continental Divide.

That day Word talked to a party of packers who were coming back from the Beaverhead mines. "They gave an encouraging account of the gold prospects in Bannack and vicinity." But he did not mention Alder Gulch, perhaps including that in "vicinity." It was seventy miles east of Grasshopper Creek.

At Ham's Fork, August 22, Sam traded his wagon for a bigger, stronger one and took the oath of allegiance to the United States government. Thirty or forty soldiers were stationed there to make sure that men did take it. Emigrants who were rooting for the Confederacy (at this safe distance from the battlefields of the Civil War) grumbled about the oath, but Sam Word was for the Union.

The War of the Rebellion was still going on, as everybody knew. It was half over, as nobody knew. Union troops—such as could be spared from the battlefields back home—guarded the westward trails and made sure that emigrants swore loyalty to the Union whether they meant it or not. The oath they took was this:

I_____do solemnly swear (or affirm) in the presence of Almighty God that I will henceforth faithfully support, protect and defend the Constitution of the United States and the Union of the states thereunder; and that I will in like manner abide by and faithfully support all laws and proclamations which have been made during the existing rebellion with reference to the emancipation of slaves. So help me God.[15]

The military detachment at Ham's Fork had more to do than to administer the oath. The soldiers also examined wagons to prevent contraband shipments of gunpowder.

As Word progressed toward Salt Lake, he was interested, as all travelers were, in the farming success and peculiar customs of those odd people, the Mormons. Then he headed up toward Bannack.

Late in September he had his bearings, had talked to enough knowledgeable people so that he had an idea about how far away the important places were. He was 85 or 90 miles from Bannack, he thought, and about 115 from Stinking Water.

Stinking Water was a vague term for the location of the new diggings along Alder Creek. All along that gulch busy camps were springing up with names like Virginia City and Nevada City. Almost any inhabited place became a "city," but names were often shortened, so men spoke casually of walking from Virginia to Nevada. It was only a mile or so.

Sam did some business for the first time in that beautiful exchange medium, gold dust. Meeting some packers from Boise, he sold them some spare bacon at 50¢ a pound in dust, figured at $16 an ounce.

Since leaving Salt Lake he had met more than a hundred freight wagons from the Beaverhead, the Grasshopper diggings, trundling down to buy provisions from the Mormons. It was late in the season for that high country. They would be lucky to get back with their freight for the hungry gold camps before snow blocked the passes.

On September 27, somebody told him, "We're on the summit of the Rockies." He parted with the other wagons, including his own, which he arranged for another man to drive, on September 28. They were heading for Stinking Water by a cutoff. But he rode his mule instead to Bannack City—because he was anxious to pick up his mail and hear that his wife and little Willie were getting along all right back home. He reached Bannack just after noon on September 29, having ridden sixty miles since he left the wagons. He looked around for a day and a half, read and reread his wife's letters, and then headed for the newer diggings. He reached Virginia City on October 3.

When Sam Word left Missouri, he was heading for Washington Territory, but his destination was in newly organized Idaho Territory before he reached it. A few months after he reached Virginia City, it was in a still newer territory, Montana.

The main thing the country needed was people. This statement, of course, is from the white man's point of view. The Indians thought otherwise. The Sioux, crowded in from the east, thought there were too many Crows. The Crows, resenting and fighting the encroachment on their hunting grounds, were convinced that there were too many Sioux. And all of them tried hard to make the pale-face go home, until a year or two later, when the Crows, figuring that any enemy of the Sioux was a friend of theirs, began to side with the white invaders.

The kind of people the country needed, if you ignore the firm convictions of the resident Indians, included men like Sam Word. He mined in Virginia City for a while and then practiced his profession, law. As soon as he could, he went back east to Missouri and brought out his wife and little Willie. He took a hand in efforts to develop some of Montana's natural resources; it had some that were less transitory, less easily exhausted, than gold. He served four terms in the territorial legislature, one of them as Speaker of the House; and he was a delegate to the Democratic National Convention in 1884.

Sam Word was one kind of man for whom the Bozeman Trail was made, and he tried to come in that way.

The Kirkpatricks were the kind the new country needed, too, fifteen-year-old James and his big brother, who came out from Wisconsin. They were young and bold, eager to follow Bozeman when he promised to take a minimum of eight wagons through Indian country, come hell or no water. Theirs was one of the wagons that pulled out to vote "We're with you!" But theirs was only one of four, so they went with the others, the long way round and over the Rockies twice.

The brothers tried Bannack for two years without much success. So they tried ranching. Then James turned peddler, taking merchandise to people who couldn't go to trading posts and settlements. In 1880 the Kirkpatricks set up as merchants in Dillon, in the Beaverhead country, and carried on their business for many years.

The Beaverhead became cattle country, with great ranches and few inhabitants, and Bannack City became a ghost town.

The Chief Justice Was Lost

Thousands of wagons were moving westward on the great road that summer of 1863. Many of them had passed Deer Creek before John Bozeman arrived to encourage travel on his new, short route to the gold fields, and others came too late. If they went to the gold fields, and not to settle around Salt Lake City or in California or in the Pacific Northwest, they took the same route (part way) that Sam Word had settled for.

One party of seventeen, mostly relatives, came from Ohio and left Omaha on June 16. These, too, were the kind of people the new country needed. They weren't looking for gold. They were looking for the capital of Idaho—and nobody knew where it was. The new Territory had been technically organized by Congress on March 3, but getting a vote through Congress in Washington, D.C., was one thing; straightening out details in the Far West took longer. Sidney Edgerton, a lawyer from Ohio, was the new chief justice of Idaho, by appointment of President Lincoln, but he frankly didn't know where he was going.

Wilbur Fisk Sanders, his nephew, was also a lawyer. He had fought for the Union and had been invalided out of the Army.

Wilbur's wife Harriet kept a journal all the way across, not bothering her head about recording distances traveled or grazing for the stock but writing things down from the point of view of an adoring wife and a doting mother. Harriet Peck Fenn Sanders was the sunniest-tempered woman who ever climbed into an emigrant wagon wearing a hoop skirt.

A week after they left Omaha, the oxen pulling the wagon she was in with her two little boys stopped smack in the river, in quicksand, and the men had to bring up two more yoke of oxen to get them out. She was very happy to be safely delivered on the far shore, but she never doubted that the Almighty and her menfolks would accomplish it.

Harriet Sanders loved the trip across the Plains. The air was wonderfully clear; she enjoyed seeing how many telegraph poles she could count without moving: 118 in one spot. She even admired the "grand lightning," sheet after sheet of it, during a thunderstorm. When her family got rained out of their wagon, they dashed into the Edgertons' tent.

"There was no use crying," she wrote, "so we all went to singing and such a time as we had. Mr. Booth [one of the drivers] said that after that demonstration we need not be afraid of Indians—he knew they would run."

With the other ladies of the party, Aunt Mary Edgerton and Sanders' cousin, Lucia Darling, and a hired girl, Amorette Geer, she went for walks while the wagons trundled along, picked and pressed wild flowers to send home, did a washing, and even starched the sunbonnets. Couldn't iron them, of course, but they dried nicely into shape when pinned over pillows. And if the family clothing didn't dry on the bushes when they did the wash at a river, it did when pinned securely to the canvas tops of the moving wagons.

They kept house comfortably, with less housekeeping to do than if they'd been back home. They unpacked and cooked and packed again, getting into the wagons and out again a dozen times a day— wearing hoop skirts.

Three weeks west from Omaha, some Indians did arrive. The emigrants fed them and they "behaved more mannerly" than expected. But then they came back with a lot more Indians, and the menfolks said no! The Indians threatened. And the besieged pilgrims found that Mr. Booth had been right. The party simply sat down, acting unconcerned, and sang songs. The Indians didn't exactly run, but they did go away.

At one place on the Platte River, Harriet and Lucia "took off our hoops, shoes and stocking" and waded across. Their passage took half an hour. When she bathed Willie, going on two, in the river, "He did not think it much sport but cried like a good fellow."

Somewhere near Julesburg in northeastern Colorado, the party met some soldiers who had at least a rumor about the capital of Idaho: There was no doubt that it would be in Bannack City, the Grasshopper diggings. Fully as important in Harriet's journal was the fine breakfast that the ladies laid out on July 28: fried venison, fried fish, cream gravy, pancakes, molasses, and splendid coffee.

At Platte Bridge they forded the river and broke a wheel on one wagon—disaster, because they had no spare. The gentlemen moved the baggage out of that wagon and into others, and Uncle Sidney headed back to a camp they had passed, where there was a kind of blacksmith shop. They could have spared an ox more handily than the ruined wheel with its spokes shattered.

The Chief Justice came back without any wheel, but someone recalled having seen a broken one by the road two or three days before. Mr. Sanders got on a horse and set forth. He was gone all night, and his wife realized wistfully that he was all alone, with the wolves howling. He came back next day with eight sound spokes in his arms. The whole party shouted for joy.

Six soldiers dropped in at their camp on August 5 with different news about the capital of Idaho: It would probably be at Castleton. (There is a Castleford on modern maps.) Nobody in the party had ever heard of that place.

They moved on, still hoping for something definite about their destination. On August 8 they said good-by to a dog named Nero, old and blind and lame, and left him behind with the best marksman.

Next day they were at the Three Crossings of the Sweetwater, where wagons crossed the river three times in one day.

Baking thirteen loaves of bread before starting off at noon was nothing remarkable, but ice frozen half an inch thick in the buckets on August 15 was. That day Harriet learned that they had gone over South Pass without knowing it.

Ten miles west of South Pass, a telegraph operator caught up with them. Knowing that they were officially interested in finding the capital of Idaho, he went to some trouble to bring the latest news: It would be at Lewiston, and this was no rumor, this was the real scoop.

The Edgerton-Sanders party was much relieved. Lewiston was far away, clear over on the western edge of the new Idaho Territory, but it was slightly older and bigger than Bannack City, and provisions should be cheaper and living pleasanter there.

Next day there was trouble. Willie burned his hand when he fell down by the stove. Mr. Sanders—his wife never spoke of him familiarly as Wilbur—was sick with a headache and a high fever. She administered Dovers powder and a blue pill. One of the oxen was sick, but that was not Harriet's department. The gentlemen cured him with a big dose of bacon and vinegar.

They were over the hump of the continent. August 21 "is Willie's birthday. He is a little two-year-old and a fine boy he is if his mamma does say it. I little thought when I left home that he would be so fat and healthy now. He can run almost as fast as Jimmie." Almost everything turned out better than Harriet expected, although she was certainly no pessimist.

Near the beginning of the journey Harriet had run out of salt, to her embarrassment, and she had been borrowing from Aunt Mary all the way. But on August 30 she was gratified to come upon an acre of salt three inches deep and beautifully white, so she could pay back her borrowing.

Now they were in rough country. They narrowly escaped disaster when they forded the Snake River because the ferry cost too much. (Not that they were poor, but exorbitant prices made the gentlemen indignant.)

Harriet Sanders never did get around to mentioning why they didn't try to reach Lewiston. On September 2 her party was at the Bannack cutoff, with 400 miles to go to Lewiston. They parted from the wagons that had only 150 miles to go to Bannack, not knowing they would soon be going there themselves.

They almost didn't go anywhere. The Frenchman at a ferry on the Snake River wanted too much money for his services, so the gentlemen went ten miles upstream and forded that reckless river. One driver misunderstood, in all the uproar, which way he was supposed to turn his team. The other teams followed—and the Sanders wagon began to settle in deep water. In that wagon were Harriet and her little boys, ages four and two, Lucia Darling, and Amorette Geer.

But Mr. Sanders saved them, as Mrs. Sanders never doubted that he would. He jumped into the water, grabbed the animals' heads, and turned them in the right direction. Other men on horseback rescued the passengers one by one.

In her journal, Harriet (probably still shivering) described this as a "rich" experience, and in those days "rich" used in that way meant funny, or even hilarious. They had all got out safely, hadn't they?

All that was on September 7. Next day the travelers met a party of packers going to Salt Lake, who reported that the new mines discovered at Alder Gulch were by far the richest ever discovered—and in connection with gold, "rich" didn't mean funny. It meant *rich*.

Five days later, Bannack was only 100 miles away, and they would stop there for a few days at least. On September 18 they were *in* Bannack, such as it was. Four-year-old Jimmie had been hearing a great deal of talk about Bannack, and thought it ought to be a wonderful place. Looking down on its shacks and cabins, little James Upson Sanders proclaimed, "I fink Bangup is a humbug." The whole party thought that was really rich.

Humbug or not, Bangup was the end of the line. Snow came early. They could not go to Lewiston, even if it was the capital of Idaho. And unless Edgerton went to Lewiston, he could not take the oath of office as Chief Justice of the Territory.

Not until September 22—four days after they reached "Bangup" and more than four months after Congress organized the Territory—did Idaho's first governor, William Wallace, announce that the capital really was Lewiston.

It turned out that Sidney Edgerton was in the right place after all. Governor Wallace, a Westerner, didn't much care for "furriners" from way back east in Ohio, so he assigned Chief Justice Edgerton to the new Territory's far eastern district, out of his way.

Edgerton never did go over the mountains to take the oath of office. On May 26, 1864, Congress organized a new Territory, called Montana, in which Bannack was included. Edgerton became its first governor, Bannack its first capital.

Harriet Sanders was not the only emigrant who enjoyed the long, slow journey across the Plains. In fact, if you read the journals kept by some of the others, you must conclude that the discomforts have been overrated in literature and motion pictures.

If a wagon train encountered hostile Indians, horror and death sometimes resulted, and there was always this danger. But for most of the westward movers the journey was something like a picnic that lasted all summer. Children played and ran, women read or knitted in the wagons. There was dancing of an evening at the larger camping places. There was card playing for sociability, although the more rigid of the "Sunday people" deplored both dancing and card playing, along with Sunday travel. People picked flowers, told stories, sang, got acquainted with strangers whom they would never have met if they had stayed at home—and whom they sometimes disliked, of course. Travel across the Plains opened up a new world of understanding. Men went hunting while the stock rested, without having their consciences nag them with the conviction that they ought to be doing something more constructive. Everybody went sight-seeing.

The big thing was that their motive power—oxen, horses, mules —needed time to graze. The result was that all the people had more time to kill than they had ever had before. One man who became wealthy said in later years that he had suffered more and had less fun on de luxe hunting trips than on his oxcart journey across the Plains.

CHAPTER 15

The Widow's Might

And there came, in the migration of '63, some who despaired, who were helpless and destitute, dependent on the kindness of others. Like Mrs. Busick from Iowa, who brought nothing but two little girls, a small trunk, and a cow.

The older child was Emma, six years old. Lizzie, who was only four, told what she remembered when she was forty-five years older —what she remembered and what others had told her afterward.

The neighbors around the farm near Des Moines kept talking of "the Land of Gold," and the Fleecers were going to join the stampede, Mr. and Mrs. Fleecer and their two sons. They offered to take the Busicks—Lizzie remembered that they insisted, even. Mrs. Busick had nothing to contribute except the cow's milk and her help. There were three covered wagons, drawn by oxen, and six men, two women, and four children. A man named House drove the loose stock.

At a crossing of the Platte, a yoke of oxen stepped off the ford into deeper water and upset a wagon, but the men labored mightily and pulled it out, with the contents somewhat damaged.

And once they met a yelling band of Indians, who pulled up their horses in a cloud of dust and shouted a greeting, "How!" They passed on, seeming to mean no harm—but one of them shot an arrow into Mr. House's back.

When he did not catch up with the wagons as expected, two men rode back to look for him. They brought him back to the wagons, suffering great pain from the arrowhead embedded deeply in his flesh. Mrs. Fleecer pulled the arrowhead out with her teeth.

After that experience, women as well as men carried guns and ammunition, but no more Indians approached.

They suffered a loss that was harder for them than for more affluent travelers: one night an ox refused to eat, and the next morning it was dead. They had no spare ox, but Mrs. Busick suggested that they hitch up her cow. The cow looked very small beside the ox that was her yoke mate, but she did her part; they drove her and milked her besides.

About the twelfth of September, as Lizzie remembered it, or remembered being told about it, they pulled into Virginia City. At the first vacant cabin they saw, Mrs. Busick had her belongings taken out of the wagon and put on the ground by the door. She found who owned it, and she rented it—ten by twelve, with a dirt floor and a sod roof, one door and half a window.

"We children felt happy, of course," Lizzie remembered, "but as for Mother, I never knew how she felt but her face was so sad that I will never forget." That is the kind of thing that a child of four *can* remember vividly, the sadness and fear in her mother's face.

Mrs. Busick got a washtub and washboard; she had not even brought those typical weapons of a widow fighting poverty. And soon she seemed happy, Lizzie recalled, washing, mending, and baking bread for the miners, and boarding several of them too.

In the spring she almost died of mountain fever. One day as she lay in bed, mice played on the sleeve of her nightgown and she was too sick to shake them off.

But she lived, and after a while she could work again.

In 1865 Mrs. Busick heard that a new mining camp, Diamond City, was very prosperous. Maybe she could do better there. She paid out of her small savings to have a two-room cabin built there, but when she arrived with her children it had no door and no windows. Nevertheless the family survived that winter, too, huddling in one room, with quilts hung over the doorway and window opening to keep out drafts. Again Mrs. Busick made a living by washing, baking bread, and sewing late at night by the light of a homemade candle.

By spring 1866 she had sixteen boarders, and the town was prospering. A year later Mrs. Busick married Christian Spiegel, a miner, a kind and considerate man. He loved the children, and he hired a woman to help his wife, but she died in May, 1868.

The little girls took care of the house for their stepfather, until the Sisters of Charity persuaded him to send them to a convent school in Helena. They stayed there for four years.

Emma married a farmer when she was seventeen. Lizzie taught a country school until, at eighteen, she too married a farmer. They had eight daughters.

Spiegel had a carved headboard placed on his wife's grave—a beautiful headboard, Lizzie remembered—and built a picket fence around it, before he went back to the Dakotas.

There were people like Mrs. Busick, too, coming to the gold camps—the desperately poor who fought valiantly and hopelessly to better their condition, or at least the condition of their children.

CHAPTER 16

Canny Trader Toponce

Gold seekers who got safely to the mines past the menace of hostile Indians, the perils of mountain travel, and the vagaries of weather faced another danger: road agents. This term was an elegant euphemism. Road agents were not humble men who peddled humble wares along the road. They were highwaymen, ruthless robbers, cold-blooded killers. And they were effectively organized, as decent men were not.

The road agents were criminals from the older mining camps in Idaho and California. They knew their own kind. There were between fifty and one hundred of them, and they even had a password, "I am innocent," which in the end didn't do any good when they used it to the wrong people. Vicious as they were, they played a childish game of dress-up, wearing their neckerchiefs always tied the same way and, most of them, wearing the same cut of whiskers.

The road agents were a bullet-scarred lot, due to their habit of shooting up one another while drunk. They circulated between the gold camps, having perfected a way to beat the high cost of living and avoid the rheumatism that beset more honest men who labored with pick and shovel in cold water and mud. The really efficient way to gather gold was not to mine it but to take it, at gunpoint, from the suckers who did the hard work. The road agents held up travelers, relieved them of their gold, and rode merrily off. Sometimes they wore masks, but a horse was about as easy to recognize as a man. Some of the more arrogant of the road agents didn't even try very hard to keep their affairs secret.

The list of men they are known to have robbed, or tried to rob, was almost a Who's Who in the Gold Camps. In addition, dozens of their victims went unsung and forgotten. One hundred and two men were murdered or simply disappeared.

Alexander Toponce was one of the lucky ones who lived to tell his story. Toponce was a freighter. Without his kind the gold camps could not have survived. He gambled greatly in buying and moving supplies and equipment, and he prided himself on his cleverness. Born in France on November 10, 1839, he crossed the ocean with his parents in 1846. Even then, not yet seven, Alex was a cagey trader.

Passengers' drinking water on the ship was awful—and the voyage from Le Havre to New York lasted forty-nine days. Little Alex discovered that the sailors had good drinking water but were short of chewing tobacco. So he took tobacco from his seasick father's pouch and traded it to the sailors—one chaw-sized piece for a gallon of good water.

He ran away from home near Buffalo, New York, at age ten and was on his own. His infant ingenuity at trading value for value increased as he grew older, and when men with whom he did business tried sharp practice, he gave full measure of the same.

Toponce came to Montana through Idaho. If he had come up the Bozeman Trail he would probably have traded the Indians out of their best war ponies. He left Denver on February 2, 1863, bound for the Grasshopper diggings at Bannack, with a bunch of men who were disappointed in the pickings around Denver and had decided to take a chance on someplace else even though it meant winter travel. There were 163 men and one woman in the train that pulled north from Fort Bridger. Toponce, just twenty-three, was elected captain of the train.

They had considerable trouble buying feed for their stock on the way, and they had to buy feed, with the grass dry and scanty even where it wasn't covered with snow. Stage station keepers refused to sell, maintaining virtuously that all the feed they had was for the stage line's own teams. Alex Toponce, a smart trader at age seven, had not lost any of his talent in the intervening sixteen years. At several stations he treated the employees with a chew of Nigger Twist and casually inquired, "How you off for grain?"

"Got plenty," they always answered. "Which is your wagon?"

"Lead wagon in the right-hand row," he would respond as he set a quart bottle of whiskey on the table. The grain was duly stowed in his wagon after he was snug in his bed.

At one station where the men were really thirsty, he picked up six sacks of grain that way. In fact, he collected so much as the train moved along that he supplied his fellow drivers and made a neat $600 on the way to Bannack.

The party struck Bear River near present Cokeville, Wyoming, and followed the Oregon Trail to Soda Springs in Idaho. Near Blackfoot they ferried across the Blackfoot River and started up the west bank. There they came upon a wagon train surrounded by Indians. The train, under the leadership of two men named Livingston and Bell, was from Salt Lake and had twenty women in it. The Bannack-bound train had fought off Indians for eight days.

"You never saw a better pleased bunch of people than they were when we drove up," Toponce remembered later. "The Indians fell back but kept in sight and followed us day and night all the rest of the trip."

They crossed the Divide to Horse Prairie, arriving in Bannack May 24. And right away Toponce's foresight and cleverness paid off. When he was loading to leave Denver, a merchant who owed him money had asked what goods he would take to balance the account. Toponce chose nails. He couldn't have chosen more wisely. He had eight pounds of ten-penny nails when he reached the Grasshopper diggings, and there he found men who were ready to trade their eye teeth for a few of them.

He got there just in time to join the great stampede to Alder

Gulch. At least 700 men took part, he estimated. As he recalled the rules later, each man was allowed, by common consent, a claim that covered 100 feet of the creek, from rimrock on one side to rimrock on the other. But a crowd of determined miners from the Kootenai country swarmed in a little later, found the creek all located, and clamored for a change. They called a miners' meeting and argued that all claims should end at the center of the stream, thereby doubling the number available.

"That's the way it's done in California," they maintained. They found plenty of disappointed men, left out in the original stampede, to back them up.

So Toponce lost half his claim, and not all of what he had left was on the pay streak. He made another good trade, however. He had with him, as freight, ten gallons of whiskey and five gallons of brandy. With these he bought scarce, expensive, needed lumber. He and two partners built what he believed was the first sluice ever set up on Alder Gulch.

The channel in which the gold occurred was about thirty feet wide and didn't necessarily follow the bed of the creek. (They never did find the mother lode. It hasn't been found yet, although hopeful prospectors still keep trying.) One rule the miners set up was that a man could take water from the stream into his sluice but had to return the water before it passed the lower line of his claim. Most of the old channel, where the gold was, had a heavy covering of dirt that had to be stripped off. This overlayer was so deep in places that the miners had to sink shafts and hoist the pay dirt up with a windlass.

Toponce and his partners had thirty-six feet of pay dirt left after the new rule went into effect. Out of it they took $20,000 in gold. He estimated that the old stream bed averaged nearly a thousand dollars to the running foot, about $5 million to the mile. Alder Gulch gold was purer and more valuable than most. It was worth $18.50 a troy ounce when Blackfoot gold from Idaho was $16 and Silver Bow gold, from present Butte, Montana, was only $13.50.

In September of 1863, Alex Toponce's quick wits and genius for trading saved him and a partner, Enos Wall, from being robbed by road agents. They were bound from Virginia City to Salt Lake with two wagons, two horses, and four mules. In Toponce's wagon was a jug of whiskey and all their gold, covered up with his bedding.

They had gone past Bannack and over the Divide into present Idaho, with Toponce's wagon far ahead of Wall's, when three men rose up out of the sage, flourished their rifles, and ordered him to halt.

"What do you want?" he asked—as if he didn't know.

"You know what we want," one of them growled. "Your money."

He reached into his vest pocket and pulled out a twenty-dollar bill, worth about ten dollars where gold was king.

"I'm sorry, boys, but this is all I've got," he apologized. (It was customary for the victim to apologize in these circumstances.) They didn't believe him, so he offered, "I've got a little whiskey if that will do you any good."

"Hand it over," he was instructed. He reached under his bedding and pulled out a flask partly filled with whiskey. He peered up the road hopefully, but Wall's wagon was not in sight.

Toponce killed time by joking with them and got them to laughing. He even had the gall to tell them they ought to "quit the road" and go to Salt Lake with him. All this time he kept an eye on the track he had passed over, and finally he saw the top of Wall's wagon coming over a hill.

Just then the road agents decided to search his wagon for gold dust. Toponce offered a proposition: "Now, fellows, here's a jug of whiskey and an empty flask. You have my twenty-dollar Lincoln skin. Why not let me fill the flask for you, and you return my money. It's no good to you around here anyway, but it will be fine for me in Salt Lake—and you need the whiskey." He added, "Hurry up and decide, because here comes our crowd and I don't want any trouble." He pointed up the road to Wall's wagon, trundling along.

They jumped as if they had been shot. "Our crowd," the man had said. There might be a dozen more wagons behind that one. The leader said hurriedly, "That's all right, pardner. Here's your twenty, and give us the whiskey."

They grabbed the flask and ran off into the brush. For a pint of drinkin' liquor, Alex Toponce had talked himself out of being robbed, and he even got his Lincoln skin back.

Toponce had a thoroughly successful journey. In Salt Lake, he and Wall loaded up with flour, tea, shovels, and picks; in Brigham City they bought butter. Also, Toponce bought a fine big hog, dressed, for 6¢ a pound and took it along, frozen. In Virginia City, where pork was scarce, he sold it to a butcher for a $1 a pound.

CHAPTER 17

Little Mollie Sheehan

The gold camps were not the best of places to bring up children, but some parents managed it. For instance, James Sheehan and his second wife, Anne, brought their baby daughter, Katherine, and Sheehan's daughter, ten-year-old Mary Catherine Caroline Fitzgibbon Sheehan, Mollie for short. They left Denver in April of 1863 and reached Bannack at the beginning of June, right at the time of the big rush to the new diggings at Alder Gulch.

When Mollie was an old lady she told her life story to her daughter, Margaret Ronan, who used the material for a Master of Arts thesis at the University of Montana in 1932.

Mollie had always supposed that her folks came up Jim Bridger's trail, because she remembered hearing "Bridger's Cutoff" mentioned over and over. Actually, however, they went by way of Fort Bridger, and that was a different matter. In May of 1863, Bozeman and Jacobs had no assurance that they were going to live long enough to reach the Emigrant Road, let alone try to bring a wagon train back, and Bridger didn't open his road until the following year.

Mollie remembered some people who made history. For example, Nelson Story, twenty-five, and his bride (Mollie thought she was about sixteen) joined the train. Everyone else in it drove horses or mules, but Story drove slow, plodding oxen. His wagon was always the last one into camp at night. Mollie Sheehan remembered him especially well because he had a pack train of little donkeys, and she loved to ride one if he came into camp in time. She sat sideways, whether using a saddle or riding bareback. She never rode "cross-saddle" because that wasn't nice, and she never even *said* "astride." That was a coarse expression.

Another man she remembered in this train was Jack Gallagher, tall, dark, and striking in appearance. Before many months had passed, she saw him dangling, dead, with a noose around his neck. When Mollie was eighty, she remembered vividly that Gallagher had been with her train. Alex Toponce remembered just as clearly, when *he* was eighty, that Gallagher had been in *his* train, which reached Bannack on May 14, more than two weeks ahead of the Sheehans'. Both narrators were probably right. If Gallagher, traveling light, started with the Sheehans, he could have ridden faster than the wagons rolled and caught up with Toponce's.

Jim Sheehan and his family arrived in Bannack just at the time of the big stampede to the new diggings at Alder Gulch. He established his wife and children in a tent and set out for the new discovery with a load of necessities for the miners. His was the first wagon to arrive there, behind the miners on horseback and afoot. Soon he moved his family to Alder Gulch.

Even children too young to grasp the full meaning of the excitement felt the fever of the gold rush. Everybody talked about staking claims, so the minute her father pulled up his team at the new diggings, Mollie jumped out, whittled a bare place on a stick, scribbled her name on it, and pounded the stick into the ground. She had staked her claim.

In the fall of '63, Sheehan set out for Salt Lake with two wagons to buy merchandise. He was carrying more gold than he could hide under his clothing in buckskin bags, and he worried about road agents, because he had been warned that they had their eyes on him. He put the bags of gold into an old carpet sack with his spare clothes and tossed it into one of the wagons, carelessly covered with bedding. He was not challenged on the road, but later he learned that, for all his cunning, he hadn't really outwitted the road agents. That dashing young multiple murderer, George Ives, had ordered them to lay off because Jim Sheehan had a nice wife and two little girls.

Mollie went to school to Thomas J. Dimsdale, an Englishman who was known as Professor because all men teachers in his time were called by that title. She admired him because he seemed to know everything. He wrote and wrote between recitation periods, and she was sure, when his account called "Vigilantes of Montana" appeared serially in the *Montana Post* (of which he was editor by that time), that that was what he had been writing.

The youngsters fooled Professor Dimsdale sometimes. Mollie and a girl friend sometimes "asked to be excused" and ran to the livery corral in the bottom of Daylight Gulch to slide down the stacked hay. This was the Elephant Corral—the children called it the elephant's pen.

There was a wedding at the Sheehan cabin on Christmas Day of '63, the first wedding in the camp. Mollie's cousin Ellen, seventeen, married William Tiernan, with Henry Edgar as best man. The bridegroom was a miner; he had bought the upper discovery claim in the gulch from Orr, Hughes, Cover, and Fairweather. Tiernan was all right, but Jim Sheehan was greatly distressed, for there was no priest. The service was strictly civil. It could hardly be called a wedding at all.

But a priest had been in the camp some weeks earlier. Father Joseph Giorda, S.J., said the first Mass in Virginia City on the Feast of All Saints, November 1, 1863. There was much excitement about preparing for this event. Two mining partners, Peter Ronan and John Caplice, offered their unfinished cabin for the service. Their friends helped finish the building and smooth the dirt floor. Ronan helped take the collection, passing a big tin cup into which the worshipers poured or pinched gold dust from their leather pokes. The gold was then poured into a new buckskin purse and laid on the altar.

When the priest was ready to leave the camp, something happened that people loved to tell about—a happy-ending little story about the innocence of Father Giorda. When he went to get his team and wagon (no doubt at the Elephant Corral), he found that the board bill for his horses was $40. Deeply embarrassed, he told Peter Ronan that he just couldn't pay it. Ronan suggested that he find out how much dust he had in the purse that held the collection. They weighed it and found that it totaled several hundred dollars.

Father Giorda came from St. Peter's Mission, about 160 miles due north. He was accustomed to ministering to the Indians up there, but he was an unworldly man who had had scant experience with Virginia City's principal product, clean gulch gold.

Mollie's cousin, Ellen Tiernan, ran a boarding house, cooking for about twenty men including the "discovery men," the famous lucky ones who had struck it rich in Alder Gulch. She also served as their banker, keeping their pokes of dust hidden inside her mattress until the owners could go down to Salt Lake with it. The bed became very lumpy.

CHAPTER 18

The Road Agents' Downfall

Some gold-bearing travelers escaped being robbed by remaining suspicious and alert. In early winter Sam Hauser (of the disastrous Yellowstone Expedition) and N. P. Langford,[16] who was part owner of a small sawmill, set out for America carrying $14,000 in dust. It wasn't theirs; they were taking it as a favor to James Stuart and Walter B. Dance, partners in a general store, who were sending it to creditors in St. Louis.

Hauser and Langford went from Virginia City to Bannack by coach and noted with surprise and dismay that Sheriff Henry Plummer was one of the passengers. They had reason to suspect that he was up to no good, so Hauser made a point of telling *all* the passengers that he was carrying treasure. In Bannack he actually turned it over to Plummer, very publicly, for "safekeeping." He got it back a few days later when he and Langford left for Salt Lake late at night with a group of eight Mormon freighters.

Sam Hauser received an unexpected gift from the sheriff: a bright red woolen scarf. "You'll find it useful these cold nights," Plummer assured him. Then Plummer left town, ostensibly to look over some silver-mining prospects. Hauser and Langford suspected that road agents might find the scarf useful, too, for identifying the wagon they would want to hold up.

Just before they left, young Henry Tilden, who had come west with the Sanders-Edgerton party and lived with the Edgerton family, rode into town with a tale of woe: a few miles out, he had been robbed by three men, and he was pretty sure that one of them was Sheriff Plummer.

Langford and Hauser rode with their guns across their knees. (Langford had a double-barreled shotgun, each barrel lethally loaded with twelve revolver balls.) When the wagons camped, Langford went to bed on the ground but was too cold to sleep.

Walking around quietly to keep warm, he saw four masked men looking the camp over. Discovered, they rode away. Later he found out who they were: Sheriff Plummer, two of his deputies, Buck Stinson and Ned Ray, and George Ives.

Hauser and Ives had been through hell together on the Yellowstone Expedition, but there was a total absence of brotherly love between them when Hauser had gold and Ives wanted it.

A few days after that narrow escape, a group of freighters with three wagons and a string of pack animals set out for Salt Lake. Owner of the wagons was Milton S. Moody, and one of the packers was John M. Bozeman. Among them they carried $80,000 in gold in buckskin sacks, divided among canteens stowed in the packs. In one of the wagons was a carpet bag containing outgoing mail— valuable mail, since the letters carried a total of $1,500 in Treasury notes.

These men were lucky, because one of them, John McCormick, had once done a favor for George Ives. That handsome young villain had warned him, the night before the train left, to be alert *all the time*. The whole bunch was wary and heavily armed, a state of affairs that displeased the two road agents assigned to rob them while they relaxed in camp. The road agents, Dutch John Wagner and Steve Marshland, took a look at the guns in sight and withdrew for a conference.

Wagner suggested that they attack at once; they could kill four men immediately with their heavily loaded shotguns and scare the rest into the brush by yelling like a mob. But Marshland got cold feet so they put off the job until morning.

In the morning, one of them did something utterly stupid: he said something to his companion about a revolver within hearing distance of the camp. Every man in the crowd cocked his weapon, and the two road agents, emerging from the brush, looked death in the face. With a hasty explanation that they were searching for lost horses, they departed.

But they tried again two days later when the packers had gone far ahead of the wagons. Marshland found the carpet bag. Just as he reached the rear wagon, still looking for gold, a man hidden inside the cloth cover shot him in the chest. He yelled, then ran like a deer. Moody shot Dutch John, who spurred his horse and departed with a wound in his shoulder.

The defending travelers were left with Marshland's horse, arms, equipment, and twenty pounds of tea that he had taken from another wagon train. Some of the packers, chasing Dutch John, found and retrieved all the stolen letters containing currency. Marshland and Dutch John were captured and hanged by Vigilantes before the new year of 1864 had grown old.

The downfall of the road agents began with a man named Palmer, who went pot-hunting in December and shot a grouse on the wing. He found the dead bird on the body of a dead man. The dead man was a popular young Dutchman, Nick Tiebalt (or Tbalt or Thibault or variations on that theme), who had disappeared a few days before on an errand to deliver a team of mules that he had sold.

Marks on the body showed that young Nick had been dragged, living, by a lariat around his neck. His clenched hands held sagebrush that he had grabbed during this agony. There was a bullet hole over his left eye.

Palmer sought help at a nearby shack—a wakiup, such temporary structures were called—and was turned down cold. The two men there, Long John Franck and George Hilderman, refused to help him lift the frozen body into his wagon. Hilderman remarked, "Dead bodies are common enough in this country. They kill people every day in Virginia City and nobody says anything about it. Why should we trouble ourselves about this man when he's dead?"

The shocked and angry Palmer loaded the body without help and drove to Nevada City. Men flocked around the wagon to stare and exclaim. Twenty-five of them rode out in a rage to look for his murderers.

At the wakiup they found one of Tiebalt's missing mules. George Ives was there, too. They arrested him, Franck, and Hilderman. The angry men from Nevada took their captives back to the gold camp (Ives, riding his own horse, joked them into a race and almost got away) and called the miners in from the gulches for a trial. This was not the unruly, scatterbrained kind of miners' court that had let the killers of Dillingham go free the previous spring. This time there was a jury. Wilbur Fisk Sanders, who happened to be at Alder Gulch from his home in Bannack, volunteered as one of the two prosecuting attorneys.

The case of the People vs. George Ives was heard first. Testimony began on December 19, out of doors, with some 1,500 bundled-up miners in the audience. It went on for two and a half days. The verdict was guilty, with one juror dissenting; he wasn't convinced that Ives had killed the Dutchman, although he agreed that the defendant was guilty of countless other crimes. The vote didn't have to be unanimous.

There were enough roughs in the audience to raise a roar of protest, and enough men who were doubtful to roar with them. Then Colonel Sanders dared imminent death by shouting out the necessary motion: "I move that George Ives be forthwith hanged by the neck until he is dead!" (Years later, when Sanders was an old man with a distinguished career behind him, that was remembered as his finest hour.)

His audacity paralyzed the roughs. They had stopped hangings before; why not again? But the mob yelled agreement: *Hang him!* Somebody ran for a rope. Somebody ran for a big packing box. Two men prepared a scaffold; it was rough, but would serve. The butt of a forty-foot pine log was wedged inside a half-finished building with the top projecting over a crossbeam, the box was set for the fatal drop, the noose was placed around the murderer's neck. At the order, "Men, do your duty!" the packing box was jerked out from under the booted feet of the condemned man. And so, on the night of December 21, 1863, George Ives swung in the moonlight at the age of twenty-seven.

George Hilderman was tried the next day, found guilty on general principles, and recommended to mercy. He was old and weak-witted, but smart enough to leave the country forever within the ten days allowed him.[17] Long John went free, too. He had testified against Ives.

The miners, some jubilant about the triumph of justice and others mumbling that Ives was really a pretty nice fellow, had a couple of drinks and plodded back to work on their claims. But two dozen angry men, knowing that one execution was not enough, gathered secretly and formed a Committee of Vigilance. They signed this compact:

> We the undersigned uniting ourselves in a party for the Laudible purpos of arresting thievs & murderers & recovering stollen propperty do pledge ourselves upon our sacred honore each to all others & solemnly swear that we will reveal no secrets, violate no laws of right & never desert each other or our standerd of justic, so help us God as witnes our hand & seal this 23 of December A.D. 1863.

Twenty-four men signed. The top space, in which someone's signature should have appeared, was never filled. Sometime later the committee adopted very detailed regulations and bylaws, obviously written by a lawyer and properly spelled.

On the same day the Vigilante Compact was signed, the men set out—poorly clothed, with scanty provisions and bedding, in bitter cold weather—to track down more road agents.

The Alder Gulch diggings, only six months old, were on the map with a bloody thumbprint when the year 1863 ended. But no matter how dangerous it was to live there, or how desperately hard it was to get there, this was where the gold was. And this was where people were still going to go.

1864

CHAPTER 1

The Rage of Decent Men

It is interesting to speculate: what would have happened if the occupants of that shack to which Palmer went for help had responded like decent men with a normal concern for human life? They might have said, if they had been more cunning and less arrogant, "My God, that's terrible! Where is the young Dutchman? Sure we'll help you get his body to town!"

How much delay would that have caused in the formation of the Vigilantes? The story would have been different in some details. Public rage at the death of young Tbalt would have boiled, of course, but the fury might have died down. There had been dozens of murders before with no punishment for the killers. But because of the inhuman reply that Palmer received, the anger of the mob focused on Ives, Hilderman, Franck, and the men with whom they associated.

The newly organized Vigilantes were so determined and so furious that they did not bother to take warm clothing or enough blankets or food. Only one of them even had any gold in his pockets with which to buy such things. They rode out on "the Deer Lodge scout" determined to catch Alex Carter (because Ives had said he was Tiebalt's killer), Deputy Buck Stinson, and Hayes Lyons. Stinson and Lyons had been tried for the killing of Deputy Sheriff Dillingham the previous June but had been freed when the rabble of a miners' court made a farce of the trial.

The men of the Deer Lodge scout failed to catch their villains, but they won a greater prize. They learned all about the organization of the road agents, who called themselves the Innocents. They suffered from cold and hunger, sickened from eating half-raw meat and, approaching Deer Lodge, found they had missed their quarry after all. The road agents had been warned. But the man-hunters found out who had warned them—George Brown had written a letter and Red Yager had worn out a horse in delivering it. The wording of the letter was: "Get up and dust and lay low for black ducks," a thinly disguised warning if there ever was one.

The Vigilantes caught both men in the Stinking Water Valley, on the way home, and questioned them. Red Yager astonished them by telling everything they wanted to know. Some of it they hadn't even suspected. The road agents were organized; their password was "I am innocent"; their chief was the smooth-talking, fast-shooting sheriff, Henry Plummer. Yager named names and indicated the specialty of each man.

This bean-spilling did not save him from the rope, and he could not have thought it would. He was not even disappointed when they told him he was going to hang right then and there. This strange fellow shook hands all around and told his captors, "Goodby, boys, and God bless you. You're on a good undertaking."

Whereupon the Vigilantes strung him up to a cottonwood bough, with George Brown dangling beside him, and pinned a note on the back of each body. One said "Brown! Corresponding secretary." The other: "Red! Road agent and messenger." Then, after a journey that hadn't been a total failure after all, they rode back to Virginia City.

This double hanging took place on January 4. On January 10, the Vigilantes who had organized at Bannack neatly rounded up Sheriff Plummer, Ned Ray, and Buck Stinson, tried them in secret [18], and performed a triple hanging.

Young James Kirkpatrick, who had been along on John Bozeman's first attempt to use his new trail, was by now living with his brother in Marysville, a mile or so from Bannack, and earning dust for his poke by setting up tenpins in a saloon. On January 11 there was excitement all along Grasshopper Creek. The news that three road agents had been hanged arrived before dawn. James noticed that the road was full of heavily armed men, "a living stream," well bundled up against the cold, all tramping toward Bannack to see for themselves. James joined them, stopping at several cabins on the way in order to thaw out.

Everything was orderly and quiet in Bannack. Lots of men were drinking in the saloons; they seemed satisfied, relieved. In later years he described what he saw:

> In the lower part of a two-story log house, not yet completed, lay on the floor, frozen solid, the bodies of the three terrors of the town. Side by side, with each a deep groove in the neck showing the marks of rope strand spirals; clad in their Sunday clothes, newly

shaved, they laid with the awful ropes lying near, a gruesome ending to lives of crime.

A year before, almost to the day, Henry Plummer had killed an old friend, or anyway a former companion, named Jack Cleveland. Shortly thereafter, Plummer and a butcher named Hank Crawford engaged in a shoot-out. Crawford shot Plummer. But whereas Cleveland's wound had been fatal, Plummer's was only a severe handicap for a man with the reputation of being the fastest gun in the Rockies. Plummer's arm was broken by the bullet, which lodged in his wrist. A local doctor judged he had to leave it there. Plummer, who should get credit for being a man who didn't give up easily, patiently practiced shooting with his other hand until, once more, he was better than most men with no handicap. After he was safely dead, some inquisitive citizens did a dissection on his crippled wrist. The lead ball was so polished by the movement of the bones that it shone like silver.[19]

The day after the triple hanging, also in Bannack, Dutch John Wagner was hanged and Greaser Joe Pizanthia was demolished. When the committee approached Pizanthia's cabin, he fired and killed one of the Vigilantes. The rest of them furiously fired a howitzer at the cabin to knock a hole in it, dragged Pizanthia out, strung him up, filled him full of bullets, and then burned the cabin. Just how did a small cannon happen to be handy in Bannack? It had probably been left there by Captain James Fisk after he guided a bunch of emigrants across the Montana plains from Minnesota.

Now the suddenly successful Vigilantes had really got into the swing of things—and their numbers were vastly augmented by men who agreed with their policies and were no longer afraid to admit it. The Vigilantes had become fashionable. The morning of January 14 found hundreds of armed men grimly lined up on the hills above Virginia City, determined to prevent the escape of six road agents who were wanted. Five were arrested. Bill Hunter escaped, but not for long. They got him later. The five were questioned privately and hanged publicly from a beam in an unfinished building on Wallace Street, the main thoroughfare. They were Clubfoot George Lane, Frank Parish, Hayes Lyons, Jack Gallagher, and Boone Helm.

In groups small or large, the Vigilantes rode out on further man hunts. They strung up Steve Marshland in the Big Hole January 16;

Bill Bunton in the Deer Lodge Valley January 19; George Shears at Frenchtown January 24; Cyrus Skinner, Alex Carter, and John Cooper at Hell Gate January 25; Bob Zachary at Hell Gate January 26 and, on the same day, Whiskey Bill Graves at Fort Owen; Bill Hunter—who had escaped on the day of the five-man execution—in the Gallatin Valley February 3.

Twenty-two men dead in a few weeks, and dozens of others scared out of the country because they saw the writing on the wall. The writing was 3-7-77, a number that, scrawled with charcoal on a tent or cabin, meant "Get out or get hung." Nobody knows to this day what the number really stood for. It may have been the dimensions of a grave—three feet wide, seven feet long, seventy-seven inches deep—but another explanation is that it told how much time a man had to leave; three hours, seven minutes, seventy-seven seconds. Whatever those numbers meant, they were effective.

CHAPTER 2

The Vigilantes' One Mistake

The Vigilantes performed one execution, in March, that they had no reason to be proud of. They hanged Joseph Albert Slade for disorderly conduct. In fact, they did not boast of *anything* they did, but they saw the cleanup of the road agents as necessary for the safety and welfare of decent men, and so they took the evil upon themselves. The first book published in the Territory was *The Vigilantes of Montana, or Popular Justice in the Rocky Mountains,* a defense of their actions written by Professor Thomas J. Dimsdale, schoolmaster and editor of the *Montana Post.* He said, "It was a dreadful and disgusting duty that developed upon them; but it was a duty, and they did it."

After they rid the earth of Bill Hunter on February 3, none remained of Henry Plummer's gang. The Vigilantes' job was finished, but in the absence of competent civil authority they set up a People's Court to try future offenders by judge and jury. Captain Slade, drunk and disorderly as he usually was, signed his own death warrant when he defied this court. He had been arrested many times, had paid a couple of fines for the damage he did when he roared into saloons and stores, but he owed vastly more than he ever paid.

After one riotous night in which he did a great deal of damage, he was arrested by the new sheriff, J. M. Fox, who began reading him the warrant for arrest. Slade snatched it from him, tore it up, and stamped on it. A member of the Vigilance Committee warned him sternly to behave, but Slade hunted up Alexander Davis, judge of the People's Court, and threatened him with a pistol at his head.

That was too much. Messengers rode to Nevada City and to the busy gold gulches, because whatever was done to Joe Slade had to be a public affair with the public concurring. After all, he was no road agent. He said, in fact, that he had been a Vigilante. He had committed no murders in Montana, although he had many killings on his record before he went there, excusable under the violent circumstances of the frontier.

Six hundred miners marched into town. The executive heads of the Vigilantes were meeting, unwilling to punish Slade by death. They agreed to do so only if the miners agreed unanimously—and the miners did. Nobody was safe with Joseph Slade on the loose.

He sent a messenger to get his wife, who was at their ranch twelve miles out of town. While he begged for reprieve, men hurried to get rope, someone with skill born of practice tied a hangman's noose in it, and Slade was marched down into a gulch where, at the entrance to the Elephant Corral, there was a high gateway with stout posts and an overhead beam. Slade's loyal wife rode down the hill, screaming, on a lathered horse, just a few minutes too late.

Dimsdale said of the late Joseph Albert Slade's past activities as superintendent of an outlaw-harried division of the Overland Stage Company: "He was feared a great deal more, generally, than the Almighty, from Kearney, west."

Dimsdale's defense of the Vigilantes in this case was:

> The execution of the road agents of Plummer's gang was the result of the popular verdict and judgment against robbers and murderers. The death of Slade was the protest of society on behalf of social order and the rights of man.

Nevertheless, it was shameful. Disorderly conduct was not a hanging offense.

The frantic, fruitless ride of Molly Virginia Slade on her black horse, Billy Bay, captured the hearts and imagination of those who saw her gallop down, screaming. Some said she came with a gun in her hand and her black hair flying. N. P. Langford, who had been a Vigilante and whose *Vigilante Days and Ways* was published in 1890, said of her:

> This ill-fated lady was at this time in the prime of health and beauty. She possessed many personal attractions. Her figure was queenly, and her movements the perfection of grace. Her countenance was lit up by a pair of burning black eyes, and her hair, black as the raven's wing, fell in rich curls over her shoulders. She was of powerful organization, and having passed her life upon the borders, knew how to use the rifle and revolver, and could perform as many dexterous feats in the saddle as the boldest hunter that roamed the plains. Secure in the affection of her husband, she devoted her life to his interests, and participated in all the joys and sorrows of his checkered career. While he lived, she knew no greater grief than his irregularities.

Her hopeless ride passed into legend. The house where she had lived, and where she is said to have kept her husband's body in a metal-lined coffin filled with whiskey until she could take him to Salt Lake for burial later that spring, gained the reputation of being haunted. Travelers who took refuge there, after it was empty and falling to ruins, maintained that they could hear in the lonely night the pounding of a horse's galloping hooves and the frantic screams of Mrs. Slade, riding forever to try to rescue the man she loved.

The Committees of Vigilance, once organized, continued their watchdog role for years. There were autonomous committees in Bannack and, after the discovery of gold in Last Chance Gulch, in Helena. They were solid organizations set up on a businesslike basis. There remain a few scraps of documentary evidence about their financial affairs, scraps that surely should have been destroyed, because the Vigilantes were sworn to secrecy.

One is a memorandum of purchases "for the Vigilant Community" from Lott & Brother, who ran a store in Nevada City. It is signed by James Williams, leader of the Alder Gulch committee. Lott & Brother were John S., treasurer of the Vigilantes, and Mortimer H. This memorandum, dated November 23, lists purchases of basic supplies such as coffee, salt, bacon, flour, percussion caps, powder, and "1 memorandan [sic] book $1.50." The total is $143.

The November date is interesting. It could not have been 1863;

the Vigilantes did not organize until just before Christmas. Their work of cleaning out the Plummer gang was completed within a few weeks. But it is clear from the November date that they were still active enough the following fall to be using fairly large amounts of supplies in their forays far from home.

February paid-outs in an unidentified year, probably 1864, totaled $332.26 and included some interesting items:

Paid Morses order for rope	5.00
Paid for repairs on pistol injured by C. Brown	3.50
Paid Mexican woman for pistol	50.00

Rope and pistols, necessary instruments for rough justice; but what peculiar circumstances prompted the payment of $50, a very large sum for a pistol, to a Mexican woman? We shall never know.

Where did all this money come from? The general public paid, perhaps under some pressure from grim collectors. John Lott kept a Treasurer's Book. A fragment of it carries this heading: "We the undersigned have paid the amt. opposite our names to the ferreting fund." The Lott brothers topped the list with $25 as a good example. Other individuals paid $10, $5, or $2.50. A subtotal is $839.05. Each mining district had a collector.

Another scrap, headed Nevada City, I.T., is a pledge:

We the undersigned citizens of Highland District agree to pay the sum annexed to our names to Reed one of a comt. to selecit [sic] funds to defray the expences [sic] ferreting out highwaymen etc.

CHAPTER 3

A Child's-Eye View of Doom

Children in the gold camps were exposed to some dreadful shocks. When Mollie Sheehan started home from school in Virginia City on January 14, 1864, she noticed that Wallace Street, the main thoroughfare, was unusually crowded. Then she saw why: In an unfinished building the bodies of five men were hanging, with their heads lolling loosely, and two of those men she knew. One was Clubfoot George Lane, who used to speak pleasantly to her from his shoemaker's bench in Dance & Stuart's store. The other was Jack Gallagher, whom she had known when her family was on the way to Bannack. Molly was so shaken that she could hardly manage to go the rest of the way home.

One day in March she had another dreadful experience. The school children couldn't get across Daylight Gulch from the school because a big crowd was in the way, gathered around the Elephant Corral, where travelers boarded their stock. From the steep hillside the youngsters could look down into a milling crowd.

Mollie recognized Joseph Slade, in fringed buckskin, hatless, with a man on each side forcing him to walk under the high crossbar of the gate. His arms were tied, with the elbows bent so as to bring his hands up to his chest. He kept opening and closing his hands as he implored (three times she heard him say it): "For God's sake, let me see my dear beloved wife!"

She saw, and some of the men in the crowd saw, a woman on a horse galloping down the hill from the east. Someone yelled, "There she comes!" A man wearing a black hat hastily adjusted a rope from the corral gate crossbar and somebody kicked the box out from under Slade. Mollie Sheehan turned away in horror and managed to get home somehow. Joe Slade's fiercely loyal wife arrived just too late.

A little later Mollie slipped away from home, wanting to tell Mrs. Slade how sorry she was. The child found her sobbing and moaning in a hotel room, bowed over a body wrapped in a blanket. Mollie stood beside her for a moment, trembling. Then she went home without saying anything.

Virginia City was a busy place, and ingenious children found ways to earn money. One youth got a job sharpening sticks. Paper was too scarce to waste in wrapping meat, so customers carried it home on the end of a sharpened stick provided by the butcher. Little girls sold bunches of wild flowers for 25¢ in dust to boarding house and hotel keepers, or lamb's quarter for greens at $1.50 for a bucket crammed full. Also they cleaned up the sluices after the owners had cleaned them.

Miners used a tin scraper for this, but Mollie and other girls used a hairbrush and got the fine gold that was left. Dried in the oven, and with the black sand blown out, the dust a child collected might weigh as much as a dollar. A blower was a small box-like contrivance into which you put the gold dust and its accompanying dirt. You gave it a shake, blew the dirt and sand away, then shook and blew it again. "Clean gulch gold," the medium of exchange, meant just what it said.

A man caught fooling around another man's sluice was likely to be shot on sight, but the miners were amused to see little girls cleaning up after the cleanup. Females were scarce, respectable females were even scarcer, and girls, big or little, were worth coddling. Children got so much jovial encouragement that they took it for granted they were doing the miners a favor by giving the sluice-box riffles a good cleaning.

Mollie once put her new straw poke bonnet, trimmed with bright pink chambray, on the crosspiece of a sluice box while she brushed. The owner of that claim, Peter Ronan, didn't notice that she was there. He lifted a sluice gate up above and let the water gush through, splashing her bonnet. She was furious. To punish the careless fellow, she cried, "I'll never, never, never again take gold from your sluice boxes!" Ten years later she married him. He was fourteen years older than she was, but their marriage was a happy one.

The Sheehans had Granville Stuart's family as a near neighbor, and Mollie was a frequent caller because she liked to play with their baby, which slept in a hammock made of a blanket folded over suspended ropes. Mollie liked to swing the hammock.

"One day," she said long after, "the incongruity of the situation struck me, young as I was. Mr. Stuart, handsome, looking the scholar and the aristocrat, sat at a combination desk and bookcase, writing. The Indian wife on moccasined feet was padding about doing her simplified housekeeping."

Mollie suddenly inquired, "Mr. Stuart, why did you marry an Indian woman?"

He turned and patted her shoulder. "You see, Mollie," he replied, "I'm such an odd fellow, if I married a white woman she might be quarreling with me."

Mollie's beloved stepmother scolded her about that, explaining that her question was rude. Mollie grieved, because she did want to be ladylike. Mrs. Wilbur Fisk Sanders was her ideal. Another thing she was reprimanded for: when the news came of President Lincoln's death, during noon recess, the Southern girls in the little school picked up their long dresses and jigged and cheered—and Mollie joined them. Her father scolded her for that.

"I'm ashamed of you," he said. "I am a Democrat, but I am first, last, and always for the Union and for Lincoln." Besides, he explained, death was not a matter for levity.

CHAPTER 4

Montana Enters History

Miners, businessmen, and professional men went on about the matter of improving their condition, but there was something else that needed doing. The capital of Idaho Territory, way over on the west side of the mountains, was ineffective for the people of Bannack and the teeming camps along Alder Gulch. They needed their own government, close enough to be useful.

Somebody had to go east and talk to the nation's lawmakers and territory organizers. Somebody had to convince them that the new camps had a substantial population—and the most effective convincer would be samples of the precious metal that had brought in all those people. Somebody needed to show them what it looked like, the nuggets and flakes and powder, and say, "Look, gentlemen. This is what we've got. This is what we're digging out of the ground. And there's lots more where this came from. We use this instead of money. There's no end to it!"

Sidney Edgerton was selected as the man to do the job. He knew the right people; he had been a congressman himself. He was a member of the right party, Republicans being in the majority.

A few days after the spectacular mass hangings in Bannack and Virginia City, Edgerton set out with a party of men on the first lap of his journey, to Salt Lake City. They rode horses, carried their belongings on pack horses, and camped out. They also carried gold, lots of it, heavy, beautiful gold. Edgerton had dust quilted into the lining of his overcoat, and in his valise he had big, choice nuggets to display for the bedazzlement of congressmen when he reached Washington.

Congress was duly dazzled. There was very little back talk about "Don't bother us—don't you know there's a war on?" The war was a sound reason for encouraging emigration to the gold fields. The Union desperately needed gold.

Congressman James Ashley [20] from Ohio, an old friend of Edgerton's, promoted the organization of a new territory. He proposed a name for it, too. "Montana" sounded good, he thought. It was Spanish for "mountainous," he explained.

But what was Spanish about an area that bordered Canada? An Indian name would be more suitable, someone urged. They had Indians out there, didn't they, as well as mountains? How about Shoshone, for one of the Indian tribes around there? The delegate from Colorado mentioned dryly that Shoshone meant snake, and got a laugh. So Shoshone was out. The names of those great men, Jefferson and Douglas, were proposed, but the Republican majority would have none of that.

The House passed the name Montana, but the Senate didn't like it. Senator Charles Sumner wanted an appropriate Indian name but couldn't think of one. Someone assured him that Montana wasn't foreign Spanish, it was respectable Latin. So he agreed, the new territory became Montana, and Congress went on with other pressing matters.

Sidney Edgerton had a talk with the President and told him a joke that made Mr. Lincoln laugh. Edgerton also applied for a job. The new territory would need a governor. Several other men wanted the appointment, too, and when Edgerton started back to Montana (Lincoln signed the Organic Act May 26, 1864) he didn't know where he stood. On June 22, Mr. Lincoln named Edgerton to a four-year term. The first Governor of Montana Territory got the news at Salt Lake, on his way home. He named Bannack the capital, because he lived there.

Granville Stuart commented later that a more fitting name for the new territory would have been Tay-a-be-shock-up, Snake for "the country of the mountains." But whether it is Spanish or Latin, Montana is a name you can pronounce.[21]

The derivation of Montana was still a touchy subject forty-five years later when Colonel Sanders' second son, Wilbur, published an article, "Montana—Organization, Name and Naming." Or perhaps he just wanted to show off his learning. (He was a mining engineer educated in the Helena public schools, Phillips Exeter Academy, and Columbia University.)

In several dozen pages he defended the name with a short course in Latin in which he gave the complete declension of the adjective *montanus,* including the vocative, in case anybody wanted to say O Mountainous! He quoted Pliny, Caesar, and Livy to prove that *montanus,* and therefore Montana, is sound, respectable Latin.

Sanders mentioned that there had been arguments about what to call the people. In his boyhood, they had been Montanians. The poet Joaquín Miller, who wrote a history of Montana, had proposed Montanese. Sanders, still under the spell of Latin, thought the term might properly be Montani. But the people of the state are now Montanans by common consent.

While Congress debated about a name, thousands of other Americans debated a more personal question: *Shall we go west to the gold fields and try to better our condition?*

But the Indians! The terrible trip—it would take all summer and would cost so much. And leave all our folks, leave the home place, start all new, among strangers.

But they won't all be strangers—my cousin said he kept running into men he knew.

Your cousin gave up and came back, no better off than he was before.

For that matter, we've stayed right here and we're worse off than we were. Times are going to get harder with the war and all. It'll cost a lot, all right. But we can raise the money now, and with conditions like they are and getting worse, maybe another year we couldn't sell the farm for love or money.

What route would we take? Your cousin said it was terrible through those mountains.

There's other ways. There must be other ways. I heard a feller talking about a new way, lots shorter. We can see about it when we get out there on the main trail. Somebody will know. And if that route is just a tall story, there's still the way your cousin went, up from Fort Hall.

So for thousands of men, some of them with families, it was westward ho! to the gold fields when the Plains greened up that spring.

CHAPTER 5

Jim Bridger Breaks a New Trail

Jim Bridger, fabulous frontiersman, guided two trips up his trail west of the Big Horns in the summer of '64. In the first train was a man who, unlike the emigrants whose admitted aim was to better their condition, went up to Montana to preach the word of God. He was the Reverend L. B. Stateler. Although bettering his condition was not his major purpose, the conditions he had left behind could hardly have been worse. Both his country and his church were bitterly divided.

Stateler was born in 1811 on the Kentucky frontier and at nineteen was licensed to preach by the Methodist Episcopal Church. He became a saddlebag preacher—a circuit rider—and a missionary to various Indian tribes. In 1844 the church divided into the Methodist Episcopal Church, South, and what the Southerners called the Methodist Episcopal Church, North. Northerners omitted the "north," maintaining that theirs was *the* church, the mother church. Southerners saw the two as sisters and equal. (By any name, the two did not get back together until 1939.) When the division came, the two branches (or the main trunk and the erring branch) were not in agreement even about what divided them. Northerners maintained it was the issue of slavery. Southerners insisted it was the power of bishops.

The Methodist Episcopal book of discipline prohibited "the buying and selling of men and women with the intention of enslaving them," and a General Conference agreed that no slave owner could hold an official church position if laws of his state permitted emancipation. This seemed reasonable, but it didn't work out. A Georgia bishop held slaves he had inherited; he was willing to free them, but Georgia laws prohibited this. His church would not let him sell his slaves, and his state would not let him emancipate them, so he was deposed from his office. The church split on more than boundary lines. A Maine bishop adhered to the Methodist Episcopal Church, South.

Stateler, dedicated to God and the South, was living in bleeding Kansas when its people were divided by more than denominational disagreement. Harassed by armed Northern sympathizers, he left for Denver, hoping for a better life. His house in Kansas was burned by arsonists, and his wife and daughter narrowly escaped with their lives. They joined him in Denver, but found that prejudice against "Secesh" was strong there. The Statelers joined a train of 62 wagons, 300 persons, heading for the Montana gold fields.

The train left Denver about May 1. It went to present Cheyenne, then on the old Emigrant Trail through the Black Hills to the North Platte River. It was here, probably (or it may have been in Denver), that they hired Jim Bridger as guide. The wagons left the main road at the Red Buttes and traveled north on Bridger's brand-new route, with the Wind River Mountains to the west and the Big Horns to the east, up through the Big Horn Basin. That was the difference between Bozeman's road and Bridger's; Bridger took his people along the west side of the Big Horns, where the Sioux didn't care. The Big Horn and the Yellowstone were too deep to ford, so the men felled trees, cut lumber with whipsaws, and built ferry boats. Cattle and horses swam.

It was soon noised abroad, Stateler said much later, that he was a preacher (no doubt he noised it himself), so the train decided to lay over on Sunday, and from then on they had regular preaching. The Statelers were desperately poor, but they had a few cows, which pulled their wagon and supplied milk. The family exchanged butter for other things that they needed.

The Statelers had a serious accident when their wagon, temporarily hitched to the back of another, overturned at the edge of a precipice. Stateler went over with it, and so did his wife, inside the wagon, which turned over twice on the way down while the stove and heavy boxes banged around. The horses pulling the wagon ahead landed on their backs. But the Statelers and their horses escaped with only minor injuries, which did not surprise the Reverend in the least. "Surely," he said, "an Unseen Hand upheld and protected us."

Before reaching the Big Horn River, the party camped in a basin with bluffs on two sides—a real trap in case of Indian attack. Next morning they found that a big band of Indians had come in during the night and camped less than a mile away. Bridger's party naturally assumed they were Sioux.

Bridger and a small party of unarmed men rode out to parley. The chief approached with a group of warriors, also unarmed. (Anyway that's what the preacher said later, but it doesn't seem likely.) Then the Indians started to yell: "Bridger! Bridger!" and galloped up, rejoicing to recognize their old friend. The whites rejoiced too, for these weren't belligerent Sioux. They were Shoshones from old Fort Bridger, out on a buffalo hunt. The emigrants gave them a feast and some presents, and Bridger gave the chief—Washakie, who became famous as a peace chief—a paper testifying that he was a friend of the whites.

That was the only Indian scare Bridger's first party had. Stateler said later, "There appeared to be a gracious Providence that watched over us, so that we went in peace and safety. Others who followed behind us had both sickness and death." They crossed the Yellowstone on Independence Day. Several trains had overtaken them, so that there were about a thousand persons in the combined party. They left the river near present Livingston, crossed through Bridger Pass, and camped at a settlement that was organized as Bozeman City a few weeks later.

They crossed the Madison River on July 8 and camped. Stateler and his family went on to Virginia City but couldn't find a house to live in, and there was so much confusion there that they proceeded to Norwegian Gulch, about thirty-five miles to the northeast, where two or three hundred miners were at work along the creek. Norwegian Gulch already had a Methodist preacher, a Missourian named Hardgrove, like Stateler an adherent of the Southern church. The two men took turns preaching. The Statelers lived mostly on money from butter that Mrs. Stateler churned and sold for $1.50 a pound gold or $3 in greenbacks. Flour cost $25 a hundred pounds but went to double that price later. An ordinary little cookstove cost $250. Coffee was $1 a pound, sugar 50¢. When snow blocked the incoming freight wagons, the Statelers lived on wild meat straight.

With the coming of winter, they moved their camp fifteen miles to the Jefferson Valley, which became their permanent home. But the Reverend Mr. Stateler traveled anywhere, preached everywhere. Montana had plenty of anti-Secesh animosity, but it was endurable. After the family was safely sheltered in Montana, Mrs. Stateler once gave vent to her loyalty to the cause of the South. While herding the cows in a canyon, she shouted, "Hurrah for Jeff Davis!" and the words came back in an echo that she thought was grand. Some twenty years later, a Southern bishop who heard the story told it to Jeff Davis, who was his neighbor. Then to Montana came a photograph of the defeated Southern leader with this inscription:

Beauvoir, Miss., December 7, 1887
To Mrs. L. B. Stateler, with grateful affection and admiration both for herself and her husband, whose devoted service in the cause of Christianity is meet for a monument higher than man could build.
Faithfully, Jefferson Davis

Mrs. Stateler died on April 13, 1889, lauded as "the matriarch of Montana Methodism." Her husband lived seven years longer, giving money—whenever he had any—to build new churches.

CHAPTER 6

More Wagons on Bridger's Road

John Jacobs piloted a train up to Montana in 1864, and this time he got there instead of being turned back by Indians. But this time he was not on the trail that he and John Bozeman had marked, east of the Big Horns, through the Indians' hunting country. No, he was on the brand-new road that the old mountain man, Jim Bridger, was opening up just a few days ahead of him, on the *west* side of those mountains, through the Big Horn Basin. There was no reason for Jacobs to feel any loyalty to his own trail. The road itself had no value to him. But there was money to be earned by guiding wagons along any route that was passable. Bridger had a peculiar genius for smelling out the lay of the land. So Jacobs went that way.

There is mention of Jacobs' trip up Bridger's road in a journal kept by Cornelius Hedges, who was with another train just behind him. Hedges, thirty-three, was an exceedingly well-educated man for his time. He had a Yale degree and had studied law at Harvard.

He had been both a lawyer and a newspaper publisher, and he was destined to be both in Montana. He did not say in his journal what other persons were in his party when he left Independence, Iowa, on April 20. He didn't say, either, that he took the Bridger Trail, but there is no doubt about it.

The train he was with traveled on the north side of the Platte; the great transcontinental road went on both sides of the river, and the branch one took depended on where one came from. Three days out from Independence, on Sunday, he wrote that he had been reading in Proverbs 22. This was good reading for a thoughtful man who was about to face danger. "A prudent man foreseeth the evil, and hideth himself: but the simple pass on, and are punished." A lot of simple men went west that year, but sometimes even prudence wasn't enough protection. "The rich and poor meet together; the Lord is maker of them all." They did meet together, and travel together. "Train up a child in the way he should go: and when he is old, he will not depart from it. . . . Seest thou a man diligent in his business? he shall stand before kings; he shall not stand before mean men." Good reading for Sunday or any other day.

Cornelius Hedges mentioned only a few place names on the main trail: May 19, Ash Hollow; May 21, sight of Court House and Chimney Rocks; May 25, Scotts Bluff. Two days later he called at Fort Laramie for mail, but there were no letters. May 28 he "bathed in the Platte and changed all over." A full bath and clean clothing were worthy of mention in any journal. May 31 they passed Deer Creek about noon. Now they had to decide: take a short-cut or go the long way, over the Rockies twice? Hedges "found that the new route was a rage." There were really two new routes, Bozeman's and Bridger's, each with its disadvantages—which, in the case of Bozeman's, were sometimes fatal to human beings. The disadvantages of Bridger's road were fatal to a lot of livestock. But Bridger's route was even newer than Bozeman's, and nobody had yet gone over it and come back to report.

On June 2 Hedges wrote, "Paid our share for pilot $5." The pilot was named Rouleau, and he rode a pony with a red feather. They camped on "Bridger's ground." Next day, with another man, Hedges rode to the cutoff. Seventy-five teams were gathered. Feed was poor and water was bad. They camped on Dry Creek, one of several watercourses that had water in them only during the spring runoff. More than a hundred teams had gathered by June 5, Sunday, and Rouleau was proving troublesome: "Guide drunk—wrangling all the afternoon." That night the drunken guide even lost track of his horse.

Hedges' party left the Oregon Trail at or near present Casper, Wyoming. On June 7, he noted that Jim Bridger was six days ahead, John Jacobs three days ahead. "Many teams gave out—great dissatisfaction—train divided; poorly corralled." But on June 8, in spite of everything, someone calculated that they had put one hundred miles of the cutoff behind them.

June 11, on the Wind River (which becomes the Big Horn on emerging from Wind River Canyon, south of present Thermopolis) they found that Bridger's train had built a boat for crossing and had buried it on the far shore. (Perhaps it was simply sunk in shallow water to keep the wood from drying out.) Etiquette did not require Bridger to make his boat available for the next comers, and anyway he would need it himself, because he was coming back. The drunken Rouleau's train built its own boat, big enough to ferry two wagons over at a time. They crossed and on the thirteenth buried *their* boat. Next day there was a final blowup with the guide; some of the wagon owners got their money refunded, and not all of them traveled together thereafter. June 15 they camped on the Grey Bull River.

On June 16 they left the river and crossed a divide. The following day Hedges' party met two men who had ridden back from Bridger's train; they said it was twelve miles ahead. On the eighteenth they crossed what was then called the Stinking Water and is now the Shoshone River and found both Bridger's and Jacobs' trains near them. Now they had come 206 miles along the cutoff.

June 23, Hedges drove down to a ford—he doesn't say on what river, but it must have been the Clark's Fork of the Yellowstone—and watched Jacobs' train pass. Then he went up a mountain and took a look at the joining of the Clark's Fork with the Yellowstone.

His train forded the Clark's Fork several miles south of the confluence on June 24. Five days later it forded Divide Creek. On July 2, Jacobs' train passed. On Independence Day, Hedges' train caught up with Bridger's, which had in the beginning been six days ahead. But Bridger had been building his new road as he went, and this had slowed him down. Hedges' train traveled with Bridger's thereafter. July 7 they "passed the headwaters of Yellowstone &

struck those of the Gallatin." Actually, the Yellowstone's source is Yellowstone Lake, and this train was certainly not in present Yellowstone Park, but Hedges no doubt meant the place where Shields River flows into the Yellowstone. They reached the site of Bozeman July 8 and two days later were in Virginia City.

It's a good thing that the estimable Cornelius Hedges was not piloting the train, because it is plain in his journal that he didn't care very much where he was as long as he got to where he was going. He identified few streams, although they all had well-known names. Streams had to have names; how else could one man tell another where something had happened or where he was likely to run into trouble? So they were named, without ceremony, imagination, or regard to duplication. Even as late as 1899, when Dr. C. G. Coutant published his *History of Wyoming*, too many streams had identical names. He urged that the Legislature provide a state board to straighten out the confusion, remarking, "There are half a dozen 'Horse Creeks' to be found on the map, and twice that number of 'Muddy Creeks,' and there are 'Sand Creeks' and 'Dry Creeks' and 'Forks' without number." Not to mention Lodgepole Creeks anywhere that lodgepole pine grows and a Stinking Water River in Wyoming and another in Montana—but both of them now have nicer names.

CHAPTER 7

Up Bridger's Road with Rocky Mountain Bob

Behind Cornelius Hedges' train on the Bridger Trail in 1864 moved one guided by Rocky Mountain Bob, not otherwise identified. To follow a wagon train required no particular talent; the trail was plain enough, the earth scarred by wheels and hooves, camp sites marked by trash and the ashes of cooking fires, the stink of occasional dead oxen. And Bridger's towering reputation for knowing land forms guaranteed that where he took wagons through, other guides could follow.

W. E. Atchison, of Polo in northwestern Illinois, kept a journal of his travels westward and up Jim Bridger's trail in 1864. His party was a mere drop in the torrent of the western migration. Early in the morning on May 13, pulling up to ferry over the Missouri River from Council Bluffs, Iowa, to Omaha, Nebraska, they found 240 teams lined out ahead of them. By suppertime there were still 120 teams ahead. Atchison and his companions (whom he did not name in his journal) were able to cross on May 16.

Atchison's party drove mules and were able to make much longer drives than ox-drawn wagons—22 miles, 27 miles, several times 30 miles a day where the ground was level and conditions favorable. Just west of Fort Kearny, Nebraska, his train let another one join up so there were thirty wagons, seventy-two men, four women. The augmented train organized, with Jonathan Mumma elected captain. The newly elected Inspector of Arms canvassed the ground and "found should a party of 'Red Skins' attack us we could meet them with 346 shots."

On June 7 they were at far-famed Chimney Rock. Atchison, thinking of home, noted:

> This is the day for the Union National Convention which assembles in Baltimore for the purpose of nominating a candidate for the presidency. We away out here on the plains of Nebraska are awaiting with breathless interest the result. We *hope* at least that firm and unflinching patriot, A. Lincoln will receive the nomination and be reelected to that proud position which he has so nobly filled the last "presidential term."

Another twenty-five miles and they were nearly opposite Scotts Bluff, towering above the level plain. After one more day of travel, on June 9, they came to "the boundary line between Nebraska and Idaho and now we are in the land of gold far-famed Idaho. As we passed the line which is denoted by a stake in the ground cheer after cheer went up from the boys which resounded along the whole line." Actually, they had crossed into present Wyoming. "Idaho" must have been a vague term, because Wyoming was part of Dakota Territory until 1868.

June 11 they camped near Fort Laramie. On Monday, June 20,

they drove forty miles to Lower Platte Bridge, "where the Bozeman's cutoff takes in. Had quite a discussion whether this or the 'Bridger' cutoff should be taken. The Bridger men prevailed and we drove 5 miles further to 'Upper Platte Bridge' and camped at 5:00 P.M."

After camping at Upper Platte Bridge, Atchison's party drove another ten miles to the Red Buttes, "high, perpendicular rocks or bluffs of a red color on each side of the Platte." There one hundred or more wagons organized for mutual protection in taking Bridger's cutoff. They hired "Rocky Mountain Bob" as guide, paying him $300. Another four miles and they set forth on Bridger's Trail.

They bore to the north, staying away from Powder River. They camped on the Tongue River June 25. That night, just after midnight, the camp was aroused by a shot and bad news: One of the guards had fired because he got no answer to his "Who comes there?" and had wounded a man who was stirring around camp.

June 27 they were bearing north-northwest through broken country. They camped where grass, wood, and water were all abundant, for the first time in days. Some of the men prospected for gold and found scanty signs of it. Rocky Mountain Bob called the 300 persons in the train together and urged them to organize more completely, because they were now in the country of the Crow and Snake Indians. The following day they could see the great Snowy Range of the Rockies—it looked cool in contrast to the boiling heat of the Plains.

They camped on the Little Horn River (now called the Little Big Horn), traveled June 29 down that valley twenty-five miles, and camped on the Big Horn. They ferried across and moved along the Big Horn, now going northeast. July 4 they camped on Grey Bull River, remembering that this was the glorious anniversary of the nation's independence. July 6 their route took them for thirty miles through sterile, barren country where nothing grew but sagebrush, greasewood, prickly pear, and weeds. They camped that night on the Stinking Water (Shoshone), traveled along it for another day, and then crossed it, traveling thereafter northwest.

Atchison's train had no Indian trouble. A few Crows camped with them July 11, and the following day 200 of them came into camp, wanting to trade. "We made some excellent trades—robes, moccasins, etc.," he wrote, without a word about this tribe's propensity for making off with anything that was loose.

The great distances traveled in a day are surprising, for surely not all the wagons in this large train were pulled by fast mule-power: July 13, twenty-two miles; July 14, crossed two branches of the Yellowstone, also the Rosebud, through very broken country, but made twenty-three miles; July 15, fourteen miles through a gulch with beautiful scenery and good water, a total of twenty miles, camped on the Yellowstone, and so forth. Atchison does not mention having to build any road or any such exasperating delays as Major Owen reported with Bridger's own second party later that summer.

On the nineteenth a party of thirty men went out prospecting and three of them almost drowned in fording the Yellowstone; the party was driven back by some 600 Indians, tribe not identified. Atchison reports this calmly, with no mention of even an argument, let alone fighting. Next day they traveled to Shields River and up that valley, twenty-five miles. The journal keeper's entry for July 21 is especially interesting:

> Broke camp at 5:00 A.M. Traveled through some of the most beautiful mountain scenery of which it is possible for man to conceive. It was beautiful rather than sublime, those mighty hills as they rise in gentle slopes away up toward the heavens covered with forests of pine and the verdure of summer. Met a party of Major Bridger's train on their return trip. As usual with "Skedaddlers" they tell a doleful tale of matters and things in the "new Eldorado." Traveled 20 miles.

On Friday, July 22, they reached the Gallatin Valley, fertile and beautiful: "Ranchmen have established themselves here and are raising all kinds of produce for the Virginia City market." They heard exciting news on July 25, on a fork of the Madison River, about new discoveries in Norwegian Gulch. Two days later they were in Virginia City. Atchison preached himself a little sermon in his journal entry this day:

> Here ends our taking notes. Our trip has been tedious and laborious and we are thankful that it is at an end. Our curiosity is now fully satisfied in regard to a trip across the plains. Hard, earnest toil must now engage us if we would be successful in our new field of labor.

There is no further entry until September 27, when—without explaining why—he wrote, "Left Virginia for the Yellow Stone." After two months, he had had enough. October 3: "Arrived at Yellow

Stone. Commenced building boat." A week later, "Sailed on board flat boat 'Miner.' Traveled 25 miles." On October 19 he came to the mouth of the Rosebud River and passed the American Fur Company's dilapidated old Fort Sarysy.

The flatboat flotilla was attacked November 2, just past Fort Berthold, by two or three hundred Sioux, and a dozen or so shots, mostly arrows, were fired into his boat, but nobody was hurt. On November 18 he reached Yankton, Dakota Territory, left the boat, and hired passage by wagon overland to Sioux City, which he reached on the morning of the twentieth. Ten days later he was home. Atchison was, after all, a "skedaddler," just like the men he had met on Jim Bridger's trail.

CHAPTER 8

Frank Kirkaldie Needed Hope

There were some, like Atchison, who reached the gold fields, faced the fact that they weren't going to better their condition there, and returned to the States, having had their adventure. And there were some who stayed in Montana, doing well at their old occupation of farming in a new land with new problems.

But there were others who could not go back but did not succeed in farming either. The story of one of them is known through the letters he wrote his wife—for five years, letters explaining why he couldn't send money, why his latest project had failed. For five years, longing to be reunited with her and the children. Five years of dismal endurance, of hope deferred that maketh the heart sick.

His name was Frank Kirkaldie. He came up with a wagon train by Bridger's cutoff. He was not prosperous enough to have his own outfit, his wagon and team. Kirkaldie had never been prosperous. He had been a marble cutter in Vermont, but the marble dust affected his lungs. He moved to Illinois, took up farming near Joliet, married Elizabeth Risley. He didn't do well there, so he moved to Des Moines, Iowa.

And he kept hearing about the gold in Idaho. Des Moines was the jumping-off place for a lot of caravans going to Idaho. A man couldn't help listening to the talk and hoping for better things. Frank Kirkaldie was thirty-six years old when he turned his face to the Rocky Mountains. He sent Elizabeth and their four children back to Joliet to live with her mother. Surely, within a year he would return in prosperous triumph and take his family out to a new and better home in the West.

Kirkaldie had to work his way out to the gold fields. He hired out as a driver for a man named Munger—Colonel Munger, he was called. Kirkaldie was permitted to take along some of the things a farmer needs, such as a plow, and he had a stove, some bedding, and things like that. He even had four cows. They worked their way, too, hitched to a wagon and pulling with the oxen.

When he wrote to his wife from Des Moines on May 1, just before starting, he was already almost out of money. He had paid $75 for a horse to ride, and had supposed it would cost only half as much. But he was sending his mother $20, and he asked Elizabeth to send her $20 more. There should be between $25 and $40 more for Elizabeth and the children when all his bills were paid. He missed the children already:

> You did not write me a word about our babies in your last. I take it for granted that they are well or you would have mentioned it. How are they getting along with their teeth and with their walking? Before this month is gone they will be a year old.
>
> I am glad that Fanny is attending school and I hope she will try hard to progress in her studies. Tell Bub that I have been writing to Grandma Kirkaldie and that I am going to send her one of his pictures in it and I am going to carry one of his and one of Fanny's with me to Idaho and I want to think of them always as pleasant and kind to each other—and always brave enough to tell the *truth* whatever it is.

Fanny was ten years old June 9. Her little brother Frank, called Bub, had turned four in January. Their father wrote to them, too:

> As we are having some nice smooth road this morning, I thought I would try to write you a little riding along in the wagon.
>
> I am driving six oxen yoked up to a large covered wagon such as we saw on our way to Grinnell. I do not ride much but walk nearly all the way so as to see that the oxen all go right. When night comes I fix up my bed in the wagon and sleep there all night and in

the morning we have to get up about as soon as it is light so as to feed our cattle and be ready to start again.

Tomorrow we expect to get to Council Bluffs. Mama will show it to you on the map.

I hope you will be kind and pleasant to each other and help Mama all you can. I look at your pictures often and wish I could see you. But I suppose you will grow so big that I shall hardly know you before I get back.

He never did go back, and when he saw the children again his fond suggestion was pitifully true: he hardly knew them. But on the way west in 1864 he could not guess that the time of separation would be so dismal and so long. He wrote long letters to "My dear Wife" whenever there was a chance to mail them, and he acknowledged letters from her—but they do not survive.

May 29 he wrote that he expected to be opposite Fort Kearny on June 1 and he hoped there would be a letter from her. At Kearny the train would leave the regular Salt Lake road, and there would be few if any chances to pick up mail before they got to Fort Laramie, late in June.

I hope Fanny will keep her shoulders straight and her teeth clean and Bub will keep well and grow big as fast as he can so that he will be a big boy when I get back.

On July 3, fifty miles beyond Fort Laramie, he wrote because it was his wife's birthday, although he probably wouldn't have a chance to mail this letter until his journey ended.

I was disappointed at not getting more of a letter from you at Laramie . . . I think you might find more to write than you have yet. . . .

You ask how Mrs M. [Munger] gets along with her boarders. She has considerable trouble with them, but it may as well be with them as with anything else. She is bound to be in a stew about something; and I think she has caused more disturbance than any six men in the train. She has managed the Col. so long with ease that she is very much disturbed if she cannot manage everything else.

Homesick Frank Kirkaldie ended this letter: "I wish I could spend the evening with you and the children. But a thousand miles is too far to go for that."

He wrote often; it was a way of feeling close to his family. On

July 7, eighty miles beyond Fort Laramie, he wrote at length about the Independence Day celebration they had had: a procession for marching, and an oration, and the reading of the Declaration of Independence, with orchestra music (two violins and a flute), the singing of "The Red, White and Blue," a very good picnic dinner, and dancing by lantern light in the open under a shade of boughs and leaves. He added:

> We heard at [Fort] Laramie that Grant had Richmond closely invested and expected to be in possession by the 4th of July. We think that perhaps we may hear something more at the Ferry which is a short distance above us. I hope to hear that Richmond shared the same fate that Vicksburg did a year ago. If that is the case, I think the 4th must have been celebrated in the Northern states as never before.

Before he finished the letter there was news, or at least a rumor of news: They heard that Grant had captured Richmond, but they didn't know whether to believe it. It was only a rumor; Richmond had been under siege since mid-June, but Confederate troops did not evacuate it until the following April.

Emigration on the main trail was so heavy that it was hard to find grass for the stock. The drivers had to move the cattle far off the road to feed, and this took so much time that each day's drive was relatively short.

The leaders of his train—Kirkaldie was only a hired driver—were talking about taking Jim Bridger's cutoff. On the other hand, there was a rumor of good diggings near the South Pass, so they might go that way, on the old main road.

He wrote again July 21, from Bridger's cutoff among the Big Horn Mountains. Kirkaldie had parted company with the Mungers. They were going by way of South Pass, the old road, the long road, and could not reach Virginia City much before the first of October, he estimated. He wanted to get there sooner. "I tried to persuade him [Munger] to go the 'cutoff,'" Kirkaldie wrote, "but I suppose Mrs. M. was determined to go the other road and he was inflexible."

They had heard before they left Des Moines that some new routes would open that year to shorten the way to the gold fields. They found that two new routes had opened, Bozeman's and Bridger's. And it looked as if a majority of the emigration was taking one or the other. So Kirkaldie arranged to put his two yoke of cows with the teams of a man named Burns and put his freight in one of Burns's wagons.

On August 1 he added:

> When I commenced writing we were some 40 miles S.E. of Wind or Big Horn River. We are now some 60 miles from where we struck a cross-road. We followed it down 45 miles on this side before leaving it. I would write more in regard to our journey, the country, etc. but we expect to meet a train today—Bridger and a company with him on their way back East and I will send what I have written by them, trusting that you get it some time. . . . We are a long way on the last half of our journey.

It is doubtful whether Elizabeth, living with her mother, looking after four children, wanting her own home, cared very much about the details of her husband's journey. But his men friends back home would care, and the letter would be read many times, and saved with his others. He added to it the same afternoon:

> We are still laying here and Bridger and train have come up and are laying here too. There are probably 15 to 20 men in it who are on their way back to the States from Virginia City. They talk very discouragingly in regard to the prospects there and say they will be perfectly satisfied to quit gold hunting if they can only get back to their homes.
>
> They say that there is only that *one* gulch by Virginia City that pays anything, that there is twenty men to every day's work there is to do and more flocking in all the time and I have not the least doubt that people who are going there nearly destitute of money or provisions will suffer the coming winter.
>
> . . . I have staked my all on this cast and I do not feel as though I could abandon the thing without a thorough trial, inasmuch as I am so far on the way. Still if I become entirely satisfied that I cannot succeed out this way I shall give it up at once—if I can, because my family have the first and more important claim upon me, although it would have a very disheartening effect upon me I am afraid. However, I still hope for better things.

Poor man. He always hoped for better things. He didn't know yet how dismally long his hope would have to last.

Virginia City turned out to be no place for Frank Kirkaldie. He was a farmer, not a miner. Provisions were very high in the gold camps, and food was scarce, especially vegetables of any kind. Very well, he would do what he knew how to do; he would farm, producing vegetables to meet the gnawing need. The Stinking Water and the gold were not for him. He went to the Gallatin and its rich land to break for farming. He had looked at it with a farmer's eye on the way to Virginia City. He settled now a mile from present Central Park.

Next year, next year—he had next year and a crop and prosperity to think about. Meanwhile he built a cabin for this winter of 1864–1865, of hewn cottonwood logs. It even had a floor of hewn logs. Frank Kirkaldie was not a lucky man, but he was a worker. He made no window, because warmth was more important than light, and in daylight hours he was not in the cabin anyway. He made a hole in the door and tacked white muslin over it, and there was his daylight. He built a fireplace, and he had his stove.

Another man, named George, took up land next to his, and they broke prairie on twenty acres with the plow he had brought. They plowed when it was so cold that their beards were frosty, but the ground was dry and broke well before the share.

He wrote on November 27:

> Today is the thirty-seventh anniversary of my birthday—surely "Time and tide wait for no man." Time is hurrying us all on some to early graves—others struggle on to middle and perhaps to old age, but still we "move on." It seems hardly possible that I have numbered so many years. We shall soon begin to be *old*.
>
> I hope we may soon secure a home and be able to rear our children with a love for it—and us. Let us remember that our children will soon notice our faults and will be sure to respect us in proportion as we deserve to be respected. Let us try to deserve their respect and love and train them up so that the world may be made better for their living in it. Let us be careful not to discourage them but encourage them all we can—praise them when they deserve it and try to be patient with them at all times. Do not think that I write thus to lecture you for I do not. But in thinking about it I am certain that there have been many times in my past experience when such advice would have been wholesome for me.

How Elizabeth reacted to this sermonizing we can only guess. That was a time of preachments, from ministers to congregations, from husbands to wives and vice versa, from the godly to the heathen, and from parents, teachers, and McGuffey's Readers to children.

Kirkaldie hoped that Fanny was taking her schoolwork seriously, and couldn't Bub have a sled that winter? He had heard a rumor that Old Abe was elected President, but he had also heard that McClellan was the people's choice. He hoped it was Old Abe. A few days later he wrote to Fanny and Bub, admonishing, preaching, advising. He was their affectionate papa, and they were very far away. He opened the letter, dated December 7, to write a long one to his wife, because he had just received two letters from her, dated August 6 and September 12. There was time between them, months of time, as well as miles of space.

Now he was sorry, and he said so, that he had written so discouragingly after meeting the retreating stampeders. Their homesickness had colored everything black for them, he felt—and his passage through 200 miles of desolate country had influenced him. Elizabeth could not yet have answered the letter he wrote August 1, but she had been getting bad news about the gold fields from other sources. He reassured her:

> The truth is that business in Virginia has been very brisk all the past season. Almost everybody there who has been industrious and persevering, have made money. ... Those who ought to know say that no man willing and anxious to work need long be idle, and wages were good, laborers getting from $3. to $6. in gold per day while $1. per day would buy their provisions. Freighters have all made money. That gulch at Virginia is probably the best paying gulch, taken from one end to the other, that has ever been discovered in any country.

But he thought that people there who had not laid in their provisions would suffer that winter—and he was right. That was the winter of the flour famine.

CHAPTER 9

Jim Bridger's Second Trip

Jim Bridger, trail-wise mountain man, guided two trains to Montana along his own road in 1864. On the second, he had with him a man who was by no means a newcome pilgrim. John Owen had been on the frontier for fourteen years. He was known as Major Owen because he ran a trading post. He had bought St. Mary's Mission in the beautiful Bitterroot Valley from Jesuit missionaries in 1851 when he was thirty-two, and now it was busy, prosperous Fort Owen.

He was a rotund man, about five feet eight, weighing some two hundred pounds. A diminutive Snake woman, whom he called Nancy, was his wife. She was less than five feet tall. Unlike many squaw men, Owen married her as legally as he could manage it on January 8, 1858, when he made this entry in his journal:

> Myself Mr. [Thomas W.] Harris & Mr. [Caleb E.] Irvine did this day Sign marriage contracts with our Indian Wives   I have often thought of the correctness of it & in the absence of any person duly authorized to perform the Marriage Ceremony We did it ourselves in the presence of Witnesses   I have been living pleasantly With My old Wife Since the fall of 49 and in case of accident I should feel Much hurt if I had not properly provided for her according to law.

In brief, John Owen was a very decent fellow. Nancy was not necessarily old; he usually called her "my old wife" in his journal, as in our time "old girl" indicates affection and stability.

Major Owen was a great traveler. Between 1851 and 1864 he covered 23,000 miles on journeys in the Northwest, usually through almost trackless wilderness. The idea of a cutoff from the Emigrant Trail was not the result of a sudden flash of inspiration in the minds of John Bozeman and John Jacobs. Several of the relatively few men in Montana thought it would be a good idea, even before the influx of people to the new gold fields, but Bozeman and Jacobs took appropriate action.

Major Owen noted in his journal for Sunday, February 2, 1862— before the discovery at Bannack, mind you:

> Wm Rogers an old Mt Trapper down   had quite a talk with him about the practicability of a Wagon road to Fort Laramie Via Hell Gate defile. [Hell Gate is about thirty miles from the site of Fort Owen. Major Owen, being there already, thought of the road as going out instead of coming in.] His opinions only go to confirm my own which have been formed by frequent conversations on the same Subject with old Mt. Men now numbd with the dead years passed & gone. It will be a valuable link in the Chain of Explora-

tion when the fact is Established that a route from Platte river can intersect the road Now being Constructed by Lt. Mullan, U.S.A.

When Major Owen joined Bridger's second 1864 train in September, he was coming home from the East. (He had left Fort Owen the previous November 12.) One thing he did there in the spring just past was to put in a good word for Sidney Edgerton as a candidate for Governor of Montana Territory. Owen introduced Edgerton to influential men in Congress and personally handed Edgerton's application to President Lincoln.

Owen's return from Washington, D.C., and wherever else he had been was late in the season. Here is his journal entry for September 18, 1864:

> Left Camp at mouth of Antelope Creek Sunday on the North Platte opposite the Red Butte five miles from Platte Bridge [about 140 miles west of Fort Laramie] Traveled four miles and struck Bridgers cut off. Camped on Antelope Creek 11 miles from the junction of the Cut off and the Salt Lake Road found good grass and plenty of Water that of the Creek strongly impregnated with Sulphur Road passed through rolling country course about W N W Saw a number of Antelope

There were about twenty-five men in the party. Owen, who was taking three wagons of freight up the trail, listed more names than that but later erased some of them for reasons not now apparent. Right away Bridger's second party ran into bad water. Owen kept erasing "alkaly" as if not sure of it, preferring to call it saline. Major Owen looked at Bridger's road with the eyes of an inveterate traveler who might want to go that way again. For the first three days the grass wasn't good; it had been eaten off by the stock with Bridger's first train. And there were dead oxen along the road, animals that hadn't made it through to the land of promise. They found deep sand but good grass and a good spring on September 23 and had a good view of South Pass from their camp. September 26 they were entering the Big Horn Basin; the water was very good, the grass pretty good, but the only fuel was willow.

On September 29, after resting the worn-out cattle for a day, they were faced with a steep and narrow road, but Bridger found a detour through a valley that cut off five miles. They stopped twice to shovel dirt into dry stream beds to get the wagons across. One wagon turned over. "The course of our 12 days drive," wrote Owen, "will be the location of the road in the future." He didn't know that Bridger's road had no future. It was not used after 1864.

Bridger found the road, but the men he guided built it as they went. September 20 they laid over to do some grading on the new cutoff. On October 1 they traveled only two miles and turned over two wagons. From October 2 through October 5 and again on the seventh and ninth they spent most of their time building road.

On the fifteenth day they camped at the junction of No Wood and the Big Horn River. Next day they left the river and plodded through heavy sand for six miles to the divide, then another nine miles through badlands to Grey Bull Creek or River. The cattle were failing from exhaustion. The only water was in one or two stagnant pools. But the grass was excellent. Indian sign was seen, but Owen noted, "Bridger Some what lost as to their whereabouts."

Bridger's best talking point for his road, in competition with Bozeman's, was the lack of hostile Indians. His road was woefully hard to travel. On October 21 the train took longer getting down one hill than in traveling ten miles to reach it. Five hours of effort passed before the last wagon got down to flat country—and then, in sight of the spot where they would camp, a wagon turned over.

Sunday, October 23, was a bad day. Twelve yoke of oxen were lost. All the water they had brought from Grey Bull Creek several days before was gone, and they were using water of the consistency and color of good cream. Owen didn't say how it tasted. Two of the men in the party had to leave three of their wagons behind. All the men suffered for water.

They found four yoke of lost cattle, but sixteen head were still missing on the twenty-sixth. The outlook was bleak on October 31 —they were short of grub and had to dole out flour by the cup. The men who had been looking for cattle came back without them. Owen's journal ended Tuesday, November 1.

Back at Fort Owen, John Owen's employee, Thomas W. Harris, in charge of the trading post during the boss's absence, was also keeping a journal. He had written a year before—November 12, 1863—that "Maj. John Owen left for Washington City D.C. via Salt Lake City. C.E. Irvine goes with him as far as Salt Lake City I fear they will have a hard trip of it as there is already plenty of snow in the mountain but Success to them and hope they will get through Safe—"

So Owen missed the excitement when the Vigilantes came to call in January, 1864. Harris wrote:

Mon 24th ... three men got in from mines in search of road agents or highwaymen found and arrested Bill Graves and have him in custody at the Fort tonight they Say they have hung four at Hell Gate and were after the 5th one Say they feel Sure he was caught and hung this morning, the names of the men hung are as follows Skinner John Cooper Alic Carter & George Sheens [Shears], the fifth one not yet caught [is] Robt Zackry

Tues 25th This morning the Vigilance party left with their prisoner went about two miles below the fort and left him Swinging to a Pine Limb this they say is the twentieth man they have hung within the last two months and if Zackry is caught he is twenty-one

Wed 27 I understand that Zackry was caught, & hung at Hellgate yesterday morning

On March 25 Harris noted: "Mr. Chaffin got in from Bannack, he brings no news of Importance only that the Vigilantes are still hanging a man occasionally."

He received a letter from Owen on June 5; it was dated March 28 and had been written in Washington. Owen wrote August 2 from Kearny, Nebraska, that he was on the way home.

Near the end of October, Harris heard on a trip to Hell Gate that "Maj Owen camped somewhere east of the Big Horn and that his teams are all give out & that he has sent to Virginia City for fresh Cattle."

This is a clue to the puzzle of why Jim Bridger's road, shorter and safer than John Bozeman's, was not used after its first and only season, while the Bozeman Trail was so popular that the Army established three forts on it. Bridger's trail didn't have enough good grazing and potable water to sustain the animals that pulled the wagons.

In November and December, Harris continued to be concerned because there was no news of the major—until a bit of gossip startled him:

Sun. (Dec.) 18th Chatfield out from Fort Says the report is that the Major and his party have all gone up by the Sioux Indians

21st ... I get no definite news from Maj Owen, Rhumer is that has been robed & murdered by Sioux Indians, but I place little credit in the report.

Sat 24th ... This is a very dull Christmas eve I took three drinks

before supper to the memory of my old friend Maj Owen who is absent which made me feel quite lively in fact almost tite   I never
missed any one so much as I do the Maj Owen, who has now been
absent from home over thirteen months   report is that he has been
killed by the Indians but I don't believe it

On December 29 he heard that Major Owen was at the Three
Forks of the Missouri and all right.

And on February 12, 1865, Owen reached his fort, much to the
relief of Harris, who was tired of his responsibilities there and had,
in fact, moved to a farm of his own. Owen had been away for fifteen months.

CHAPTER 10

The Troubles of the Townsend Train

One train that encountered real trouble on the Bozeman Trail in
the summer of '64 had A. A. Townsend as its captain. Benjamin
William Ryan, thirty-eight years old and married when he left Shef-
field, Illinois, April 13, kept a journal on this trip. Ryan was an
objective journal keeper. He noted the facts as he saw them and seldom commented. When he was sick, he said so, but he did not
mention worry, disappointment, fear, or delight. His complaints
were few.

Ryan and two companions started with two yoke of cattle and
bought another yoke in Moline for $115. They bought provisions on
May 12 at Council Bluffs, where they found about forty wagons
camped. He noted the purchase of 700 pounds of flour at $3 a
hundred (a little less than a year later the hungry men in the gold
camps paid $1 a pound for flour if they could get any), 200 pounds
of ham and bacon at 15¢; 150 pounds of sugar at 24¢.

A tremendous lot of people were going west. There were 180
teams ahead of Ryan's party waiting to cross the Missouri by ferry
on May 14, and by the end of that day there were 300. Ryan and
his friends stayed in line overnight and crossed on May 16, camping

near Omaha, "a fine flourishing town of about 2000 inhabitants and the capital of the territory." They reached Fort Kearny (Nebraska) May 28. Ryan noted: "Man keeps a kind of trading post. Telegraph crosses the river."

"Emigration immense; constant stream of teams," he wrote June 6 as they moved along the Oregon Trail. They reached Fort Laramie June 18 and Ryan found three letters waiting. He did not comment on this historic, storied fort, which impressed most travelers if for no other reason than that they felt they were getting somewhere.

On June 29 some of the great emigration left the Platte and took the Bozeman Cutoff. July 1 they were camped on the Dry Fork of the Powder, waiting for more wagons to come up to form a stronger party. Here they elected officers and hired two guides, Raphael Gogeor (there's no telling how the man's name was really spelled) and John Boyer,[22] at $4 a wagon to take them to the Big Horn River. The guides agreed to find a passable road, wood, grass, and water, and act as interpreters if Indians were encountered.

The businesslike Ryan listed an inventory much like the kind that was later required by commanders in charge of Army forts along the Bozeman Trail.

Wagons   150
Men   375
Women   36
Children   56
Oxen   636
Cows   194
Mules   10
Horses   79
Shots (from all firearms
    without reloading)   1,641
Valuation $130,000
Captain   A. A. Townsend of Wisconsin
Lieutenant   Blasedale
Orderly   Vanderly
Wagon Master   Van Sickles

Ryan was making notes not simply to jog his memory but also to help his friends if they should follow. His oxen had trouble keeping up, so he wrote: "Should have cattle for this trip not less than 5 year old & not more than 6 & weigh about 2500 to yoke, straight legs & round bodys."

The train had to stay on Dry Creek for a few days because so many cattle were sick from alkali water. The antidote administered consisted of fat bacon, vinegar, and cream of tartar. On Independence Day, six or seven hundred of those carefully counted shots available without reloading were fired to celebrate, and Ryan opened a box of cake he had brought from home. "Found it all right," he noted.

On July 7 they ran into trouble after leaving Powder River and driving two miles to reach good grass. While they were stopping for breakfast, a party of armed Indians rode up, telling the guides they didn't want to fight; they just wanted food. The party fed them but couldn't lose them. They rode in the same direction the train was going.

One man had gone back to their last campground; seven others rode back to see that he was all right—and half a mile out they were attacked by thirty Indians. One man was badly wounded with an arrow in the back. The seven fought their way back to camp and Captain Townsend immediately ordered the wagons to corral. The fight went on in earnest—and it lasted five hours, with the white defenders firing from high points of land to keep the Indians away from the wagons. Ryan listed one man killed in the fight, another killed who had gone off hunting, and two more missing. One of these had gone to search for a lost cow, the other to prospect.

These Indians were Cheyennes—or said they were. On August 8 some of the prospectors came upon a camp of five or six hundred Crows, who begged for provisions and told them frankly to stay out because they scared the game away.

The Townsend train camped August 19 on "Gallatin bottom near a small stream." There were about a dozen cabins with nice gardens, and potatoes and peas were growing well, "but they have to irrigate the land," Ryan observed. This was brand-new Bozeman City.

A few days later Ryan and some of the others found Virginia City a bustling place with lots of men at work and mines paying but all the claims taken up. They disposed of their animals and wagon, and six of the men bought a claim, at least partly on credit, four miles up the gulch from Virginia, for $2,500.

Ryan kept track of the man-days of labor invested in that mine and the return in gold. On September 6, eight men worked the mine, ran the sluices part of the day, and took out only $11. Another day, "Run the sluices 9 hours. Took out $65.70, 8 hands to work." They weren't getting rich at that rate. On September 18— Sunday, and hardly anybody mined—he noted, "There was a man hung yesterday for stealing 700 dollars. Today there was a prize fight about 2 miles from here in the hills. 2 Dolls. a ticket. They say there was a large crowd to see it."

The following Sunday they divided their take for the week. Ryan's share was $100—not a great return for the money and labor invested. Then he got a sore throat (he had suffered from pains in his face and teeth on the way up the trail) and the misery hung on. He could seldom work. He hired a man to do his share of the labor for $5 a day. Some days the gold in the sluices was gratifying: $128.75, ten hands to work; $177.15, nine hands to work. But expenses were high. Ryan paid $5 for a pair of pants, $4 for a vest, $1.25 for dinner, $2.50 to the doctor, and $3 for medicine.

Eleven men working took out only $58.25 on October 6. Ryan's throat got worse; he feared the ailment might permanently injure his speech. He bought more of that three-dollar medicine. Eight men working, running the sluices all day October 11, took out only $38.25. But you never could predict—the next day the take for seven men's labor was $177.75.

And so it went; some days they worked; some days there was no water for the sluice or it froze. It was late October now. Virginia City is high and cold in any season. Often Ryan's companions stripped topsoil off their claim—necessary labor, but only sluicing washed out the gold. Ryan, miserable with his ailing throat, spent his time mending. He restored a pair of pants by covering them entirely with tanned antelope hide and burlap sacking. On most days in November and December, the men stayed in their cabin. It was cramped and dismal, but warmer than the great outdoors.

At the end of 1864 Ryan noted some things that he had learned were needed by anyone coming to Montana by wagon:

Gallon and half-gallon milk cans with tight covers (no doubt for carrying sweet water in the dry stretches or where water was foul with alkali)

Fraziers Lubricator for wagon grease

2 dozen boxes of Preston & Merrills infalable [sic] yeast powders

Vinegar

Crackers

Benjamin Ryan had not noticeably improved his condition by daring the perils of the wilderness and fighting Indians along the Bozeman Trail, but he was the kind of emigrant for whose protection the forts were built in 1866. Without noticeable repining he went back to Illinois in 1865. Fifteen years later he moved to Nebraska. In 1895 he spent some time in Sheridan, Wyoming (safe from Indians by that time), with two of his sons who worked for the Burlington Railroad. He died in Nebraska in 1898, on May 14, just thirty-four years after the day when his party waited with 180 teams ahead of them to cross the Missouri River at Council Bluffs.

Another adventurer with Townsend's train was T. J. Brundage, traveling with his brother George. T. J. kept a journal more detailed and exciting than that of the laconic Benjamin Ryan. He was one of the men who went looking for the man who was looking for his cow. Their camp site was about three miles west of the site where Fort Connor (later Fort Reno) was built in 1865.

When the small party of whites charged the Indians in an attempt to get back to the wagons, young Brundage and Asher Newby were in the lead. They won a short, close-up fight with some Indians. It was Newby who was struck by an arrow, steel-tipped, that went three inches into his back and struck his left lung. He dropped from his horse. Brundage looked back through the melee after he had managed to return close to the wagons and saw three white men on foot trying to help Newby. Brundage hastened back, dismounted, and hoisted the wounded man onto his horse. Newby, with blood gushing from his nose, was pale as a sheet. A French doctor in the party failed to extract the arrow, but another doctor, named Hall, succeeded. Newby recovered.

Another man, shot through the bowels, died early the following morning. Mills, who had been searching for his cow, was killed and scalped. The train behind Townsend found the cow—and Mills' scalp hanging in a tree. The man who had been out hunting was found dead with eleven arrows in him and a shot through the head. The man who had gone prospecting was not found.

After they crossed the Big Horn River on July 20 with great difficulty, the train divided. Fifty wagons went on to Virginia City. The Brundage boys and others scattered after a while to seek their fortunes in their own way. Later that month twenty men went prospecting and ran out of provisions. Four of the men nearly died on the road but were rescued by their friends, who missed them after making camp. Another group of twenty ran into some four hundred Indians and turned back.

On the Yellowstone again, a man named Donuelson accidentally shot himself August 13 and was buried on a high bluff. The Brundages reached Virginia City August 25, but they had "seen the elephant." They went home in October by way of the Yellowstone and the Missouri. Later both brothers went west again. George became a pioneer of Sheridan County, Wyoming, and T. J. settled in California.

CHAPTER 11

Some Found Gold Fast

Some pilgrims struck pay dirt so fast that they could hardly believe their own luck. For example, David B. Weaver, twenty-four, and his partners. They reached Curry's Gulch on August 27, 1864, and discovered a richer placer three days later. They named it Emigrant Gulch because they *were* emigrants.

Weaver was in the coal business in his native Pennsylvania when he and David R. Shorthill and three other men decided to go west. They outfitted in Iowa, five men with one wagon, one yoke of cows and two of oxen. They crossed the Missouri at Omaha and left there May 21. They were at Fort Kearny on June 2, and June 25 they were across the river from Fort Laramie. By this time their train had increased to twenty wagons, but this wouldn't be enough to stand off Indian attacks so they moved slowly, waiting for others to catch up.

They crossed the North Platte (between present Casper and Glenrock) July 6 on a toll bridge kept by one Reshaw—one of the ubiquitous Richard family. Here the Bozeman Trail began, Weaver said plainly. And here they heard that a large train with a man named Townsend as captain had set out a few days earlier. David Weaver and his companions started up the Bozeman Trail July 17 with sixty-eight wagons divided into four companies, all under the leadership of Cyrus C. Coffinbury as captain.

The Coffinbury train corraled July 22 at the same spot where Townsend's train had camped on the ninth.[23] They noticed that at this point Townsend had diverged from the Bozeman Trail and, assuming there was some good reason for this, did the same. As the wagons were moving into corral, Weaver noticed arrows tipped with iron scattered around in the grass. This was peculiar; Indians didn't usually waste iron except under unusual circumstances. It was hard to get and hard to shape into arrowheads. Weaver saw one of the men pluck from a tree branch a dark object that, from a distance, looked like a dead crow. But it turned out to be a fairly fresh scalp—and it wasn't from an Indian. (Later, in Virginia City, the brother of the man in Townsend's train who had gone looking for the cow exclaimed as soon as he saw it, "That is my brother's hair!") The finder—stupid fellow—showed it to some of the women in the party. Terror and panic ensued among the women and children. Before long another ominous sign was found: on the blazed surface of a big cottonwood there was a written message: "Captain Townsend had a fight here with Indians July 9, 1864."

Next morning, a few miles away, the Coffinbury group found three graves, with markers made of boards. The graves had been torn open and the bodies were naked. Wolves might dig up graves, but they didn't steal clothing and blankets. Indians did. (Later the Crows said the Sioux were responsible, but some whites felt that the Crows knew too much about it to be innocent.)

They camped August 4 on the Big Horn, 234 miles from the Platte. There they found colors while doing a little prospecting, but they went on to the Yellowstone and up the first canyon to about 150 miles above the point where they first struck the river. They camped August 25 and divided up their outfit. Two of the party went on to Virginia City. Weaver, Shorthill, and a man named Norris heard there was activity at Curry's Gulch, so they went there and found two miles of it staked off in claims. The miners there had put a great deal of labor into their claims, but there wasn't much gold and bedrock was very deep. Placer gold, if there was any, might be in deep gravels, so a tremendous amount of digging and earth-moving was required.

Thomas Curry, for whom the gulch was named, had arrived the preceding winter with two companions about where Chico, Montana, is now. After being robbed by the Crows, they returned to Virginia City to refit and came again in the spring. Curry, hearing that there were white men down the valley, went down and met Bridger's first train as it was coming up to the Gallatin Valley. He induced some of the men to join him at his gulch, and these were the miners Weaver found there, thirty-six of them. They had constructed a long string of sluice boxes, but the best any of them could do was $2 a day—with flour selling at $28 a hundred pounds in gold dust. Some of them were already pulling out, disgusted, when Weaver arrived.

Where did the gold come from? Where there is some, there may be more—if you can find it. Shorthill and Weaver began to prospect the side gulches and ravines. Nothing there. They went farther up the main gulch on August 30, taking along another man, Frank Garrett. This was in very rough country in the Snowy Mountains. At the third waterfall up the gulch Shorthill dug under a shelving rock in the water—and in the first pan found a dollar's worth of gold. This was coarse gold, easy enough to extract with the primitive equipment they had or could build; these were little nuggets worth maybe a quarter of a dollar apiece, instead of the finer dust that they had found before.

They staked their own claims, with advice from Shorthill, who had mined in Colorado and knew something about it. Then they spread the word. They sent an excited messenger after their friends in the wagon train that had gone on toward Virginia City. To prove they weren't talking through their hats, they sent along four or five dollars' worth of gold in a little box that had held percussion caps. The messenger overtook the wagon on the divide between the Madison River and Alder Gulch, actually in sight of Virginia City. Some of the men turned back at once. Those who were on foot traveled almost night and day to stake claims early.

The lower gulch was the Curry District, the new discovery was the Shorthill District, and the whole thing was Emigrant Gulch because men from Bridger's and Coffinbury's emigrant trains swarmed in. Shorthill District was formally organized at a hurried meeting September 12, and the usual mining laws were adopted. The secretary didn't sign them, and the adjourned meeting was never held because everybody was too busy digging dirt or building sluices.

(Forty-two years later, just for fun, Weaver got in touch with the secretary and had him sign the bylaws.) They had seven weeks of mining before ice froze in the sluices October 20. The time saved by coming up the Bozeman Trail, rather than through Idaho, had proved that time is money.

A settlement called Yellowstone City mushroomed, and the men settled in for a hard winter. Freighters didn't come as far as Emigrant Gulch, so prices were higher there, and supplies were scarcer, than in Alder Gulch and the Grasshopper diggings. Plug tobacco sold for $5 a pound, and smoking tobacco was actually worth its weight in gold: on one side of the scale, gold; on the other, tobacco. With gold at $18 a troy ounce, and twelve troy ounces to the pound, a pound of tobacco was worth $216. When any man went to Virginia City, he took outgoing letters at 37¢ apiece to that destination. The C.O.D. price for letters brought to the gulch was 75¢. The distance was a little over one hundred miles.

CHAPTER 12

South Pass Seemed Safer

Most of the women who went west were competent in cooking and making do, although there were a few, raised in the lap of luxury, who literally couldn't boil water because they didn't know how to regulate the heat in a portable sheet-iron stove.

Albert Jerome Dickson, thirteen in 1864 when he drove a team from LaCrosse, Wisconsin, to Virginia City, was a lucky boy. He traveled with Joshua ("Dad") Ridgley and his wife Rebecca, who was a remarkably good cook. Albert had been bound out to Dad Ridgley at the age of ten and was obligated to work for him until he came of age.

Mrs. Ridgley was the ideal helpmeet for a westward-bound pioneer. Their group ate well. She took along dried apples and peaches, cereals, dried pumpkin and sweet corn, beans, some root vegetables (including onions—an onion worked wonders in the limited diet), a year's supply of bacon and lard, enough flour to last until the next year's wheat crop could be harvested and ground. Mrs. Ridgley packed her glass jars of home-canned goods in a barrel of flour, which kept the temperature uniform and protected the jars from breaking.

The Ridgleys looked ahead and packed things that would be scarce on the frontier, such as seeds, cuttings, window sashes, and a cookstove. Mrs. Ridgley jubilantly put up jam and jelly whenever the wagons stopped long enough where wild chokecherries, currants, gooseberries, and wild plums were ripe.

This party guessed wrong on one thing. They planned to buy potatoes before setting off on the prairie, but wagons ahead of them had cleaned out the available supply. Way out in Idaho, they camped with some freighters who were hauling potatoes to the Montana mines. The freighters were out of flour, so Dad Ridgley traded fifty pounds of his for potatoes, pound for pound. Potatoes would sell at the mines for 28¢ a pound in gold, twice that in greenbacks.

Dad Ridgley, like many another emigrant, had trouble earlier on the road with alkali water that poisoned his stock. One ox died; the others and the two milch cows were miserably sick. "Bacon," Ridgley was advised; "give 'em bacon." But the animals didn't want any bacon. The men had to snub them to the wagon wheels, prop their mouths open, and poke the slices of fat meat down their throats with sticks while the critters struggled, bucked, and bawled. Travel the next day was very slow, with the sick oxen staggering along, but they did recover.

In that year, 1864, John Bozeman must have recruited emigrants at Fort Laramie. Everybody stopped there to pick up mail, news, and rumors, to wash clothes, repair wagons and harness, and bake bread. While the Ridgley party was there, early in July, Albert Dickson found a note from some friends from home who had started ahead of the Ridgleys. These were the Phillips brothers. That such notes were found, stuck in cleft sticks somewhere around the huge camping area, seems remarkable, but it happened often. Everyone who saw such a note read it (or had some literate person read it for him) and, if it was for someone else, carefully replaced it.

The Phillips boys' note was dated a week earlier. It said that a man named Bozeman was gathering a train bound for the mines by way of the east side of the Big Horns. This shorter route sounded very appealing. The Phillips boys left another note, dated July 1, at present Douglas, Wyoming, where wagon ruts left the main trail and turned north.

The idea of saving time was very appealing, but Bozeman's train was six days ahead. Would these latecomers ever be able to catch up? Bozeman's people would move as fast as they could, and those following could go no faster. The Ridgley party decided not to chance it. They were too few to fight off Indians—and there was Indian trouble right around where they were, two days east of Platte Bridge Station. There were graves all along the way. There were horror stories about trains attacked, men killed, women captured.

Some of these stories were true. One of the true ones, the Ridgley party learned later, became so entangled with fiction that *they* were all mourned back home. This was the story of Fanny Kelly. On July 12, a band of Sioux attacked a wagon train on the great Emigrant Road eighty miles west of Fort Laramie. Some men were killed, some wounded. Four persons were taken captive: Mrs. Kelly, aged nineteen, her little niece Mary, Mrs. Sarah Larimer, and her small son Frank. On the third day Mrs. Larimer escaped with her little boy. They managed to reach Deer Creek Station, where they found Mr. Larimer and Fanny's husband, Josiah Kelly. News of the disaster spread.

But Fanny wasn't dead. She had left a trail of tiny paper scraps, from torn-up letters, as her captors forced her to ride with them through the wilderness. Terrified but determined to save Mary, she sent the child back along the paper trail one night. Someone, surely, would rescue her when she reached the Oregon Trail. But she never saw Mary again. The child's body was found pierced with arrows—and Fanny, during her long captivity, once saw a scalp with long, fair hair that she was sure was Mary's.

Fanny was delivered from her terrible experiences in mid-December when a group of Sioux handed her over to officers at Fort Sully in present South Dakota. She was later reunited with her husband, who had been trying valiantly to arrange for her ransom.

Her capture had become a *cause célèbre* because Mrs. Larimer had reported it. The story reached the Wisconsin community whence the Ridgleys had come. There it spread with believable but untrue details: Mrs. Ridgley had been captured by the savages, and the males of her party had all been killed. Not until six months later —thanks to the slowness of mail across the plains—did Mrs. Ridgley's grieving daughter and young Dickson's frantic mother learn that all was well.

The Emigrant Road was dangerous enough; on that, the Kelly-Larimer party had been overcome by hostiles. But John Bozeman's road was *terra incognita* and might be even worse for a small party such as the Ridgleys would have with them. They didn't take the cutoff, after all. They crossed over South Pass and departed from the main trail on the Lander Cutoff, with eighteen or twenty other wagons. At one camp the party had an unforgettable experience: a troupe of professional players, on their way to the mining camps, put on a performance on the jerry-built stage illuminated by a big bonfire, and everybody dressed up in his best clothes. There was a sentimental play, an acrobatic feature, a ventriloquist act, and songs and instrumental music.

The Ridgleys went on up by way of Fort Hall, Idaho, and reached Virginia City about September 5, four months after they had left home. They looked around a bit, and Dad Ridgley decided he could handle a plough better than a gold pan. He heard great tales of a new farming settlement in the Gallatin Valley, and to that valley he went. As his wagons toiled up the ridge, leaving Virginia City, young Dickson could see the row of white-painted wooden markers on the graves of the five road agents who had been hanged the previous January.

In the Gallatin the men took up claims and built cabins. The Phillips boys from back home had arrived a few weeks earlier, up the Bozeman Trail, and had their cabin built already, about twenty miles from the Ridgleys' claim. The brand-new town of Bozeman City, laid out August 9, had several cabins.

One night the Phillips boys stopped at the Ridgley cabin. Their journey with John Bozeman hadn't been at all exciting, they reported, except for a stampede when their loose stock joined a herd of buffalo and went kiting off across country for twenty miles before Bozeman and the other men could catch them. They hadn't really had any trouble with Indians. Twice, roving bunches of them had crept up within gunshot of camp, but they left when they saw that the wagons were heavily guarded.

The first settlers in the Gallatin learned fast that they'd better irrigate. Dad Ridgley joined with thirteen other farmers to build a ditch. When his first crop was ready in 1865—rutabagas, early cabbage, and potatoes—he loaded two wagons and headed for Helena, ninety miles away to the northwest. That gold camp was booming, and miners needed food.

A party called "the four Georgians" had made a rich strike there on July 21 of the previous year. Two of them, John Cowan and John Crab, really were from Georgia. Reginald ("Bob") Stanley was from Cornwall, England, and D. J. Miller hailed from California. Discouraged at poor prospects in the Prickly Pear Valley, they were ready to give up when they decided to take one last chance. It was worth taking. The jubilant discoverers called the place Last Chance Gulch. But a few months later, when the camp began to look permanent, its name was changed to Helena (accent on the Hel), after Helena, Minnesota. Ridgley and young Dickson found it a flourishing place, second only to Virginia City in population.

At threshing time in the fall of '65, the farmers near Bozeman City suffered a horse raid, losing about fifty head to a fast-riding bunch of Indians. The Crows maintained virtuously that the horse thieves were Flatheads and even went so far as to bring in a Flathead captive. They were going to punish him by burning him at the stake, they said, and everybody was welcome to attend the festivities. When the day came, however, the captive was gone. The embattled farmers started to build a stockade on the East Gallatin near the Ridgley place.

In May, 1866, Ridgley took his wife and young Dickson up to Fort Benton, thence to Sioux City by Missouri River steamboat; then to their old home in LaCrosse, Wisconsin. But the following year they went back to Montana, where they prospered. Ridgley died in 1870 and was buried in the Bozeman cemetery next to John Bozeman's grave.

Years later, someone asked young Dickson, who had become old Mr. Dickson, whether he would prefer to travel by ox team or airplane. He said he'd choose oxen.

CHAPTER 13

Alex Toponce to the Rescue

Freighters on the frontier were more than skilled handlers of mule and ox teams. A man who was only that was simply a teamster. Freighters hauled on contract for pay, but often they invested their own money, guessed at what commodities would find ready sale at their destinations, and took chances that what they had for sale would still be in demand after the passage of weeks or months required to deliver it. Freighting required heavy investments in wagons, stock, and merchandise. A freighter needed brains as well as brawn. The mining communities were completely dependent on freighters for staple foods, clothing, tools, equipment, and such comforts as they might hope to get.

That smart-as-a-whip trader, Alex Toponce, sold his whole freighting outfit in Virginia City at the end of 1863. It was good business to sell out at the mines and buy new wagons and oxen in Salt Lake. He could hire plenty of men in Utah to drive wagons to the mines, but once there they stayed there. Anyway, there was no freight to take down to Salt Lake, so there was no revenue. But there was always a market for wagons and stock in Virginia City.

So on January 2, 1864, Toponce headed for Salt Lake with a large company of travelers and a great deal of gold. He had $20,000, and the others in the group made the total $125,000. They traveled light, without wagons—that is to say, on horseback, with a maximum of discomfort.

They were camped near present Dillon, Montana, and Toponce was on guard while others kept up a roaring fire, when he noticed some riders at the edge of the timber, apparently sizing up the camp. He challenged them, and they asked whether they could get some hot coffee. Of course they could. In bitter weather the Golden Rule sometimes operated. But as they approached, Toponce stopped them some fifty yards from camp with orders to leave their guns and horses and come in one at a time. The first one in was Buck Stinson, one of Sheriff Plummer's deputies. The three visitors warmed at the fire, and Deputy Stinson announced that he had a warrant for George Forbes, who was with Toponce's group.

Forbes was crippled, putting him at a disadvantage if it came to a fight, and everybody knew he had a lot of gold with him. Toponce refused to let Stinson arrest Forbes or anyone else, and he saw to it that the intruders left camp as they had come, one at a time. Stinson had been involved in the public murder of Dillingham.

An hour later three more men rode up. Toponce made them come in one at a time, too. But these were men of good repute, men who could be trusted—if you could trust anybody. They were little X Beidler, soon to become famous as the Vigilantes' hangman, and two other fearless, reputable men who became Vigilantes, John Featherstun and Neil Howie. They were trailing Buck Stinson and his friends.

Toponce heard later that the pursuers caught Buck and two other men in a cabin on Rattlesnake Creek (in present Missoula) and hanged them all, one on each corner of a cabin. He heard wrong. Stinson was hanged, along with Henry Plummer and Ned Ray, in Bannack by that settlement's brand-new Committee of Vigilance, on January 10. Neil Howie, single-handed, arrested Dutch John Wagner after a bunch of fifty or sixty travelers refused to help him. Wagner was hanged January 11. Featherstun helped take him to Bannack.

Toponce and his friends suffered greatly on that winter journey. They kept overtaking half-frozen travelers along the Snake River, men who had lost their horses and were out of food. Their group grew until it included twenty-three men and one woman. Food ran out entirely near present Malad City, Idaho, and the few horses and mules they had either died or were so badly frozen that they had to be left to die. The nearest place where help could be found was Call's Fort, forty-five miles away, and the only way to get there was to walk.

They came to an agreement: It was every man for himself, and the first one to reach Call's Fort should send back a relief party. They buried their bags of gold dust in the snow and marked the place with sagebrush. Carrying their blankets, they started to struggle through crusted snow that broke under a man's weight at every step. Toponce and his wagon boss, Hawkins, went ahead. They lost sight of the others the second day. Then Toponce left Hawkins behind. He crossed the Bear River on the ice and reached Call's Fort on the morning of the fourth day. He never could remember much about that dreadful trip. Whenever he lay down in the snow, exhausted, he remembered the sufferers behind him and got up again.

At Call's Fort, Chet and Carl Loveland, father and son, immediately began to organize a relief party. The women set to frying beef and cooking other food. By the time they were ready to leave—with six or eight sleds drawn by teams, and a lot of saddle horses— Toponce was able to go back with them. He slept in the bottom of one of the sleds all the way.

First they met Hawkins. Then they picked up the lone woman, with her blankets on her back. They sent one sled back to the fort with those two. Then they picked up some more half-frozen men, including the lame George Forbes and another lame man named Matthews. Most of them hadn't got even halfway to the fort. Some of the rescued travelers went on with the last sled and retrieved the hidden gold. Everybody in the party was saved, although some were in agony with frozen hands, feet, and ears.

CHAPTER 14

How Things Were in Alder Gulch

X Beidler and some of his friends marked Independence Day by putting up a pole to fly the United States flag. During the night, Secesh men cut the pole to pieces. Beidler and his friends raised a taller pole and put up a flag, but that night the Secesh poured kerosene against the wood and set it on fire.

Molasses was a great delicacy, expensive and scarce. Sam Hauser took his meals with Granville and James Stuart and some other men. One evening they came in, hungry and tired, to find Hauser contemplating a molasses-dripping mouse that he held by the tail. They lost their taste for sweetening then and there. Their stomachs churned as, during the next several weeks, they watched Sam spread molasses on his bread at meals until it was all gone.

Then he asked innocently why they had suddenly lost their taste for the camp's favorite sweetening. James Stuart replied, "I like it well enough, but not after a mouse has drowned in it."

"But it hadn't drowned," Hauser explained with a happy smile. "I killed the mouse and smeared it with molasses just to see how you boys would take it."

Is it any wonder that smart Sam Hauser became prosperous as a banker?

A big event took place on Saturday, August 27, 1864. Montana Territory's first newspaper, the *Montana Post*, published its first issue. Now there was news—late, but better than mere rumor—of the war in far-away America, news of local affairs, editorials telling people what to think and do about public problems. In September, the miners were informed that mail contact was cut off east of Salt Lake because of Indian depredations; Sherman was at Atlanta; the draft called for half a million more men; potatoes in the Bitterroot Valley were $3 a bushel. Thomas Dimsdale, an educated Englishman, was opening a school; the *Post* editorialized in favor of building a schoolhouse. Neil Howie, well and favorably known for his courage in apprehending road agents some months earlier, had been appointed sheriff by Governor Edgerton.

And on September 24 the *Post* warned that a food shortage might be in the offing, because more supplies were being used than were coming in. Truer words were never printed—but what could anyone do about the situation? The December 3 issue reported that wagon transportation had entirely played out. Now no more food would be coming up from Salt Lake City until next spring. What was coming, during the deep-snow months of January through March, was the Hungry Winter.

1865

CHAPTER 1

The Hungry Winter

When 1865 began, Montanans were proud of their status, with a full-fledged territory of their own and a relatively peaceable populace. Arrests were now made by proper law officers (with the Vigilantes keeping watchful eyes on such matters) and for relatively minor misdeeds. Murder and robbery were no longer the only crimes worth punishing.

The year opened in Virginia City, the Territory's metropolis, with a historic prize fight. Scheduled for Sunday, January 1, it was postponed until the next day at the urging of Chief Justice H. L. Hosmer, who didn't like prize fights anyway, especially on Sunday.

In this corner, Hugh O'Neil, age thirty-four, 190 pounds, five feet eight and a half. His opponent, Con Orem, age twenty-nine, 138 pounds, five feet six and a half. O'Neil was taller and heavier, but Con Orem was faster and, although he was a saloon keeper, he didn't drink. Gloves were not required, but both men wore them—ordinary snug buckskin gloves without padding. The fight went 185 rounds, lasted three hours and five minutes, and was declared a tie. It was stopped by mutual consent of the backers.

The Territory's first legislature was in session in Bannack—in a dirt-roofed cabin lighted with a coal-oil lamp and heated with a stove—and no doubt some of the elected representatives of the people rode the seventy miles between camps to take in the fight.

Culture abounded. Professor Thomas J. Dimsdale edited the *Montana Post*, ran a subscription school for children ($2 a week per child), and held singing school for adults once a week. Local-talent lecturers took part in a lyceum series. There were two churches, both with Sunday Schools, and a strong Masonic Lodge. The Montana Historical Society was organized that year by men who knew they were making history. Colonel Sanders was president, Judge Hosmer historian, and Granville Stuart secretary.

A daily mail and stage service operated (when possible) between Virginia City and Salt Lake by way of Bannack. A. M. Smith came to town and opened a photographic gallery over Con Orem's saloon. For $5 a man could have his tintype made and neatly framed in a little black case lined with red velvet to send home to the States. He would prepare for this by spending some time in Thomas White's hairdressing parlor, a place somewhat fancier than a mere barber shop.

But above all this bustle of civilized activity hovered two ancient enemies of man, winter and starvation. That was the Hungry Winter, the year of the flour riots, when the have-nots took from the haves and friend turned against friend.

As early as the previous September, the *Post* had warned that a food shortage might be in the offing, because more supplies were being used than were coming in. A prudent warning—but what could a man do to be saved? Perhaps a few people bought and hoarded, but about all the warning really accomplished was to show people that the *Post* was alert to public problems.

In its December 3 issue the *Post* reported that wagon transportation had entirely played out. Snow came early and lay deep. Now no more supplies would be coming up from Salt Lake City. Salt Lake flour, cheaper than that freighted across the Plains from St. Louis or "States" flour brought up the Missouri by steamer to Fort Benton, was $25 a hundred pounds, wholesale price quoted by Rockfellow and Dennee. That was about normal.

The next week's paper reported that a storm had left a foot of snow, followed by a hard wind and 18-below temperature. Five teamsters, hired by Edward Hardester to drive freight wagons from Salt Lake to Virginia, were stopped by snow on the wrong side of the Rockies. Hardester callously fired them, without a grubstake. They spent the small amount of money they had for grub and started on foot for the Beaverhead. One of them froze to death.

December 24 Rockfellow and Dennee reported that the majority of freight wagons were holed up on the Snake River for the winter and were not expected before the latter part of February. This expectation turned out to be overoptimistic. The middle of March, some mail came in by Overland Stage, twenty days from Salt Lake City. The *Post*'s correspondent at Silver Bow City (near present Butte) wrote on March 18 that a "bread riot" had occurred at Dorain's store. Some Irishmen with no money seized flour there—and then demanded canned oysters.

The April 1 issue reported real increases in the price of flour. St. Louis was up $8, Salt Lake $11, States $15. The paper came out on

Saturday. The next day there was a riot in Nevada City. The editor scolded about it the following week without telling what really happened. Why should he? Everybody along the gulches knew it already.

Flour had gone to more than $40 a sack. A gang of "self-appointed regulators" bought flour by force from merchants who had it, at the old prices, $25 for Salt Lake and $28 for States. They paid for it in clean dust, all but two sacks.

That happened on Sunday. Angry mass meetings were held in Virginia City that day and Monday. A committee went to call on the merchants, pleading that the people were destitute. The committee "inflamed the crowd," said the *Post,* and the crowd, angry but unorganized, tried to take flour by force from the Newbanks store.

Inside the store, barricaded behind sacks of flour, were twenty-three armed men. Outside was Sheriff Neil Howie, one of the bravest men who ever lived, with twenty hastily deputized policemen. They would have been mowed down by rifle fire if Howie had not been persuasive as well as courageous. He talked the mob out of its violent intentions. The *Post,* provoked at the whole affair, scolded merchants in an editorial headed "Speculation" and scolded the mob in one called "Two Wrongs Never Make a Right."

The April 15 issue published some news that had leaked in somehow from back in America: Richmond had fallen. Rockfellow and Dennee said flour was becoming very scarce, which everybody knew, and that consumers should economize, which everyone was doing already if there was any flour in the cupboard to economize with.

The *Post* gave the surrender of General Robert E. Lee just nine lines of type in its April 22 issue, because the end of the Rebellion, way back East, was of less vital importance to its readers than the drama right around home. There had been real excitement, and this time the editor straddled no fence. In a long editorial he soundly scolded the "monopoly." Merchants had run the price of flour up to $100 a sack—a dollar a pound!—and boasted that they had a right to sell as they pleased.

Some outstanding citizens had taken part in this second flour riot. The *Post* commented, "Unlike the outbreak on a former occasion, which we consider wholly unjustified, there were many respectable men in command and in the ranks." That made a difference. Rockfellow and Dennee were staunchly on the side of the monopoly. Their weekly comment on prices included a remark that they knew of flour selling at $5 a pound within a few hundred miles. The implication was that anything less was entirely reasonable.

This is what had happened, although the *Post* prudently did not tell all the details: A mob of exasperated miners, hungry for that staple of life, common bread, and worried for the women and children of the camps, gathered for a stormy mass meeting. S. R. Blake, chairman, whipped the meeting into order long enough to bring sense out of chaos. He must have had a powerful personality—angry miners were not easy to calm down. They could have swarmed through the town and taken the remaining flour. There would, of course, have been fighting, with dead men lying in the bloody snow. But there was no fight. A planned invasion took place. Tension had been mounting with the price of flour. On April 16, it was $65. Next day the price was $90, and people who could were paying that much. On the morning of April 18, the price was $1 a pound. At noon the remarkably disciplined second bread riot began.

Four hundred and eighty men marched from Nevada to Virginia. Their leader rode a horse and carried a symbolic banner: an empty flour sack. They were divided into six companies, each with its captain. They were ominously silent. Most of them did not even answer when bystanders jeered or cursed. They searched the town—stores, warehouses, restaurants, boarding houses, even some haystacks—and collected eighty-two sacks of precious flour. They handed out promissory notes, printed up in advance at the *Montana Post*, promising to pay for the flour at a price it used to sell for, Salt Lake $27, and States $30.

Three opportunists, aiming to get while the getting was good, went into a store on Content's Corner and began to pick out clothing. A messenger ran for Sheriff Howie, who strode in with his pistol in his hand and announced that the first man who stole from a store or a saloon would be shot or hanged. "Stealing" was different from taking flour that would be paid for.

Colonel Sanders and others addressed the milling crowd, advising them to be orderly in their search for flour. An armed group marched to the Sanders home after a rumor spread that a wagonload of flour had been delivered there. The mild Mrs. Sanders invited them spunkily to come in and search.

The riot could not have been a surprise to Sheriff Howie. He had to resign himself to keeping order on the ragged fringes of the silent, surly mob. He was quoted, years later, as having made this speech: "Gentlemen, this uprising is to get flour and pay a reasonable price for it; it is not to sack the town. . . . The same men that fought for law and order a few months ago are prepared to fight for it now."

Those men were the Vigilantes. Which side were they on during the flour riots? On all three sides—and there were three: people who had flour, the marching searchers, and the armed volunteers who helped Howie keep the peace. The Vigilantes had been of one mind about hanging road agents, but this was a new conflict in which their individual interests differed. One Vigilante, Charlie Beehrer, who was a brewer, boasted later that he bootlegged four sacks to a baker at $70. As a reward, he was allowed to buy four loaves of bread for $16.

Mollie Sheehan's freighter father, Jim, used one room of his house for storing merchandise, including flour. He had freighted most of it to Last Chance Gulch just before the Alder Gulch men rebelled and started to confiscate available supplies. Mrs. Sheehan hid the flour she had for her own family: she emptied part of a barrel of beans, filled it half way up with flour, and poured the beans on top.

There was some free-lance looting. A freighter named William Lambert was planning to leave for Salt Lake as soon as he could get through the mountains. Someone stole four of the eight sacks of flour he had stored for provisions on the journey. Later someone broke down the door of the storage shed and took the remaining four sacks. Lambert not only could not set out for Salt Lake—he even had to pay $10 for a new door.

The searchers took eighty-two sacks back to Leviathan Hall (where the notable prize fight had been held) and let the applicants line up. If a man could prove he had no flour, he could buy eighteen pounds, more if he had a family. As the supply ran low, the ration was cut to ten pounds. Then it ran out entirely.

The flour committee paid back the former owners, but all this ruckus was very embarrassing. When it was over, Mayor Pfouts published a notice in the paper that he would proclaim martial law if there were any more disturbances. Sheriff Howie warned in print that male citizens were subject to call to disperse unlawful gatherings and that demonstrations would be dispersed at all costs. "All costs," of course, meant shooting. There were no more riots, because flour began to come in. Some single men shared their flour with those who had families. Others were quiet, unsung heroes who voluntarily went without bread or flapjacks and lived for weeks on a diet of beef and coffee.

The next issue of the *Montana Post*, April 29, had such terrible news—from the point of view of *some* of the Territory's people—that no local riot could have crowded it out: President Lincoln had been assassinated. The news had come in by horseback messenger from Bannack. The *Post* was still making do with any kind of paper, and this issue was printed on dirty pink, but it was a mourning issue just the same, with heavy black rules between the type columns. There was one small item of good news: fourteen sacks of flour had come in from the beleaguered wagon trains on the far side of the Rockies. It was high time, because rice, beans, and hominy, those poor substitutes for bread, were almost gone.

J. WILKES BOOTH SHOT! was the headline on the big national news story in the May 6 issue. Locally, more flour had come in—sixty-four sacks on Monday—and the price dropped to $65. This flour had been unloaded three times, with terrible effort, to lighten the wagons for the straining oxen, floundering in deep snow where the crust had melted. Men carried the sacks on their shoulders two hundred yards at a stretch. On Thursday, 107 more sacks had come. Someone had offered to pay 20¢ a pound to get in some choice freight, not identified, from just twenty-two miles west of the Divide, but even a mule carrying a load of mail hadn't got through.

The food shortage at Silver Bow City was worse than at Alder Gulch. There was *no* flour, and miners were living on straight beef and coffee. Beef was cheap. Coffee was $1 a pound. Potatoes were 35¢ a pound and scarce; sugar and rice, 75¢.

There was joyful weeping in the streets of Virginia City when the first flour wagons rolled in. Women and children cried, and men hitched up and drove out along the road to escort the wagons. The *Post* for May 13 said flour was arriving every day. The editor wrote gaily:

> The road is now open to Salt Lake. Some parts do not much resemble the Macadamized causeways of the East, but the collective

energy of the beef persuasion can now overcome the difficulties of the passage. The Hee Haw minstrils [sic] also are making the hills vocal with their wild psalmody, digging their toes into the gravel and making ground fast. May their ears never grow shorter.

The newspaper's paper shortage was still desperate. Even its colored stock was running so low that the May 27 issue was only half its normal size—a single unfolded sheet, printed on both sides. By June 10, a supply of white paper had got through, and there was plenty of flour for everybody at the satisfactorily low price of $15 a sack.

There was still plenty to worry about. Gold had been up to $36 an ounce, was now worth about half that. Goods ordered from the States at the old price, and due to come up the Missouri to Fort Benton, would have to be paid for with twice as much gold as had been expected. A dozen people had been killed by Indians near Fort Benton, and Governor Edgerton was calling for 500 short-term volunteers to fight the Blackfeet up there. Two white men had been found scalped within twelve miles of Last Chance Gulch, and Indians had captured a girl of twelve. But spring had come after the long and dreary winter, and there was bread again.

What happened to Alex Toponce during the long, harsh winter of 1864–1865 was typical of the trouble freighters had. He had bought a train of wagons in Salt Lake City and loaded them with flour at $24 a hundred. But getting the flour from the seller took longer than he had allowed, and he didn't start north until about November 10.

At first the wagons moved right along at fifteen to eighteen miles a day, but where Dubois, Idaho, is now a snowstorm struck. Before it stopped there was nearly three feet of snow on the ground, and the oxen could move the wagons no farther. Four other trains, belonging to the firm of Coe and Carter, were stuck ahead of them, near the crest of the Continental Divide, but Coe and Carter were near enough the top to get over. They took their cattle down to Horse Prairie and wintered very well.

Toponce took his, 175 head, to an island in the Snake River and turned them out to rustle for themselves. He left his wagon boss to look after the wagons corraled on Dry Creek, and he and the other drivers went on to Virginia City by stage.

In March of 1865, with the flour shortage acute, he hired a pack train of horses and mules, struggled back to his stranded wagons, and loaded the flour on the pack animals. He paid the packer $20 a hundred pounds for moving the flour, and in two trips they moved it all. But so did other freighters. The price had dropped to as low as $30 before he was through. He figured that he would have been just as well off if he had left all the flour in the wagons back in Idaho.

In April he went to the island in the Snake River where he had left his oxen and found only one alive. The rest of them had starved and died, frozen into the hard crust of snow that froze after a chinook wind melted it. He left the one thin survivor there, with plenty of grass coming up and nothing to do but eat it.

A story was told years afterward about another unprofitable flour transaction. At the height of the excitement in Alder Gulch, a man sold his meek, long-suffering wife to an old admirer for $100 gold and two sacks of flour. After a quick divorce, the lady married her new owner. They settled down on a ranch, raised a family, and presumably lived happily ever after. But the ex-husband hung on to his flour a little too long. He got only $27 a sack for it when the market broke.

At Emigrant Gulch that winter they ran out of flour, as other gold camps did. In the spring David Weaver's partner, Shorthill, learned on a trip to Virginia City about the flour riots that had taken place there. He heard that freighters coming up from Salt Lake had halted along the way for fear of having their loads seized. This may have been true in some cases. Freighters did not favor hijacking. But the basic reason for halting was that the wagons couldn't get through the snow.

Meanwhile, back in the cabin at Emigrant Gulch, with raw elk hides carpeting the dirt floor, David Weaver carefully dusted out discarded sacks and retrieved a few spoonsful of flour. In the woods one day he heard a noise that scared him. It could have been made by a grizzly bear, but the bear turned out to be a man gathering pitch from spruce trees. He had discovered that chewing it like gum relieved his craving for bread and biscuits. Emigrant Gulch didn't get flour until May.

CHAPTER 2

The Camels Are Coming,
Hurray! Hurray!

A remarkable event occurred in Virginia City in early June: a camel train came to town. This was less astonishing in 1865 than it would be now. Experiments with camels for pack trains in arid country had been carried out in parts of America, notably the Southwest, for several years. A camel could carry six to eight hundred pounds, travel thirty-five miles a day, live on brush, and get along six to ten days without water. An "express" dromedary with a light load could briskly cover seventy-five miles in a day.

The *Montana Post* for June 3 announced that a long-heralded camel train had arrived and there would be free rides for children. But mules and horses hated the smell of camels, and owners of runaway teams detested them. By the end of July the camels had been moved to Helena, where they were used for moving freight, such as merchandise and gold dust in nail kegs. After a few months they were put on a freight run from Hell Gate over the mountains to Walla Walla, Washington.

By that time the original seven camels had become six. The seventh was shot for a moose while grazing. The shooter, James McNear, a crack shot from Kentucky, was just about to down another "moose" when the irate owner came roaring up. McNear went free only after he handed over his gun, ammunition, watch, and most of his money plus the deed to a gold claim. Then the owner stood over him while he dug a grave to bury the beast.

The Bad Luck Boys
on Powder River

John Bozeman's idea that people bound for the gold fields needed a new, shorter route was sounder than he could have guessed. While he and his partner, John Jacobs, were finding and marking their road to get wagons to Bannack, Alder Gulch opened its riches—and Alder Gulch was seventy miles closer for emigrants along the Bozeman Trail.

The next year, 1864, Last Chance Gulch was discovered, and Helena sprang up there. In 1865 there were probably 18,000 white persons in Montana, as contrasted with the 500 during the first winter after discovery at Bannack.[24]

There was all that gold to be had, and Bozeman's road went to it, and there were thousands of men anxious to get the gold or to raise crops or freight merchandise to serve the miners. There was also, at long last, the end of the Civil War. The United States Army was all through fighting Rebels. Now it could get busy with the Indians who defended the Powder River country and blocked the Bozeman Trail. The Indians had done more than that. They had stopped *all* movement across the plains on the great Emigrant Road for a while in 1864.

The Army, what there was left of it after a lot of weary veterans went home, was now free to fight the redskins. Citizens intent on bettering their condition by going to Montana demanded that the Army do so. What's a government *for* if it doesn't help the people get what they want?

Marching around in the Powder River country in the summer of 1865 were two ill-fated expeditions. One was commanded by Brigadier General Patrick E. Connor, whose assignment was to punish the hostiles so they would *have* to keep the peace and leave the

Bozeman Trail open. The other, authorized by the Department of the Interior, was a civilian road-building crew with a military escort. Boss of this expedition was James A. Sawyers, a Sioux City man who had been a lieutenant colonel in the Iowa militia. His job was to find and build a wagon road from Sioux City to Virginia City.

Bozeman's road cut off some hundreds of miles from the old route, along the Oregon Trail and up through Idaho; Sawyers' road would be even shorter and did not involve the old Oregon Trail at all. Emigrant wagons and freighters would move west from Sioux City, whose merchants hankered for the profitable outfitting business that was enriching Omaha.

General Connor had distinguished himself in the war with Mexico, emerging as a captain of dragoons. He went back to civil life but left it again when the Civil War broke out. As Colonel of the 3d California Infantry, he learned a great deal about Indian fighting. He was a hero to frontier settlers and traders after he soundly defeated a combined group of Bannacks and Shoshones at the Battle of Bear River in northern Utah in January, 1863.

Major General G. M. Dodge said something unintentionally funny in one of his letters giving orders to Connor about the Powder River campaign:

> You of course understand that we settle the Indian troubles this season, and at such time as you consider it proper and for the interest of the government you can make an informal treaty for cessation of hostilities, appointing some place for meeting the Indian chiefs for having a full understanding with them, and myself or such persons as the government sees fit to go there. You must be the judge when it is proper to do this, and the Indians must be given to fully understand that when all hostilities cease, any act of robbery, murder, etc., by their people will precipitate our whole force on them.

You of course understand that we settle the Indian troubles this season—ah, the serene assurance of it! Indian troubles along the Bozeman Trail hadn't even really begun. There were graves of white men along that road already in June, 1865, when Dodge wrote that letter. But there would be more, many more, and General Connor never had a chance to shake his finger at the Sioux and threaten to "precipitate our whole force on them." He was lucky to get out of the Powder River country as well as he did. What the Indians fully understood was that hostilities weren't going to cease until the palefaces agreed to stay out.

Both Sawyers and Connor had trouble with Indians. But that was by no means the only trouble they encountered. Government red tape encompassed them; if supplies were available, there weren't enough wagons to haul them or the supplies were in the wrong place. Sawyers couldn't get all the men he had been promised for an armed escort. Connor infuriated his superiors in the Army. And both ran into mutiny among their men.

Mutiny was the order of the day that spring. General Robert E. Lee had surrendered April 9. Most veterans of the War of Rebellion, from either side, wanted to go home. Some yearned to go to the goldfields. Almost none of the enlisted men, except a few career noncoms, wanted to stay in the Army. On the other hand, many career officers were hanging on by tooth and nail. Promoted fast during the war, and given even higher brevet grades for gallantry in action, they endured demotions afterward lest Othello's occupation be completely lost.

Major General G. M. Dodge wrote to Connor from Fort Leavenworth on July 21 that infantry troops and some cavalry had mutinied, but he got them going. "All troops are giving me great trouble," he said. On the same day, Connor wrote from Fort Laramie that part of the 1st Nebraska Cavalry back at Fort Kearny claimed they were entitled to discharge because the war was over. "I have ordered Colonel Heath to suppress it with grape and canister," he said, "and bring the leaders to trial."

Captain H. E. Palmer, Connor's acting quartermaster, recollected in later years that at Fort Laramie "we had a lively little matinee with the Sixteenth Kansas, who mutinied, the entire regiment refusing to go after the Indians." They said their terms of enlistment would be finished before the expedition was, they hadn't enlisted to fight Indians, hadn't lost any red devils, and were not disposed to hunt for any. Connor appeared on the scene with two companies of California troops who were devoted to him, two pieces of artillery, and some cavalry. He formed them in line ready to attack, and the Kansans gave up their mutiny in five minutes.

Connor was having exasperating delays because of contractors' failure to do as they had promised. He expected to establish a post on the headwaters of either the Tongue or the Powder River near the Bozeman Trail. (The one he did establish was on the Powder, and he named it for himself. Later it became Fort Reno.) His expedition consisted of three columns, the right one commanded by Colonel Nelson Cole; the center by Lieutenant Colonel Samuel Walker; the left by Colonel J. H. Kidd. Connor himself went with that one. His orders to Cole July 4 and to Walker July 28 landed him in hot water. They included this clear statement of policy: "You will not receive overtures of peace or submission from Indians, but will attack and kill every male Indian over twelve years of age."

This was not a new policy with Connor. On July 3, instructing Colonel C. H. Potter about keeping the transcontinental mails moving, he had said: "Treat all Indians found near mail route as hostile. . . . Show no quarter to male Indians over twelve years of age." The same day he told General Dodge in a letter about Indians: "None of them are to be trusted. They must be hunted like wolves."

His July 28 letter to Walker attracted the attention and the wrath of Major General John Pope in St. Louis. Pope hit the roof. He ordered General Dodge to take immediate steps to countermand such orders and threatened, "If any such orders as General Connor's are carried out it will be disgraceful to the government, and will cost him his commission, if not worse."

In another letter Pope wrote Dodge:

> General Connor is ignoring the quartermaster and commissaries, and violating law and regulations in making contracts himself and forcing officers to pay public money on them. Stop all this business at once, and order all officers to conform to law and regulations.

The orders caught up with Connor in August, and he replied to General Dodge from "near Fort Connor," with the equivalent of "Yes sir! I'll explain everything when I get back." But he never did. When the Powder River Expedition was finished, Connor was a bitter, disappointed man who felt that he had been disgraced.

Cole was to march from Omaha to Columbus, Nebraska, where the Loup Fork flows into the Platte, then around the east base of the Black Hills to the Little Missouri, in the northeast corner of present Wyoming, then across the Powder and the Tongue to a rendezvous on the Rosebud River. He would have about 1,400 cavalry and 140 six-mule wagons.

Colonel Samuel Walker was to march from Fort Laramie up to the Black Hills, taking wagons, then go on with pack mules through the Hills and northwest to Powder River and the rendezvous. He would have 600 cavalry.

Connor would direct the left column, which he divided into two sections. He went with the main body, commanded by Colonel J. H. Kidd. With his cavalry were ninety-five Pawnee scouts. He also had the very best of the guides, Jim Bridger and Mitch Bouyer. Connor and Kidd would move up the North Platte to Horseshoe Station, then north to the Powder and down that river. A wagon supply train with 195 teamsters and wagon masters went with them.

The west section of the left column, commanded by Captain Albert Brown, detached at Horseshoe with 116 cavalrymen and 84 Omaha scouts. It would go up the North Platte to Platte Bridge, then northwest to Wind River, then eastward to the new post that Connor would establish on the Powder.

Connor, with about 675 men, crossed the North Platte August 2 near LaBonte (or Bridger's) Crossing and marched up the north bank. Near present Douglas, Wyoming, he turned north. He reached Powder River August 11 and built, on the Bozeman Trail, a supply depot that he named for himself: Fort Connor. This was his base of supplies when he marched north.

His Pawnee Indian scouts had a brisk battle with twenty-four Cheyennes and killed all of them, capturing their horses (some of them government property) and clothing that included two infantry coats that Colonel Thomas Moonlight had given away at Fort Laramie the previous spring. It was stupid to give Army uniforms, even worn-out ones, to Indians. Hostiles often disguised themselves as soldiers when approaching white men's camps.

Connor attacked an Arapaho village of some 1,500 persons—who had not been hostile before that—destroyed their lodges and winter supplies, and killed over sixty warriors. Then, too short of ammunition to go looking for more Indians to "punish," the troops moved down Tongue River to meet Cole and Walker, but they were nowhere to be found. Just about everything that had been planned went wrong.

Cole and Walker had the major share of the trouble. Their men were unwilling to fight, their officers were ignorant of Indian warfare, they had no competent guides, and their maps were inadequate. An extremely cold storm broke over Cole's column September 2 after it had marched twenty-six miles in searing heat. In the next few days, hundreds of horses and mules died from the weather, exhaustion, and starvation. Too-close herding had kept them from grazing, but loose herding would have let the Indians get them.

With no animals to pull the wagons, these had to be destroyed, with great quantities of quartermaster's stores. Before long, Cole's men were starving along on less than quarter rations. After terrible difficulties, Cole reached newly established Fort Connor, expecting to find clothing and shoes for his ragged, limping men—but there were none. His men's feet were swollen and bleeding from marching over cactus and rock. Cole had been out eighty-two days, had traveled 1,200 miles on rations sufficient for sixty days.

Colonel Sawyers expected an escort of at least 200 cavalry for his road-building project, but in May he found that only 118 *infantry* had been assigned, with rations for only three months, and no wagons to haul civilian supplies. Finally he got twenty-five cavalrymen, ammunition and rifles for his civilian employees, and authority to draw rations for six months.

When he left Niobrara on June 13, after exasperating delays, his train included five wagons of emigrants. His military escort was not nearly big enough, and the men didn't want to go anyway. They were Galvanized Yankees,[25] the war was over, and they wanted to go home. His road-building party included fifty-three men with fifteen wagons, six oxen to each. The escort had twenty-five mule-drawn wagons. A private freighting concern, C. E. Hedges and Company, had thirty-six wagons loaded with merchandise for Virginia City. It was bossed by Nat D. Hedges, nineteen years old.

Sawyers had trouble all the way. He and Captain George W. Williford, commanding the escort, feuded constantly. Some of the emigrants and civilian employees turned back because the escort was so meager. Only July 15, Williford sent Lieutenant Dana with fifteen men to Fort Laramie, seventy-five miles away, to get shoes and other supplies for his nearly barefoot soldiers. The resulting delay angered Sawyers—especially when Dana and his men rejoined them August 1 without the supplies they had gone after. Dana had sent the wagon and supplies to join the military force on the Powder River and planned to meet that group later.

Williford maintained that Sawyers' guides were incompetent. Sawyers said Williford's soldiers were cowards. Indians harassed all of them frequently, stealing or stampeding the stock. The train headed northwest to the Powder River around the north side of Pumpkin Buttes—and got into badlands country where both animals and men suffered for lack of water. The expedition had to curve back.

On August 13, young Nat Hedges was scouting for water a mile or so from camp when a bunch of Cheyennes got him. His body was found, scalped and mutilated. Next day, Indians tried to make off with the horse and mule herd but failed. The men corraled the wagons and dug a grave for Nat Hedges, then drove the stock over it so the Indians wouldn't find it and dig it up again.

On the fifteenth, Sioux and Cheyenne Indians attacked at sunrise. Sawyers wrote in his official report:

> The bluffs around at sunrise were covered with Indians to the number of 500 to 600, and fighting was commenced by their charging down over the plain and shooting into the corral; each charge was repulsed, however, and at about noon they called for peace. After some parleying I decided to treat with them, and for some bacon, sugar, coffee, flour, and tobacco, they agreed to let us go on our way. The minority, however, were discontented with this treaty, but were restrained by the majority from fighting.

This was a bland understatement of the situation. It wasn't only a minority of the Indians who were discontented, no doubt because they wanted more supplies than were offered. Captain Williford objected strenuously to giving the enemy any presents at all. From the beginning Sawyers, commanding the expedition, and Williford, commanding his escort, disagreed about almost everything. By trying to buy off the hostiles, Sawyers laid the foundation for mutiny among his men.

While the Indians were still close by, Privates Anthony Nelson and John Rawze ventured among them—and turned up missing. After the Indians departed, a party sent out from camp brought in Nelson's body. The other man was never found.

Williford and all the other officers but one wanted to go back to Fort Laramie. Sawyers preferred to send scouts to ask General Connor for protection. Two scouts were willing, but there were no volunteers among Williford's soldiers, and Williford refused to order men to go along. The scouts—J. F. Godfrey, a former lieutenant colonel who had signed up with Sawyers, and Charles W. Sears—set out for Powder River with two guides but no military escort.

Sawyers wrote in his report for the seventeenth that "the cattle were herded during the day by the drivers and pioneers, there seeming to be an indisposition on the part of the escort commander to expose his men as pickets; he seemed, in fact, indisposed to do much of anything, except to go to [Fort] Laramie by the shortest route."

Sawyers' intrepid scouts came back on the nineteenth after riding 150 miles, having spent fifty hours almost constantly in the saddle, to report that Connor had passed down the Dry Fork of the Powder about two days earlier. The unhappy expedition moved on, south of Pumpkin Buttes—they passed between the two southernmost of them—and arrived at the Dry Fork. An ox died, several mules gave out, and Captain Williford refused to go any farther.

Sawyers sent his scout Godfrey out again with a guide. They found new Fort Connor thirteen miles away, but the general had gone on to Tongue River. When the train reached Fort Connor, Williford received orders to stay there with his command. Colonel J. H. Kidd, commanding the fort, provided a cavalry escort to take Sawyers' party to the Big Horn. They moved along the Bozeman Trail, and on the last day of August lost another man: Captain Osmer F. Cole, a volunteer in the escort party, was shot dead by an Indian as he explored ahead with another officer. The expedition took his body along in a wagon. Now Sawyers had only thirty-five men in his military escort.

On the first day of September, the Battle of Tongue River began. (This siege by the Indians was about halfway between present Ranchester and Dayton, where the Bozeman road crossed the Tongue.) A bunch of Arapahoes stampeded some of the stock and, while the wagons were corraling for defense, two men were killed. They were Dilleland, a driver for Sawyers, and an emigrant driver named Merrill.

The chiefs of the attacking redskins wanted to talk. Connor had captured their ponies a few days before; they wanted them returned. Sawyers wanted something, too: more men for defense. An uneasy truce prevailed while three Arapahoes and three white men set off to catch up with General Connor.

Captain Cole's body was buried secretly September 3 in a rifle pit. On the sixth, the two drivers' bodies were buried in the wagon corral while members of the expedition danced gaily to fiddle music so the suspicious Indians wouldn't guess what was going on and dig up the bodies later. The expedition waited and waited to hear from General Connor. On September 12, Sawyers faced mutiny and had to give in before the combined anger of his employees. His story for that day is brief:

> Fine day; some Indians came in sight towards night. As our present escort could not in any event go further than the Big Horn by their orders, a large majority of the men refused to proceed beyond that point without escort, (only twenty men of the command being willing so to do.) No reinforcements appearing, I was constrained, to my great regret, to announce that on the morrow we would retreat to Fort Connor.

Thus he glossed over a dramatic confrontation that one of his mutinous drivers, A. M. Holman, described in more detail in later years. The men were keyed up because Sawyers trusted the Indians too far; too many of them wandered into camp with the excuse of wanting to talk to the chiefs who were conferring in a tent with Sawyers. The employees simply deposed Sawyers by a vote of sixty to five!

"As a successor to Colonel Sawyer [sic]," Holman recalled when he was an old man, "we selected one of our number, a brave and fearless leader, and he followed out the wishes of the majority." The brave and fearless leader's identity is lost, because neither Sawyers nor Holman named him. In more detail, Holman told about this event in a book:

> We were wrought up to a high pitch of excitement for this was a critical time and we felt that we must do something to prevent total annihilation. Some suggested a change of leaders. It was quickly put to a vote and a new leader was chosen. He with a few men immediately ordered the straggling Indians out and away from the corral. We then voted on the question of disposing of the seven Indians held in our camp. . . . So our newly elected captain went to the tent and ordered the Indians to get out. He warned them that if they or any of their number came again within shooting distance of the corral, they would be fired upon.
>
> Since we had acted so impulsively in electing a new commander, it was suggested by Col. Sawyer that another vote be taken, and so the men were told to step on either side of an imaginary line, but the verdict was the same as before. . . .
>
> After consultation with the men, our newly-elected captain told our former commander that if he would destroy all but thirteen wag-

ons we would proceed and fight our way through. The men did
not feel called upon to sacrifice their lives any longer in order to
protect a large train, which was chiefly government property, but
with only thirteen wagons there would be men enough to afford
protection to the teamsters. Seven lives had already been lost and
there was no one who felt it necessary to risk his life in order to
protect superfluous wagons and stock. Col. Sawyer would not consent to the proposition of destroying the wagons, so the other alter-
native was to endeavor to get the train back to Fort Connor.

Accordingly we started next morning in two columns on our back
trail.

Sawyers was saved from his mutinous civilian employees after
only one day's march back toward Fort Connor. A company of cavalry showed up, under the command of Captain A. E. Brown. The
men of Sawyers' small cavalry escort were sent on to Fort Laramie
to be mustered out, since their enlistments had expired. Captain
Brown helped Sawyers suppress his insurrection and went with
him, now heading back toward Virginia City.

Colonel Sawyers noted no more Indian encounters, but Holman
recorded one, in camp at the crossing of an unidentified creek, that
was sheer entertainment. "We never before in our lives had experienced so much fun and excitement," Holman recalled. Dust was
sighted in late afternoon while the white men were loafing and the
Winnebago scouts were eating supper. Was the dust raised by hostiles? The white men ran for their weapons. The Winnebagoes ran
for their ponies. Some forgot their guns. As each one mounted, he
rode up the valley yelling. "We felt ashamed of ourselves," said
Holman, "when we saw that any one of them was brave enough to
fight the entire Sioux nation."

The dust was caused by hostiles, all right—400 of them, with
some white flags of truce waving to show they were peaceful. Captain Brown, in charge of the Winnebagoes, ordered their chief, Little Priest, to halt them. The chief said he couldn't. His warriors had
come to fight Indians and that's what they were going to do. Brown
pulled a gun on the chief, who decided he *could* stop his men, and
did.

The new arrivals maintained they were just out hunting (400 of
them?) and were not the hostiles who had fought on Tongue River.
They went into camp near Sawyers' outfit. The Winnebagoes were
terribly disappointed to be done out of a fight, and the whites were

downcast because they had expected to watch it. The Winnebagoes kept up a noisy war dance all night, and some of them sneaked out and brought back seven fresh Sioux scalps.

Sawyers' expedition forded the Big Horn on the nineteenth near the site where Fort C. F. Smith would be established the following year. The expedition was lucky with the river. Fording was often impossibly dangerous. Here Captain Brown and his supply wagon turned back, but he sent eight of his horse soldiers on as an escort for Sawyers.

On the Yellowstone, September 29, they met a fleet of Mackinaw boats heading back to America from the gold fields; they would float down the Yellowstone and the Missouri to Omaha. On October 5 Sawyers passed Bozeman City. His men admired the sight of fields and fences—civilization at last! A week later they were in Virginia City. They had traveled 1,039 miles. Sawyers paid off his men and put his stock and equipment up for sale through a commission merchant. He was back in Sioux City on December 3, having gone by way of Salt Lake.

Sawyers was enthusiastic about the possibilities of his new road. It made travel to the gold camps 600 miles shorter than the Salt Lake route; a stage that took sixteen days from the Missouri River to Virginia City should make the trip on his road in half that time, he claimed. The War Department, which had co-sponsored his expedition with the Interior Department, was not enthusiastic, however.

Virginia City's *Montana Post* praised Sawyers' road in a news story October 14, commenting: "When the war with the savages is over, this will be the best road from the Missouri to Montana. . . ." But when the war with the savages was over, many years later, there were railroads, and they were not where Sawyers had built his road.

The District of the Plains, which had been established for General Connor to command, was abolished without warning. In an order dated August 22, Connor was ordered to Salt Lake City to command the new District of Utah. This order reached him a month later, September 22, near Fort Connor. He was furious. He had had no warning of this. He had battled red tape before he started, he had battled redskins in the Powder River country; he was eager to go on fighting. He had taken some of the heat off the stage stations and the wagon trains on the Emigrant Trail by keeping many of the hostiles occupied north of there. Now he was suddenly removed from the task to which he had been assigned, and this was more than a slap in the face. It was a blow to the heart.

Embittered, he obeyed the order to go to Salt Lake, but he never did turn in an official report on the Powder River Expedition, which ended September 23 when he left with a small escort. His notes were destroyed in a fire, and he was mustered out of the Army April 30 of the following year.

When he and his escort started out of the Powder River country, the Indians assumed he was retreating and they were rid of him. Accordingly, they hurried down to the great Emigrant Trail to pillage and massacre. They moved so fast that they passed him.

General Dodge wrote to General Pope on September 15; he had been to Powder River himself and looked things over. He thought the new post that Connor had established was well located. The Indians' trails all crossed at or near the site. A good deal of work had been done there; a stockade had been built and a beginning had been made on the quartermaster buildings, but there wasn't much to store in them yet. Stores for the new post hadn't even reached Fort Laramie. They did later, and were freighted on to Fort Connor in such quantities that the post became permanent instead of temporary. There was simply too much stuff to move.

General Dodge commended the Bozeman Trail without naming it:

> From [Fort] Laramie to Powder River, then to Virginia City, is an excellent wagon road; good grass, water, and wood all the way, and the most direct road that can be got. The travel over it in another season will be immense; it saves at least 450 miles in distance.

But Sawyers' expedition was a failure as far as making a road was concerned, Dodge said bluntly:

> It had a heavy train belonging to private parties, and while its ostensible object was to survey and make a road through a country comparatively unknown, its real purpose seems to have been to take the train through, and to that end its efforts were devoted, instead of making a road, building bridges, etc.

What Connor achieved, at great cost in money and untold misery to his men, was to stir up the Indians like a bunch of hornets. But he did build rickety Fort Connor, which was not intended to be a permanent post, and he left stores there to be guarded by two companies of Galvanized Yankees.

Sawyers did not leave that much of a monument. His road was never used again except by himself, the following year, when he took a smaller expedition to improve it for the hordes of emigrants and freighters who decided not to go that way.

CHAPTER 4

Meagher of the Sword

The most colorful character ever to set foot in Montana arrived in September, 1865. His name was Thomas Francis Meagher, and his title was Territorial Secretary, by appointment of President Andrew Johnson.

Meagher was world famous as an Irish revolutionary; he gloried in the sobriquet he had earned with a fiery oration in his native land when he was twenty-three: Meagher of the Sword. Two years later, as a result of other speeches, Queen Victoria's government tried him for seditious libel, and he was sentenced to be hanged, beheaded, and quartered. The sentence was, however, commuted to banishment to Tasmania. He escaped early in 1852 (with lots of help) and arrived in New York May 26 of that year.

Meagher was always a storm center, always dead sure he was in the right, always able to change his mind in five minutes about what *was* right. He was outspoken in favor of the South and slavery. After Fort Sumter was fired upon, he said impulsively in an argument, "I tell you candidly and plainly that, in this controversy, my sympathies are entirely with the South!" But a short time later he organized a Union company of Irish Zouaves in New York. Then he organized the Irish Brigade and was its brigadier general. He was a gallant leader and much luckier than his men, most of whom were killed in action. But at least once when orders were delivered to him, he was too drunk to understand them; and he was relieved of further duty before the war was over.

His political record before he came to Montana was interesting. He had been a Democrat in New York but later said in a letter to a newspaper that to be a Democrat was to favor "a selfish and conscienceless faction" that would cripple the nation if it could. He was to change his mind again in the brief time that remained to him.

Sidney Edgerton, first Governor of Montana, could do more good for his Territory—whose people now clamored for statehood—in the East than he could by staying home. Anyway, he wanted to put his older children in school. He took out of his coat pocket the skimpy bunch of papers that represented the Territory's three-months-old government, handed them over to Meagher, and behold! the new Secretary was Acting Governor. There was a drawback: Only the Secretary could sign government vouchers, and while Meagher acted as Governor there was no Secretary. So the poor man, always hard pressed for money, never could collect his salary.

The turbulent Territory's first legislative assembly, called by Edgerton in December of 1864, had passed a lot of laws but had not produced a proposed constitution for the proposed state of Montana. The enabling act had expired. The government was, therefore, shaky; there was considerable doubt that it had any right to exist.

A group of citizens asked Acting Governor Meagher to call an election for a territorial legislature. In December, he wrote Secretary of State William Henry Seward that he was opposed to calling a session because Southern sympathizers would surely be in control. Within a month, however, Meagher did an about-face on this. The Southern element was perfectly reliable, he assured Seward. It was the radicals and extremists among the Republicans who were dangerous. This change of stance naturally infuriated the Republicans. The Democrats were delighted.

Then the Acting Governor—who became known, with a curl of the lip, as "the Acting One"—ran full steam into the most powerful force in the Territory, the Vigilantes. They had never intended to run the government, but they closely watched those who did. After the Territory's first election they had warned Governor Edgerton very clearly not to sign the election returns from a precinct that they had reason to believe did not exist. They were not going to put up with any nonsense from Meagher.

In December, 1865, one James Daniels killed a man in Helena over a card game. The Vigilance Committee there seized him and turned him over to the legal authorities. Daniels was duly sen-tenced to three years imprisonment. Acting Governor Meagher hated prisons, having had too much personal experience with them when he was younger, and he had a mistaken notion of the power of his office. He appalled the Territory's leading citizens by order-ing Daniels released.

Judge Lyman Munson, proclaiming angrily that Meagher had been drunk, demanded that he revoke the pardon. Meagher re-fused. Daniels was accordingly released from jail in Virginia City and headed for Helena, thundering threats of vengeance on the men who had testified against him.

He still had Meagher's pardon in his pocket when the Helena Vigilantes hanged him—within an hour of his arrival. Someone pinned this warning on the back of his coat: "If our acting governor does this again, we will hang him too."

Thomas Francis Meagher was a fighter, but the men whose anger he incurred were fighters too. As Thomas Dimsdale wrote in his apologia for the Vigilantes, "Middling people do not live in these regions." The Acting One decided to call a legislative session of the men elected during Edgerton's regime. This "extraordinary" ses-sion, legal or not, was set for March of 1866.

CHAPTER 5

To the States by Mackinaw

Getting to the Montana gold camps was difficult: going back to America by water was a little easier. There were those who needed transportation to go home for a winter visit with the folks, or to lay in a stock of merchandise to be brought up the Missouri River by steamboat during high water in the spring, or to take gold out and say good-by forever to the gulches from which it came.

During late summer of 1865 this advertisement ran in the *Mon-tana Post*, published in Virginia City:

TO THE STATES BY MACKINAW

HO! FOR THE STATES!

20th of September, 1865

600 Passengers Wanted

A fleet of Mackinaw boats will leave the mouth of the Yellow-stone Canon, for the States. The boats are from thirty to thirty-five feet long; sharp at both ends, and built so as to be proof against all injury from obstructions to river navigation.

FARE—From Virginia City to St. Joseph, Mo., $40.00; from the place of embarkation, $30.00.

Experienced navigators of the Yellowstone and Missouri will act as pilots, and the whole will be in charge of a man well acquainted with Indian affairs.

Tickets for passage can be obtained from A. M. Torbett, at the Clerk's Office, Virginia City, and at Taylor and Thompson's, Helena.

TERMS—Ten dollars in advance, and the balance on embarkation.

Tickets must be secured by the 1st of September.

R. C. Knox & Co., Proprietors

Among the passengers were Judge H. F. Hosmer, chief justice of Montana Territory, and his family, going home for a visit. They had come out the year before. Two years after the Mackinaw trip, Judge Hosmer's son Allen published a book about it, *A Trip to the States,* in Virginia City. Only three copies of this little book are known to exist.

Allen was born September 15, 1850, in Toledo, Ohio, and the Hosmers' journey from Virginia City began six days after his fifteenth birthday. The book is very good for a teen-age boy, and when you get to the end you realize that it would have been even better if his type hadn't been so limited. He not only wrote the text, he set the type himself and printed it one page at a time on a small hand press. Even so, he couldn't use full stops in many places where he knew he should have them. His supply of type was short of periods, so he used commas. And he had very few capital letters —only one upper-case W.

The family, with other passengers, left Virginia City by wagon September 21, 1865, and reached Bozeman City just before noon on the twenty-fifth. Next day in the Yellowstone Canyon they found 300 people camped, waiting for the boats to be finished for trans-portation down the Yellowstone River to the Missouri and down that river to wherever they could get better transportation back to America.

There were thirty-six boats, divided into four fleets under various owners. Not all the boats were "sharp at both ends." The Hosmer family, including two ladies, were in a party of ten in one of Fleet No. 1's ten boats. Their Mackinaw was sharp at the bow, 3 feet high, 32 feet long, 8 feet wide at the center, and 4 feet at the stern. There were nineteen flatboats, some with cabins. Another fleet of nine included common flatboats with a small cabin on the stern. Each fleet belonged to a different builder. Fleet No. 4 had only four boats, sharp at both ends as in the Knox advertisement.

It was "Ho! For the States!" on September 27. Passengers and boatmen lived on wild game, had trouble with rapids and gravel bars on the river, slept sometimes on shore, worried about Indians, and cooked on small portable stoves. Sheldon Schmidt, "a dutch-man from Iowa," fell into the river while trying to take a rope ashore. He grabbed wildly, got a grip on the stove, then managed to seize an oar. Another man saved the stove. From then on they all joked that "Schmidt when he went into the Yellowstone took the stove along for a life preserver."

On October 2 they passed the mouth of the Big Horn, which made the Yellowstone muddy. Young Hosmer commented that there was a pretty site for a town there and foresaw that before many years it would be the metropolis of Montana. This was, in fact, the same Big Horn City that James Stuart had laid out so hopefully in 1863. It is now Bighorn, and has a population of about ten.

The boats traveled with the current, sometimes helped by oars, sometimes also by sails if no rapids were ahead and the river was clear of sand bars and rocks. Sometimes they even traveled at night. On October 7 they reached the great Missouri, and ten days later the Hosmer family left the fleet at Fort Sully in present South Dakota. There the menfolks sat in on a council between an Indian commission and a bunch of Sioux. They left October 27 on the steamboat *Calypso*. On November 10 they reached Sioux City, Iowa. They were finally in the United States. From Sioux City they traveled to Chicago and Detroit by stage and train.

CHAPTER 6

Kirkaldie Struggles On

And how was Frank Kirkaldie, that homesick, hard-working farmer, getting along this year? He yearned for letters and newspapers in his Gallatin Valley cabin. He was very tactful in hinting that his dear wife was not writing as often as she might; he suggested that the mail must be delayed somewhere—as it certainly was. On January 24 he received two letters from her, one written in July and the other November 27.[26]

Everything was going to get better as the country settled up, he assured her. There would surely be a regular express service next season, with no more need to depend on chance travelers who picked up the mail in Virginia City. The weather was beautiful, the stock was doing well without winter fodder, and there had been some parties—one, at Bozeman, had more than twenty ladies in attendance! He didn't go to the parties, but his wife could look forward to some sociability when she came out.

Transportation was getting better, too. He heard that a company had applied to the Territorial Legislature, then in session, for a charter for a toll road from the Gallatin to Fort Union, near the junction of the Yellowstone and the Missouri. That was only 350 miles from the Gallatin Valley, and steamboats of 330 tons would be able to make two trips a season to Fort Union during high water from St. Louis. If those bits of rumor were true, the States would be much closer than in the past.

There were stories of new stampedes to new diggings, but Kirkaldie's problem was to get seed for spring planting. He had failed in a project to trade a plow for wheat; but he sold the plow for $80 gold, or he could take part of it in seed potatoes.

Something his wife said put him on the defensive:

Perhaps I am mistaken but it seems as though I detect in the tone of your letter . . . an impatient or discontented state of mind—

for instance you say that 'the water, the fish, the timber, and the gold are all very fine—get as much of the latter as you can and hurry back and get us a home any where but in Joliet.' I have endeavored in my letters to you—to give you as correct an idea of this country as I could—partly because I thought it might interest you and partly because I had not much else to write about. As to the gold I shall most assuredly use my best endeavors to secure all I can of it honorably—in as much as that was my sole object in coming here—But I have not yet secured it and I am fully convinced— as indeed I always have been—that in my case at least, it will require time.

He explained that most miners didn't get rich—but this was a good country just the same. He *had* to believe that. "I am very sorry," he wrote, "if any new cause of unpleasantness has arisen in your intercourse with your mother or anybody else which renders your stay in Joliet more irksome to you than formerly."

He would send money from time to time, but probably not until the next fall. He was trying to turn everything he had into money for seed, and it was expensive. He had engaged twenty bushels of seed barley for nearly $160 in gold to sow ten acres. He had bought three bushels of seed potatoes at $10 a bushel; that should sow half an acre or a little more. He would sell his horse and one more cow; the white cow would come fresh in March, and then he could have butter. He hadn't had any for six months.

His claim of 160 acres, half a square mile, was on the east side of the Gallatin River about eighteen miles above the Three Forks of the Missouri. It had considerable timber, a fine spring a few rods from the cabin; it had a hundred acres or more of nice level prairie, good plough land, and it looked like rich soil. He was going to fence fifteen or twenty acres and cultivate all he could of it.

Kirkaldie worried. "You mentioned in your July letter," he said, "that Willie had crooked legs—but have not alluded to it in any of your subsequent letters that I have received. Have they—or are they likely to become straight?" Bub's fifth birthday was coming in a day or two. Kirkaldie was glad to have a good report of his health and behavior. "I have no doubt he will take good care of papa and mama when they get old."

He had a new address, care of Davis & Housel, Virginia City, and he hoped this would get the mail to him more expeditiously. He had not received any copies of the *Chicago Journal*, and his neighbors suspected that someone in Virginia City was selling newspapers as they came in. Latest war news received in the Gallatin Valley was that Sherman had captured Savannah.

On March 3 he wrote that he had received no more letters from his dear wife, and it was nearly eleven months since he had seen her. The babies must have changed a great deal, he thought. The most exciting news about mining was the discovery at Last Chance Gulch (July 14, 1864). The new town there had 300 houses, and two stage lines were running between the new diggings and Virginia City.

He had been mending his clothes, patching them with buckskin, and had used up more than half the thread he brought. He planned to buy a pair of buckskin pants if he could raise the money. They lasted two or three times as long as cloth. If his wife got a chance to send him anything by some friend who might be coming out, he wanted all the plum and cherry pits and apple seeds he could get, because when she moved to Montana they would want fruit trees.

March 18 he wrote from the booming new town of Helena, in Last Chance Gulch; he had gone there with two other men to look for work. They had passed through Gallatin City, where there were forty log cabins, unfinished, only two or three of them occupied. This was a desolate monument to a big idea. Someone had dreamed of making it a port on the Missouri River. But a railroad was needed to portage freight around the Great Falls of that river, and nobody built the railroad.

Helena, Kirkaldie thought, would become the headquarters of gulch mining for the whole territory. Already it had hotels, stores, law offices, express offices, jewelers' shops.

March 26 he wrote again. He had met some men from back home. He and his companions had taken up a lot in Helena and were building a cabin 16 by 20 on it to live in while they stayed there; they would sell or rent it when they went back to their farms. A few days later he speculated again, this time buying a small mining interest in Nelson's Gulch. He carefully did not tell his wife, who needed money, how much he gambled on this, but he did mention some current prices: flour, scarce, was $50 a sack (one hundred pounds), and bread $1 a loaf in gold; a pie cost the same. Butter was $1.50 a pound and wonderful fat beef from 18¢ to 25¢ a pound.

Eight hundred dollars in gold had been sluiced out of twenty-three loads of dirt in Dry Gulch, but he still believed that farming was the best undertaking for him. He hadn't had a letter since Lizzie's of December 3, and no newspapers had come at all.

He didn't do well in Helena. He wrote April 17 that he was leaving. He had done some trading and got a yoke of cattle and a wagon, part cash and the balance payable when his crop came in, but it cost him his little mining interest. It was more than a year since he had parted from his wife and children, and the last letter he had received was still that one dated December 3. He wrote:

> I hope before another year rolls around to be able to report some progress at least—I wish I might make enough to go to Illinois next fall; but everything is uncertain and I do not allow myself to make any extravagant calculations.

News had come that Richmond had fallen, and it looked as if the Rebellion was about played out. (This time he wasn't wrong.) "I hope," he said, "that peace will soon be restored within our borders and a peace on a good sound substantial basis. And we shall be indeed as we profess to be a Free nation."

When he wrote June 19, he was gleeful at the mail that had come —"A perfect feast of good things." There were letters his wife had mailed February 28, April 29, and May 1; some others from relatives; and a clipping about the murder of President Lincoln. He had heard about that, but this was the first he had seen about it in print, and he sincerely mourned:

> Never in the history of this country I think was the loss of any public man so keenly felt by the whole nation, never any, whose loss was mourned so sincerely and extensively as that of Abraham Lincoln. We did not know until he was taken from us *how much* we loved and respected him—or how we leaned upon him as a pillar of strength in these troublous times—And felt that whatever others might do or say—that *he* at least would not be influenced by passion or prejudice—that *he* could be relied in every emergency that he would go calmly and steadily forward—governed by the soundest reason in everything and always inclined to the side of mercy. If traitors expected or hoped for mercy they should have spared him alive—for no other man in power will have his forgiving spirit.

Kirkaldie refuted without anger his wife's recent suggestion that he had abandoned his farm and gone prospecting. He had, he explained, gone to Last Chance to try to earn some money. His deal on the yoke of cattle and a wagon was successful, he maintained—but he hadn't got his crop in as early as he would have liked. More bad luck: two frosts in June had destroyed squash, pumpkins, cucumbers, melons, and garden beans. His onion seed wasn't good; the cabbage seed didn't do well, either.

In his next letter, July 23, he had to admit that his grain crop wasn't good. He hadn't commenced irrigating until too late. Nobody in the Gallatin knew very much yet about irrigating. "But I suppose," he commented optimistically, "that land that is cultivated this year will bear a much larger crop next year & with less irrigation." The potatoes and rutabagas looked good. He hoped for $6 a bushel, 10¢ a pound, and it looked as if he might have 200 bushels or more.

Mining was booming, although Emigrant Gulch, over on the Yellowstone, was playing out. A nine-pound nugget worth $2,070 had been taken out of Nelson Gulch, he heard; it came from about a mile below the claim he worked.

"I hope the Govt is taking measures to close up the Indian troubles? I think as soon as the Indians find out that the South is conquered & there are any amt of soldiers at the disposal of Government—that they will soon become as docile as kittens." In this, as in many other things, Kirkaldie was wrong.

On September 22 he wrote a hasty note: a Mr. Murray was leaving for Omaha by Mackinaw boat on the Yellowstone, so Kirkaldie sent his wife twelve ounces of dust, which should bring $20 an ounce in the States. He hadn't had a letter from her since the end of June.

October 8 he wrote a letter to his children, about taking a load of potatoes to sell in Confederate Gulch to get the money he sent to Mama. His oxen, put out to graze the first night, went all the way home instead. The children of course would want to know about Indians, so Papa told them about nine Indians who rode dramatically into camp where he and three other drivers were armed with only an old rifle and two small pistols. The party of farmers had a little scare, but the Indians left after being given some potatoes.

He was careful to make the story interesting for the children without scaring his wife to death. The Indians, he said, were "Pondurays"—a tribe that lived away to the northwest near the British Possessions. The Pend d'Oreilles, also called Kalispels, still live in northwestern Montana on the Confederated Selish and Kootenai Reservation. They were not troublemakers from the white man's point of view. Nine Indians who could be bought off by four poorly armed white men for a few potatoes were not fierce red devils like the Crows, Sioux, and Cheyennes.

October 29 he wrote his wife that he had a letter from her and some other mail. He was finding out what vegetables grew in the Gallatin and specified the kinds of onions and cabbage seeds he would like to have her send. His potatoes had sold for only 8½¢ a pound, after all his high hopes, but some farmers got even less. His crop wasn't very good, only 175 bushels, but the quality was first rate. He hoped to send his wife $150 in the spring.

Kirkaldie could see all sorts of possibilities for making money—if a man had money to begin with, as he never did. A man with two four-horse teams, a threshing machine, and two good reapers could earn $3,000 to $4,000 in the Gallatin Valley in four months and then sell the outfit at a good profit. If his wife had been there, and if they had twenty or thirty cows, he could have made $100 in gold from each of them in one season.

"But I see no way of getting you here now—in the shape I wish —until the season after next," he wrote sadly. "And even that is dependent on my success next season—It makes me impatient to be so cramped for means when there is such a good chance to use means to advantage." But he felt that he had accomplished something. He had learned something about farming problems in this new country. Tom Coover (Cover), who had a new mill operating in the valley, was going to go back to the States to get machinery for another flouring mill. More people were moving in, looking for land.

Unlucky Frank! He wrote November 12 that he had bought a splendid yoke of oxen for $100 cash and $60 on credit, but he had them only two or three days when the best ox took sick and died. He worried about the possibility of another cholera epidemic in the States. It had been terrible along the Oregon Trail, decimating emigrant parties and Indians alike.

On November 26 he was pleased with the improvement in mail delivery—a letter from his wife and one from his mother had taken only thirty-six days from Joliet. He had never received mail so fast before. The Mackinaw boats had reached Omaha in twenty-five days. He was starting for Helena with another man, each of them taking a load of potatoes and beets to sell. They would pack the vegetables in chaff to keep them from freezing and, if the nights got really cold, would keep a fire going on each side of the wagons.

He asked for his wife's ideas about how their milkhouse should be arranged, although he didn't expect to build it until she got there—sometime, sometime. He wanted at least ten cows to start with. Butter was $1.75 retail in Virginia City.

He mailed this letter in Helena December 7, having arrived safely and sold his produce to good advantage—but he didn't say how much he got for it. And so ended 1865 for hard-working, unlucky, lonely Frank Kirkaldie.

CHAPTER 7

Moving the Supply to the Demand

Not the least of a farmer's problems was getting his crop to market. W. W. Alderson and his brother John, who settled in the Gallatin Valley in 1864, bought seed potatoes from neighbors at prices ranging from 25¢ to 40¢ a pound; they traded a $250 horse for 1,000 pounds of them in one instance.

The first crop, raised on sod ground and well cultivated, was excellent. Late in November of 1865 they loaded two wagons, one drawn by a span of "American" horses—that is, stout animals they had brought from the States, not the smaller ponies that ran wild— and the other wagon drawn by three yoke of young oxen. Burlap bags cost $2 apiece, so the brothers did without them and simply loaded the potatoes loose in their wagon boxes.

They set out about November 21 for booming Diamond City in Confederate Gulch—and within hours the mild weather gave way to a blizzard that bedeviled them until they made their last camp, eight or nine days later. The brothers spread their bedding over the potatoes, which didn't even have wagon sheets over them, and a foot of snow that covered the load before the first day ended gave additional protection from frost.

At night the men took shelter in heavy timber and snaked logs up to the wagons for big fires. Having no blankets that weren't already in use, the brothers couldn't go to bed, so they stayed up all night to keep up roaring fires. And so it went for the entire journey, with catnaps instead of sound sleep and, for meals, roasted potatoes with fresh butter they had brought along to sell.

On the way they passed a load of frozen potatoes that an unlucky rancher had dumped by the road. If he had kept on going, he could have sold his frozen potatoes for 6¢ a pound in Diamond City. The miners were not fussy about their provisions. The Aldersons sold theirs, unfrozen, two tons of them, for 12½¢ a pound wholesale. Their thirty-six pounds of butter brought $2 a pound.

CHAPTER 1

The Sunday People

There were plenty of problems, large and small, to rile emigrants. Sometimes they just plain didn't like one another's looks or manners. Some trains were too slow, and the drivers behind cursed in their dust but couldn't get around them. Most dangers and big annoyances brought the people in a wagon train together in spirit: Indian scares, the Platte River, bad weather, bad water, sick oxen, stubborn mules, and the United States Army, which was seldom able to provide the individual protection that every emigrant considered was his God-given right.

There was one problem, however, that often divided them, causing hard feelings and sharp talk. This was the question of laying over on Sunday. Even a preacher, if there was one in a train, couldn't always persuade the majority of drivers to stay camped until Monday. There were often sound reasons for moving on.

There were both men and women who felt deeply that the commandment "Remember the Sabbath day, to keep it holy" should be obeyed on the trail as it was at home. They could quote chapter and verse: Exodus 20:8—and often did. But men were more likely to be practical, although they might shake their heads sadly when the decision was made to move on, Sabbath or no Sabbath. Women were more vociferous. A train of emigrant wagons was liable to suffer from grievous internal dissension between strong-minded "Sunday people" and sinners.

One train that went up to Montana in 1866 almost a month ahead of Colonel Henry B. Carrington and his fort-building troops of the 18th Infantry included Mrs. Ellen Fletcher and members of her family. She was typical of Sunday people who carried their convictions to extremes. Her letters to relatives in Cuba, New York, were long, detailed, and pleasantly lacking in complaints about discomfort and danger. But on remembering the Sabbath day she was a fanatic. One not only camped; one also refrained from doing the family wash. On Sunday, May 29, she wrote:

The men were much more quiet in camp today than I expected them to be. There was no rude boisterousness manifested. On the contrary, they seemed to be stiller than usual. One of the men washed his clothes today, and one woman (the only one in the train besides ourselves) did out her washing. She is an Oregon woman, and has been there for 15 years. She says that she has crossed the plains before and shall wash when she gets the opportunity. Chell and I preferred not to have our washing done for the present, rather than employ our Sabbath in that way.

In June they "came to the new road called 'Bowsman's Cut Off'. . . . The Indians don't like to have us travel this road, as it is called their best hunting ground." On the Bozeman road, the train had more women in it. In a journal entry dated "Sabbath, June 24th, 1866" Mrs. Fletcher noted:

Last night the captain took a vote among the men to decide whether we should start today or not. The majority were in favor of resting, accordingly we have the day to ourselves and God. . . . Nearly every woman in camp except ourselves has been washing today. They make the excuse that they haven't the chance to wash only occasionally and as the water is good and the wood plenty [the train was a day or two beyond Crazy Woman Fork] they thought that they were excusable for washing. I preferred to leave my clothes until some other day, even if not quite so convenient.

We can imagine for ourselves the discussion between the godly Mrs. Fletcher, doing her Christian duty in reminding the other women what day it was, and their startled, defensive explanations —also their muttered comments about "Who does she think *she* is, trying to tell *me* what to do?"

The next day a Mr. Smith hit his wife over the head with the butt of his whip and narrowly escaped being strung up to the nearest tree, but it turned out that Mrs. Smith was only stunned, not dead. Mrs. Fletcher didn't say so, but it's possible that she felt Mrs. Smith had only got what she deserved for being so ungodly as to wash on Sunday. Mrs. Fletcher washed in camp on Monday, and the clothes were dry by morning, proving that the Lord looked after His own.

Two Solutions Collide

Two powerful forces were in opposition in America in 1866. We can call them doves and hawks, although nobody did at the time. The hawks wanted to end the Indian problem in a hurry by using force to conquer the Indians. The War Department, some high-ranking Army officers, and most frontiersmen were hawks. The only good Indian was a dead Indian, kill every male over twelve years of age, nits make lice—such ideas were common. If enough Indians could be killed, the remainder might be placed on reservations where they couldn't do much harm.

The doves were officials of the Interior Department, which was supposed to take care of the Indian problem, and half a dozen do-good organizations in the East called, in general, "Indian friends." Their idea was that if the wild, free, buffalo-hunting Indians were treated tenderly they would quite soon settle down to be happy, industrious farmers. The doves overlooked the fact that farming was the last thing a Plains Indian wanted to do. He liked the life he had. All he wanted was to be let alone so he could go on that way.

Next time you get news that makes you roar, "That is the stupidest thing that ever came out of Washington!" look back at something that happened at Fort Laramie in 1866 because of decisions in Washington. There was something *really* stupid, and disastrous to a great many people, both red and white. The problem was to keep the river of emigration flowing undammed up the Bozeman Trail. There were two solutions, and they collided. The Indian Bureau sent a commission of doves to Fort Laramie to get a peace treaty signed by several tribes to keep that road open. At the same time the hawks of the War Department dispatched a military force to build forts along the road, with or without a peace treaty.

Somebody was very stupid indeed, and it wasn't the savages. The military force, under Colonel Henry B. Carrington, arrived while the peace talks were going on. It was plain to the Indians that the Great Father in Washington was talking out of both sides of his mouth. He was cooing, through his treaty-peddlers, "My children, please let the settlers pass through your hunting country, and in return I will give you all these fine presents. Now play nicely together!" At the same time, with the voice of the hawk, he was warning, "The emigrants are going through whether you like it or not, and my soldiers will fight you if you try to stop them!"

The Indians—Sioux, Cheyennes, some Arapahoes—who needed that hunting country because they lived on game, did the obvious, natural thing. They fought for it. And John Bozeman's cutoff became "the bloody Bozeman" until the Indians won that war and the trail was closed in 1868.

Colonel Carrington commanded the expedition to establish forts to protect the trail. His superior, in Omaha, was Brigadier General Philip St. George Cooke. Carrington had part of the 2d battalion of the 18th U.S. Infantry to build and man three proposed forts that would protect the road to Montana.

The original plan was to move Fort Reno (formerly Fort Connor) [27] and rebuild it about forty miles farther up, also to build two new forts, one on the Big Horn River and the other on the upper Yellowstone. It didn't work out that way. Carrington found too many supplies at Fort Reno to move, so he decided to leave that where it was and strengthen it. He built a second fort at the forks of the Piney; this became Fort Phil Kearny. On the Big Horn he built the third and most isolated post, Fort C. F. Smith, in Montana. No fort was built on the upper Yellowstone—he didn't have enough troops to spread them that far.

Carrington gathered his troops, civilian employees, equipment, and supplies at Fort Kearny, Nebraska (near Kearney City, then known as Dobey Town). He had to transport a multitude of things: a steam sawmill, mowing machines, shingle- and brick-making machines, carpenters' tools, doors, sash, glass, nails, and locks. He had to collect ammunition, firearms, supplies of all kinds, wagons and stock to move them. Most of his soldiers were infantrymen, recruits, but he did pick up some very much needed horses. He improvised cavalry, and most of the men actually made their first horseback trip to water without being bucked off.

In the long train of wagons were rocking chairs, churns, primitive washing machines, turkeys, chickens, and a couple of hogs. There was even a church bell. The "Sunday people" of the emigrant trains would have approved of Carrington; he stopped on Sundays if at all possible.

With all this, 220 wagons drawn by six-mule teams, and some ambulances, Carrington set out from Fort Kearny on the nineteenth of May. Someone called the outfit "Carrington's Overland Circus." The column followed the south bank of the Platte River, which the colonel's wife, Margaret, called "the most unaccountably contrary and ridiculous river the world ever saw." They reached Fort Sedgwick, near Julesburg in northeastern Colorado, May 30.

There for three days the command labored mightily to cross the South Platte with a huge flatboat rigged up as a ferry, because no ford could be found. As soon as the ferry was put into operation (it took twenty yoke of oxen to get the cable across), the river level fell more than a foot, as if that cranky stream knew what was wanted and refused to cooperate. (Margaret Carrington suggested that the disposition of the river resembled the natural depravity of man.) Then followed vast labor of unloading, of rebuilding wagons so they would float, and hitching up double teams of mules.

"To be sure," wrote Margaret Carrington, "the lead mules would be swimming, the middle team pulling, the wheel team floundering, and the wagon would be rolling in quicksand; but the expedient of double teams always left some one or more span on the earth's surface, to pull on or push the others."

And so they crossed the wickedly changeable South Platte. On May 29, just before they won this struggle with nature, the Peace Commission had passed them, on the way to Fort Laramie to make everyone happy and safe by giving nice presents to the Indians.

Two days and thirty-five miles after the crossing, the column reached Louis's ranch. Now it was heading for the North Platte, for Court House Rock and Chimney Rock and Scotts Bluff, those famous landmarks on the trail along the river's south bank. When the command camped four miles east of Fort Laramie, two sergeants drowned while swimming in the North Platte, which was unpredictable like its southern sister.

While they were in camp there, a Brulé Sioux named Standing Elk came to call. When he learned where the expedition was going, and why, he said frankly that he would sign the Peace Commission's treaty and so would Spotted Tail (the Indians had doves and hawks, too) but that many Sioux weren't even going to come near

Fort Laramie. They would not sell their hunting grounds and the whites would have to fight them. He was absolutely right.

Carrington sent wagons to Fort Laramie for the 100,000 rounds of rifle ammunition he would need—and found that not even 1,000 rounds were available for the kind of arms his infantrymen had. Twenty-six wagons loaded with provisions were ready for him, but not a single driver. Providing drivers from among his enlisted men cut down his effective fighting force in case of trouble on the way.

Plenty of Indians were at Fort Laramie, but most of them were the peaceable ones who weren't going to dispute passage along the Bozeman Trail. Red Cloud and Man Afraid of His Horses, whose good will was most needed, made no secret of their hostility.

With considerable difficulty, Red Cloud had been coaxed to attend the peace conference. He had visited Fort Laramie in March with great pomp. Messages had been exchanged between him and E. B. Taylor, who was president of the Peace Commission and was in Omaha at the time, but the presents for the Indians, bribes to pay for their agreement, couldn't get there until June. Red Cloud departed, promising to gather his scattered people for the postponed conference in June. Everything looked rosy when the meeting opened June 5. Apparently Taylor promised the chiefs that the whites would simply pass through the Powder River country without disturbing the red men's food supply, the wild game. This was plain deceit on Taylor's part, or else he didn't know anything about emigrants and freighters. They liked to hunt, too.

On June 13 the conference blew up. Red Cloud understood very well that Colonel Carrington and all those soldiers were not simply going to pass through the Powder River country. They were equipped to stay there. Red Cloud refused an introduction to Carrington, threw his blanket around himself, and remarked, "The Great Father sends us presents and wants us to sell him the road, but White Chief goes with soldiers to steal the road before the Indians say Yes or No." It is hard to stamp out of a meeting while wearing moccasins, but Red Cloud and some other Sioux leaders gave that effect. After that, he was harder to catch for any more peace conferences.

Carrington wanted to wait at Fort Laramie until the Peace Commission's parleys discovered whether there *would* be trouble, but his orders were to hurry. He hurried on. Taylor, on June 29 (one day after the column reached Fort Reno), telegraphed D. N.

Cooley, Indian Commissioner, "Satisfactory treaty concluded with the Sioux and Cheyennes. Large representations. Most cordial feeling prevails." He overlooked the rage of the chiefs who had walked out and were preparing to defend Powder River against all comers.

At Fort Laramie, Carrington picked up his chief guide, Jim Bridger, and an assistant, H. Williams. This was the same Jim Bridger who had set up in competition with Bozeman and Jacobs to guide pilgrims into Montana. Jim Bridger had tried just about everything in the frontier West since the great days of the fur trade had died away. He had been out there for more than forty years. He belonged there, like the sagebrush and the buffalo herds. He was something to write home about, like seeing Cloud Peak for the first time or crossing the Platte.

The stories about him were wonderful, especially the stories he told about himself. He had seen a diamond in the Rockies that was so bright it enabled him to travel thirty miles on a dark night. He remembered when Scotts Bluff, nearly four hundred feet high, used to be a deep valley—or sometimes it was Laramie Peak, which had grown up from a hole in the ground.

Bridger couldn't read, but he enjoyed being read to. He didn't believe the Bible story about Samson's tying foxes by the tails and turning them loose to set fire to the Philistines' grain. If Bridger told a tall story, that was all right, but when someone else was the narrator, he wanted believable facts.

After a taste of Shakespeare, he sent for a set of the plays, but the murder of the little princes in the Tower, in *Richard III*, made him so furious that he burned the books, commenting, "Shakespeare must have had a bad heart and been as devilish mean as the Sioux, to have written such scoundrelism as that."

Someone started to read him "Hiawatha," but he couldn't stand it. No such Indian ever lived, he said, and he wouldn't listen to any more lies. More important to Colonel Carrington, Jim Bridger knew all about the Indians of the Plains. They weren't like Hiawatha.

The command passed Fort Laramie June 17 and on June 20 reached Bridger's Ferry. Here they had to cross the North Platte. The beef herd swam the river. Wagons and people crossed in a ferry boat worked by the current; a round trip for one ferry load took eleven minutes. June 22 the command marched sixteen miles; June 23, fifteen miles, turning north in the morning to pass through the Red Buttes, lofty sand hills and rocky ridges. Travel was difficult for the heavier wagons. Camp that night was near the mouth of Sage Creek.

Just before reaching the basin where the Fort Reno road (the Bozeman Trail) turned northward along Sage Creek, and the Mormon road went on west toward Salt Lake City, they found a rude shed made of lumber, where Louie Gazzous, known as French Pete, had a little store catering to emigrants and freighters. His Sioux wife, half-blood children, and several employees were with him. He and his employees would be victims of the Sioux before long, in spite of his close ties with that tribe.

The column marched fourteen miles June 24 and camped at the head of Sage Creek. Next day they covered fifteen miles to camp on the South Fork of the Cheyenne. About the middle of this day's march they had a good view of Laramie Peak.

On June 26 they covered twenty miles, using a short cut that cut five miles off the old trail. Early in the morning of the twenty-seventh they had their first view of the Big Horns, eighty miles away. They camped, after twenty-one miles, on Dry Creek, also called the Dry Fork of Powder River. Next day they passed Buffalo Springs and went down the Dry Fork sixteen miles, and one more divide took them to Fort Reno. The road ran along the bed of Dry Fork.

Now, at Fort Reno, they were on Powder River. The fort was barren and ugly, most unprepossessing. From here clear to Bozeman City in Montana there was not a single white man except travelers trying to get somewhere else. The only good thing about poor Fort Reno was that timber was plentiful. The water was alkaline, and the vegetation was cactus and sagebrush. Warehouses and stables were protected by a rough stockade, but the men's quarters and the magazine were on an open plain nearly 130 feet above the river, from which water had to be hauled by wagon. On Carrington's second day there, however, someone found a spring of decent water that was easier to reach.

Three wagon trains of emigrants were waiting there impatiently for permission to move on. Even their womenfolks weren't worried a bit about Indians, believing implicitly that there were no bad ones on the route. Carrington posted an order in the sutler's store, instructing the emigrants how to corral their trains and keep out of trouble. They came to read, with every intention of doing just as they pleased. Later, when the other forts were in operation, every train had to check in at each of them, and if there was much of a discrepancy between the size it was and the size it had been, it had to wait for more wagons to join up.

The waiting pilgrims at Fort Reno had their peaceful illusions shattered one morning by a breathless messenger who came in yelling, "Indians!" The sutler's horse and mule herd was galloping off with a bunch of Indians behind, heading for Pumpkin Buttes. The colonel sent two officers and eighty mounted men in hard pursuit, but they came back the next day, after riding nearly seventy miles, with none of the stolen stock. They had picked up an Indian pony loaded with tobacco, brown sugar, bolts of calico, and other items —presents given at Fort Laramie in return for signing the treaty to let the white man use the Bozeman Trail. The obvious conclusion to be drawn from that was that some of the same Indians who had so recently promised to play nicely had hurried back to Powder River to harry the whites.

Carrington spent ten busy days at Fort Reno. Nothing much had happened at that dull place since General Connor left it in the fall of the previous year. Captain George W. Williford had settled down there with two companies of the 5th U.S. Volunteers— "Galvanized Yankees." The War of the Rebellion was over, but their enlistments were not. The homesick troops had unenthusiastically built barracks and storerooms, had worked hard as woodcutters and carpenters. There had been little military routine except for sentry and guard duty. Indians came in sight often, and early in November, 1865, a band of Arapahoes stampeded the horse herd and killed a herder.

Life was dreary there, brightened only by the weekly mail from Fort Laramie. Aside from that one Indian attack, the most interesting events were desertions. In March a sergeant and eleven other men deserted. In April another sergeant and four men took off for parts unknown.

When Carrington arrived June 28, Captain Williford was not there any more. He had died April 29 at Platte Bridge Station from an ailment diagnosed as dropsy. On July 6, the remaining men of the two companies of Galvanized Yankees gladly marched away toward Fort Laramie. A company of Winnebago Indian scouts had wintered at the shaky post, departing shortly before Carrington arrived. He met them near Fort Laramie on June 17. His wife wrote:

Many of them wished to go back with us, but there was no existing authority to employ them, and it was generally understood and
directly affirmed by Major Bridger that some of the Sioux at Laramie expressly demanded, as a condition of their own consent to
peace, that these Indians should leave the country. If this be true, it
was sharp in the Sioux, for the service lost its best scouts, and no
depradations had taken place around Reno while it was known that
they were there. . . . Being deadly enemies of the Sioux, it is not to
be wondered that the latter should wish them out of the country.

The command started out again on the Bozeman Trail on July 9,
leaving two officers and one company as a guard. Now the procession included only three officers' wives, who had to be company for
one another at Fort Phil Kearny. They were Margaret Carrington,
Mrs. S. M. Horton, wife of the post's surgeon, and the wife of Lieutenant William H. Bisbee.

That first day's travel took them twenty-three miles to Crazy
Woman Fork or Crazy Woman Crossing, where the water was always muddy and yellow; it was a good camp site, however, although dangerous. A nasty battle took place there later that month.
Carrington had no trouble there, probably because his force was so
very large that the Indians thought it wasn't wise to attack. The
column stayed there a few days to mend worn-out wagons. On the
twelfth, Carrington left at Crazy Woman the four companies that
would later move way up north to build Fort C. F. Smith. For the
time being, they would finish mending wagons while the rest of the
command moved on.

Carrington camped at noon on the Clark Fork, twenty-three
miles farther on. The water was very swift there and hard to cross.
On Friday the thirteenth, after passing Rock Creek, the column
sighted a few Indians, and somebody up front came upon a crude
sign, two pieces of a crackerbox with a message penciled on them.
An emigrant train had been attacked there the previous Tuesday,
and another one the Friday before, and both had lost some stock.

About 11 A.M., after passing Lake De Smet,[28] they camped on
Big Piney Fork, "just east of the crossing of the Virginia City road
[the Bozeman Trail] and about four miles from the Big Horn
Mountains." Fourteen miles past Clear Fork of Powder River, they
came suddenly upon the two Piney Forks of the Clear Fork. This
was where Fort Phil Kearny was built.

TWO SOLUTIONS COLLIDE

The roll call of the streams that were landmarks for travelers included Peno Creek (now called Prairie Dog), Goose Creek, Tongue River, Rotten Grass Creek, the Little Big Horn, the Big Horn River, where Fort C. F. Smith was built and someone built a rickety ferry that was a real money-maker.

All this was splendid game country, and this was where the hunting Indians had to hunt or give up their freedom. Of course "freedom" for the Indians was "hostility" as interpreted by the whites. Here were elk, mountain sheep, antelope, two kinds of deer, rabbit, sage hen, prairie chicken, water birds, grizzly and cinnamon bear— and tens of thousands of buffalo. Wolves and beaver abounded; both provided fur for the native red men.

Most of the command stayed in camp on the Big Piney Fork while Carrington and a mounted escort went to take a look at the beautiful Tongue River Valley. About nine o'clock in the morning, the officer of the day discovered that several men had deserted, bound for the Montana gold fields. The detail sent after them returned before noon; a band of Indians had blocked their way and sent them back with a message to the white chief: he must take his soldiers out of the country.

In spite of the horrors that the hostile Indians perpetrated on the Bozeman Trail, they must be given credit for speaking with a straight tongue (except those who had promised to be good and then stole horses). From the beginning of the treaty parley at Fort Laramie and even before, certain chiefs had made it clear that they would stand for no encroachment from the invading whites. There was nothing sly or subtle about it. They would defend their last hunting grounds. And they consistently did.

The turned-back detachment had met French Pete's traveling store about seven miles out, and a young teamster with him had been drafted by the Indians to take the message and bring back Carrington's answer. Their message was a clear statement of intention with no shilly-shallying: If the whites wanted peace, they must go back at once to Powder River. The Indians would not bother the old post (Fort Reno), but they would not let the white man build any new ones.

These threatening Indians were reported to be Oglala Sioux with Red Cloud as their chief policy maker. They had been talking to some Cheyennes, trying to get those Indians to join them. They wanted the white chief—Carrington, who was not in camp—to go with Jack Stead, his interpreter, to their village and settle the question of war or peace.

Brevet Captain John Adair put the messenger in a tent that passed as the guardhouse and waited for Carrington to return. He did, with Jim Bridger and his escort party, after thirteen hours' absence, late in the afternoon. He had looked over a lot of country without seeing any Cheyennes or Sioux. Carrington sent French Pete's teamster back, with Jack Stead, to invite the Cheyenne chief and some of his men to meet with them after two sleeps. Stead came back the next night. The Cheyennes had become alarmed and had moved thirty miles away to Tongue River, but he had their promise to make the visit.

Carrington's ride had decided him against the Tongue River Valley for the new fort. It was too far from pine timber needed for building and fuel, and it would have left the major Indian trails untended. So on Sunday the fifteenth the command moved to the plateau at the forks of the Piney. The new fort would be built there. The men were kept busy staking out streets, building sites and a parade ground. A mowing machine began to cut down grass. A horse-powered sawmill was being readied for use until the steam-powered mills got there, and details of men were digging, chopping, and ditching. They were building Fort Philip Kearny.[29]

When the Indians arrived around noon on the sixteenth, the tents and the activity indicated that the white men meant to stay there. The command dressed up for company: the officers were grand with hastily unpacked epaulettes and dress hats, and the regimental band played. The Cheyennes were dressed up, too. One tall warrior, on horseback, wore beaded moccasins and a breechclout and carried a big, fancy umbrella.

They met Carrington and his officers in a big tent, with the three officers' ladies peeking out from headquarters tent nearby. There was much solemn smoking of a red sandstone pipe, there was handshaking, there was dramatic oratory, translated by Jack Stead. And there was Jim Bridger, that paragon of the frontier, whose scalp the Cheyennes would have enjoyed taking.

The Cheyennes wanted to be friends, they told Carrington, although Red Cloud had been pressuring them to join his Sioux. They accepted presents—tobacco, some secondhand clothing, and some rations—and departed. This band apparently never bothered the whites from then on. But there were plenty who did, and some of them started the very next morning by stampeding the horses and mules with the bell mare in the lead so the rest followed. Brevet Major Henry Haymond and an orderly rode off in hot pursuit, leaving orders for the men with horses to saddle and follow. Two companies of infantry and fifty mounted men went after them. Two men were killed and three wounded.

The Sioux were making good on their threat to oppose the white man's passage. Besides small attacks that drove off a few mules, on July 22 a train of emigrants was attacked on the Dry Fork of the Powder, with one man killed and another wounded; on July 23 an attack on another train there killed two men, and in still another attack one man was killed; July 29, four miles east of the East Fork of the Cheyenne, nine white men were killed. All these people had been assured at Fort Laramie that they could safely proceed through the peaceful Powder River country!

French Pete's traveling store was found, the wagons plundered, the trader himself and four other men killed and mutilated. Gazzous' Sioux wife and her five children had escaped by hiding in the brush. The same Sioux who had stolen the post's mule and horse herd had attacked Gazzous. Furthermore, they had whipped some of the more peaceable Cheyennes, including Chief Black Horse, with their unstrung bows in punishment for treating with Carrington.

Carrington abandoned the idea of a fort on the upper Yellowstone; he didn't have enough troops to man it. Early in August he sent Captain N. C. Kinney with two companies ninety-one miles to the Big Horn to establish Fort C. F. Smith. Indian depredations continued—soldiers and citizens killed, stock stolen. At the two new forts on the Bozeman Trail, men labored mightily to build their own protection. A party of Crows, whose hunting grounds the Sioux were now claiming and defending, called at C. F. Smith to offer 250 warriors to fight the Sioux. But the officers there had no authority to hire that many and no money to pay them or feed them.

Jim Bridger learned from friendly Crows that the fighting men from 1,500 Sioux lodges were preparing to attack Phil Kearny and C. F. Smith. As indeed they were; a few dozen at a time in the beginning, but hordes of them in December.

CHAPTER 3

The Inspector Comes to Call

Carrington's superior, General Philip St. George Cooke, was in a hurry to find out how well Carrington was proceeding. General William B. Hazen, acting Inspector General, and escort reached Fort Reno August 19. Hazen didn't think much of that post—old Fort Connor, hastily built the year before. He found that the only new structure there was a stockade. The fort sorely needed it, but the logs were "of uneven lengths, leaning and generally frightful." Furthermore, the garrison was poorly organized and badly managed. The officers at Reno blamed this on the confusion resulting from cancellation of the plan to abandon the fort and move its contents.

The general soldierly appearance of the bewildered enlisted men there was nothing to boast about. Most of them were green recruits who were kept so busy fortifying the place against Indians and getting ready for winter that they hadn't begun to learn how to be soldiers. They had no drill, no bayonet practice, no target practice. None of the three forts yet had enough ammunition for target practice anyway, but it was pretty bad that when the night guard went off duty the men emptied their rifles by firing at nothing.

Hazen left detailed recommendations for improvement and departed August 23 for Phil Kearny with a big train of government wagons and emigrants. He spent August 28 and 29 at Phil Kearny. He noted that the garrison had 381 officers and men; it was headquarters for the 18th Infantry Regiment, and for the Mountain District of the Department of the Platte, with Carrington commanding both. It was also headquarters for the 2d Battalion of the 18th. Captain Tenodor Ten Eyck commanded the battalion and the post.

Things were really humming there. Virtually all the enlisted men were working on construction. More than sixty civilian employees were cutting timber, hauling logs, running the sawmills. All that activity was admirable, but nothing had been completed except the log stockade. Supplies and equipment were in a huge pile, not under cover. The barracks might be finished by winter, but Hazen predicted that most of the officers would have only temporary huts —except Colonel Carrington's house was almost finished. That was being built by the regimental band.

Hazen commented: "Had there been no officers' wives with the command, and the fullest interests of the service understood, I believe the labor on the stockade would have been first applied to storehouses and quarters for the men, which would by now be properly enclosed." That was a reflection on Carrington's decision about what should be done first, but Hazen couldn't very well criticize General William Tecumseh Sherman, who had advised the officers to take their wives along. Hazen had fought Indians in Texas in the 1850s, but he hadn't fought the Sioux in the Powder River country or he might have understood why that stout stockade looked good to the garrison at Fort Kearny even if they still lived in tents.

Judgment, judgment—Hazen was supposed to judge, to criticize, but his comment on the Indian situation must have infuriated Carrington: "With care nothing should have occurred, and the whole character of affairs here has been greatly exaggerated, resulting greatly from the fault of not communicating promptly and regularly with Dept. Hd. Qrs.; Col. Carrington appearing to think only of building his post."

Carrington had been communicating, but it hadn't done him much good. It never did do him much good. Because when the Sioux chief Red Cloud had promised at Fort Laramie to keep the white men out of that country, he meant exactly what he said. The only "care" that could have prevented disaster on the Bozeman Trail would have been to close it to emigrant travel and to cancel the building of the forts.

Hazen did have high praise for Carrington's plan of Fort Phil Kearny. He left that post on August 30, taking along twenty-six men and horses as an escort. This decreased Carrington's improvised "mounted infantry" by one-third. The mounted infantrymen, not trained as cavalry, were overworked anyway. They were escorts for mail, which was supposed to go once a week; they were couriers between forts; they were used for picket and outpost duty and to communicate with wood parties in danger. The departure of Hazen's escort left less than forty horses at the post. Awkward as the untrained riders were, the temporary loss of so many horses was something to worry about.

James D. Lockwood, an enlisted man in one of the companies sent to build and garrison Fort C. F. Smith, was impressed almost to ecstasy by the Big Horn Valley, about two miles wide, "with the towering peaks of the Big Horn mountains standing in awe-inspiring majesty at the head of it; with the river issuing from its protecting shadow, through a mighty rugged walled cleft or canyon, and then flowing peacefully upon its course, taking nearly the center of the valley and shimmering like a stream of silver in the sunlit distance." He wrote this description many years later, but the sight was still vivid in his memory.

He remembered hard work, too: "After some delay and difficulty in getting the heavily loaded wagons down from the rugged bluffs into the valley below, a march of eight miles further brought the little expedition upon the ground chosen for the erection of Fort C. F. Smith in Montana territory."

Captain Kinney's two companies had been toiling there for a couple of weeks when Hazen inspected the post. They were building in what he considered the proper sequence. They had cut a lot of logs and were ready to construct storehouses for supplies. Hazen and his escort left Fort C. F. Smith September 4, did some exploring, and inspected a new post, Camp Cooke, at the mouth of the Judith River about one hundred miles down the Missouri from Fort Benton (which was an old trading post and busy inland port for steamboats but had no troops). From there he went to Virginia City and then to Camp Douglas, near Salt Lake City.

In Hazen's judgment, based on fighting Comanches and Apaches on the Texas plains, Carrington was wrong in feeling that he was on the defensive. Attack! Attack! That was how Hazen had succeeded in Texas, by surprising the Indians in their villages. The troops should punish Indians by constantly harassing them. Some of Carrington's officers were strong proponents of the *toujours l'attaque* theory, too. Captain William J. Fetterman, who arrived in November, was especially restive under the cautious policy of his commanding officer. He let it be known that in his opinion one company of Regulars could whip a thousand Indians, and a full regiment could clean out *all* the hostiles. Captain Fetterman based this judgment on the way things *ought* to be. He knew nothing whatever about fighting Indians. Before he had time to learn very much, he was dead.

CHAPTER 4

Carrington Quells a Mob

An example of the Indians' constant harassment of Fort Phil Kearny came on a bright September morning when a little snow had fallen. The timber train went out to the pinery; a water party was loading at the creek in front of the fort; men were digging, hewing, setting the bases of logs in a trench for the stockade. Others were working on the construction of barracks, and the sawmills were busy.

The alarm came: "Indians!" Seven of them were seen riding hard toward the mounted picket on Pilot Hill.[30] A relief party—some horses were always kept saddled and ready—lit out on a run through the east gate. But they obviously weren't going to get there in time to save the men on picket. Carrington ordered his howitzers into action. A case shot with eighty balls in it hurtled through the air, and some of the Indians actually stopped to watch it. Then the shell exploded over their heads, and they scattered. The "gun that shoots twice" was pretty impressive. A second shot knocked one of the attackers out of the saddle.[31]

Meanwhile, across the Piney, some fifty Indians made a dash for the horse herd of a party of miners, who fought them off without loss. A case shot turned aside a party of attackers coming from another direction, but a much larger band came in sight on Lodge Trail Ridge, apparently ready to attack the wood train. Carrington sent out a detachment to the rescue, but the Indians signaled to one another with the flashes of small mirrors and then disappeared.

Two men felling trees in the woods were killed, and one poor fellow, with arrows in him and scalped, dragged himself nearly half a mile to the blockhouse after breaking the shafts off the arrows. He died the next day.

The afternoon of that eventful day brought more action. The whistle of the more distant of the two sawmills shrieked, and at the same time pickets on the hills signaled a warning. Fifteen Indians were galloping toward the four-man picket on Pilot Knob. Two officers set out with a relief party. The pickets turned their horses loose and, with rifles ready, backed down toward the rescue detachment and were saved. The relief party returned that evening with some rather pathetic prisoners, eight Cheyenne men and a squaw, with broken-down horses and nothing much to eat. They said they hadn't done any attacking; they had just happened to get in the way of the Sioux while trying to reach the fort. They wanted permission to hunt in the Tongue River Valley. Carrington let them camp near the fort and gave them some bacon and coffee.

But his men began to mutter: *Some of that lot was with the redskins that attacked our pickets! The boys with the wood party recognize 'em!* Carrington found out about this growling just in time to avert a massacre. Ninety armed men in the fort were about to take vengeance into their own hands and wipe out the little Cheyenne camp. Carrington ordered them back and emphasized the command with three pistol shots just as they were preparing to surge out through a gate. He punished the men only by chewing them out (what else could he do with so many?) and earnestly warned the visiting Cheyennes: *Stay off the roads. My soldiers can't be expected to tell friend from enemy.*

Among the civilians at Phil Kearny was Ridgeway Glover, a too-eager photographer for *Frank Leslie's Illustrated Weekly.* He did as he pleased, sometimes going off into the mountains alone for five or six days. When he wasn't wandering, he lived with the post's wood choppers. Glover threw caution to the winds just once too often. On September 17, Sergeant Fessenden and two other men, out hunting deer, found the artist's body. His back had been split open with an axe, and the Indians had taken his long yellow hair. The hunters, understandably excited about their discovery, rejoined the train of wood wagons with which they had come out of the fort on the way to the pinery. This train was attacked by Indians, but men sent out from the fort rescued it.

Even when the Sioux did not attack, they watched. Margaret Carrington described them thus:

> In ambush and decoy, *splendid;* in horsemanship, *perfect;* in strategy, *cunning;* in battle, *wary* and careful of his life; in victory jubilant; and in vengeance, fiendish and terrible.
>
> Too few to waste life fruitlessly; too superstitious to leave their dead to the enemy; too cunning or niggardly of resources to offer fair fight; too fond of their choice hunting-grounds to yield willing

possession to the stranger,—they wait and watch and watch and wait, to gather the scalps of the unwary and ignorant. . . .

Growing conscious of the white man's power, knowing how vain is an open field struggle, they avoid such determining issues, and waylay in detail. . . .

The Indian comes as the hornet comes, in clouds or singly, yet never trying to sting until his ascendency is assured and his own exposure is slight.

CHAPTER 5

Sawyers on an Empty Road

Again in 1866 Sawyers went to build his road. Again, as in the year before, the Army and the Department of the Interior disagreed. This time the military decision was made by General U. S. Grant himself, who ruled that the Army was spread out too thinly, protecting emigrants on the main-traveled roads, and that no escorts could be spared for anything else.

Sawyers did get firearms for the civilians of his road-building crew, but he headed west June 12 with no escort. He had fifty-seven men in his party, with seven scouts and guards. They improved some stream crossings, built some rough bridges, and fought Indians. July 16 they reached Fort Reno, which had been Fort Connor the year before. Four emigrant wagons and fourteen persons joined them for protection, and every night the Indians tried to steal or stampede their animals.

July 21 they reached the spot on the Piney Fork of Powder River where Carrington's seven infantry companies had begun work on Fort Phil Kearny. Carrington could spare no men for an escort, but thirty-two wagons and sixty-one emigrants were glad to join them on the way up the Bozeman Trail. There were more Indian attempts at scattering their stock, but they got through all right and ferried their wagons across the Big Horn. Sawyers had *forded* the

Big Horn very near this point in 1865 on September 19. His men had found a place where the water was only three and a half feet deep. Earlier in the summer, however, the river would be deeper. The identity of the builder of the ferry is lost in time. Probably it was A. C. Leighton, sutler at C. F. Smith, who knew a good thing when he saw it.

Sawyers shortened his road on this second trip by about a hundred miles—but it was never used again.

CHAPTER 6

The View from the Ranks

William Murphy was a lowly member of A Company, 2d Battalion, 18th U.S. Infantry. He was in Carrington's Overland Circus on the march to Powder River, but some of the things he told in "The Forgotten Battalion" in *Annals of Wyoming* years later may have been based on scuttlebutt. Anyway, he had a somewhat different view than the colonel's lady, Margaret Carrington, who wrote a book, *Absaraka, Home of the Crows.*

At Fort Laramie, Murphy said, Red Cloud was in council with Army officers (actually, the Peace Commission), and he heard that the Oglala leader had threatened to kill every white man who crossed the North Platte. That is somewhat stronger than other reports. Murphy was impressed by some bow-and-arrow shooting he saw at the fort; young Indian boys could hit a button with an arrow at thirty yards. Combine Red Cloud's threat with that kind of marksmanship and you had something to think about.

After the command arrived at Fort Reno a hailstorm struck while the picketed mules were grazing under guard. Hailstones were as big as pullets' eggs. The mules pulled their picket pins, and in spite of their hobbles they stampeded. The herders' horses went right with them. The herders stopped their mounts after two or three miles, but by the time they and a company of cavalry from the fort caught up with the herd, the mules had got clear to Pumpkin

Buttes, some forty-five miles away. If there had been a few Indians around just then, Murphy thought, Forts Phil Kearny and C. F. Smith would never have been built.

Murphy was detailed to help load wagons with provisions from the log storerooms built by Connor's men. The mud chinking had dropped out, the roofs leaked, and everything was a muddy mess. On July 3 the troops received four months' pay, and understandably a few men celebrated by getting drunk. Murphy commented:

> One method I saw here for punishing drunkenness was on this day, and one of the worst cases of cruelty I saw in the army. At the guard tent four stakes were driven into the ground and the drunken soldier was stretched at full length and tied to them. This was called the "Spread Eagle." The sun was beating down on him when I saw him, and I thought he was dead. Flies were eating him up and were running in and out of his mouth, ears and nose. It was reported that he died, but in the army one can hear all kind of reports.

Murphy saw another man punished; his head was shaved, he was branded with a hot iron, and drummed out of the Army. That was punishment indeed, because it was suicide to go a mile from the fort.

Travel was misery for officers' wives, but it was much worse for foot soldiers. The Army issued only wool socks, no matter what the weather, and the marching men had sore feet. There was only one ambulance available for sick or blister-footed soldiers; the women and children had the rest.

Without really complaining, Murphy got the point across in his memoirs that he didn't think much of the site chosen for Fort Phil Kearny: "For some reason they picked out a location about seven miles from the timber and five to eight miles from any hay bottom." He heard that a former Federal judge, partner in a freight outfit, had some influence on that decision. Other rumors blamed the choice on Mrs. Carrington. Ah, well, the site was something to grouch about when there was nothing better to do.

For two or three days at Phil Kearny they never saw an Indian, and they began to think the stories about Red Cloud's threat were nonsense. But from July 17 up to December 21, when the Fetterman "massacre" occurred, hardly a day passed without a sight of hostiles at Phil Kearny, and they heard it was the same at Forts

Reno and C. F. Smith. Soldiers were always having to make a forced march to the relief of an emigrant train or freighters—but usually the Indians were gone when they got there.

On July 17, the day Indians killed French Pete Gazzous and his five men, hostiles also ran off Fort Phil Kearny's "dead herd," the slow-moving mules and horses that were crippled or had sores. Three men were wounded and two killed. Mounted soldiers pursued the stampeded herd but found only four animals, dead.

Murphy helped build the stockade of logs set three feet into the ground. Two sides of each log were hewed flat so they fit tightly together. He well remembered worry and hardship. So serious was the shortage of ammunition for a considerable time that there was no target practice at all. The men who buried the dead after the Fetterman fight were badly frozen, but the fires they warmed by were of green cottonwood. The tops were fed to the starving mules, which gnawed holes in the logs of their stables. The officers burned good pine wood, brought from seven miles away by the same soldiers—or was he just grouchy because rank has its privileges?

Corn for the stock had to be freighted from Fort Reno; the journey took three or four days, and at 25 to 40 degrees below zero the men suffered. Burlap sacks were much in demand for wrapping the men's feet over their shoes of cheap split leather.

CHAPTER 7

The Crazy Woman Fight

Carrington's command had reached Crazy Woman Crossing July 9 and camped there a few days to mend worn-out wagons. They had no Indian trouble. But eleven days later a smaller group, bound in the same direction, had a brisk, bloody battle that would have wiped out men, women, and children if rescue had not come by chance in the nick of time.

This detachment included five officers (First Lieutenant J. M. Templeton in command), the wife of Lieutenant Alexander Wands, the wife of Sergeant F. M. Fessenden of Carrington's prized regimental band, a Negro woman servant, and some small children, including the Fessendens' baby, born at Fort Sedgwick a few weeks earlier. Their escort was a meager ten men, considered sufficient by the people back at Fort Laramie, who took the official position that everything was peaceful and calm in the Powder River country.

The party passed Fort Reno. They traveled sixteen miles in the cool hours before dawn, hoping to find good water. At Dry Creek they found none. But they did find a scalped, naked, bloody body with a fragment of shirt clinging to it. The scrap of shirt identified the dead man as a soldier. Hastily the men buried the body. They drove their thirsty animals on. About nine o'clock in the morning they topped a rise and could see the forks of Crazy Woman—and moving shapes that could have been buffalo. But the buffalo turned out to be mounted Indians, who sheltered in the timber and swooped down to attack as the men labored to get the wagons through heavy sand.

Lieutenant N. H. Daniels had ridden ahead to look for a suitable camp site. His horse came galloping back, riderless, with four arrows in its body and the saddle turned under its belly. Lieutenant Templeton came running with an arrow in his back, bleeding from a bad wound in the face.

With superhuman efforts, the teamsters and the infantry escort yanked the wagons and ambulances out of the sand and corraled them in a defensive position between Crazy Woman and Dry Creek. The hostiles—fifty of them—maintained their attack and did considerable damage. Two mules in the cook wagon's struggling team fell dead. Men hastily cut them out of harness—and then another mule was disabled and had to be cut out while eight men held off the attacking Sioux.

Now the soldiers abandoned the cook wagon, and drivers lashed the teams into a run for higher ground. There they corraled the remaining wagons, with the mules and the ambulances inside. Several men were wounded and everyone was frantic for water. By late afternoon a detail of volunteers made a successful dash to the creek with canteens.

Chaplain David White, a practical fellow of the praise-the-Lord-and-pass-the-ammunition sort, did as much damage as anyone in firing at the redskins. Then he and Private William Wallace volunteered to ride back to Fort Reno, on two of the surviving four saddle horses. They galloped out as the sun was going down. Both horses died of exertion, but the frantic couriers reached the fort with their story.

Before the two riders were well out of sight, the embattled detachment saw dust to the northwest and naturally assumed it meant more Indians. But this was a rescue party, coming along without knowledge that rescue was needed. This was a good strong contingent, thirty-four wagons and an escort of forty-seven men, bound from Fort Phil Kearny to Fort Reno to pick up supplies. In command was Captain Thomas B. Burrowes. He had left Phil Kearny July 20, nooned four miles southeast of Clear Fork Crossing, and pushed on toward Crazy Woman. When he sighted Templeton's train, he moved faster. On the way he found by the road the body of Private Terrence Callery, who had gone off without permission to hunt buffalo. Burrowes took command of the corraled defenders and had everything set up for further defense about nine o'clock that evening.

At daybreak next morning, July 21, he sent out men to search for Lieutenant Daniels. The body was found stripped, scalped, and mutilated, pierced with twenty-two arrows. Men buried Callery's body and loaded Daniels' into a wagon for later burial. The outfit was almost ready to leave Crazy Woman when more help came: Lieutenant T. S. Kirtland and thirteen men, up from Fort Reno in response to the desperate message carried by the chaplain and his companion.

Captain Burrowes took the whole lot of them to Reno Sunday morning, July 22. Chaplain White officiated at the funeral of Lieutenant Daniels. Late that afternoon Indians tried to stampede Burrowes' mule herd but didn't get a single one. Next day at dawn the whole train set out for Phil Kearny and, at Crazy Woman again, they overtook two trains that had started out from Reno the day before. Hugh Kirkendall was captain of forty-two mule teams and William Dillon headed a train of thirty-five ox-drawn wagons. In camp that night two teamsters had a fight. One was stabbed. Burrowes dressed his wounds (there was no doctor along) and put the other teamster under arrest.

At daylight July 24, they started north again, with Kirkendall's and Dillon's trains following the military. Near the Clear Fork Crossing, Indians were sighted. Burrowes corraled his outfit and barked orders to prepare for defense. But these Indians were

friendly; they were Cheyennes (many of whom were most un-
friendly) with protection papers signed by Colonel Carrington. Burrowes decided to camp on Clear Fork. More Cheyennes poured in,
some 300, including women and children, all demanding food. Burrowes handed over hard bread, three sacks of flour, one hundred
pounds of sugar, and fifty pounds of coffee in return for their promise to leave camp.

The evening was still young when a messenger rode in from Dillon, back on the trail, saying that Kirkendall's train was under attack by a large force of Sioux. Burrowes sent couriers up to Fort
Phil Kearny and dispatched a sergeant and fifteen men back to help
Dillon and his teamsters. But Dillon himself had been wounded fatally. Help came from Fort Phil Kearny the morning of July 25, a
captain with sixty men and a mountain howitzer, all welcome indeed. The whole bunch of them pressed on up to Phil Kearny, arriving about two in the afternoon.

One wonders: would the terrified women in the ambulances have
been more frightened, or less, if they had known of a decision made
by their protectors? If the Indians overwhelmed the little band, the
white men would kill their women. Perhaps the women did know.
So great was the fear of capture by Indians (and with good reason)
that such knowledge was probably a comfort.

CHAPTER 8

"All Killed and Scalped by Indians"

All along the great Emigrant Trail and on the Bozeman Trail travelers became indignant and sometimes furious when the military required them to wait until a strong train could be accumulated for
defense through Indian country. But in Montana, travelers were
supposed to be safe once they crossed the Big Horn at Fort C. F.
Smith. That they weren't always safe is shown by what happened to

a Methodist preacher named William K. Thomas, his eight-year-old son Charles, and a hired driver, Joseph Schultz.

They were on their way from Illinois to join William Thomas's brother George, who had a farm in the Gallatin Valley. (William's wife and two infant daughters had died a year or two before.) What happened after his wagon reached a supposedly safe area was told mutely by two arrow-punctured bodies at their last campground (near present Big Timber), where the ashes of their fire were still hot when other travelers found them August 24. Schultz had been fishing; his body was found in the Yellowstone River. Another man, named Wright, was buried with them. William Thomas's diary and sixteen arrowheads (thirteen taken from his body and three found in his little son's) were duly delivered to his brother.

With their fine big prairie schooner, drawn by a $500 team of mules, they had gone from St. Louis, where they outfitted, to Atchison, Kansas; they left on May 28 with Weller & Longworthy's train. They left Fort Reno on the Bozeman Trail July 22; Indians were lurking around but left when fired upon. The train reached Crazy Woman the next afternoon. A government supply train of 100 wagons caught up with them there, and they felt better. Two teamsters got into a fight and one was mortally wounded when the other stabbed him.

Thomas was obviously traveling in the long and sorely beset column of wagons that moved along during and after the Crazy Woman fight. Here is the order of departure as shown by his diary entry July 24: The government train went ahead, followed by three citizens' wagons including his own; then an ox train (this would be Dillon's); then Kirkendall's mule train. The ox train stopped three miles behind the rest, with Kirkendall back of it, and was attacked by Indians. Six men went back to see what was wrong and ran into a fight before reaching the train. Wagonmaster Dillon died that night. Next day, July 25, they reached Fort Phil Kearny.

"This is the most beautiful place for a fort that I have seen west of Fort Leavenworth," the Reverend Mr. Thomas wrote. "Its mountain scenery is most striking and majestic, with its beautiful range of hills on either side, north and south, as it were throwing their arms around and clasping one in their bosom."

Funerals were held that night for the knifed teamster and Wagonmaster Dillon. The party rested the stock while waiting for more wagons to strengthen their defensive abilities. Forty wagons came July 28 with a report of two men killed and one wounded by Indians between the Platte and Fort Reno.

Mr. Thomas wrote on July 31: "No hopes of leaving here for several days by order of headquarters ... I am meditating upon the adventure that I am about to take, counting the cost, summing up the danger, cold chills run through my blood." This was the proper frame of mind, surely.

The train of 112 wagons moved August 2 but not very far, because a wheel broke and they all had to stop. Next day they went about a mile and stopped for breakfast, having received orders to wait for forty government wagons and two companies of infantry. This was Captain Kinney's outfit, on the way to establish Fort C. F. Smith. Half a mile from camp they noticed a grave. The bodies of five men, killed a few days before, had been dug up and chewed by wolves. Mr. Thomas was shocked at the depravity of men who would perform so inadequate a burial.

They found a lone grave August 7, and Thomas wrote: "We could not make out his name, part of the headboard being gone. He left Chambersburg, Pa., May 8th 1864 and was killed here by Indians." He had been scalped and wolves had gnawed the flesh from the face. This shallow, hastily made grave, with only a few shovelfuls of earth tossed in, shocked Thomas again.

August 11 they camped on the Big Horn, where Kinney and his troops stayed to unload the government wagons and to build the new fort. One man was drowned while trying to find a ford, and two others barely escaped the same end. After all, they had to cross on the ferry. They swam the stock, and three mules drowned. A big train of 350 wagons caught up.

It was on August 17 that Thomas made his fatal decision to go on ahead because one of the freight wagons had broken down. He wrote, "I determined trusting in the Lord to go ahead." After coming safely through the Crazy Woman fight, his little party was wiped out because of this decision. Someone came along who knew him and those with him, someone who took the time to dig graves and put up headboards, which another traveler noted September 8 and later told his brother about. The headboards carried these inscriptions:

Rev. W. K. Thomas, age 36 years of Belleville, Ill.
Chas. K. Thomas, age 8 years of Belleville, Ill.

James Schultz, age 35 years of Ottawa Co. C.W. [Canadian West]
C. K. Wright
All killed and scalped by Indians on the 24th day of August, 1866.

CHAPTER 9

The Burial Party

A day or two behind the wagons that were involved in the Crazy Woman fight was a party in which Perry A. Burgess traveled with two of his uncles. There were various ways of paying for passage on the journey to Montana. Perry worked his way, for $25 a month and his keep. His employer was his uncle, Mansel Cheney; the other uncle, Lewis, was travel-wise, for he had gone overland with an ox train in 1850 and stayed in the West four years.

Perry and three other young men, not burdened with much of the world's goods, had one saddle horse among them. They took turns riding it. Safely across the South Platte, they camped one night among a large party of emigrants and some friendly Sioux. The chief had supper with the whites—bread, molasses, fresh milk —and the emigrants entertained their visitors with violin music. What nice, peaceable people those Indians were! The emigrants encountered another kind later.

July 8 they crossed the Laramie River at Fort Laramie; six days later they crossed the North Platte at Bridger's Ferry. One man came near drowning while they swam the stock across. The train increased as they caught up with more wagons.

They traveled a dreadful thirty-two miles July 21, a night drive without water on the Bozeman Trail. They camped on the Dry Fork of the Powder with a train of freighters, and here Perry Burgess picked up an Indian arrow by the road. Next day they pulled out very early, looking for decent water and grass. Six miles down the canyon they found a little poor water. Mansel and Lewis scouted on ahead. Nine Indians rode down from behind a hill, very friendly, and started to shake hands with everybody. Then one drew a pistol from beneath his blanket and shot Mansel dead.

Lewis's horse jumped and ran back to the astonished men who were watering the loose stock—they were totally unprepared and unarmed except for revolvers; even those weren't all loaded. But the young men charged at the Indians, firing, and drove them off. The whites dashed on for another half mile toward the wagons, which stopped when their drivers heard gunfire. The young men grabbed their rifles from the wagons, gathered up the cattle, and turned back.

They could see twenty-five or thirty Indians on the hills, shooting arrows. Back where Mansel had been killed, they found that the Indians had stripped him and shot arrows into some of the stock. The train of freight wagons came up. After the men got the dead Mansel decently laid out, Perry and six others returned to the place where they had been attacked, armed now and yearning to kill Indians, but they were gone. They had plundered the wagon, destroying what they didn't take. Perry had lost his watch, clothing, and everything else, except his violin and rifle, which were in another wagon. Later they found some of the clothing and another man's violin, dropped by the fleeing Indians.

On July 23 the travelers were more careful. One man rode on each side, some distance out from the train, as a scout. When the train stopped for noon after twelve miles, they dug a grave and buried poor Mansel as well as they could. They moved eight miles farther that day and found Fort Reno, old Fort Connor, where there was plenty of water for the thirsty stock. Perry Burgess noted, "The soldiers are very much alarmed on account of the Indians and are building a log stockade around the fort. Distance today 20 mi."

On the twenty-fourth they moved twelve miles; next day they traveled sixteen miles without water and camped on Crazy Woman Fork, that ambush spot favored by the Indians. Feed there was poor, so Perry and five other men herded the stock half a mile from camp. They were relieved by two other men, to whom they handed their guns, and started back to camp. Halfway back there, they heard the yell, "Indians!" and saw mounted redskins coming like a whirlwind, into the herd and out of it again with all the ponies and saddles except two ponies that weren't worth taking. The two herders emptied their weapons but didn't bring down any Indians.

Travelers on the Bozeman Trail obviously needed protection from the Army. On July 26 these wagons passed a battleground where low breastworks had been thrown up with small stones. Some bloody garments lay around, along with two dead ponies and a mule. Perry Burgess and the train he was in reached Fort Phil Kearny on July 28. A great many wagons were waiting there for reinforcements against the Indians. Three men were hired to guide them: Lewis Baker and James and Thomas McGarry. A total of 110 wagons pulled out on August 2, including Kirkendall's mule train. There were 171 men, 6 women, and 5 children.

Next day they passed the spot where French Pete Gazzous and five other men had been killed. Wild animals had dug up the bodies. Men from the newly arrived train covered them up again. On August 7 they did the same thing for a man who had been killed a few days ahead of them. They camped on the Little Big Horn.

They spent August 11 trying to find a fordable place on the Big Horn, deep, swift, and about 250 yards wide. One of Kirkendall's men, named McGear, was drowned. The party found more graves, and dug one for McGear. They gave up trying to ford the river and moved five miles upstream to the ferry, which they had to repair. "The ferry boat here is a sorry affair," wrote Perry Burgess. "It is constructed of rough planks hewn from cotton wood logs, covered with rags and barely large enough to carry one wagon."

There were a few wagons and men on the far side of the river; Indians had run off most of their stock, and they were waiting for more animals to be brought from Virginia City.

Kirkendall's train crossed on the thirteenth; four of his mules drowned. Other wagons crossed the next day. Perry's group crossed on the fifteenth after unloading some of the freight and carrying it over in two dugouts fastened together. Other trains caught up, so that at one time 300 wagons were waiting to make the perilous crossing.

"Some of the men prospected a little for gold," wrote Burgess, "but could not raise the color." He was learning the lingo of mining fast. On the eighteenth, one of Kirkendall's men was severely injured by a wounded buffalo. He had an arm and a leg and several ribs broken.

The emigrant outfit, thirteen wagons in all, pulled out ahead of the freighters and reached the Yellowstone River. They found two men and a boy dead there and the campfire still burning. This group dug graves for Mr. Thomas and his companions, suddenly alert to the possible consequences of pulling out ahead of the comparative safety of a large train.

They crossed the divide between the Yellowstone and Gallatin valleys on August 31 and noticed with gratification that the country looked civilized. They actually saw men traveling alone and unarmed! Next day they nooned at what Burgess called "Couvier's Mills," near Bozeman City. "Couvier" was Tom Cover, one of the original discoverers of Alder Gulch.

CHAPTER 10

The River of Wagons Flows On

There were plenty of opportunities for an adventuresome young fellow to go west in 1866, even if he was more interested in clerking in a store than in get-rich-quick-maybe mining for gold. George Fox, who worked for a man named Raymond in Davis County, Iowa, gave the boss notice in April that he was quitting. Raymond, who had other stores, offered him a job clerking in a sutler store at a frontier post for $125 a month or a partnership in one that would open at a fort 150 miles west of Fort Laramie.

Fox said he'd think about it. Anyway, he was leaving Iowa. He went over to Omaha to pick up some express, and a Mr. Kinney told him about another opportunity: $40 a month to go with Colonel Sawyers' second expedition to Virginia City, Montana Territory. Fox said he'd think about it.

Then he met a freighter, A. Bernard, who offered opportunity but no pay. "He is going to Montana with ox teams, said I could go; think I will," George Fox wrote in his journal. "Terms, I furnish my own provisions and pay for hauling them."

While waiting for Raymond to pay his wages, another chance for travel came up. Two young fellows who had a mule team were going to Denver. He liked that idea, but Raymond didn't answer his telegraphed demand for his wages. The mule-team owners went without him. On May 30, Fox was helping Bernard load up when Raymond arrived with his money, and the next day they pulled out: Bernard, five drivers, a cook, and George Fox.

They joined other movers and reached Fort Kearny on June 20. Four days later, more freight wagons and emigrant wagons caught up. They now had thirty-four wagons, forty-nine men, twelve women, ten children, and eighty head of cattle. There were some disagreements, because the emigrants wanted to go faster than the freighters with their heavy-laden wagons, but it was safer to keep together and complain.

Fox noted how many rattlesnakes he killed but soon stopped counting their rattles. When a man shot himself accidentally on the Fourth of July, Fox wrote: "A lady handing him the pistol, it went off, hit his hand and went into his side. They don't think he will live." But the following day the man seemed to be getting better.

Ten days later his party met a big bunch of Indians, who had made off with some of their oxen but paid for them with a buffalo robe and some ponies. Fox noted, without comment, "They had a white girl seven years old." Before reaching Fort Reno on the Bozeman Trail they came upon bloody signs of an Indian fight and four graves of men Fox thought he had met at Fort Kearny. The grave markers said the fight had been July 24. About sunset on August 2 they came in sight of Fort Reno.

In the same train with Fox was Benjamin Dailey, who left a fragmentary diary. He noted, the day before they reached Fort Reno, that the train "found a pair of bloody pants with sixteen bullet holes in them concluded the Indians had been around"—certainly a logical conclusion. But their train had not met any hostiles yet, and this was noteworthy. The soldiers told them that all the other trains that had passed so far had to fight Indians. But a man with a government train coming down from Phil Kearny reported that Indians were "not very troublesome."

An officer came down to their camp from Fort Reno and took the customary census of wagons, men, women, children, stock; counted the firearms in the party; noted how many shots they could fire without reloading in case of sudden attack; and warned them to stay together and corral the wagons every night. Right away there was friction between civilians and the military. Benjamin Dailey noted sourly:

The Rockies, the Great Falls,
farmers' and miners' tools, timber,
and a boast about treasure.

Last Chance Gulch, busy main street of Helena, Montana Territory, in 1869, when the future state capital was five years old.

Fort C. F. Smith, Montana Territory, in 1866. Drawn by Captain I. D'Isay from a sketch by Anton Schonborn.

(Top) *Graves of the five road agents hanged in Virginia City
January 14, 1864.* (Bottom) *Drawing of
Fort Reno, Dakota Territory (now Wyoming), in 1867
by Anton Schonborn.*

FORT PHILIP KEARNEY

Plan of Fort Phil Kearny, Dakota Territory (now Wyoming), with buildings and areas identified.

*Road agents once propped their booted feet on the balcony railing
of Robbers Roost while waiting to rob travelers
coming from Virginia City, twelve miles away. The building still stands.*

This forerunner of trains and buses was called a Concord mud wagon.

2000 DOLLARS
REWARD!!

Proclamation by the Governor!

Helena, Montana Territory,
July, 5th, 1867.

Information having been received by me, that the body of General Thomas Francis Meagher has not been recovered from the Missouri river, and it being desirable that the same should be done, in order to proper and christian burial; now therefore, I, Green Clay Smith, Governor of Montana, do offer a reward of One Thousand Dollars ($1000) for the recovery of the said body, and its safe delivery at Fort Benton, St. Louis or either of the Military Forts on the Missouri river, where it can be procured by friends.

In testimony whereof, I have hereunto set my hand and the great seal of the Territory, this, the day and date above written, and the Independence of the United States of America, the ninety-first

GREEN CLAY SMITH,
Governor of Montana Territory.

At a Meeting of the Citizens of Helena, held on the evening of the 4th day of July, 1867, the following Resolution was unanimously adopted:

RESOLVED, That N. P. Langford, Esq., Chairman of the Meeting, be, and he is hereby authorized—in behalf of the citizens of Helena—to offer an additional Reward of One Thousand Dollars, for the same purpose.

Now, therefore, in accordance with said Resolution, I do hereby offer a reward of One Thousand Dollars, ($1000,) pledged by the citizens of Helena, in meeting assembled, for the recovery of the body of

GEN. THOMAS FRANCIS MEAGHER,

and its delivery at either of the places designated in the foregoing Proclamation of Governor Green Clay Smith,

N. P. LANGFORD, Chairman

In spite of determined search and offers of rewards, the body of General Meagher was never found.

Thomas Francis Meagher

*World-renowned Irish revolutionary, Acting Governor of
Montana Territory, maker of warm friends and bitter enemies, he
plunged into the Missouri River under mysterious circumstances.*

Frontier characters drawn by Charles M. Russell: Sioux hunter, Flathead woman, scout, prospector, trapper (center).

RED CLOUD

The Sioux chief was old and bitter when he posed for this
photograph, but he remembered winning a war
against the United States.

HENRY B. CARRINGTON

The colonel was a retired brigadier general when this picture was made, about 1908.

MARGARET I. CARRINGTON

His first wife died at thirty-nine, four years after leaving Fort Phil Kearny.

FRANCES (GRUMMOND) CARRINGTON

Widowed in the Fetterman Fight, she married Carrington a few years later.

FINN BURNETT

*A civilian teamster, he lived to
tell about the Hayfield Fight
at Fort C. F. Smith.*

PATRICK E. CONNOR

*The general's expedition to whip
the Sioux along Powder River
was a disaster.*

WILLIAM FAIRWEATHER

*He found danger and
gold, lived hard, drank hard,
died broke at thirty-nine.*

JIM BRIDGER
*Mountain man and maker of
legends, he was Carrington's
chief of scouts.*

JOHN "PORTUGEE" PHILLIPS
*He rode by night to
Fort Laramie carrying news
of the Fetterman disaster.*

GRANVILLE STUART
*It was said of him:
"Granville Stuart was the history
of Montana."*

HARRIET SANDERS

The sunniest-tempered lady
who ever climbed into
an emigrant wagon.

WILBUR F. SANDERS

His bronze statue in Montana's
capitol is inscribed,
"Men, do your duty."

JAMES STUART

In his finest hour, he led the
Yellowstone Expedition
through danger.

The soldiers at the Fort stole one of our cows, when the owner went after it, they threatened to shoot him. He said he could shoot too. So they let him have the cow. our captain asked for an escort of 10 men to Fort Philip Kearny, but he could not have it. They have 150 men here. all they do is steal from emigrants eat Uncle Sam's rations & play cards. if a dozen Indians comes around they shut themselves up in the Fort and watch them. There is no fight to them.

On August 5 the train camped at Crazy Woman Crossing but had no trouble. Next day they passed a recent battleground but saw no Indians. When they reached Fort Phil Kearny, a picket came down and told them where to camp. An officer visited the camp, took the census, checked firearms, and let them move on. He reminded them that no party could go forward without at least sixty armed men, but he assured them that if they kept a sharp lookout and didn't straggle there was absolutely no danger under God's heaven.

Both Fox and Dailey commented favorably on the splendid thirty-piece brass band that contributed much to the morale of the post. "The music sounded well, something like civilization," Fox remarked.

They caught up with several trains consolidated into one big one of 200 wagons. All had had trouble with Indians, and Fox learned that a man he knew had been killed. In spite of the assurance of the officer back at Phil Kearny, they were all a little more comfortable to be in a large party for defense. But the size of the train caused complications and slowed everybody down. There was brisk competition to get started first and let the late starters eat dust. When Bernard's wagons rolled at five o'clock one morning, another group was ahead of them anyway. Another day they got up at two and moved at four. That time they were first, but it was quite a race, with everybody hustling and yelling.

On August 15 they camped six miles below Fort C. F. Smith. The Big Horn River was too deep and too swift to ford; ferry prices were out of sight, but there was no other way to get across. George Fox wrote: "Five dollars per wagon and swim the stock. It is a rickety boat made out of hewed plank, leaks some and will hold one wagon. They run it with oars, the crossers doing the work. There is 150 wagons to cross before ours cross."

Benjamin Dailey was sourly critical:

The ferry is a concern made after the fashion of a skow on the Mississippi. Hewn timber put together with wooden pins. It looks as if it would sink at anytime, but it don't, it is propelld [sic] by 4 oars, hewn out of a pine tree very roughly, the proprietor lives at the fort, and lets the skow to emigrants and pilgrims at the rate of five dollars per wagon, the pilgrims furnishing their own motive power, in the last three days there has been 256 wagons crossed, netting the proprietor the nice little sum of $1280.00 all he done was set and look on. he is protected by the commander of the Fort, so he can charge pilgrims what he pleases.

Dailey estimated that C. F. Smith had 300 soldiers; they were living in tents with no buildings of any kind. Those 300, he thought, were more afraid of Indians than his train of eighty men, which had fourteen women and eight children to worry about. "Afraid" was perhaps not accurate. Call them cautious, the men at Fort C. F. Smith. They had fought more Indians by the middle of August than Dailey had.

One by one—ferrying took a minimum of ten minutes per load—the drivers and the unwilling rowers got their wagons across. On August 18, George Fox's twenty-eighth birthday, they weren't finished yet. The big train split up, too hard to handle, too much squabbling. Thirty-four wagons constituted the outfit with which Fox traveled. They ate very well indeed, because hunting was great: buffalo, antelope, bears. Bear meat tasted very good, Fox noted, "a little porkish."

On August 26, beyond the farthest fort, they sent a man out on picket to guard the stock. They never saw him again. On August 30 they passed the graves of the Thomas party. They used another ferry August 31, this time across the Gallatin. John Bozeman owned this one and charged $6 a wagon. The ferry didn't amount to much, but at least it didn't operate with oar-power provided by the paying passengers. It worked with ropes, pulleys, and the river current. Prudently, the drivers went looking for a ford, because the wind was blowing too hard to work the ferry anyway. On September 2 they did ford the river with the wagons chained together.

Now they were getting relatively close to Bozeman City. There were lots of wagons on the road. "Can see several houses," Fox noted. "Looks like civilization. Saw a reaper running and men stacking wheat. Came to Bridger Creek, 2 rods wide, 1 foot deep, in 1 mile more and Boseman [sic] town is 3 miles more on the East

Gallitin [*sic*]." The town had about a dozen cabins, a couple of small stores, a blacksmith shop, and Cover's mill. There was some irrigation.

"I saw Boseman, the man that laid out one of the roads," Fox wrote. "Don't like his looks." John Bozeman was a good-looking man. Did he seem arrogant? Did he say something irritating? Fox didn't explain why he didn't like Bozeman's looks. Nowhere else in his journal did he seem irked at any individual. Benjamin Dailey was the diarist who didn't like a lot of people.

The day before they reached John Bozeman's city, Dailey talked to a wagon driver who was going down to the Yellowstone with lumber to build boats for that year's flotilla back to the States. He said the mines were played out, cattle weren't worth anything, and you couldn't get a good price for anything you wanted to sell. The next man who came along said mining was the best business in the country, miners with gulch claims were making $25 a day, and common laborers were collecting $5. A pilgrim who wanted to find out whether he could better his condition couldn't find out anything for sure—what he learned depended on the personal experience and prejudiced opinion of his informant.

Dailey reached Virginia City with Bernard and two other men on horseback ahead of the wagons. He was more enthusiastic now. He learned something about quartz mining, saw a flock of 500 sheep, stopped with the other riders for a fine breakfast of new potatoes (ah, potatoes! the great Gallatin Valley!), fish, venison, and coffee. They were curious about a hot spring that one of the men said was the devil's teapot and hell couldn't be far off. They passed the house of the notorious Joseph Slade—still notorious, still talked about, although he had swung at the hands of the Vigilantes more than two years before.

But soon Dailey was—of course!—disappointed in Virginia City. He found it a small town of small, poorly built log cabins, with several stores that had good stocks of merchandise, but not a good house in town. Next day was Sunday, September 9, and he had assumed—being ignorant of mining camps—that the Sabbath would be quiet. But no, the racket started at eight in the morning, the stores, billiard rooms, and grog shops were all open, and auctioneers were yelling their wares everywhere—horses, dry goods, pistols, saddles, bridles, anything a person wanted to buy.

George Fox got there a little later, with the slower-moving

wagon train. In the Gallatin Valley he enjoyed new potatoes at 10¢ a pound and butter at $1.25. Greenbacks, the money he carried, were worth 85¢ on the dollar compared with gold. His party met a couple of hundred men heading for the Yellowstone, going back to the States by boat. They gave a poor report of the country. They'd had enough. On September 11, Fox reached Virginia City and went to work unloading wagons at a grocery store and a commission house. "Not much business at the place," he commented; "looks dull."

CHAPTER 11

He Traveled in Style

One of the movers who had a relatively easy journey to Montana on the Bozeman Trail was twenty-six-year-old Thomas Alfred Creigh, who went as "managing clerk" of a freighting outfit to take boilers and quartz-stamping machinery to the Alder Gulch mines. Placer mining was still going on, but hard-rock mining had begun, too. This was rich-man's mining. It required costly machinery to crush the rock and extract the gold.

Creigh's outfit hauled eighty-one tons of machinery, including two boilers. The wagons carrying the freight for which he was responsible left from Nebraska City in a train that included fifty-two wagons and 235 yoke of oxen. Creigh, in the 1866 equivalent of a white-collar job, did not drive or herd stock. He read books quite comfortably while traveling in a wagon called the "Reading Room" because it contained the library. The book collection included a good supply of cheap Beadle novels and some current best sellers. One of these was *Jane Eyre* by Currer Bell, published in 1847. Many a journal keeper mentioned it that summer on the way across the Plains. They didn't know and wouldn't have cared very much that Currer Bell was an English clergyman's daughter whose real name was Charlotte Brontë. What they did know was that *Jane Eyre* was a startling novel.

Creigh's Reading Room, hauled by four yoke of oxen, was also a small arsenal, with rifles, revolvers, and pistols hung up in handy places, along with a violin. Heavy machinery was the basis of the load, with bedding, carpet sacks, old boots, and canned goods tucked in. On the front bow of the wagon, a three-foot United States flag whipped in the wind.

Crossing the Platte at Julesburg was a terrible experience, as it was with every train. Creigh's outfit crossed nine teams at a time, with ten to twelve yoke of cattle to a team. Just to get his boilers across required the labors of twenty-six yoke of oxen and fifteen men. "Crossing the river has been a grand scene," he wrote, "one seldom witnessed, may I never have to cross it again." That river crossing, he calculated, would be the worst one on the whole route. The crossing was complicated by an incipient mutiny of the men, who made "certain demands (silly ones)," but the mutiny was no surprise. The reliable men in the party were ready for it, and the "conspiracy" was settled in good order.

Once the dissident drivers were quelled, Creigh went back to his reading. He finished *The Neighbors,* by Mrs. Bremer, and remarked that it was "a first rate novel written in easy conversational style"; it made him homesick.

On August 4 they were near Fort Laramie. Creigh rode over to the fort to pick up mail and to get the dispute with the drivers settled for good. They were threatening to strike because of Indian scares.[32] The commander at the fort sat in judgment and ruled that men who left a train on the road were not entitled to *any* pay.

The train forded the North Platte four days later, then waited for several days, with everybody getting more and more irritated, because the military authorities wouldn't let them go on. Creigh commented cynically, "Emigrants have to protect U.S. troops. Would that there was no military force in this country. Our delay costs more than ten times their protection, for it amounts to nothing." Ninety wagons were camped and waiting. Creigh finished reading *John Halifax, Gentleman* by Mrs. Murdock and termed it "good."

After ten more wagons pulled in, the train left the main trail on August 15. Next day they passed the four graves that previous travelers had mentioned, graves of men killed July 24. And someone picked up a piece of paper with an ominous message: "A train of 36 wagons 40 men some women and children corraled by Indians two days."

They were at Fort Reno August 20, at Crazy Woman next day. There were a couple of Indian scares and one fight. They reached Phil Kearny August 25. At Fort C. F. Smith they found, as others had before them, that the Big Horn couldn't be forded, so they paid $4 a wagon for the rickety ferry. Either the price varied or the sour Benjamin Dailey may have been wrong when he mentioned $5 a wagon.

After that, they kept running into Crow Indians, who were friendly but insistent beggars and accomplished thieves. September 16 they passed the graves of the Thomas party. Two days later they had trouble fording the Yellowstone. They watched three of their cattle drown and the next day lost seven more. On September 20 they passed hot boiling springs, about twenty of them in an area some 200 feet square. And on September 26—ah, civilization!—they passed through Bozeman City and corraled the wagons by a fenced field of shocked wheat. "It seems like a new world," Creigh wrote.

They were in Virginia City on October 4, starting to move the machinery to the mill to which it was consigned. The journey from Nebraska City had taken 107 days and they had traveled 1,115 miles.

Creigh was continually interested in the variety of men in the train. There were officers and men who had fought on opposing sides in the late war; they came from Maine to Michigan and even Texas. And one, an Englishman, had been twice wounded in the fall of Delhi, India.

CHAPTER 12

The Grummonds Head for Tragedy

While Carrington's troops were setting up in business as protectors of emigration on the Bozeman Trail, Lieutenant George W. Grummond of the 18th U.S. Infantry was ordered to join his regiment at Fort Phil Kearny. Grummond had started his military career as a captain of Volunteers, and after the Battle of Bentonville, North

Carolina, was breveted brigadier general for gallant and meritorious service. With the end of the war he was moved back to second lieutenant as a career officer in the reorganized Regular Army.

He took with him on the westward journey his young wife Frances, a Tennessee girl. Theirs was the kind of wartime romance that did occasionally take place: the young Union officer courted and married the daughter of a Secessionist who had been a well-to-do slave owner. The Grummonds celebrated their first wedding anniversary on the way from Fort Kearny to Fort McPherson (Nebraska). That was the only anniversary they ever had. When they went east again, Lieutenant Grummond's body was in a box.

Frances Grummond was the only woman on the journey of more than a thousand miles to her husband's new post on the Bozeman Trail. Their little wagon train consisted of two Army ambulances and a baggage wagon. Six men went along part of the way, carrying mail.

Most travelers recalled with varying degrees of horror some details of the dangerous crossing of the South Platte at Fort Sedgwick in northeastern Colorado. Frances Grummond remembered mostly that she would have felt safer on horseback than in a wagon. She had once crossed a swift, swollen river back home on a blind mare, clinging to the animal's neck to keep from drowning.

General Sherman himself had urged officers' wives to accompany their husbands to the West and establish a pleasant garrison life in the new country; it would be an interesting experience for them— and absolutely peaceful, too. He was neither the first general nor the last to be wrong about a prophecy, but interesting—yes, that it really was.

Being the only woman in the party caused complications for Frances Grummond, especially at rest stops on the open prairie with no brush to hide behind. Once she left the ambulance and unobtrusively took a walk, wearing cloth slippers. The wagons trundled slowly but steadily on. Returning to the road, she stepped in a cactus, but the wagons were so far ahead that she dared not stop. She ran, screaming, for almost a mile with the soles of her feet full of cactus spines before the driver of her ambulance heard her. She spent the next two days pulling cactus spines out of her feet.

The detachment reached Fort Laramie in September and moved on after a brief stop. At Fort Reno there were no officers' ladies, but two officers turned their rough quarters over to the Grummonds during their short stay there. Reno was having no Indian trouble at all except for occasional cattle and horse raids. This was the deadline that the hostiles had established. The white man could go that far up the trail, and usually did so safely, but he had been clearly warned to go no farther.

Nobody at Reno knew much about conditions up at Phil Kearny. There was no travel by troops between the posts just then, except for mail parties risking their lives, riding at night. There wasn't even any Indian trouble at the blood-stained crossing of Crazy Woman. The party did come upon a lone white cow there and wondered (while butchering her to have fresh meat) where she came from. The beef was too fresh, and Frances Grummond vomited what she had eaten. She was pregnant.

Two campfires later, at Phil Kearny, there was a little delay about getting through the gate. They noticed a picket guard on a high point waving a signal, and it was lucky that Frances couldn't read the message. Actually, the picket was sending two signals: a wood train had just been attacked by Indians west of the fort, and a small party was approaching from the east. Detachments were sent out in a hurry in both directions.

The small party was the Grummonds and the mailmen; an escort came out to meet them. Just before they passed through the gate, they halted to let another wagon in, carrying the scalped, bloody, still-warm body of a soldier from the wood train. Frances was half sick with horror, and the feeling of apprehension never left her as long as she lived at Phil Kearny. That was not a very long time. She left, a widow, in January.

Phil Kearny was a beehive of activity. It was not finished, but construction was progressing. Officers' houses—except the Grummonds'—enlisted men's quarters, warehouses, the sutler's store, a guardhouse, and a fine parade ground were ready or would be soon. The most reassuring touch was the presence of the mountain howitzers, ready for action. And there were markers outside the fort showing how far a howitzer's charge would carry; also, how close to let the Indians get before firing with rifles so as not to waste ammunition. Ammunition was very scarce indeed. There wasn't enough for any target practice at all. And more than a hundred of the rifles available were beyond repair by the armorers.

The infantrymen worked at chopping down trees, hauling logs, running two small sawmills, digging ditches, building, and fighting

Indians, who attacked almost every day. But Phil Kearny had the regimental band, a great morale builder. The measured crash of band music pushed the savage wilderness away for a few rods beyond the stockade. At guard mount on Sundays the band played hymn tunes, such as "Old Hundred" and "Nearer, My God, to Thee," and songs of home and security like "Annie Laurie" and "When the Swallows Homeward Fly."

The ladies, protected prisoners who dared not go outside the stockade, made do with what they had. The fresh meat was wild game, juiceless and sometimes tough. Frances Grummond had never made butter, but she learned to remake it. The sutler sold butter for 75¢ a pound. Its outstanding characteristic was strength. By kneading it in hot water, she could freshen it up to taste pretty good.

Desiccated vegetables were available, dried and compressed into a very solid cake. These were the only vegetables provided to the Army on the Plains. (Colonel Carrington had taken along some garden seeds, but there is no record that anything came of this idea.) Desiccated vegetables consisted of onions, cabbage, beets, turnips, carrots, and peppers steamed, pressed, and dried in cakes twelve inches square and an inch thick. The cakes came sealed in tin cans and weighed about the same as a block of wood of the same size. Men out on scouts carried chunks of this stuff and nibbled it as they traveled. When Frances Grummond first tried to make soup, the solid vegetables swelled and swelled. Frantically, she kept ladling them out until all her cooking pots were full.

Carrington's Overland Circus had brought along several hundred head of cattle for beef and a few milch cows, but in the few weeks that Phil Kearny had been abuilding the Indians had run off almost all of them in spite of the armed guards who herded them as they grazed. A very few hens and turkeys remained. Eggs were scarce and precious.

So that was how things were in the Powder River country, which was supposed to be perfectly safe for emigrants and a fine place for Army wives. Now there were six officers' ladies, the wives of Colonel Carrington, Captain Tenodor Ten Eyck, Lieutenant Alexander Wands, Lieutenant William H. Bisbee, Surgeon S. M. Horton, and Lieutenant Grummond. The Carringtons had two little boys, James and Harry; the Wandses had a son, Robert; the Bisbees had a daughter, Jean.

A country mile apart from the officer class were the wives and children—a surprising number of both—brought out by enlisted men. Several enlisted men's wives and at least one daughter worked at one time or another as hospital matrons or laundresses. They kept strictly apart from the officer class. A superficial reading of the books Margaret Carrington and Frances Grummond wrote later makes them seem nonexistent.

The Negro servants receive more mention. There were three. Mrs. Carrington's was a man who, when dressed up, looked like an elegant headwaiter. Mrs. Wands had a maid who looked like a Pawnee Indian. Captain Ten Eyck's wife was the happy employer of a maid who became locally famous because she could make tasty sausage of any kind of meat that came to hand—a fine skill indeed, since there was no pork.

And in a class all by herself was a woman known as "Colored Susan," laundress of Company H, who earned a special order from Colonel Carrington. The order he posted said she sold whiskey to the soldiers; she sold pies made of government flour and fruit; was of bad repute before she even arrived, and she "must observe better behavior or she will not be tolerated in the garrison."

CHAPTER 13

The General Insists

General Cooke's temper was boiling. From Omaha he issued orders to Carrington: mail *must* be sent once a week, and the mail carrier *must* travel not less than fifty miles a day. That was reasonable—*if* the weather was decent, *if* the mail party didn't have to take time to hide from Indians now and then, *if* there were enough men to carry the mail and horses for them to ride, horses in sound enough condition to get them through.

But by fall half the horses at Phil Kearny had been driven off by Indians, there was trail-blocking snow even in September, and one round trip journey to Fort Laramie that month took nineteen days.

At one time in October so many horses were on the road that the post had only twenty-eight for emergency use, and they were not sufficiently well fed to last long under hard usage. Pickets outside the post had to be mounted. The civilian contractors had their own horses and mules, but the Army couldn't call on them.

Carrington's posts were short of men. General Hazen had gone off with twenty-six men and horses; they were away for two months. The pinch up at Fort C. F. Smith was severe. At one time that fort had only ten rounds of ammunition per man. A civilian contract train heading up that way with supplies and ammunition included thirty-one wagons—but their drivers had only five firearms among them. Carrington had to send an armed escort, taken from his already depleted force at Phil Kearny.

But General Cooke obviously didn't believe Carrington's reports about the problems in the Mountain District. In fact, he fumed that he wasn't getting reports. His telegram dated November 12, carried by horseback courier from Fort Laramie, demanded that Carrington send certain monthly and tri-monthly reports since July, and threatened, "If not immediately sent, with explanation, this matter must be brought before a general court-martial." There was another telegram with it. The courier carrying the second one had caught up with the first rider, after fifty-five miles of hard riding, at Bridger's Ferry. The second one acknowledged receipt of some of those missing returns. Carrington had been sending them right along, by riders who had to skirt Indian camps. Cooke had sent still another telegram, ordering Carrington to hurry up and get even with the Indians for the "large arrear of murderous and insulting attacks by the savages on emigrant trains and troops."

Around that time, Cooke made another decision: Fort Phil Kearny's military reservation must be restricted to twenty-five square miles. Carrington sent him a map of the area with a letter that said the equivalent of "Surely, sir, there is an error in issuing this order? Twenty-five square miles is an area only five miles square. That restriction cuts us off from all the best grazing for our stock and for cutting hay, also from the timber we need constantly for building and heating."

The restriction *must* be observed, Cooke replied, hinting that if Carrington just tried a little harder he could find plenty of grass and timber inside his five-mile square. Cooke had never been there, of course. This order meant that Phil Kearny was more heavily dependent than ever on civilian contractors. They could go anywhere they dared, while all Carrington's men could do was try to protect the wood trains from Indian attacks. The time was coming, in early December, when a wood train sorely needed protection.

CHAPTER 14

Old Glory Waves in the Wilderness

The most heart-lifting event at Fort Phil Kearny in that fall of 1866—which was to become tragic winter—took place on the last day of October. That was the regular muster day for pay and inspection, made very special by the formal dedication of a flagstaff that Chief Musician Barnes and Private William Daley had been making.

The tip of the flagstaff loomed 124 feet above the parade ground. A bandstand was built around its base, with a platform for the ladies. When the adjutant's call sounded, the well-polished men, all in new uniforms, formed in companies before their quarters, then in line of battle; the divisions moved to their allotted positions.

The chief bugler sounded "Attention." The colonel barked "Order arms" and "Parade rest." Chaplain White offered a prayer. Colonel Carrington made a speech, reminding the men of how much they had accomplished in three and a half months. He named the dead: Private Livenberger of F Company was the first, on July 17. Then Lieutenant Daniels, Private Callery of G Company, Gilchrist and Johnson of E Company, Fitzpatrick of H Company, and Oberly and Hauser.

"In every work done," he told his listeners, "your arms have been in hand. In the pine tracts or in the hay fields, on picket or general guard duty, no one has failed to find a constant exposure to some hostile shaft, and to feel that a cunning adversary was watching every chance to harass and kill. . . .

"Stockade and blockhouse, embrasure and loop-hole, shell and bullet, have warned of danger, so that women and children now notice the savage only to look for fresh occasion for you to punish him and, with righteous anger, to avenge the dead. . . .

"The crowning office, without which you would regard your work as scarcely begun, is now to be performed, and to its fulfillment I assign soldiers, neither discharging the duty myself nor delegating it to some brother officer; but some veteran soldiers of good repute shall share with a sergeant from each of their companies and the worthy men whose work rises high above us, the honor of rising our new and beautiful Garrison Flag to the top of the handsomest flagstaff in America. . . ."

That was the first full garrison flag to float between the Platte and Montana—"a new impulse to your own future exertions; a new source of courage to each traveler westward, and a new terror to foes who dare to assail you. With music and the roar of cannon we will greet its unfoldings."

The chaplain invoked the blessings of the Almighty. Daley held the halliards, with the group of selected sergeants and enlisted men around him. The men stood at parade rest with right hands raised to their hats. The rest of the gathering stood reverently during the prayer.

Then the orders rang out: "Attention! Present arms!" The long roll of the combined drum corps growled with the snap of presented arms.

"Play!" The full band rang out with "The Star-Spangled Banner."

"Hoist!" The great flag with its 36-foot fly and 20-foot hoist rose to the top of the pole and broke out at full length.

"Fire!" And the guns roared defiance to the wilderness.

Cheers were not permitted on this solemn occasion, but the ladies couldn't help clapping.

The unusual noises from within the stockade aroused the red guardians of the Powder River country, and long before the evening gun was fired unusually large numbers of Indians were seen on the hills, flashing signals with mirrors, but they did not attack.

In November, Carrington received word that reinforcements were coming, but not nearly the strength he had asked for, not nearly so many men as he needed. At Phil Kearny he had infantry, the foot soldiers whom the Sioux called walk-a-heaps. Now he got sixty-five men of the Regular Cavalry. More than half of them were raw recruits who were just beginning to find out how to get on a horse. They didn't have cavalry carbines. Something had gone wrong as usual, so that when they left Fort Laramie they were armed with long, awkward, muzzle-loading Springfield rifles.

Carrington received some infantry reinforcements, too, but not trained men from other companies of his own regiment. He got ninety-five recruits to be divided among the three undermanned forts in his Mountain District. Too little, of course—and not because headquarters in Omaha didn't know of the need or have more men. Carrington had kept headquarters informed in detail about the continuing attacks on his forts. At Fort Laramie, where there was no immediate danger, there were twelve companies.

Another exasperation: with tension high, an order came from the Department Commander, General Philip St. George Cooke, safe back in Omaha, to fire that great scout, Jim Bridger, who knew all about Indians. His services cost too much. The government was paying him $5 a day—a big sum indeed when a private soldier's base pay was $13 a month, but only average for a day laborer in the gold fields. Carrington endorsed the order "Impossible of execution" and sent it back.

Fort Phil Kearny went on getting ready for winter, preparing to protect next season's wagon trains, preparing to attack the Indian watchers on the hills. Carrington has been criticized for his failure to march his men out and clean up on the redskins once and forever. He has been accused of spending too much planning and manpower on the meticulous construction of his fort, of fussing too much about such details as keeping the men off the grass of the parade ground. He never did fare forth to attack in strength.

But he intended to attack. He just never got around to it. He felt he had to get his forts ready first. Winter was the time to attack, to march his men out and catch the hostiles snug in their camps. Winter was not the season when Indians looked for chances to fight and gain glory by counting *coups*. Winter was a time to pull in and endure, to stay in tepees and keep warm if they could, to eat the meat they had made in the fall hunt—and often, toward spring, to get lean and hungry because the meat was gone and game could not be found.

What Carrington did not guess was that hundreds of angry, determined warriors were coming together, contrary to all custom, for a concerted attack in winter. If the white intruders were permitted to settle in and stay, then hunger would come oftener and earlier in another winter because game would be harder than ever to find. They were preparing a winter war of utter fury.

Carrington was no fire-eater, but he had some officers who were. Among them were Captain William J. Fetterman, Captain Frederick Brown, and Lieutenant Grummond. Fetterman, a brevet lieutenant colonel, had recently arrived from recruiting duty. Impatient with the delay in cleaning up the redskins, he once boasted in the presence of Carrington and Jim Bridger, "I can take eighty men and go to Tongue River!"

Jim Bridger told Carrington, "Your men who fought down south are crazy! They don't know anything about fighting Indians." Of course eighty men, and even less, *had* gone to Tongue River en route to the Big Horn, in the past three summers, armed civilians with wagon trains. Some of them had been attacked, but most of them got through, with hair-raising tales to tell. That, however, was before the Sioux were really heated up.

Fetterman, Brown, and Grummond had faced shot and shell in the recently concluded War of the Rebellion, as Carrington had not. They had been on the winning side against courageous, civilized men of their own race, men who used the same kind of weapons and the same traditional military tactics. Surely they could whip a bunch of savages! Why not get the business started without further delay?

The fire-eating Fetterman proposed a plan for fooling the Indians: he would take a detachment at night to a cottonwood thicket along Big Piney Creek in front of the fort, hide his men, and leave some hobbled mules as live bait to decoy the Indians into making a raid within howitzer range. With official permission, he tried it on a bright moonlight night, but no Indians took the bait. Within three hours of Fetterman's disappointed return to the fort, Indians drove off a herd of stock less than a mile away.

One late-night alarm—wagon train carrying mail corraled just below Lake De Smet, surrounded by Indians—brought almost a full company out of the fort with a howitzer to the rescue. The mail and its escort were brought safely in, but part of that mail was enough to make the beleaguered occupants of Phil Kearny blink and shake their heads. Here were documents from the Fort Laramie peace commission assuring them that a satisfactory treaty had been made with *all* the Indians of the Northwest, and the Indians should be advised to go to Fort Laramie to get their presents! Every white man along the Bozeman Trail had his own opinion of where the Indians ought to go. It was not Fort Laramie.

Winter moved into the Powder River country. The men shivered in their warmest clothing. They wore leggings of buffalo skin with the hair inside. The few women had them, too, but with shoes attached, made of harness leather by the post shoemakers. These "buffalo boots" reached to the knee and fastened with straps and buttons. They weren't pretty, but they were warm.

At Phil Kearny there were between 350 and 400 men, including civilian employees and teamsters, prisoners in the guardhouse, sick and wounded in the hospital, and those absent with mail parties— sometimes 236 miles away at Fort Laramie. Surrounded by thousands of Indians who had no intention of settling down cozily in their tepees for the winter, the fort had less than a box of cartridges per man. Obviously there could be no target practice even for the untrained recruits.

On December 6 there occurred a heart-stopping event. A wood train was attacked about nine o'clock in the morning. The warning came from mounted pickets on Pilot Hill, who kept wheeling their horses in rapid circles, which meant that an attack in force was expected. Carrington immediately started the eager Captain Fetterman to the rescue with a detachment of mounted infantry and part of Lieutenant Horatio Bingham's cavalry to drive the Indians north over Lodge Trail Ridge. Carrington himself, with Lieutenant Grummond and thirty mounted men, moved to intercept the Indians' retreat if the first rescue party repulsed them.

Fetterman's men drove about two hundred Indians north, but Carrington saw something peculiar: fifteen cavalrymen, dismounted and without any officer, separated from the rest. They explained that Lieutenant Bingham, with Lieutenant Grummond and a few men, had gone forward. The colonel ordered a bugle sounded to guide Fetterman toward him. Carrington himself emptied one Indian saddle in the fighting.

Confusion reigned. Lieutenant Wands by mistake had joined Fetterman instead of Carrington. He had a slight wound, but his cool use of his Henry rifle saved Fetterman's men after Bingham left them. Nobody ever knew why Bingham had done that, because he was dead. With him was Sergeant Bowers, still alive although a hatchet had cut into his skull. And where were Grummond and three men with him? They were riding like the wind; seven Indians had spears at their backs. Grummond and his men escaped.

When it was all over, the fort on the Piney had two more bodies in its new cemetery, for Sergeant Bowers was dead by that time, and the post hospital, not quite completed, had five more wounded patients. One officer at Phil Kearny showed himself as no fire-eater that day. Captain James W. Powell was ordered, in writing, to bring fresh troops along with an ambulance to join Carrington. But Powell told Captain Tenodor Ten Eyck to send a lieutenant instead, and Powell stayed in his quarters.

That was December 6. On the nineteenth, Captain Powell redeemed himself. The Indians again attacked a wood party. Powell commanded a detachment ordered out to rescue the woodcutters. He rescued them and reported having seen two or three hundred Indians.

One more wagon train load of logs was needed to finish the hospital, so on the twentieth Carrington himself commanded a party of eighty men to guard the woodcutters. He built a small bridge across the Big Piney for easier access while the log cutting went on. One more day of work would complete all the outside labor for the winter. But that day, December 21, brought historic disaster.

CHAPTER 15

The Fire-Eater Extinguished

On December 21 occurred a battle that shocked the nation. It has become known as the Fetterman Massacre, although it was not a massacre. It was a fight between two armed forces, one of which was totally annihilated.[33]

The furious Indians who watched every move at Phil Kearny were mostly Sioux with some Cheyennes. Their leader—who may not have been present at the Fetterman "massacre"—was the great Oglala, Red Cloud, a remarkable man. War was a way of life with the Plains tribes. There was no way for a young, ambitious fellow to gain glory except to risk his life in battle and to count *coups* against an enemy. A war chief, therefore, had no trouble rounding up men to fight. His problem was to hold them back so the overeager young men, with reputations to build, wouldn't try to dash out ahead of their companions and upset his long-range plans.

Red Cloud did make long-range plans, and this was remarkable. Furthermore, he was able to persuade his fighting men to do things his way. Carrington could *command* his forces. Red Cloud had to depend on oratory and his reputation for success as a leader. He was the great defender of the Bozeman Trail against the invading whites.

But whether or not he was present on December 21,[34] he had been field marshal of the combined Sioux and Cheyenne forces for at least six months, and he had been seen and identified during the December 6 attack.

On December 21, the red defenders carried out a decoy plan that worked, as Fetterman's plot with staked-out mules had not. The Sioux-Cheyenne warriors even had a briefing, with mystic overtones, the day before. A *berdache*, a half-man–half-woman (perhaps a hermaphrodite, perhaps simply a man who preferred to do women's work because he didn't want to be a warrior), carried out a strange ceremony at a point near the scene of the planned ambush, five miles from the fort. Three times he rode out with a black cloth over his head, and fell off his pony, proclaiming that he had a small number of soldiers in his hand. Each time the leaders sent him back to try again. The fourth time, he yelled that he had both hands full, lots of enemies. Then the chiefs were satisfied.

The wood train and its escort, about eighty men altogether, left the fort a little after ten o'clock on the twenty-first. About eleven o'clock a picket signaled that the train had gone into corral and was under attack. Colonel Carrington immediately ordered out a rescue party with Captain Powell commanding. But Captain Fetterman insisted that his senior rank entitled him to command it, and Carrington agreed. Lieutenant Grummond wanted to get in on the fight; the colonel let him go with a force of cavalry. Captain Frederick H. Brown, who had been reassigned and was ready to leave Phil Kearny, was determined to kill some Sioux while he still had a chance at them. He went along. There were also two civilian frontiersmen, James S. Wheatley and Isaac Fisher. Altogether, there were eighty-one men including Fetterman—just what he had said he wanted to ride clear to Tongue River.

The order Carrington gave Fetterman was clear: "Support the wood train, relieve it, and report to me." To Grummond he said, "Report to Captain Fetterman, implicitly obey orders, and never leave him." Frances Grummond, trembling with worry, heard these orders. Before the relief party rode out, Carrington mounted the sentry walk inside the stockade, halted the column, and repeated his orders, stressing, "Under no circumstances must you cross Lodge Trail Ridge."

Then they rode out. Carrington realized that they had gone without a surgeon, so he ordered one to follow. The surgeon returned to report that the wood train had broken corral and moved on safely, but Fetterman had gone over the crest of Lodge Trail Ridge and could not be reached because there were so many Indians there.

Fetterman had marched right into the Indians' trap.

Carrington sounded the general alarm. In a few minutes he had Captain Ten Eyck on the way out with a supply wagon and all the soldiers who could be spared. Those left in the fort heard shooting for a while. Then it stopped. The colonel's orderly, who had gone with Ten Eyck, galloped back with a written message: Reno Valley was full of Indians but nothing could be seen of Fetterman's command.

The women at the fort congregated, breathless with terror for their men, in Mrs. Wands's cabin. Night was coming on when they heard the crunching of wagon wheels. The gates opened. The wagons came in, loaded with mutilated, bloody bodies, forty-nine of them. There would be no more that night, but there were many more to come. Fetterman and all his eighty men were dead. Frances Grummond was a widow. From then on, she was under the sympathetic protection of Margaret Carrington.

Everyone in the fort expected a heavy attack by Indians the next morning if not before. Carrington had to try to get word out to the world, for there was a distinct possibility that nobody would live to tell the story. There enters here on the stage of history a civilian, a foreigner, employed by the quartermaster. His name was John Phillips. His nickname was "Portugee." He volunteered to carry a message from Carrington, through bitter cold and snow and wind and waiting, triumphant Indians, with the odds against him something like 100 to 1. Carrington's chaotic dispatch, written in grief and exhaustion, was for the Adjutant General, Department of the Platte, at Omaha:

> Do send me reinforcements forthwith. Expedition now with my force is impossible. I risk everything but the post and its stores. I venture as much as any one can, I have had but today a fight unexampled in Indian warfare; my loss is 94 killed. [So it seemed in the confusion.]
>
> I have recovered 49 bodies, and 35 more are to be brought in, in the morning, that have been found. Among the killed are Brevet Lieutenant Colonel Fetterman, Captain F. J. Brown and Lieutenant Grummond. The Indians engaged were nearly 3,000, being apparently the force reported on Tongue River, in my dispatches of 5th November and subsequent thereto. This line is important, can and must be held. It will take four times the force in the spring to re-open it, if it be broken up this winter. I hear nothing of my arms that left Leavenworth September 10. The additional cavalry ordered to join me has not been reported; their arrival would have saved us much loss today.
>
> The Indians lost beyond all precedent. I need prompt reenforcement, and repeating arms. I am sure to have, as before reported, an active winter, and must have men and arms. Every officer of this battalion should join it. Today I have every teamster on duty, and but 119 men left at post. I hardly need urge this matter; it speaks for itself. Give me 2 companies of cavalry, at least forthwith, well armed, or 4 companies of infantry, exclusive of what is needed at Reno and Fort Smith.
>
> I did not overestimate my early application of a single company. Promptness will save the line, but our killed shows that any remissness will result in mutilation and butchery beyond precedent. No such mutilation as that today is on record. Depend upon it that the post will be held so long as a round or a man is left. Promptness is the vital thing. Give me officers and men. Only the new Spencer arms should be sent; the Indians are desperate; I spare none, and they spare none.

All that Portugee Phillips had asked was to choose the horse he would ride. He chose a Thoroughbred belonging to Carrington and took along some iron rations for himself and a small amount of grain for his mount. Carrington let him out through the sally-port gate into the bitter, dismal night and bade him God-speed.

The only cheer at Phil Kearny throughout that night was the relief the anxious, sleepless inmates heard every half hour when the sentries called the time, the post number, and the words "All's well." When dawn came, Carrington called in his remaining officers to arrange an expedition to search for the remaining bodies. He faced some arguments: a small party wouldn't be safe, but a large one would leave the undefended post open to capture. Carrington insisted: "I will not let the Indians entertain the conviction that the dead cannot and will not be rescued. If we cannot rescue our dead, as the Indians always do at whatever risk, how can you send details out for any purpose?"

In addition, failure to bring back the bodies would convince the enemy that the fort was too weak to stand against attackers. Carrington won. Every single soldier who was fit for duty begged to go along. He took Captain Ten Eyck, Lieutenant Winfield Matson, a surgeon, and eighty men.[35]

Before they left, Carrington made arrangements for mass destruction of the women and children in case Fort Phil Kearny fell. He cut the fuzes of the spherical case shot in the magazine and adjusted the store of ammunition so that with one match the whole magazine would be exploded. Secretly, so as not to terrify the distraught women any further, he left these instructions: "If, in my absence, Indians in overwhelming numbers attack, put the women and children in the magazine with supplies of water, bread, crackers, and other supplies that seem best, and, in the event of a last desperate struggle, destroy all together, rather than have any captured alive."

All day the women waited, and the sentinels walked their posts. And somewhere to the south Portugee Phillips spent most of the daylight hours in hiding; there was more chance of getting through if he traveled at night, off the Bozeman Road. The sunset gun had sounded before the wagons came back to Phil Kearny. Soldiers brought out their best uniforms to cover the hacked, tortured bodies of their comrades for the last sleep. And Carrington brought Mrs. Grummond an envelope containing a lock of her husband's hair.

For days, then, the making of coffins and the digging of graves went on, in cold so intense that the men could work only fifteen minutes at a time. Snow fell so heavily and drifted so badly that it was possible to walk over the top of the stockade, so along with their other labors the men kept clearing a ten-foot trench on the outside, in case the Indians took a notion to walk in. There was no gaiety at Phil Kearny for Christmas of 1866.

And where was the intrepid Portugee Phillips? Had he reached a telegraph station where he could send Carrington's frantic message? He stopped at Fort Reno to rest and get fresh supplies. General Henry W. Wessels, who had recently taken command there, gave him a brief dispatch to carry. At Horse Shoe Creek telegraph station he delivered Wessels' message. Apparently it never reached Fort Laramie at all. The Horse Shoe Creek operator would not promise to handle the long dispatch from Carrington, so Portugee Phillips rode on.

On Christmas night he reached Fort Laramie. A talented stage director could not have made his arrival more dramatic. His horse was staggering when Phillips was challenged by the guard. Brigadier General Innis N. Palmer was attending a ball, a gay Christmas affair at Old Bedlam, the bachelor officers' quarters. Into the lights and music, among uniformed officers and ladies in their best gowns, stumbled Portugee Phillips, bundled in his buffalo overcoat. He found General Palmer and handed him his message. The news of the disaster spoiled the Christmas ball.

Legend says that Colonel Carrington's Thoroughbred horse dropped dead as Phillips dismounted at the door of Old Bedlam. He had good reason. So long a ride in only four days—the night of December 21 to the night of December 25—would be fantastic even in good weather and daylight. Portugee Phillips had neither, although he may have changed horses somewhere along the way—at Horse Shoe Station, perhaps.

While the sorrowing men at Phil Kearny built coffins and dug graves in the frozen earth, General Palmer at Fort Laramie sent a telegram and Carrington's dispatch to General Cooke in Omaha. Cooke wired back orders to send two companies of cavalry and four of infantry to relieve Fort Phil Kearny. Wessels, commanding Fort Reno, would move from his post with the reinforcements to assume command of Phil Kearny. Carrington was relieved of command and ordered to Fort Caspar (now Casper, in east central Wyoming).

The weather was so bad, with a blizzard raging, that Palmer could not move the relief out of Fort Laramie until January 3.

CHAPTER 16

Nelson Story Defies Everybody

Emigrants and freighters muttered or roared their protests when commanders at the Bozeman Trail forts required them to wait a while until more wagons came up to strengthen the train—but with all their complaining, they obeyed orders. One party that came up the trail not only disobeyed but got away with it.

The leader of that outfit was Nelson Story. He had no pilgrims along. He had a couple of wagons freighted with stock for a store he was going to open in Bozeman, a lot of longhorn cattle, and some two dozen fighting cowboys. Story had made good in the gold camps since '63, when Mollie Sheehan enjoyed riding the burros he used as pack animals on the way to Bannack. He had made good $40,000 worth, according to some accounts, and had invested it in Texas cows to drive north to the vast grasslands of Montana. He had 500 or 3,000 head (depending on which old-timer's account you prefer to believe) and he was not a man to be stopped either by Red Cloud's Sioux or Colonel Carrington's soldiers.

One of those who told of Nelson Story's dramatic drive up the Bozeman Trail was John B. Catlin, who was interviewed by A. L. Stone in 1912. Catlin was a young veteran of the Civil War when he and a friend, Steve Grover, gave up farming in Indiana in favor of adventuring in the far West. In the spring of '66 they got a job driving bull teams from Nebraska City to Montana. The first day Catlin managed to tip over the mess wagon, but profiting by experience and the blue language of the wagon boss, he learned fast.

"The trouble with Steve Grover and me," Catlin recalled, "was that we felt sure we were the men who had put down the rebellion. This made us overconfident, perhaps. But we were not overconfident more than twenty-four hours after we joined that bull train."

When they got ready to leave the main trail at Fort Laramie to head up to Montana, the two young men had quit their new profession of bullwhacking and had their own small outfit: a mule team, a wagon, and two saddle horses. Nelson Story was at Fort Laramie, so they joined his parade. Their first Indian trouble occurred about ten miles short of Fort Reno, where they had a brisk little engagement in which two drivers were wounded and some cattle driven off. Story's stubborn cowboys followed the Indians into the badlands, surprised them in camp, and got back all the cattle. Three head of cattle were wounded; they furnished beef to the outfit. A couple of men rode on to Fort Reno to get an ambulance for the wounded men, who were left there to recover. One of them was the trail boss.

About an hour before they ran into Indians, they had met a Frenchman and a boy who were making camp. The Frenchman refused to camp with them, arguing that he wasn't half as much afraid of Indians as he was of some white men. After the fight, Story sent back a couple of men to see how the Frenchman was doing. They found his body and the boy's, scalped and mutilated, their wagon burned and their horses missing. Story's men buried the bodies.

After a rest at Fort Reno, Story's herd moved on toward Fort Phil Kearny. Soldiers stopped them three miles out, with orders to come no closer because Colonel Carrington needed the meadow for grazing Army stock. In addition, he ordered them not to go on because of danger from Indians. They were far enough from the fort so that the soldiers couldn't have helped them in case Indians did attack, and no escort could be provided to help them move on. Nelson Story fumed. His crew built two field corrals, one for the bull teams and one for the Texas longhorns. They settled down to wait for Carrington's permission to move on. Story was certainly not going to turn back. It was already October, and winter was coming fast.

After two weeks, Nelson Story called his men together and proposed that they move ahead without permission. If they started in the night, they could get far enough before morning so that the soldiers wouldn't dare follow them. Every man but one saw it Story's way. The one who voted No was immediately placed under guard so he couldn't report to the fort. After one night of travel, they turned him loose to go back to Phil Kearny.

Story's party had twenty-seven men armed with Remington breech-loaders. They traveled at night the rest of the way and had only two or three minor skirmishes with Indians. The only man killed was a herder the Indians got while they were still at Phil Kearny.

After Story's herd reached Fort C. F. Smith, on the Big Horn, they could relax a little and travel in the daytime, because the Crow Indians were rated as friendly. The herd forded the Yellowstone at a place where Carrington's fourth fort would have been built if he had had enough manpower to spread out that much. Then it was a fairly easy journey through Emigrant Gulch to Bozeman City. Story paid off his men there and left his cattle. He went on with the rest of the train to Virginia City, getting there December 9.

John B. Catlin had the greatest admiration for Nelson Story. He said:

> Even after three years on the skirmish line in the Civil War, I had never seen a fighting man like Nelson Story. He hunted a fight and when he found it he knew how to handle it. He never carried a rifle, but there were always two big navy revolvers on his hips. He was always splendidly mounted and would ride like the wind. He would say, "Come on boys," and ride away. Of course, we'd follow him—we'd have followed him to hell—but accustomed as the Civil War had made me to following almost any daredevil leader, there were a good many times when Nelson Story had me guessing. The Indians soon got to know him. Also they feared him. They knew he would go through with whatever he undertook and they had no time to bother with him.

CHAPTER 17

The Eager Beaver

Alson B. Ostrander was unique among the enlisted men at the Bozeman Trail forts. He *wanted* to be there. He had used influence to get there. He had used influence to get into the Army in the first place. He succeeded in 1864, at age eighteen, when draft dodgers, deserters, and bounty jumpers were doing everything they could to get out or stay out.

Ostrander was born in Poughkeepsie, New York, in 1846. When he was fifteen, at the beginning of the Civil War, he was already on fire with the idea of becoming a soldier. But he quieted down temporarily, attended school, and took a six-months business course at Eastman's Commercial College in his home town.

There he developed skill in penmanship that opened up the way to later adventure. Ostrander could write legibly and fast, a skill that was in great demand before there were typewriters. Everything that wasn't printed (with hand-set type) had to be hand written. There were no copying machines, so when ten copies of a document, for example, were required in a hurry, ten men sat down with pen, ink, and paper and wrote while another man dictated.

Young Ostrander, with help from his father, who knew the right people, enlisted in the Army March 4, 1864. Twenty-one was the legal age for enlisting, but at eighteen he could be a "Music Boy." He was sent to Governor's Island in New York Harbor for training as either a fifer or a drummer. Within ten days he was detailed as a clerk at post headquarters; the Army needed someone with legible handwriting more than another fifer or drummer. Ostrander worked in the Recruiting Bureau until June 1 under Colonel D. A. Loomis. Then Loomis was relieved by Brigadier General Philip St. George Cooke, who moved headquarters to 24 East Fourth Street in New York City.

This kind of soldiering was better than nothing, but Ostrander still yearned for something exciting. In March, 1866, news came that the War Department had created a new military department in the West to be known as the Department of the Platte. Headquarters would be in Omaha, Nebraska, and the commander would be General Cooke. Cooke read about it in a newspaper before his orders came.

Ostrander immediately wrote a letter to the Adjutant General of the Army requesting to be transferred from General Service to some regiment serving in the Department of the Platte. General Cooke approved—and wrote his own letter asking for his penman's transfer. That night the boy rushed home to Poughkeepsie by train to ask his father to help. His father was going to Washington anyway and would call on a congressman he knew. The boy's request was turned down officially, but the father went straight to Lieutenant General Ulysses S. Grant. Although Grant had a few other things on his mind, he approved the transfer. Alson Ostrander caught up with General Cooke finally and went to work for him again as a clerk in Omaha.

But in Omaha he only heard about action on the Indian frontier; he couldn't *see* any of it. Twice he requested transfer to his own regiment, the 18th U.S. Infantry; twice he was refused. The third time, General Cooke asked him why he was so insistent and Ostrander answered frankly, "I have only a very short time before my enlistment expires and I don't want to go back home and have to say I served three years in the army and never saw my regiment or company!"

His dream came true. He was ordered to Fort Reno. From end-of-track on the Union Pacific, at Kearny Station, he was one of a party of thirty regular soldiers, two officers, and a captain's wife traveling by wagon and ambulance. Nobody ever enjoyed the adventure of going west more than Alson Ostrander.

From Bridger's Ferry on the Oregon Trail they started up to Fort Reno on November 19. Always on the lookout for Indian trouble, the ambulance kept tight to the cavalry and each wagon driver kept his team's noses close to the tailboard of the wagon ahead, while the infantrymen marched beside and behind. Young Ostrander, who had heard some very bloody stories by that time, found that his enthusiasm for fighting Indians had seeped away. He missed a chance to kill an immense elk but covered himself with lesser glory by shooting an ox that some passing train had lost. That saved him from being nicknamed "Buck" for buck fever.

Just short of Dry Fork he had his first experience with a blizzard —November was not too early for that. Thanksgiving found them still on the Bozeman Trail; five men in Ostrander's mess shared one sage hen for dinner. The next day they reached Fort Reno, and Ostrander was ready to begin soldiering. Here he drew his very first uniform—after more than two and a half years in the Army! Clerks in the office where he had worked in New York wore citizens' clothes.

It is pleasant to visualize this eager young fellow, the only enlisted man in the Bozeman Trail forts who was delighted to be there. He thoroughly enjoyed soup made of desiccated vegetables, which he had not encountered before. The other men had encountered them too often. He was, we must admit, pretty well spoiled.

Back in Omaha, when he was sick with typhoid fever, General Cooke himself had brought him goodies. "Imagine, if you can," Ostrander wrote in *An Army Boy of the Sixties*, "a brevet major general in the regular army, of the old school, walking eight or ten blocks through the streets of Omaha, carrying a pitcher of lemonade to a private soldier!"

That Private Ostrander had not been whipped into shape by the Army is proved by the fact that he tried to revolutionize the Army's way of handling mail. Fort Reno usually had two or three hours' notice that mail was coming, because sentries watched all approaches. The mail carrier (who had a small escort) would turn the bag over to the post adjutant, Lieutenant T. S. Kirtland, who had the only key to it and kept the key locked in a drawer. Ostrander thought this was pretty silly. He and another headquarters clerk, Clarke, did all the sorting and separating.

They spread a blanket on the floor and dumped the bag's contents on it. Then they placed the bag so they could throw everything into it that was going to the forts beyond Reno. Clarke and Ostrander, on their knees, tossed mail with both hands, keeping out everything for Reno. Then they tossed the rest back. Clarke restrapped the bag, the lieutenant ceremoniously locked it, and the mail carrier went on his way.

The first time Ostrander took part in this performance, he had big ideas about a better way to do it. He remarked (in the presence of Lieutenant Kirtland and Montgomery Van Valzah, the mail carrier), "This mail ought to be put up separate at Fort Laramie. They could make one big bundle for us and for each post up the trail. Then all we'd have to do would be to take out our own bunch and let the rest go on."

Clarke suggested that he shut up and mind his business. The lieutenant explained, more gently than was required of him, why that wouldn't work: There would be four separate bundles, including Bridger's Ferry, and they would vary in bulk and weight, so the carrier would have trouble balancing the sack on his horse. Still sorting, Ostrander urged, "They could put them in separate sacks. Then there'd be no delay here."

Lieutenant Kirtland, still sunny-natured, said it would be hard to balance separate sacks on the horses. Private Ostrander, still trying to improve the Army's way of doing things, argued that each of the three or four men in the carrier's escort could carry a sack. Kirtland reminded him that the carrier was responsible to the government and was paid $10 a day while on the trip (even the fabulous scout Jim Bridger up at Phil Kearny was paid only $5 a day), and nobody else was allowed to handle the bags.

How, Ostrander wondered, did the rules allow him and Clarke to handle all the mail at the post if it was important that only the carrier could touch the bag on the way up there? He noticed two letters for himself, exclaimed happily, and put them in his pocket.

"Throw them out," ordered Clarke, and he had to put them with the other Fort Reno mail—to read after everybody else got theirs, because the headquarters staff came last in the order of things. He gave up his project of trying to improve the Army's mail-sorting system.

At Fort Reno he had a soft detail. He did not build or cut wood or drill or fight Indians. He did not live in barracks with B Company; he lived at post headquarters, in comparative ease, with another clerk. He saw a man named Blair tomahawked and scalped right outside the fort, but danger came not nigh to Ostrander.

Still, he had the satisfaction of being where the action was. He awoke around midnight a few days before Christmas at a sentry's challenge; he heard the answer: "Scout with message," and a horse's hoofbeats. Next morning he learned the reason for the brief excitement: Portugee Phillips had stopped long enough to report the bloody news of the Fetterman fight and had galloped on through the night.

CHAPTER 18

A Soldier Watches Torture

James D. Lockwood, a soldier at Fort C. F. Smith, was a young fellow of perhaps more than average curiosity. One day after the Crows won a little battle with Sioux near the fort, Iron Bull, the respected winter mail carrier, rode up dragging a captive Sioux at the end of a rope. The other Crows howled their delight. Iron Bull decided to turn the fellow over to the women and invited the white chief and his soldiers to watch the performance. The commandant refused but couldn't talk Iron Bull into releasing the captive. Lockwood wanted to watch, though, so he sneaked out and did. Here in his description:

> The tribe was assembled in a level flat of land, from which arose abruptly a high, rocky cliff. The squaws, with their prisoner, were in this flat, the poor wretch in the center, and the tormentors in a circle around.
>
> The chief's warriors and children lined the cliff, from which they could obtain a full view of the entertainment. There was a small fire burning near. The prisoner was entirely nude. A large strong rawhide rope was about his neck, with four or five squaws swinging to the opposite end. Occasionally they would jerk the poor wretch to his knees or flat on the ground, and then he would be encouraged to rise by a woman running up with a piece of bark with hot ashes and coals of fire, which she would place upon his reclining body; no sooner would he regain his feet, than he would be jerked this way, that way, slapped, beaten and kicked; burning fire brands were thrust into his ears, and, in fact, outrages too shocking and horrible to narrate, were perpetrated.
>
> This treatment was prolonged until, thinking that death would soon relieve the poor victim from their hellish cruelty, they began dismembering him; cutting off his toes, fingers, ears and nose; no part of the miserable being's human anatomy escaped their horrible attentions, and they were constantly encouraged and directed to greater cruelties by the warriors and children.
>
> Our hero [Lockwood means himself], having been trained from boyhood among scenes of war and bloodshed, found that this was too much even for him, and with a feeling of sickening faintness, he rushed from the spot and returned to the garrison. Not long afterward, a party of warriors came riding up, dragging the armless, limbless trunk of the poor prisoner, by means of the rope which was still fastened around his neck. The commandant, shocked and disgusted, drove them from the place.

Frustrations of "the Acting One"

The first extraordinary legislative session called by Acting Governor Meagher met in March in 1866 and continued for forty days. He called a second session that met during November and December of the same year. At the same time, a constitutional convention was held, because Montana could not become a state until it proposed a constitution acceptable to Congress, and Montana would have no vote in Congress as long as it remained a territory. It did have a delegate to Congress, Samuel McLean, who had defeated Wilbur Fisk Sanders for that post in the Territory's first election in October, 1864. But Delegate McLean could only advise and argue. He couldn't vote.

The convention came up with a constitution, all right, but to this day nobody knows what was in it. The delegates produced a single document with no copy. It was sent to St. Louis to be printed, but with no money to pay for the job. The constitution simply disappeared. (Montana held its second constitutional convention in 1884 and didn't become a state until 1889).

The acts of Meagher's two special sessions of the territorial legislature came to nothing, like the proposed constitution. Congress in 1867 invalidated every one of them—a move unprecedented in American history. Many of them were for the benefit of self-seekers who wanted, and received, charters for toll roads and bridges. The men of Montana were busy trying to better their condition.

Acting Governor Meagher entertained hope that he might be appointed Governor in fact if Sidney Edgerton resigned. Edgerton did resign at last, without returning to Montana, but a Kentucky man, Green Clay Smith, received the appointment that Meagher coveted. Smith arrived in Montana early in October. The *Montana Post*, in Virginia City, editorially rejoiced "most heartily that Governor Smith has assumed the gubernatorial chair and that General

Meagher who has brought disgrace upon himself, his race, the Territory, and the country generally, has been superseded."

A few years earlier, in New York, Meagher had publicly whipped one newspaper editor who offended him and had received the apology he demanded from another. In Montana he found himself in a different league. He gave Henry N. Blake, editor of the *Post*, a choice of retracting or fighting a duel. Blake calmly refused to do either. He published news of the challenge in his paper, heading it blithely "Pistols and Coffee for Two."

Blake maintained that as editor he had the right and duty to criticize the official conduct of public men, and he was going to go right on doing it. Furthermore, the "code of honor" was a relic of barbarism and ignorance, murder was illegal, and he was not going to let Meagher make a criminal of him. In case anyone thought he was a coward, Captain Blake called attention to his own record in the Union Army and to his honorable wounds, which still bothered him in bad weather.

Acting Governor Meagher must have been the most frustrated and furious man in Montana.

CHAPTER 20

A Tax Collector Looks at Montana

A man who is pleased with the way he is handling a hard job naturally wants the boss to know about it. Therefore, on May 20, 1866, N. P. Langford sat down and wrote a long letter to his superior, J. W. Taylor, Commissioner, Internal Revenue Service. Taylor was in Washington. Langford was in Virginia City, and he had a rousing tale to tell. He began:

> I have often been minded to write to you, giving you some idea of what I have been doing in Montana—the difficulties I have had

to contend with and annoyances to bear with in organizing this Collection District; and while I do not claim any undue credit for what I have accomplished—for I have done no more than faithfully discharged my official duties, I nevertheless feel a pride in the fact that a greater success has been attained than the most sanguine could have anticipated; and I am convinced that few men would have undertaken what I have in such a community as this.

He attributed much of his success in enforcing the revenue law to his understanding of Montana men and manners—and to the fact that the men he dealt with knew that threats of personal violence wouldn't prevent him from doing his duty. Langford had been one of the earliest Vigilantes, although he soon traveled out of the Territory and was absent during most of their excitement.

The curse of new territories, said Langford, is the inefficiency of officials. Men accept political jobs in the hope of moving up to better ones. As a result, they court popular favor. "Especially," he pointed out, "does this fact apply to two classes of officers: the judicial and the financial." A tax collector had better be a man who is not looking forward to a career in politics! He continued:

Considerations such as these determined me to give up all thought of anything else and devote myself solely to the duties of my office, ignoring all political prospects, so far as they related to myself, although they were flattering: probably more so than of any union man [36] in Montana; for reasons connected solely with law and order; to maintain which I ran many risks of life. The "History of the Vigilantes" [37] details these facts fully and I need not farther refer to them.

The first obstacle he encountered, before he even tried to wring taxes out of his unwilling neighbors, was lack of lawbooks and forms. The assessor had a copy of the law, but he lived sixty-five miles away. Langford had read it one day in Washington, but he needed to have it to show doubters. After six weeks he borrowed a copy from a "pilgrim." He had only twenty blank license forms; he borrowed four hundred from Utah, but these were not enough. So he got some printed locally. Upon receiving his first assessment list, he put a notice in the *Montana Post* and tacked up a couple of hundred notices of the date around the country. So what happened?

Within two or three days after posting these notices some twelve or fifteen men came into my office to talk with me about the collection of revenue. They generally went over about the same ground: said they were "loyal and believed in paying their taxes," but there were many who didn't believe in it and wouldn't pay. They wanted to know what would be done with delinquents, if I'd try to enforce the law, if I thought I could do it without the aid of a regiment of soldiers and other such questions. I told them that I should enforce the law, after giving full notice to all persons, and that I didn't think that I'd need any military force, but if I did I'd get it. They advised me not to "press the matter" on the start for fear of trouble. They came, they said, "to advise with me as friends." These men did not all come together, but in parties two or three at a time, and at first I thought nothing of it, but the questions asked by different parties were so similar, my suspicions were aroused, and I plainly saw that it was a preconcerted plan. Sometimes a man was more violent than the others and would say that he owed no allegiance to any government but that of Jeff Davis and that I need not expect to collect a tax from him, for he wouldn't pay it.

The date for paying taxes came and went. Langford had more than a hundred delinquents. He gave each one a personal notice (he had no official blanks even for that) that he would seize the property if taxes weren't paid in ten days. This brought in about fifty more. Then he issued warrants for the remainder and seized the property. Many of the warrants were returned unsatisfied, although he knew the men had money.

Then he gave notice that every delinquent would be indicted at the next term of the U.S. Court. This produced loud talk and some threats. Some of Langford's friends urged him to forget collections this time. He said he was supposed to collect taxes, and he was going to collect taxes.

As the time for the sitting of the Court drew near, I had some stormy times in my office, and to tell the truth I was not without anxiety at times concerning the results. I was in a Territory more disloyal as a whole than Tennessee or Kentucky ever were. Four-fifths of our citizens were *openly declared* Secessionists. Virginia City was first called Varina, in honor of Mrs. Jeff Davis. Then we had Jeff Davis Gulch and Confederate Gulch. . . .

At Bannack, I had seen a Secesh flag flying, and men standing nearby with revolvers, daring any bystander to say that he didn't like to see that flag, or that he didn't support Jeff Davis. Only two months before these assessments were made, our Delegate in Congress McLane [Sam McLean] discussed the issues of the campaign under a *white* flag, on which was embroidered an olive branch.

In our local matters we were completely under the rebel rule—the rule of what is familiarly known here as "the *left wing* of Price's Army"—that is, the wing that left his army. So you see that I had not the support of one fourth of our people, and threats of violence were the rule, and not the exception.

I often thought of your counsel while I was east: that it was not expected by the Department that I would place myself in jeopardy in the discharge of my duties. But I determined that I would at once settle the question whether I should yield to them, or they to the law; and at the session of the Court I had every delinquent indicted—sixty or seventy in all. This really astonished them, and they concluded that Montana was in the United States instead of Secessia.

Langford had proved his point: the law was going to be enforced. And having proved it, he asked the judge to fine the defendants 5¢ and costs. The fine could have been $100. Two of the men were abusive. Langford ordered them not to say another word in his office or he would thrash them as they had never been thrashed before. They quieted down and left.

Forbearance sometimes ceases to be a Christian virtue, Langford remarked, adding, "The rebels may hate me, but they shall not despise me. I will have their respect, even if I have to flog it out of them."

The embattled revenuer told briefly of the flour riots of April, 1865. The organized mob that searched for flour threatened, in their disappointment, to confiscate money as well as flour, so Langford cannily cached (hid) his collections. A few days later he caught a man tearing down one of his official posters. He arrested the man, who was fined for hindering a revenue officer. "He turned out to be a captain of 100 of the rioters," Langford related; "very brave at their head, and believing himself to be equally brave when alone by himself, but he was terribly frightened on being brought into court."

The fly-by-night traders who set up business from their wagons at the site of each new gold stampede were hard to catch. He and his deputies hired assistant collectors for this, even when the cost of collecting was higher than the law allowed. The principle of the thing was important—and besides, the settled merchants in the older camps complained if they thought their wagon-dealing competitors weren't paying their share.

Even when the Federal government imposed a $10 license on miners, effective May 1, 1865, Langford did not quail, although he was warned that some miners would absolutely refuse to pay. Small wonder! They had come to the gulches at the risk of their lives, with the blessing of the government and, on the great transcontinental trail, some protection from the Army. Now they were about to be penalized for doing what they had come to do, what the nation wanted them to do! Again, it wasn't the money (although $10 was two days' pay for a hired hand in a mine in Alder Gulch); it was the principle of the thing. Langford wrote:

> Miners are the most independent class of people in the world—extremely jealous of the privileges they have always enjoyed—and they looked upon this requirement of the law as an aggression upon their privileges. . . .
>
> I posted notices in the gulch setting forth the requirements of the law, and a few days thereafter five gentlemen came into my office and told me that they were a committee appointed to inform me that the miners did not believe it was right to be required to take licenses and that it would lead to bloodshed if I persisted.
>
> I told them that it was useless to talk of resistance, that the law must be enforced and that I would enforce it. They urged me to consider it well before acting. Our conversation occupied about an hour during which not an angry or excitable word was spoken on either side. They were gentlemen—Secessh of course—and I really feared the result of the advice of these men more than the threats of a hundred loud talkers.
>
> It was just a few days after we had received the intelligence of Lee's surrender, and as the Committee rose to go, one of them said, "I am in favor of paying these duties but was put on the committee and had to act." I replied that I supposed that he was forced into it by his neighbors, as Gen. Lee was into the rebellion. He said, "I suppose so." I responded, "I don't think you can hope for greater success in resisting the law than Gen. Lee attained." The conference ended here and they went their way—and the miners came up and took licenses a few days after.

A miners' meeting at German Gulch resolved that no taxes should be collected from miners. Langford had a bunch of them indicted at the next term of the U.S. Court. They frightened the assistant assessor, a man named Cross, so thoroughly that he resigned. One of the delinquents became so noisy and abusive that the U.S. marshal handcuffed him and sent him to the Madison County jail, seventy-five miles away. Langford's posted notices were torn down or defaced.

Delinquent miners at Last Chance Gulch were indicted. At Confederate Gulch, the miners let it be known that revenue officers would be met with physical violence. U.S. Marshal Pinney advised Langford not to go there. He didn't go—but only because he couldn't spare the time. His office was 165 miles away. He sent word that they should see his deputy in Helena—and they did. Langford described the territory he was required to cover:

> The District of Montana is one of the largest in the United States —that portion of it containing settlements, and over which I have repeatedly traveled, and which my Deputies occupy, being as large as the State of New York. The circuit of the mining camps at the present time is about 1400 miles, of which about 300 may be traveled by coach, the balance 1100 miles on horseback, and this distance cannot be traveled over, at best, in less time than 15 days, for a constant ride, day after day, of 75 miles each day is all a man can bear. To organize this vast District was no easy task, and I ran the risk of losing my scalp on two different occasions. One of my first Deputies, Frank Angevine, ... was killed at Ophir by the Blood Indians.
>
> It has been necesssary that I should have thorough and brave men as Deputies—men who can take care of themselves if trouble arises.

He couldn't notify a community that he was coming, because such an advertisement would be a notice to all the road agents that a man carrying money would be on a certain road on a given day. Getting money back to the States was as hard as collecting it. Langford had only a small safe, in whose burglar-proof qualities he did not repose much confidence, so he slept near it. He wrote:

> Early in the spring parties could be found by whom money could safely be sent, but after the robbery of the coach on the Salt Lake road last June, in the Port Neuf Canon, of $60,000, and the murder of the passengers who carried it, it has been difficult to find persons willing to take the risk for any pay. In the States you have some guaranty of protection while traveling, but not so here. This coach was driven into the ambusch [sic] by the regular driver, who was

suspected a few months later, was arrested, confessed his crime and was hanged by the Vigilantes. He said there were thirteen of the robbers.

Langford explained that he had to pay well to get competent deputies and hoped he would be reimbursed. He was sure the U.S. Treasury was at least $30,000 richer, because of his policy of paying good salaries, than it would otherwise have been.

He was pleased with the effectiveness of his work. "I can get the same salary ($4,000) in occupations carrying with them no such responsibilities as those which attach to my office," he told his superior, "but I have the vanity to believe that I can collect 10 percent more revenue in Montana than anyone else can. I have collected, under all my difficulties, 96 percent of the assessments. The remaining 4 percent, for peculiar reasons existing here—as they do not in the States—is not collectible."

The reason was that laboring men with families spent every cent they earned. A man earning $6 a day for 300 days had an income of $1,800, of which $1,200 was taxable. He therefore owed $60, but he simply couldn't pay it because he had spent it all. To instruct the distant commissioner in the facts of Montana life, Langford went on to say:

> The Vigilantes are the main stay of this Country and we all trust in that body for safety. The only murderer ever tried by a Court in Montana [James Daniels] was sentenced to 4 years imprisonment for manslaughter. Genl. Meagher, acting as Governor, reprieved (?) him until the will of the President could be made known and ordered him set at liberty. The U.S. Judge ordered him to be rearrested, but before that could be done the criminal returned to Helena where the murder was committed and was immediately taken by the Vigilantes and hung. If it were not for the Vigilantes no man's life would be secure. Even with them, it is far better to "keep a close mouth" and not express an opinion concerning the character of the men we meet here. . . .
>
> I have endeavored to give you some idea of the situation of affairs here. In this Godless country, this country of lawlessness, highway robberies and Vigilance Committees, this country where a U.S. Grand Jury recommended that the court turn over all criminal business into the hands of Vigilantes, this country where every man takes his life into his own hands wherever he goes, it is but a record of a common experience—very tame in comparison with my experience during the two previous years, when, for upholding the law

and publicly denouncing a gang of desperadoes with our sheriff their secret Chief, a price was set by them upon my head.

Better times were coming, he assured the Commissioner:

But these scenes of violence and threatened violence are fast passing away. The millennium is dawning. The reign of peace is drawing nigh—and with our fertile agricultural valleys and rich resources in mineral wealth, when throughout our Territory shall rise those twin pioneers of civilization, the Church and the School House, this land will be the fairest of the fair.

CHAPTER 21

Kirkaldie: Still Hoping

As 1866 opened, Kirkaldie was thinking of moving again. He liked the Gallatin Valley very well, especially as a home for his family, and wanted to keep his place there, but he hoped to get nearer to a market for his crops. He and his partner, Batchelder, might move to Confederate Gulch and specialize in raising vegetables on ten or twelve acres. Would his wife please send seeds?—cabbage, cucumber, melon, but no onion. Only Mexican onions did well in Montana, he had been told.

"I would like to eat hickory nuts—apples and popcorn with you occasionally this winter," he said. "I think I shall know how to appreciate a few of those things if I ever get back. We occasionally substitute a raw turnip for an apple here—but it hardly fills the bill."

A weekly express had started between the Gallatin and Virginia City. He could send letters to that camp free but paid 50¢ each for letters received and 10¢ for newspapers. He wrote again February 13, disappointed that the promised photographs of the twins, Willy and Nelly, hadn't come. His wife had not been able to get a good price for the dust he had sent her, and that was another disappointment. The man he sent it with sold some in Omaha for $14 an ounce.

He and Batchelder were going to move to land six or seven miles from Diamond City (Confederate Gulch); they had already laid up logs for a cabin sixteen feet square. Now he wanted his wife to send him by express, before April 1, fifteen pounds of Hungarian grass seed and various kinds for garden truck.

In the same month he wrote that he had contracted with Batchelder to work twelve acres at the new place, Kirkaldie furnishing the team, tools, fifty bushels of seed potatoes and other seed, the proceeds to be divided equally. And Kirkaldie would then get the whole ranch. In one letter after another he wrote about the seed he needed; he was nervous about receiving it in time, but he couldn't blame his wife if it came too late for planting or never came at all. April 2 he wrote that he had paid $22.30 for half a pound of Mexican onion seed, and his early peas were coming up. Between planting and planning, he was about at his wits' end. He wrote:

> I am very anxious to make enough this season so I can go home in the fall—you ask how much an outfit would cost for us to come to this country—I dont think I could get such an outfit as I should be willing to start with short of 2000.$ in dust—and I would much rather have 3000. It is not very probable that I shall be able to make the last mentioned sum this year—& perhaps not the other —I shall do the best I can—

He worried about the cholera back home, about the children (he noted with delight that little Fanny's writing and spelling were improving). He sympathized deeply with his wife's problems in a letter dated April 28 and addressed "My Dear Lizzie"—more intimate than his usual "My Dear Wife." She worried about the seeds, and she had been cheated on a knitting machine. (Even fifty years later, desperate people were being rooked on Make Big Money at Home offers. The items they made on such machines were never up to the standards of the machine manufacturer who had promised to buy the resulting socks and sweaters.)

"To be so cramped for a little money, as you have been," he wrote, "I know is extremely embarrassing, annoying and unpleasant to say no worse of it. And I regret very much that you should be reduced to such straits." If the seeds never came, it wouldn't be her fault. But sympathy was all he could send. He could not spare any money. Next season—next year—

His seeds hadn't come yet when he wrote again May 6. He was

worried about grasshoppers. The price of flour was down to $15 in Virginia City; as a result of the shortage in early spring of the previous year, everybody had laid in a big supply. Three to four thousand acres of wheat would be grown in the Gallatin Valley in 1866—enough, he thought, to supply local demand. And two years before, there hadn't been five acres!

On the twenty-seventh, he soothed Lizzie, assured her that she did write wonderfully interesting letters. "I think you would do well," he said, "to have a little better opinion of your own powers in this respect, and a little less exalted one of mine." He reminded her, not for the first time, that he hadn't yet received pictures of the children—and he wanted her in one picture with all four of them.

In his next letter, July 4, he acknowledged with joy receipt of the likeness of the babies. He had looked at the picture twenty times a day and showed it to everyone he knew. He enclosed with his letter $100 in currency; he had sold a cow for $75. Peas were in full blossom, early potatoes were in bud. The grasshoppers hadn't done much damage. Emigration from the States was beginning to go by.

When he wrote August 9, hail had done considerable damage to his potato crop. He wanted so much to go home—but how could he manage it? He would have to give it up for this year. He fretted about affairs in a greater world than the Gallatin Valley, too:

> I see by the papers that the great Indian council at Laramie has been a failure—that no treaty with the Indians was effected—& they are now preying upon the emigration as usual—When will the U.S. Gov. quit fooling with the Indians? And nearly the whole world seems to be at war or preparing for war—in Mexico—in various parts of South America & all over Europe—the nations are gathering themselves to battle—The different branches of the U.S. Gov. are arrayed against each other where will it all end? The most quiet spot to live in for the next few years may be in some valley of the Rocky Mountains.

The price of potatoes was distressingly low—some farmers had sold the early crop for only 3¢ a pound in Helena—when Frank wrote August 30. And his wouldn't be ripe enough to keep well for three or four weeks yet. He was thinking of selling his new ranch. He still couldn't see his way clear to going home in the fall. In contrast to his situation, there were stories of a man who had recently gone down the river with 700 pounds of gold, and two or three who took a *ton* of dust back to the States. "But all this enormous wealth," he added sadly, "goes into a very few mens hands."

When he wrote September 9, he hadn't sold any of his potatoes for less than 6¢ a pound. He faced the farmer's typical problem: to sell at a time when the market wasn't glutted. His potatoes were big, but they averaged only three to a stalk. Still, he hoped for 75 bushels an acre.

"I wish you would ascertain what it will cost to send books here by mail," he wrote, "—how much pr. lb.—I do not feel like staying here another winter without something to read in the long, long winter evenings. How I wish I might spend those winter evenings with you and the children."

He had to sell most of his crop for only 3¢ a pound after all, he reported in a letter dated October 5. He hoped to raise $200 or $300 to send home. He wanted to go home—how much he wanted that!—but it was best to stay where he was. He had faith in the new territory. He told of two partners on Montana Bar who cleaned up $60,000, seven gold pans full of gold.

Kirkaldie made some bitter comments about the President of the United States, Andrew Johnson, successor to the assassinated Lincoln. Johnson was a Southern Democrat but a strong Unionist; in the fall of 1866 he was on a speaking tour, opposing the Fourteenth Amendment to the Constitution, which gave Negroes the right to vote.

"If the coarse—denunciatory & egotistical speeches of the president do not succeed in killing both himself and his party—politically—why nothing else will," Kirkaldie commented. "I think the republican party need no better thing to insure them success in the coming elections—than these vaporings of President Johnson on his western tour."

He wrote again less than two weeks later, because he was depressed, and the best thing to do during a blue spell was to write home, where he wanted to be. He had contracted to sell 200 bushels of potatoes at 4½¢ and 5¢ a pound, didn't think he could sell his present ranch near Confederate Gulch as he had hoped, was thinking about raising strawberries. But after he had written a long letter, he was still blue: "I have come too far—& have spent too much time—deprived myself of the comforts of home etc. in attempting to better my condition—to abandon the enterprise without a persevering struggle."

He was able to send some money in November, a draft on New York for $270; with what he had recently enclosed in letters, that made $300, which he believed would carry his family through the winter if economically used.

Frank Kirkaldie always had ideas, a few of which worked out. Perhaps he had too many ideas—he was always changing, hoping for improvement. If he had stayed in one place, with one sound idea, he might have been better off. But we are too far from his problems to decide that.

He wrote December 1 that he had taken a family to his old place on the Gallatin on some kind of share-cropping arrangement that he does not explain. He was to supply a plow, three yoke of work cattle, and seed for thirty-five or forty acres of grain. He was going to move from his place near Confederate Gulch and go partners with a man named Lawney on land near Deep Creek (present Townsend), putting in about a hundred acres of wheat, oats, and barley. He now had more faith in grain than in vegetables. He had settled with his former partner, Batchelder, who had soured on farming.

In his last letter of the year, dated December 16 "near the mouth of Deep Creek"—but his address was now Indian Creek, via express from Helena—he told of hauling poles to build fence at Lawney's ranch; they had to haul fifteen miles and the trip took two days.

"I hope," he wrote, "that in my *third* attempt at farming I may be more successful than in the two preceeding ones."

The telegraph was completed from Salt Lake to Virginia City "so that Montana is in communication with all the civilized world '& the rest of mankind' by lightning." And when the railroad was finished across Wyoming they wouldn't be far from anywhere. Frank Kirkaldie had to keep faith in the future, because his present, without his family, was pretty bleak.

1867

□□□□□□□□□□

□□□□□□□□□□

CHAPTER 1

Good-by to Phil Kearny

The relief of Fort Phil Kearny after Portugee Phillips' famous ride has been romanticized so much in print that one might suppose the sole purpose of the troops from Fort Laramie was to rescue the fort's garrison and take them to safety. That was not the way of it. The troops were reinforcements that Carrington should have had long before. Colonel Carrington and his family and the shocked, grieving widow of Lieutenant Grummond were not "rescued." Carrington was simply being transferred, and Mrs. Grummond went along because she could not stay.

The relief brought orders for Carrington to move to another post, Fort Caspar (now Casper, Wyoming). The orders required Lieutenant Colonel Henry Wessells to proceed from Fort Reno to Phil Kearny and take command of the three Bozeman Trail forts. Carrington would take command of Fort Caspar and the new 18th Infantry regiment. The 18th was being reorganized. The 2d Battalion, on the Bozeman Trail, would become a new regiment, the 27th. The 1st Battalion would become the 18th Regiment. The order to move could not have surprised Carrington. He had asked the previous July for command of the new 18th.

On December 21, the day of the Fetterman disaster, orders were issued transferring headquarters of Carrington's new command to Fort Caspar. The transfer was not a result of the disaster. But public indignation and horror at news of the Fetterman fight were so great that the outside world jumped at the conclusion that Carrington had been transferred in disgrace. General Cooke did nothing to clear him of this suspicion. Carrington *was* disgraced in the eyes of the world, and he spent the rest of his life in strenuous efforts to get the facts before the public and clear his name. For twenty years the powers-that-were in Washington kept papers relating to the facts buried in a basement.

Weather was so dreadful on the Plains that troops could not leave Fort Laramie until the third of January. The six companies of the relief column (and two officers' wives in a wagon) plodded through the white hell of winter for thirteen days. One man froze to death on the way. The reinforcements were just what Carrington had asked for—two companies of cavalry and four of infantry. But there wasn't room for so many newcomers, and they had brought supplies only sufficient to maintain them on the way. Carrington and the regimental band had to leave without delay. With them went a detail of sixty men to bring back needed supplies from Fort Reno.

The reinforcements brought a tremendous lot of mail that had piled up at Fort Laramie. It included newspapers that told the story—outrageously untrue—of the Fetterman disaster. Enough time had elapsed since Portugee Phillips delivered his message for the news, as told by Carrington, to get to the States and to be twisted into unrecognizable lies. In the book that Frances Grummond wrote later, she said:

> It was marvellous to see how enterprising and original certain news editors could be, when removed from all access to real facts, when they set their brains at real work. General news, already stale in the States, was remarkably fresh to us, and certainly very novel, as concerning ourselves. No correct accounts could have reached them except through the commanding officer's [Carrington's] courier to Laramie, 235 miles from his headquarters. ... Mr. Lewis V. Bogy, Commissioner of Indian Affairs, on the 4th of January, informed Congress of his own views, as follows:
>
> "Now, I understand this was the fact. These Indians being absolutely in want of guns and ammunition to make their winter hunt, were on a friendly visit to the fort, desiring to communicate with the commanding officer, to get the order refusing them guns and ammunition rescinded, so that they might be able to procure their winter supply of buffalo. It has been reported that some 3000 to 5000 warriors were assembled to invest the fort. This is not and cannot by any possibility be true. The number of Indians is not there. The whole is an exaggeration, and although I regret the unfortunate death of so many brave soldiers, yet there can be no doubt that it is owing to the foolish and rash management of the officer in command at that Post."

Of course Commissioner Bogy hadn't been near to Fort Phil Kearny, but safe in Washington he knew all about how things ought to be. The Great Father's red children were playing nicely, he was sure. He had protested to General Augur that in the December 6 fight, before the disastrous one of the twenty-first, the Indians had been attacked by the whites while on a friendly visit to the fort. It was cruel, he maintained, not to let the poor hungry Indians have firearms and ammunition for hunting. One of the many things that Bogy didn't know was that the Indians hunted very effectively with bow and arrow. But for killing men, they preferred rifles.

No newspaper had a correspondent on the Bozeman Trail, but several Eastern papers passed along "reliable information" to their eager readers. Particularly infuriating to Carrington and all the others who *knew* what had happened at Phil Kearny was an entirely fictional account in an Albany newspaper, claiming that he had refused to open the gates to let in the survivors of the Fetterman fight. There *were* no white survivors, but the story built up to this climax:

> When the last band of survivors were driven to the gates of the fort, knocking and screaming in vain for admission; when the last cartridge from revolver, carbine, and rifle was expended; when the sabers and butts of muskets were broken; and when, leaning against the gates, weary and bleeding and all resistance fruitless, all fell in one heap of mangled humanity, unsupported and uncared for.

Because, the imaginative writer raged, the commanding officer was afraid either to fire or to open the gates!

Before the facts could possibly have reached the East, just about everyone who could read had a completely wrong idea of what had happened, and the blame was put squarely on Colonel Carrington. Three large-circulation newspapers claimed that Carrington was always giving powder to the hostiles, and that the ladies of the garrison tossed packages of coffee and sugar over the stockade to the squaws.

On January 23, Carrington and his escort and the band began to grope their way down the trail through continuing blizzards. The suffering was fearful. Wagon ends had been built up of boards with a hinged door in the back, but the wagon covers, though double, were only cloth. A small sheet-iron stove with a pipe for smoke did not provide much comfort. The two little Carrington boys were so miserably cold that they cried. Carrington's servant, Dennis, kept the stove red hot, but mercury froze in the thermometer. No real cooking was possible. The best that could be done was to thaw and slightly warm the food. For the soldiers, unprotected even by wagons, the torment was even worse. Mrs. Carrington's driver, who rode one of the mules in his team, had to be lifted from the saddle because his legs were frozen. At Fort Reno he and another man had both legs amputated. Both men died.

One morning the suffering soldiers refused to come out of their blankets in spite of repeated bugle calls. The colonel ordered their legs lashed with whips, not as punishment but to start up the circulation. Frances Grummond, six months pregnant, learned to lie on her bed of furs and quilts in the bottom of her wagon and hang on with both hands when drivers lashed the mules to a gallop during Indian scares or ascending steep hills. Her husband's coffin was in another wagon.

The party stayed at Fort Reno three days, long enough for surgery on frozen hands and feet. Most of the escort then returned to Phil Kearny with supplies. Carrington's party moved on toward his new post. At Deer Creek, that busy place where John Bozeman had recruited his first party of emigrants to go up his new trail, they found that the telegraph station had been burned by Indians. Six miles short of their destination, Fort Caspar, the drivers whipped their mules into a fast trot. Indians had just been sighted. They had run off some horses from the fort.

The journey to Fort Caspar was wasted, after all. Carrington was now required to go to Fort McPherson (near present Maxwell, Nebraska) but his orders had not reached him. So back he went, eastward. At Sage Creek, on the way to Fort Laramie, there was an Indian alarm. While Carrington was galloping to hasten the corraling of the wagons, his recently repaired revolver discharged, shooting him in the left leg. He ordered the train to go on to Fort Laramie anyway, although a return to Fort Caspar would have been quicker. He traveled lying in a litter suspended by leather straps in the ambulance.

A little joy brightened Frances Grummond's life when the column reached Bridger's Ferry. Her brother William was there, waiting for her. He had come out from Franklin, Tennessee, as soon as he read about the tragedy at Fort Phil Kearny. Frances parted from the Carringtons at Fort Laramie. With her brother she reached her old home in March. A month later Lieutenant Grummond's posthumous son was born.

CHAPTER 2

The Eager Beaver Is Discharged

Alson Ostrander's discharge papers came while he was at Fort Reno. Now he was a civilian again, He had his heart's desire: he had been a uniformed soldier in Indian country. He wanted to go on up the trail to Virginia City, then on to Portland, Oregon. But this was winter, and nobody could go even as far as Fort C. F. Smith. Nothing had been heard from that isolated post for weeks. For all anybody knew at the lower forts, the whole garrison at C. F. Smith might be dead.

Ostrander settled for a trip up to Phil Kearny with two companies of cavalry, ordered up from Fort Laramie. They left Reno February 21 with the temperature at twenty below, but Ostrander, whose luck was consistently good, rode comfortably in a wagon with the captain's dog to keep him warm. He was not, of course, the only civilian accommodated at Phil Kearny. There were dozens of them, including the great Jim Bridger, with whom he got acquainted as soon as possible. Ostrander bunked with a bunch of teamsters. He had the greatest regard for these hardy men, who not only fought Indians along with the soldiers but had, in addition, the responsibilities of looking after stock, equipment, and freight. Citizen Ostrander listened, open-mouthed, to the hair-raising stories they told. Almost every stick of timber and stone that had gone into building the fort had been obtained under fire.

Without even trying, Ostrander got a job in the office of the district quartermaster, Captain George Dandy, as a clerk at $75 a month. He paid for his meals at the Washingtons' cabin about a hundred yards outside the stockade. The sturdy frontier couple who ran this boarding house were both good shots, as they needed to be, and Mrs. Washington was a good cook. Civilian employees boarded there, and on pay days, which came whenever the paymaster was able to get to Phil Kearny, the cabin was full of hungry soldiers reveling in home cooking.

The only Indian "attack" while Ostrander was at this fort was a visit from a bunch of friendly Crows who wanted to trade. Ostrander got some fine furs in exchange for chewing tobacco bought at the sutler's store. Jim Bridger handled the trading for him. The worst scare Ostrander had at Phil Kearny came late in March when he was hunting up Little Piney Creek, a few hundred feet from the fort. He saw an Indian on a galloping horse. The Indian, naked to the waist and with his hair streaming, was covered with splashes of blood and so was his pony. But he was only a friendly Crow who had killed and dressed out a deer and carried it on his shoulders.

Ostrander never did go on to Virginia City. On April 23 he started for home, back down the Bozeman Trail in a small train of four wagons and an ambulance, escorted by twenty cavalrymen. Fifteen miles short of Fort Reno, someone sighted Indians. The train corraled in a hurry—as well as five vehicles *could* corral—and the men started shooting. The Indians—twenty-five of them—circled the embattled whites, yelling, and rode on out of sight. And that was that. Ostrander would have a real story to tell when he got home!

The garrison at Fort Reno was worried about mail. Portugee Phillips, with southbound mail, was two days overdue from Phil Kearny. Montgomery Van Valzah was even later coming up from distant Fort Laramie. He never reached Reno at all. Ostrander's party started on, expecting to meet Van Valzah, but he and his escort had made their last fight. The detachment found mail scattered over an acre of ground but no trace of the men at all. The assumption had to be that they had been captured alive and taken away to be tortured at the Indians' leisure.

Ostrander shared blankets on that trip with an old trapper known as Big Sam. The only tent in the outfit was for Major James Van Voast, in command. One night, to make sure Indians couldn't get his two saddle horses, the major staked the picket pins inside his tent—but an Indian stole the horses without waking him. The man reached inside the tent and pulled up the picket pins. What woke the camp was a shot and a shout from a sentry. Ostrander started to raise up on his hands and knees—and had his face ground into gravel and prickly pear by his alert bedmate, Big Sam, who growled, "Never get up when you hear a shot. Lie still till you can guess where it came from!"

No damage was done by Indians that night except that the major lost his horses, and that was embarrassing as well as inconvenient. Alson Ostrander had the only wound of his military career. His face was on fire with pain from sand, gravel, and cactus needles. Thereafter for some time he rode in the ambulance and wore a handkerchief over part of his face. When he reached Fort Sedgwick, someone who saw him peering out of the ambulance spread the rumor that the poor fellow had been scalped.

CHAPTER 3

The Story of the Sergeants

When fresh vegetables came to Phil Kearny, just twice before the first winter clamped down, they were admired and carefully distributed. Captain N. C. Kinney, commanding Fort C. F. Smith, sent down a few sacks of potatoes that had come from Bozeman. Most of the potatoes went to the hospital, where, in November, men were already sick with scurvy. Once the paymaster brought up half a cabbage and eleven onions, a great treat.

Food for enlisted men was unbelievably bad. Early in July of 1866, at Fort Reno, Private William Murphy had helped load supplies left there the year before by General Connor. The bacon, in slabs from three to five inches thick, was so old that the fat had commenced to sluff off from the lean. It was yellow with age and bitter as quinine. The flour even had dead mice in it. The men sifted it through an improvised sieve of burlap.

The Army had no cooks or bakers. Men cooked their own rations —or ate them raw. If a company included a man who had been a baker in civilian life, his fellows were lucky. Private Murphy's company at Phil Kearny included such a man—not that any fancy cooking resulted.

"We cooked soup, bacon and coffee and dished it out to the men in their cups and plates," he recalled. "We boiled everything. I believe the bacon would have killed the men if it had not been thoroughly boiled. As it was, it surely came near to it that winter."

Murphy volunteered to work in the kitchen for a good reason of his own. He and a sergeant had quietly bought two fresh cows from an emigrant train and made some side money by selling milk. Murphy, wise to the virtues of keeping his mouth buttoned, didn't let anyone know that he had a financial interest in the sergeant's cows. Working in the kitchen at a job nobody else wanted gave him opportunities to do the milking and take care of the milk.

By January of 1867, after the Fetterman battle, the food situation was really bad at Phil Kearny. Enlisted men and civilian employees went on half rations of bitter bacon, hardtack, and flour. If Portugee Phillips was dead somewhere in the snow, as seemed inevitable, nobody outside knew of their problem and they couldn't expect either relief or supplies until after the spring thaw. After their relief came, and Carrington's party headed southward through bitter weather, the food problem was worse than ever. The post now had more men to feed, but they had not brought additional rations.

There was, however, some corn for the mules, and Finn Burnett, citizen teamster, remembered how the slave women back in Missouri used to make hominy. Finn made lye of wood ashes and water, soaked corn in it until the husks could be rubbed loose. Soaked and rinsed in six changes of water, then fried in the fat from the stinking bacon, hominy made from the mules' corn made a welcome change in the restricted diet.

If food was short at Phil Kearny, the garrison wondered, how bad must the situation be at C. F. Smith, ninety miles farther from supplies? Lieutenant Colonel Wessells tried five times in January to get men through to that isolated post. Five times they turned back because the road was blocked by snow or they were attacked by Indians. The Bozeman Trail wound only a few miles from some of the Indian winter camps.

For four months, between November 28, 1866, and March 26, 1867, Fort C. F. Smith received no mail, no letters from home, no military dispatches, no newspapers to tell what was happening back in America. Friendly Crows did bring news of a big fight at Phil Kearny, with much slaughter on both sides. As the winter crawled by, morale was poor. Finally officers erected a bulletin board and every day someone posted clippings from old newspapers. That eased the monotony a little. Rations were low; some of the men boiled grain from the animals' feed.

But the garrison was remarkably healthy. Many men were

wounded, and frostbite was common, but an officer who wrote to the *Army and Navy Journal* from Fort C. F. Smith estimated that the number sick did not average 2 per cent. Sometimes the post hospital had not a single patient.

Wessells, at Phil Kearny, tried to persuade civilians at his post to make the journey up the trail, but none of them, not even Portugee Phillips, would undertake it for less than $1,000. In February, two sergeants volunteered. They were George Grant and Joseph Graham. They rode a few miles on mules; then a man who had accompanied them that far returned with the mules and the sergeants went on snowshoes, carrying six days' rations (hard bread and lard) on their backs.

They left Phil Kearny early February 4. Each night they cached one day's rations for probable emergency need on the return trip and left a note with it. In case they *never* came back, someone, sometime, might thus learn how far they had succeeded in going. They did get through, after much suffering and hunger, about four o'clock in the afternoon of the seventh. Four days on snowshoes. Ninety miles of misery.

The C. F. Smith garrison wasn't dead after all. The men were ravenous for tobacco, but they were alive. After resting for two days, Sergeants Grant and Graham started back the night of February 9, accompanied by a half-blood guide, Mich Bouyer. All three men were mounted, and they led two pack mules carrying mail and their provisions. About nine o'clock the next morning they found moccasin tracks around a bloody patch of snow where a buffalo had been killed. The men with their animals headed at once for the hills. Some five miles later, they stopped to let the horses blow after going up a hill—and saw fifteen Indians coming.

The horses were about done for. Grant had to shoot his mount. Bouyer let the pack mule go. Bouyer and Graham panicked, kicked up their horses, and left Grant afoot. He ran for shelter in a clump of pines some 500 yards away, but on the way the snow collapsed under him and he fell into a hole. He had been running on the edge of a precipice with a 200-foot drop beneath, but he was a lucky man. He fell ninety feet and landed on a small rock ledge. He sat down under the cliff and waited. He had his Spencer carbine, breech-loading, and eighty rounds of ammunition.

He was out of sight and out of reach but the Indians of course followed his tracks to the hole he had fallen into. He heard them yelling, and they began to throw stones down the hole. One bold Indian jumped down the hole, gripping a Henry repeating rifle. He was so startled at the sight of Grant that he yelled, dropped his gun, and backed over the ledge. Another Indian let himself down. Grant shot him and tumbled his body over the ledge.

It was nearly dark before the rest of them gave up and left. When Grant emerged, a heavy fog had come up, but he followed their tracks in the snow to the frozen Little Big Horn River. Sergeant Grant tore up enough of his overcoat, cold as the weather was, to wrap around his shoes. Then he plodded up the river on the ice.

The evening of the fourth day, Sergeant Graham and Mich Bouyer panted into Phil Kearny with the news that Grant was killed and all the horses gone. So was the outgoing mail, except one letter from Captain Kinney, in Bouyer's pocket. An hour after their breathless arrival, Sergeant Grant himself slogged in, sheathed in ice and still carrying the captured Henry rifle. Graham thought he was seeing a ghost. Grant went into the post hospital, a very sick man, suffering from pleurisy and exhaustion. But they were all right up at C. F. Smith.

A cavalry detachment left Phil Kearny June 4 for Fort C. F. Smith and returned the sixteenth—the first party to get through, except those two lion-hearted sergeants, since November 30, almost seven months. Captain Kinney returned with them. His resignation from the Army had been approved January 7, but he could not get out and his successor could not get in until June.

CHAPTER 4

The Harsh Life of a Soldier

At Phil Kearny, scurvy was a curse second only to hostile Indians. (It caused 15 per cent of the deaths during the War of the Rebellion.) By the spring of '67, *all* the men who had been at Phil Kearny since the beginning were suffering from it. Some lost teeth; some were paralyzed in the legs. When the country greened up, the "scurvy gang" was ordered out to search for and eat wild onions. Then they were ordered not to, because word came that some of the men at Fort Sedgwick had been poisoned that way. But the soldiers went right on searching for wild onions on hands and knees. They figured they might as well die fast of vegetable poison as die by inches of scurvy.[38]

The three forts got a new commanding officer that spring, Colonel John E. Smith. He was tough, but he was just. Rations were better after he came, and in general things went more smoothly. Besides, in June supplies arrived, much-needed supplies, and 700 new breech-loading Springfield rifles to take the place of the old muzzle-loaders. With the fine, fast-loading new guns came 100,000 rounds of ammunition. Some of this went on up to Fort C. F. Smith.

The men were as pleased with their new arms as if Santa Claus had come with a shower of gifts. The Springfields were single-shot guns, like the old ones, but there was no more delay in reloading, no more tamping down a charge with a long, awkward ramrod.

One important change that followed Colonel Smith's arrival was that, whereas there had been neither drill nor target practice, now there were both. (However, the soldiers at Phil Kearny, at least— right where Smith was—had had no practice at all in using their new breech-loaders before the desperate battle, early in August, that became known as the Wagon Box Fight.)

Target practice was expensive, Private William Murphy remembered sadly, "as the government charged twenty-five cents per cartridge to the men if they were short." This was a lot of money to men whose extra pay for building and other labor was only thirty-five cents a day. Their frustration, after they learned something about shooting, must have been awful. Murphy remembered that they had a couple of orders from a commanding general far away *not* to fire at an Indian unless he fired first. He assumed this was to save ammunition. Probably the real reason for the order was an official hope that Indians not shot at might tend to be peaceful.

In May, the Indians resumed their attacks on wagon trains, but now Fort Phil Kearny could afford to send escorts—at least part of the way up to C. F. Smith—of twenty soldiers instead of the seven men who were all that could be spared the summer before.

One thing did not change. Soldiers still had no first-aid training and carried no first-aid equipment. If a man was wounded while escorting a train, he could expect not even half-skilled bandaging or other action to stop bleeding. "Usually," wrote Murphy, "the wounded man was put on top of the freight wagon on the goods in it, and in the summer this was next to the wagon sheet where he would burn up from the rays of the sun, while in winter it was freezing cold. Often it would be several days before the wounded man could see a doctor."

Summer or winter, a soldier's life was hard. In 1867, Henry Morton Stanley—the Welshman who earned immortal fame four years later by saying, "Dr. Livingstone, I presume?" in darkest Africa— was a newspaper correspondent traveling on the American frontier. He reported some horrors at Fort Sedgwick, Colorado, on June 16:

> Flogging appears to be revived in the army on the plains, and citizens are shocked at some un-American scenes which have been witnessed here, and it is said that we are drifting to the time-hallowed institutions of Russia and Egypt, where the lash, the knout, the bastinado are still in vogue. . . . Within the limits of the military reservation of Fort Sedgwick, and within one mile of the fort, a soldier received twenty lashes for stealing a gun. . . . In the same week a soldier of the 30th Infantry, by orders, was laid out on the ground under a hot broiling sun, and a stake fastened at each limb, to which he was firmly bound, thus laying him out according to a mode well known to military officers, and which is entitled "spread-eagle fashion." He was left in that position for two hours; in the meantime the buffalo gnats covered his face by thousands, causing intense suffering to the unfortunate fellow. "For two hours he screamed, cried, entreated for the love of God to be let loose. For two hours he roared; I couldn't stand it any longer; I tell you, sir, his face was perfectly bunged up." Such were the words of his lieutenant to a group of officers, who expressed deep commiseration for the man's sufferings.

Stanley was present, the day before he wrote, when a sick civilian, accused of giving a bottle of whiskey to soldiers, was ordered to receive one hundred lashes as punishment. He was not tried, and nobody listened to his defense, which was that the men who wanted the whiskey were not in uniform and he didn't know they were soldiers. Stanley said he was tied to a cross, almost naked, while two men lashed him:

> Before sixteen strokes had been administered blood was welling in streams down his legs and pouring into his shoes. Blood was

splashed over some of the spectators. After the fiftieth stroke the body assumed a livid colour, and the skin hung in strips and flakes. Men stopped their ears, and turned away from the horrid sight.

If a civilian could be thus punished by the military, enlisted men couldn't hope for any better treatment. Of course a man captured by hostile Indians could expect something a whole lot worse.

Private Murphy was still bitter, when he was an old man, about the way crippled soldiers were treated when several of them were discharged at Omaha in March, 1869. They received no pension because they had not served out their time. The Army got rid of them instead of pensioning them for disability. One man, whose legs were stiff from the hips down, got drunk a few days before his enlistment time was up. He received a "bob-tail" discharge, with the section commenting on character clipped off—an indication that he was not discharged honorably.

Murphy's old bunkie, John Donovan, suffered three arrow wounds, one from a poisoned arrow that left a running sore. His application for a pension was rejected several times. He finally got $16 a month.

CHAPTER 5

The Hayfield Fight

At the beginning of August, Red Cloud's Sioux struck twice and they struck hard. This time the story was very different from that of the Fetterman fight. The palefaces won in two bitter battles.

The hay camp that supplied Fort C. F. Smith was in a great natural meadow two and a half miles from the post, three miles by rough road. The camp was set up for defense; men stationed there often repulsed four or five small, quick Indian raids in a day. The hay crew consisted of civilians employed by A. C. Leighton, who had a contract with the Army to supply hay for stock at $50 a ton. They were protected by soldiers, and all the men lived at the camp.

The morning of August 1, 1867, started out about like any other day. After breakfast, the drivers of the hay-laden wagons (with racks on them instead of wagon boxes) hitched up their mules, and the outfit went trundling down the road with its armed escort walking warily alongside.

Out in the natural hay meadow, mowing machines moved along. The men remaining in camp—one officer, eight enlisted men, and nine teamsters, as Finn Burnett later recalled—took care of their chores in a leisurely way, always with an eye out for hostiles. They aired their bedding and watered thirty-one mules. They played cards, pitched horseshoes, and talked, but not very seriously, about the party of twenty excited Crows who had ridden in a couple of nights before, warning that the Sioux were planning something big. The palefaces thought the rumor-mongering Crows were crazy.

The soldiers lounged around, estimating how many redskins they could bring down with their new breech-loading guns. A sergeant remarked that he wished the boss haymaker hadn't left so much drying grass right around camp; a fire in it would be a bad thing.

About nine o'clock Finn Burnett remarked, "The Injuns haven't paid their usual morning call yet." But they were about to do so. Shots sounded down in the valley. The mowers began to rattle toward camp with their mule teams at a gallop and Indians yelling behind them. The men in camp seized their rifles and ammunition. They glimpsed the men from a picket point on a bench some 700 yards downstream galloping toward them.

The whole valley to the northeast was a moving mass of Indians. Lieutenant Sigismund Sternberg barked orders. One was "Man the rifle pits!" But already it was too late for that. The rifle pits were three half-moon trenches *outside* the corral barrier that had been built earlier in the summer. The corral was made of heavy posts set in the earth, with a string of logs on the ground at the base, horizontal poles part way up, and the whole thing lashed with green willow branches, which had tightened as they dried. The barricade wouldn't keep arrows or bullets out, but men behind it couldn't be easily spotted by the attacking enemy. Inside this were the canvas-topped boxes from the hay wagons, the three Army tents the men slept in, and the picket line to which the mules were tied. The kitchen was just outside, at the corral's one exit, near Warrior Creek. But there was a huge barrel of drinking water inside.

The defenders threw themselves on the ground behind the big logs at the base of the barricade and started to fire as the Indians rode around outside, yelling and shooting. One Indian came racing with a torch of burning hay and tried to thrust it through the dried willow branches on the barrier fence. Zeke Colvin, a citizen who had been a captain in the Confederate Army, fired at him but the Indian was too close. The bullet struck his horse in the chest. The animal fell against the corral logs, catching his rider's foot. When the Indian got loose, Zeke shot him in the back.

Lieutenant Sternberg, a Prussian who had fought in the War of the Rebellion, had definite ideas about warfare. "Stand up, men, and fight like soldiers!" he yelled. That was the last thing he ever said. While he was standing up, setting a gallant example of how not to fight Indians, he got a fatal bullet in the head.

One soldier, caught in crossfire between two Indians, knocked over one of them but the other got him through the head while he was reloading. A teamster named Hollister was shot in the stomach. Other men cautiously carried him to the frail protection of a tent, where he remained, living but in agony, all day. Sergeant Norton yelled; he had a bad shoulder wound. Men carried him into the same tent. Too crippled to handle a rifle, he could still use his revolver. At every new attack he lurched out to fight and then was helped back into the tent.

Zeke Colvin's brother Al had been a captain in the Union Army. Perhaps on the grounds that his side had won the war, Al took command of the defenders. "We'll probably never get out of this alive," he said, "but let's give those Indians something to remember us by!" He used a sixteen-shot 44-caliber Henry rifle and he made every bullet count. The Indians gave him special attention. Finn crawled over and got him the end gate of a wagon for protection.

Still hoping to get out of this alive, the men fought valiantly against the yelling swarms of attacking Sioux. Fire became a hazard as the attackers set fire to the dried hay outside. Flames came in rolling billows with the Indians whooping behind. Fire was within twenty feet of the barricade, Private John D. Lockwood remembered, when "it stopped as though arrested by supernatural power. The flames arose to a perpendicular height of at least forty feet, made one or two undulating movements, and were extinguished with a spanking slap, like the flapping sound of a heavy canvas in a hard gale." Wind carried the smoke away from the corral into the faces of the Indians, who seized the opportunity to carry away their dead and wounded.

Shortly after noon, the enemy firing almost died away. During this lull, the water barrel was found to be empty. Some of the defenders concentrated along the south side of the enclosure, covering a water party that crawled out under the wagon at the corral gate. They made several dashes to Warrior Creek and filled the barrel without having a shot fired at them by the temporarily inactive Sioux.

And what was going on back at the post? Finn Burnett, who stayed furious about it until he died sixty-seven years later, said the post commander, Lieutenant Colonel Luther P. Bradley, couldn't have been ignorant of the battle at the corral. Captain Edward S. Hartz, commanding a wood train that day, had climbed a high point and, with field glasses, had seen the mass of Indians surrounding the hay corral. He had galloped to the fort and asked permission to go to the relief of the defenders with three or four companies of the seven at the post. But the commander, Bradley, ordered everyone into the stockade and had the gate closed.

Back at the corral, with the Indians out to lunch or in conference, the men used whatever implements they could find—such as tin plates from the kitchen outside—to dig trenches behind the foundation logs. They passed around ammunition, repaired firearms that had become clogged, and snatched a bite to eat. They fully expected to be dead by evening.

When the Indians came back, everybody started shooting again. The way Finn Burnett remembered it, there were huge heaps of dead Indians all around, but most of these had grown in his imagination during the years that passed before he told the story for publication. The living Indians kept dragging off the dead, and there was much grievous howling from the women who tended the wounded.

Finn kept feeling a tug on the seat of his pants. He had drawn those pants from the quartermaster a few days before, and they were too big for him (he was a small man), so he had hiked them around his waist and bunched the excess fabric together at the back. Now, whenever he raised himself a bit to fire, a hidden Indian marksman was shooting at, and hitting, the baggy seat of his pants without hitting Finn. He raised up enough to see gun smoke coming from behind a cottonwood stump forty yards away. He fired and got his man.

Al Colvin figured that the next attack would come from the direction of the creek. He shifted most of his force to that side, and when the Indians did attack there, they met withering fire. Then most of the Indians, except for a few snipers, rode off. Private Charles Bradley had kept asking Colvin for permission to ride to the fort for help. Now Colvin agreed. There was one horse on the picket line, unwounded; all but three mules were wounded or dead. Colvin wrote a message to Colonel Bradley at the fort while somebody saddled the horse.

If the message Al Colvin wrote was half as bitter as Finn Burnett remembered, it must have curled the commandant's mustache. Colvin reported that he had dead and wounded in the corral who must have help, because the living would have to leave after dark. Finn remembered that the note also said that if Colonel Bradley was a man, he would send relief. If he wasn't, he could go to hell where he belonged. Private Bradley leaped on his horse and set out for the fort with the note.

Eyewitnesses sometimes disagree. Finn Burnett said Private Bradley didn't know how to ride a horse but got there safely anyway. Private Lockwood attributed the soldier's success to the fact that he was an excellent rider. Colonel Bradley, when he reported the fight a few days later, didn't mention Private Bradley. He gave the impression that he hadn't even known about the fight until he sent out a lieutenant with twenty men to make sure the hay wagons could move out. Then he dispatched Captain Thomas B. Burrowes with two companies and a howitzer.

Bradley certainly had ordered the gates closed after Captain Hartz galloped to the fort to report the hayfield attack. He said it was to keep out some Indians who were molesting a wood train. Whatever his reason, it would seem that he was willing to leave the men at the hayfield to be slaughtered by the hostiles. Maybe he thought it was necessary. He was never officially reprimanded for this, but the hayfield fight was something that just wasn't discussed among officers at C. F. Smith. Captain Andrew Burt's wife, who arrived only three months later, seems not to have mentioned it in her journal, from which Merrill J. Mattes wrote *Indians, Infants and Infantry*.

Finn Burnett gave scant credit to Captain Burrowes for coming to the rescue. He said the officer commanding the foremost company halted his column and prepared to go back because of Indian snipers, but the lieutenant in charge of troops behind him told him to go ahead or else get his men out of the way.

From Finn Burnett's recollections it would seem that almost as much conflict existed between civilians and the military as between red man and white. But Burrowes did get there, at sunset, and found two men dead—Lieutenant Sternberg and a private—and three soldiers and a civilian wounded. The civilian died after surgery at the fort.

The conflict between Army versus civilians flared again when the group prepared to return to the fort. Finn was determined to save as much of his employer's property as possible (collecting reparations from the government took years), but Burrowes was determined to move out of there. Finn said Al Colvin drawled: "If you're afraid to stay here long enough for Burnett to pack up Leighton's property, you'd better take your outfit and go on without us. We've fought Indians all day, and I guess we could fight our way back to the fort without you."

The Indians did destroy everything left behind and hacked the wounded mules to death. The defenders won that battle, though. The Crows reported that there was much mourning in the hostile camps. If there had been as many dead Indians as Finn remembered, they would have been stacked up ten feet high.

CHAPTER 6

The Wagon Box Fight

The crew of civilian woodcutters and their military escort working a few miles from Fort Phil Kearny were a little jumpy the morning of August 2. That was C Company's first day out there; they had marched to the woodcutters' main camp the night before to relieve A Company, which had been on duty for a month. C Company's commanding officer was Captain James W. Powell. That morning when a picket detail came off duty, Sergeant McQuiery asked whether they had seen any Indians. One of the men replied, "No, but we thought we could smell them."

The sergeant snorted, "Smell, hell!" Just the same, Private Jack McDonough's dog had smelled something that night. The sentries, one at each end of the corral, said he kept making mad dashes down toward the Big Piney Valley, barking furiously. The men had seen nothing. They had orders to fire on anything that looked suspicious.

The civilian contractor had set up two camps when he started cutting timber for the post. One was on Piney Island at the foot of the mountains. The main camp was across Big Piney Fork from it, six miles west of the fort on a level plain. A crude corral to keep the stock together at night had been made there by taking the boxes off fourteen wagons and forming them into an oval enclosure. Tents for the woodcutters and the guard detail were pitched just outside. Every man was instructed, in case of attack, to get to that corral and defend it until the fort sent out relief.

While the men had breakfast, two men remained on picket around the corral. When the sun came up, there wasn't a sign of an Indian anywhere—but they were watching in the hills all around. Right after breakfast, one train of wagons with a detachment of twenty men, including a lieutenant and a corporal, headed for the fort with logs that had been brought out of the pinery the day before. A second train pulled out for the lower pinery with a thirteen-man escort.

Before seven o'clock, Private Samuel Gibson, age eighteen, was detailed to take two other privates and relieve the picket on the Little Piney. Gibson fixed up a sunshade of willow branches stuck in the ground with a poncho over the tops. He and Private Deming were lounging under this—sensibly enough, because they had been on guard duty all night—when Private Garrett yelled, "Indians!"

The other two leaped up and, off to the west, counted seven yelling Indians, riding single file at a dead run. They weren't coming straight toward the picket post but at an angle. The defenders had their fine new breech-loading 50-caliber rifles, but not a man in the company had yet fired one. Gibson set his sights for 700 yards, steadied his new gun on a stone breastwork, and fired at the Indian in front. His bullet ricocheted off a stone and wounded the pony. The Indian was thrown off but sprang up and was taken up behind another warrior.

The soldiers looked around and saw more Indians than they had ever laid eyes on before. Deming gasped, "My God! There's thousands of 'em!" Shots sounded from the smaller wood-choppers' camp, and Gibson sent Deming to see what was going on there. He told Garrett to watch for signals from the main corral. Should they return or shouldn't they? Indians were coming across the foothills like a swarm of bees.

Deming soon came back to report that Indians had run off the stock and all the men had run for the mountains except one civilian herder who was coming toward the picket post, leading his pony. They could see a commotion in the main camp—men running here and there. No signal came for the picket to come in, but Gibson decided to start for the corral anyway and, if Indians took after them, they would take turns stopping to whirl and fire a couple of shots. Gibson went last. They started at a brisk walk, but Indians cropped up from the creek bottom in several places. Gibson fired at one, knocked him off his pony, and heard his answering shot whiz by.

Garrett stopped, down on one knee to fire. Gibson ran past him and saw Deming also shooting. The herder who had joined them couldn't make his pony move fast enough; he wanted Gibson to encourage it with a bayonet point. But the Indians seemed to be rising out of the ground like a flock of birds. Gibson told him to let his pony go. The men remembered vividly the mutilated bodies they had helped piece together and bury after the Fetterman fight. They all broke into a run, including the pony, which by now had half a dozen arrows in its flanks.

Sergeant Max Littman ran out a hundred yards from the corral and dropped on one knee. Littman could certainly shoot, and he had the heart of a lion. He knocked several Indians off their horses and saved the four men's lives.[39] They almost fell between the wagons, exhausted. Gibson reported to Captain Powell, panting apologies for leaving the picket post without orders. Powell told him, "You've done nobly! You couldn't have done better. Men, find a place in the wagon boxes. You'll have to fight for your lives!" Grateful for plenty of ammunition and the new rifles, they got into the wagon boxes and started shooting. The heaviest of the planks that protected them was no more than an inch thick, but the men could at least duck out of sight.

Private Tommy Doyle piled up some neck yokes for oxen to make a breastwork between wagon boxes. Gibson saw three or four of his comrades taking the shoestrings out of their shoes; he did the same, knowing their purpose. With the strings tied together, a loop over one end to fit over a foot, and a smaller loop for the trigger, a man could use his rifle for suicide—and would, rather than face capture and torture.

Hundreds of Indians were in sight, riding their best war ponies, chanting and yelling. Captain Powell yelled, "Men, here they come! Take your places and shoot to kill!" He didn't need to say any more. The whole plain was alive with Indians, riding and shooting with guns or bows.

In a few minutes, the Indians got a surprise. A bunch of them rode in close and waited for the embattled soldiers to pause between shots to reload with ramrods. But the Springfields didn't require any such delay. Throw open the breechblock to eject the empty shell, slap in a new one—and boom! The Indians on their ponies came and fell, and more of them came. The tops of the wagon boxes were slivered with bullets and iron-tipped arrows. Gibson, remembering that terrible day in a quieter time long later, said:

> After recovering a great number of their dead and wounded at a fearful sacrifice of life, the Indians withdrew to a safe distance, but while recovering their injured we witnessed the most magnificent display of horsemanship imaginable. Two mounted Indians would ride like the wind among the dead and wounded, and seeing an arm or leg thrust upward, would ride one on each side of the wounded savage, reach over and pick him up on the run, and carry him to a place of safety. This was done many times, and we could not help but admire their courage and daring.

The attack slowed for a few minutes. The beleaguered white men crawled to get more ammunition. None of them said a word. The silence in the wagon corral was awesome.

Gibson, back behind his barricade, watched First Lieutenant John C. Jenness fire earnestly at some partially concealed Indians. He heard Sergeant McQuiery—the one who said "Smell, hell!"—ask in a whisper whether anyone was wounded or killed. Nobody near him knew. The men inside the corral watched red-skinned couriers riding like mad; they saw the flash of pocket mirrors as their enemies signaled. As they waited for another attack, the August sun beat down on the soldiers' bare heads, for their caps were on the ground beside them, holding ammunition.

As the Indians made another rush, someone yelled, "The tents!" Men ran to tear them down. The tents were no protection and they hindered vision. The whole plain swarmed with Indians moving in for another charge. Now the barrels of the fine new guns in the corral were overheating; they burned the men's busy hands. In a lull, Gibson crawled again for ammunition—and saw Lieutenant Jenness lying dead.[40] Word was passed that two privates were dead, too. One of them had been shooting steadily for two hours, although a wound in his shoulder had left his left arm useless. A bullet in the head finished him.

Sergeant Littman waited his chance, and when it came, crawled over to where Lieutenant Jenness lay and tried to move a dead mule to protect the body from further bullets. He failed, so he went back to his steady firing.

Now thirst had become an enemy, and so had choking smoke. Arrows tipped with burning pitch rained in, setting fire to scattered hay and dried manure. Gibson and Johnny Grady crawled across to two big camp kettles into which the company cook had put used coffee grounds, with water on them, to make coffee for a meal that might never be cooked. The other men kept up a steady fire to protect them. A bullet tore through one kettle, but the black, dirty water remaining, divided among the defenders, relieved thirst.

The men were sure they knew who was commanding the innumerable force that opposed them—Red Cloud himself, who had promised to keep the palefaces off the Bozeman Road. The firing went on, and the wild yelling and the charges. In midafternoon there was a new sound, the sound of many voices below in the Big Piney Valley. It was a humming—or was it a chant? It came from hundreds of Indians swarming up a ravine in a wedge-shaped formation. The white men fired at the leader, Red Cloud's nephew (they learned later), resplendent in a gorgeous war bonnet. He fell. The rest came on, no matter how many fell.

They came so close that the defenders could see the whites of their eyes—but suddenly they broke and ran. There was a new sound, the welcome boom of a field howitzer! One of the men screamed, "Here they come! Hurray!" They could see the McClellan caps as the long skirmish line moved in. They yelled and laughed and cried and hugged one another. The splendid boom of the big gun, the gun the Indians feared, was music in the smoky air. Behind the skirmish line marched the main body of troops from the fort, then the big brass howitzer pulled by mules, then the train of ten or a dozen six-mule teams pulling ambulances and empty wagons.

Captain Powell ordered, "Get back in the wagon beds!" But the redskins were scattering, getting out of range of the howitzer. Major Benjamin F. Smith was in command of the rescue party. The post surgeon, Dr. Samuel M. Horton, came along. When they were a couple of hundred yards away, the men who had expected to die ran out to meet their comrades, to yell, to shake hands. Dr. Horton, bless him, had even brought a small keg of whiskey so that the survivors could have a drink.

And when everything was finished, the prudent men who had prepared for suicide threaded their shoelaces back in their shoes. The battle had begun at about half past seven and ended early in the afternoon. Sergeant Littman said the men could not have held out for another half hour.

Private Gibson, who became a sergeant, served forty-eight years in the Army. He was on active duty in the Sioux campaign of 1876 and in the Wounded Knee campaign of 1890–1891 which broke the spirits of the Sioux forever, but he never again went through such an ordeal as the fight against Red Cloud's warriors in the wagon-box corral. In 1908, he and Littman got together in St. Louis and peacefully fought the Wagon Box battle all over again.

Fort Phil Kearny's official post return showed six soldiers killed (three of them apparently not at the corral) and two wounded. Counting four civilians who managed to reach the corral just before the fight started, the defending force consisted of thirty-two men. The attackers numbered anywhere between 1,500 and 3,000, and their leader was Red Cloud himself. The jubilant survivors believed they killed hundreds.

CHAPTER 7

One Man's Solution
to the Indian Problem

What did the men of the garrisons think about the value of the job to which they had been assigned? Lieutenant Alexander Wishart got a load off his chest now and then by writing a letter to his home town newspaper, the Washington (Pennsylvania) *Review and Examiner.* His name did not appear, but the publishers spoke of him as "our correspondent at Fort Phil Kearny, Dakota." Here are parts of his letter dated August 5, 1867, and published in the issue of September 4:

> After a careful survey of things as they are, here, and as far as Fort C. F. Smith, (from a trip to which I have just returned) and with full conversations with both officers and citizens with whom I have mingled, I am prepared to say that it is almost the unanimous opinion that the Indian Bureau should be consolidated or else abandoned, or that more troops should be sent out to make a success of the ostensible task for which we are here.

He pointed out an "immence swindle"—Indian commissioners and Indian traders, and nobody else, were appointed to trade with the Indians at the forts. Enough troops to protect them, but not the travelers on the trail, were provided.

> That the road is not kept open all who have been on it lately know full well. No train can be sent along it without from two to three companies of soldiers, one of which is generally a Cavalry company, and one piece of artillery, and at the present time the safety of Government trains, even with these large escorts, is considered questionable. It is true a few citizens bound for the gold region are protected on their way as far as Fort Smith, beyond which point, after crossing the Big Horn and reaching the Gallatin Valley,

they are considered comparatively safe; but these trains only come along the road semi-occasionally, and the consequence is that nearly all the miners take the Salt Lake Route....

Now, if the Bureau of Indian Affairs were abolished, and the whole trouble turned over to the War Department, we are satisfied that there is sufficient vigor in that quarter to accomplish some result; or if but comparatively few regiments of frontier men were formed, (which could be easily done) and allowed to clear the country, (if extermination should be determined upon) the whole trouble would end in a shorter time and with far less expense, even if a bonus were paid for scalps, than it can possibly otherwise be done.

As to the necessity of the consolidation, or else the abandonment of the two extreme posts, but little explanation will be necessary to satisfy any intelligent man, unless it may be one who is blinded by the hope of filthy lucre, at the expense of the Government, the Indian, or the soldier.

Phil Kearny, he reported, had five companies of infantry and one of cavalry, not quite 400 men. C. F. Smith had about 325 infantry. So many details were required for wood trains, garrison, picket, extra duty, and police duty that hardly enough were left to hold the posts in case of attack. But at Phil Kearny guards were no longer needed to protect hay crews—the Indians had burned all the grass for miles around, up to 200 yards from the stockade, and were now trying to starve the stock at C. F. Smith the same way. He added:

On Friday last, on the return of a government train, which had gone up to C. F. Smith with supplies, and with which I was, about 20 or 25 miles from this post [Fort Phil Kearny] we commenced to discover the late presence of large bodies of Indians on "the war path," and so recently had they been there, that the grass for acres around was still burning.... About twelve miles out we were horrified to find amidst the burnt and burning grass a white man's scalp fastened to a pole erected near the road, and, near by, a hat the only remnants of some poor unfortunate who had fallen into the hands of the blood-thirsty savages. Further along we found dead cattle, logchains, etc. which satisfied us at once that the wood party had been attacked, and looking forward toward our destination, we saw immense columns of smoke, which led us to believe that the garrison itself had been destroyed.

The garrison had not, but Lieutenant Wishart's party had arrived just after the Wagon Box Fight. The moral was, he maintained, that the two upper posts must either be consolidated or abandoned—or more troops sent to both. The government must either prosecute the war vigorously or give up to the Indians the hunting grounds for which they were fighting so desperately.

He wrote again August 30, from the pinery near Fort Phil Kearny; his letter was published October 30.

> ...As you will perceive by the date of this letter, we are now occupying the ground which was the scene of the terrible struggle of the 2nd inst. Before that time it was thought that Indians did not care about oxen, and therefore but small parties were sent out here to guard the men who supply the Post with lumber; but as they succeeded at that time in driving off about 250 cattle, and carrying with them yokes and log chains in abundance, the policy has changed, and two companies with a piece of artillery are now thought a small enough "wood-party."

After the Wagon Box Fight the defensive corral had been strengthened. Wagon boxes had been placed in a circle with earth thrown against the outside, and then a ditch was dug outside that. They gave their miniature fort a name: Dreadnaught. When he wrote, Lieutenant Wishart had been on duty at Fort Dreadnaught since August 5. Indians had been approaching in groups ranging from two to two hundred but had not attacked. Their visits did, however, break the monotony of life at the pinery, where officers and enlisted men stationed for a month at a time longed for the relative graciousness of life at Fort Phil Kearny.

CHAPTER 8

Ordered to Fort C. F. Smith

Army wives—Margaret Carrington and Frances Grummond, for example—who accompanied their husbands to the Bozeman Trail forts marched into unknown perils with their chins up. For those who came later the prospects were even more terrifying, because the danger was better understood.

Captain Andrew S. Burt and his family were at a good duty post, Fort Bridger, in southwestern Wyoming, when rumors came, just after Christmas of 1866, about a great Indian victory at Fort Phil Kearny.

They couldn't believe the wild tales that sped over the mountains by the mysterious "moccasin telegraph" and were delivered in broken English or through interpreters by friendly Indians who came to trade at the sutler's store. But the rumors were true. Some of the men who had been cut to pieces in that horror were old comrades of Andy Burt. The Burts, when they went to Fort Bridger, had traveled part way with Colonel Carrington.

On top of the confirmation that made the rumor into fact came another shock: Major Burt was ordered to Fort C. F. Smith, even farther into the wilderness than Fort Phil Kearny. Should his family go with him? Sensible people said no. Elizabeth Burt was pregnant and sick. She *should* take little Andrew Gano, four years old, and her sister, Kate Reynolds, and the cook, Maggie, back home to Ohio. But travel, apart from military wagon trains, was dreadfully expensive. If she went home to her mother she might not see her husband again for years. She resolved to accompany him.

They left Fort Bridger in June with a military wagon train. The family cow, Susie, was shod for the trip. A flock of chickens—a rooster and his harem of twelve hens—clucked and inquired in a coop fastened to the back of a wagon. They arrived at Fort Sanders early in July and settled down temporarily in the fort's blockhouse, with two cannons in their dining room. Here Elizabeth Burt took into her family a girl of twelve, Christina, whose parents had more children than they could feed and clothe. Christina, with careful training, might be helpful in homemaking under the hard conditions of life at a frontier fort.

In August, at Fort Sanders, the Burts' second child, Edith, was born. Three weeks later, Major Burt was ordered to Omaha to take charge of recruits destined for the Bozeman Trail forts. His wife was not well enough to travel then, but in October she and Kate packed up the family, the two servants, and the livestock for another move. They rejoined Major Burt at Fort D. A. Russell en route to his new post at C. F. Smith.

In November they reached a new fort, named for Captain Fetterman, whose bull-headed conduct had been fatal to himself and eighty other men the previous December. Fort Fetterman was under construction on the south bank of the North Platte at the point where Carrington's Overland Circus had turned north a year before. Lieutenant Colonel Wessells, in command there, lived in a dugout cut into the river bank. Other officers lived in tents. Here was scant comfort for the travel-weary Burts. And to top off this disappointment, Maggie the cook quit and could not, by any argument, be persuaded to go any farther. She simply kept saying, "Too many Indians."

After leaving new Fort Fetterman, Major Burt had the other wagons of the train corraled around his family's wagon every night, with the tongues pointing inward. The mules, after grazing, were driven in and each team tied to the tongue of the wagon to which it belonged. Burt had been warned (but he didn't worry his wife with the information) that Indians were watching closely. Crazy Woman Crossing, where so many victims of the redskins were buried, was still the Indians' favorite place to attack. And they did.

They struck shortly after midnight. The bell mare's bell clanged as the mules followed her into the corral at a run, hastened by a yelling guard. Indians whooped. Rifles cracked. Mrs. Burt's heart almost stopped—for little Andrew Gano was sleeping in his father's tent *outside* the corral. But the party's surgeon, Dr. J. H. Frantz, appeared at the door of Mrs. Burt's wagon, carrying the little boy, and assured her that everything was all right. The redskins hadn't got the mules.

Shooting continued. Mrs. Burt and her sister lay flat on their mattress on the floor, hugging the children, protecting them with their bodies, until the captain came to assure them that nobody was hurt and there was no danger of another attack. Then Mrs. Burt cried a little.

The Burt party camped near Phil Kearny on arrival November 17; Mrs. Burt met the officers' ladies and was delighted with a dinner served by the quartermaster's wife, with real linen and pretty china—a big change from the meals they had in camp. At this stop the Burts learned the awful details of the Fetterman fight; they heard the stories of heroism at the Wagon Box battle, less than four months earlier. Mrs. Burt began to think maybe she shouldn't have come, after all. Not just one but two generals had tried to dissuade her.

The Burts left Phil Kearny November 21, and the second day out suffered another Indian scare. But these were not hostiles; they were too-friendly Crows. The encounter was not altogether pleasant. After the Indian women made a great, admiring fuss over baby Edith, Chief Crazy Head tried to buy her! In sign talk he offered twenty ponies. When the child's astonished father refused, the chief raised the bid to thirty. No! Then he offered his own squaw. No, no, NO. From that time on, Elizabeth Burt had the possibility of kidnapping to think about.

The evening of the fourth day out from Phil Kearny they camped for the last time. Next morning they marched into C. F. Smith at the end of a journey of almost two months. Captain Burt was warmly congratulated: he hadn't lost a man, a mule, or a wagon.

CHAPTER 9

The Mysterious End of Meagher

Governor Smith went east on January 7, 1867, and Meagher of the Sword was again Acting Governor, with all the personal problems he had had before. Republicans with influence in Washington detested him, and he returned the compliment. The Vigilantes had threatened him. The editor of the *Montana Post* had humiliated him.

Along with all this, a public problem plagued him. Many Montanans were worried to death about Indians. News of the December attacks down at Phil Kearny seeped into the Territory and lost nothing in the telling. Rumor said that Red Cloud's fighting Sioux would be out in force as soon as the grass would sustain their ponies, that Red Cloud was going to drive all the white settlers out of the Gallatin Valley. Newspapers shrieked. The *Helena Herald* complained with polysyllabic profundity about the way the Department of Interior was handling Indians. An editorial in the January 10 issue said:

> Nothing can be more sickening and unsatisfactory to the intelligent pioneer and settler in our great west, than the sentiment and

recommendations promulgated from year to year by our Commissioner at Washington, still adhering to the fallatial [*sic*] policy of the government on the question of Indian affairs. . . .

The year 1866 will be memorable as one in which the roadways and trails of the unoffending pioneer and emigrant were continuously marked by more fresh-made graves—the victims of the tomahawk and scalping knife in the hands of merciless savages—than any former season since the discovery of California!

The year 1866 will be memorable as one in which a large number of farcical, compromising, degrading and dangerous compacts were entered into between brazen robbers of the government annuities, and the outlaws, renegades and bribed halfbreeds from the various bands of offending Indians. . . .

Revenge—extermination; a rigid enforcement of grape, shrapnel, canister, fire, sword and bayonet, is the only treatment we can recommend for those untamable, treacherous, savage fiends of earth.

John Bozeman wrote a letter to Acting Governor Meagher; anyway he signed it. Bozeman was literate, but barely. The letter, dated March 25 at Bozeman City, went this way:

General:—I take the responsibility of writing you a few lines for the benefit of the people of Montana. We have reliable reports here that we are in imminent danger of hostile Indians, and if there is not something done to protect this valley soon, there will be but few men and no families left in the Gallatin Valley. Men, women and children are making preparations to leave at an early day. If you can make arrangements to protect them, they will stay; if not, the valley will doubtless be evacuated.

Now "the Acting One" had a solid foundation for demanding help from the Army. He telegraphed General U. S. Grant that danger was imminent. Until regular troops on the Yellowstone were reinforced, could he please raise a thousand volunteers to be paid for by the Federal government?

Grant thought maybe there really was some danger, but volunteers should take care of it in self-defense. They should expect to be paid later by the government if their services warranted it. So iffy a proposal as that held no attraction for most of Montana's population. They were all gamblers, after a fashion, or they wouldn't have been there, but who would gamble on getting back his bare expenses in return for doing something so dangerous when there were no Indians in sight of the cabin where *he* lived?

Most of them had been soldiers in one army or the other, and now a dream had come true: as civilians, they were perfectly safe in saying no to a general. By keeping silent, they said no to General and Acting Governor Meagher.

The *Helena Herald* in its April 4 issue had a story about T. W. Cover—one of the lucky discoverers of Alder Gulch, now prospering with a flour mill at Bozeman and other enterprises. The paper said:

> Mr. Cover contemplates starting soon on a tour to the military posts along the Yellow Stone and as far as Fort Phil Kearny; to lay before the commandants of those garrisons the situation of the Gallatin and other settlements, to secure, if possible, the co-operation of the troops, and to arrange with those commands terms upon which the Gallatin settlements may supply them with flour, grain and beef, to the advantage of the government as well as relief to the settlers.
>
> He will make it a part of his mission also to visit the Crow Indians who have applied to be located near the Gallatin Valley and inform them that the whites at those settlements do not want them to come, that they (the whites) are preparing for war, and that as they cannot discriminate on sight, between a friendly and a hostile Indian, they will be obliged for their safety to treat all as *hostile*, and make war upon any and all that appear in the settlements, until these difficulties shall have been permanently settled.

Tom Cover did indeed set out on his mission of selling supplies to the government. His companion on the journey was John M. Bozeman. They found that it was true that they couldn't tell a friendly Crow from a hostile of any tribe. What happened became known, as rumors spread, as the Bozeman Massacre, which sounded as if the whole settlement that bore his name had been exterminated in a murderous raid. Actually, only two men were killed, John Bozeman and an anonymous Blackfeet Indian. But *everybody* had heard of John Bozeman. If a famous man like that got killed, it could happen to anybody.

Tom Cover took pen in hand on April 22 and wrote a letter to General Meagher. The *Montana Post* published it May 4:

General T. F. Meagher, Virginia City
   Sir:—On the 16th inst., accompanied by the late J. M. Bozeman, I started for Forts C. F. Smith and Phil Kearny. After a day or so of arduous travel, we reached the Yellowstone River and journeyed on

in safety until the 20th inst., when, in our noon camp on the Yellowstone, about seven miles this side of the Bozeman Ferry, we perceived five Indians approaching us, on foot, and leading a pony.

When within, say 250 yards, I suggested to Mr. Bozeman that we should open fire, to which he made no reply. We stood with our rifles ready until the enemy approached to within 100 yards, at which time B. remarked: "Those are Crows, I know one of them. We will let them come up to us, and learn where the Sioux and Blackfeet camps are, provided they know."

The Indians meanwhile walking toward us with their hands up, calling "Ap-sar-ake," (Crow.) They shook hands with B. and proffered the same politeness to me, which I declined by presenting my Henry at them, and at the same moment B. remarked, "I am fooled —these are Blackfeet. We may, however, get off without trouble." I then went to our horses (leaving my gun with B.) and had saddled mine, when I saw the chief quickly draw the cover from his fusee, and as I called to B. to shoot, the Indian fired, the ball taking effect in B.'s right breast, passing completely through him. B. charged on the Indian but did not fire, when another shot took effect in the left breast, brought poor B. to the ground, a dead man. At that instant I received a bullet through the upper edge of my left shoulder.

I ran to B., picked up my gun, and spoke to him, asking if he was badly hurt. Poor fellow, his last words had been spoken some minutes before I reached the spot; he was "stone dead."

Finding the Indians pressing me, and my gun not working, I stepped back slowly, trying to fix it, in which I succeeded, after retreating, say fifty paces. I then opened fire, and the first shot brought one of the gentlemen to the sod. I then charged and the other two took to their heels, joining the two that had been saddling B.'s animal and our pack horse, immediately after B.'s fall.

Having an idea that when collected they might make a rush, I returned to a piece of willow brush, say 400 yards from the scene of action, giving the Indians a shot or two as I fell back. I remained in the willows about an hour, when I saw the enemy cross the river, carrying their dead comrade with them. On returning to the camp to examine B., I found, but too surely, that the poor fellow was out of all earthly trouble. The red men, however, had been in too much of a hurry to scalp him, or even take his watch—the latter I brought in.

After cutting a pound or so of meat, I started on foot on the back track, swam the Yellowstone, (a cool bath) walked thirty miles, and came upon McKenzie and Reshaw's camp, very well satisfied to be so far on the road home and in tolerable safe quarters. The next day

I arrived home with a tolerably sore shoulder and pretty well fagged out. A party started out yesterday (Sunday) to bring in B.'s remains.

From what I can glean in the way of information, I am satisfied that there is a large party of Blackfeet on the Yellowstone, whose sole object is plunder and scalps.

Yours etc., T. W. Cover

Gallatin Mills,
Bozeman, April 22, 1867

The *Helena Herald* roared this long headline for its big story May 2:

Killing of Col. Bozeman and Wounding of Thomas Cover by the Blackfeet Indians! The panic among the Gallatin settlers! Their apprehensions of a general attack upon their homes! Their appeal to Gov. Meagher and the people of the Territory! Prompt and friendly response by the Governor, and Minute Men called for to meet the emergency! The people of Madison County rallying! 300 men from Edgerton, and 100 from Deer Lodge wanted! Let these counties do their whole duty!

The *Herald* issued a clarion call:

War Meeting at the Court House! 300 mounted men wanted from Edgerton County to march out to the defense of the Gallatin settlements! Rally! Rally!! Everybody!!!

Meagher shouted for volunteers, 600 of them to serve for three months. He got a few, but no supplies from storekeepers. The Territory's credit standing was not encouraging, and who could promise that the Federal treasury would ever pay the bills?

And the town of Bozeman had *not* been attacked by marauding Indians. John Bozeman and Tom Cover had been fifty-five miles from home, on the way to the Bozeman Trail forts to get a government contract for the sale of flour and vegetables. A Helena man named Nowland wrote to General Sherman in St. Louis, giving this information and suggesting that the two salesmen had been pretty rash when they set out with no protection but their own rifles.

Sherman decided the situation did not require him to use his authority to call out volunteers. But Acting Governor Meagher telegraphed the Secretary of War about "citizens murdered," urging authorization to recruit 800 volunteers. There wasn't an hour to be lost, he cried. He bombarded Washington with frantic telegrams.

On May 7 Sherman telegraphed Meagher: "If Indians enter the

valley of the Gallatin, organize 800 volunteers and drive them out. These troops should be used only till the regulars reach the Yellowstone."

By the time the message was published in the *Montana Post*, it authorized Meagher to organize the militia if Indians *threatened* the Gallatin. More demands, more telegrams. Murders and depredations were being committed daily, Meagher warned Sherman.

General Sherman finally told Meagher to stop telegraphing collect. But he did authorize 800 volunteers for two months, to furnish their own horses, at 40¢ a day. That might look like money to a private in the Regulars, but in the gold camps it wouldn't even buy tobacco.

Major William H. Lewis, who was ordered up from Salt Lake to take charge, interpreted one of Sherman's messages as permission to go ahead at the Federal government's expense. The merchants were glad to interpret it that way too. They supplied the unenthusiastic volunteers with everything from horses to whiskey, all on tick to Uncle Sam. Meagher busily issued vouchers to pay for horses and immense amounts of supplies. He did not live to find out that the Territory's debt for all this came to $1,100,000 and that it was not honored until five years later, when Congress unwillingly paid the clamoring creditors at fifty cents on the dollar.

The general caliber of the Montana militia was nothing to brag about. Thomas H. Leforge, who was a member, described his brief military experience in *Memoirs of a White Crow Indian*. Leforge joined up for ninety days when he was not yet eighteen, but two men who were recruiting said his age didn't matter. Leforge's outfit had only their own firearms and clothing, scant food, no shelter and no horses. Leforge's company mutinied a day or two after he was inducted, refusing to leave their temporary camp and head for the Yellowstone River, where the hostiles were. General Meagher ordered the whole company arrested and brought before him.

When Meagher started to lecture them, a man known as Chris leveled a rifle at him and said they had heard enough. The unruly militiamen of the other companies yelled, "We're with you, boys!" General Meagher had to cut his lecture short.

Most of the men, Leforge recalled, were ex-ruffians from the Missouri-Kansas border. One company drowned its first captain by roping him and dragging him back and forth through a river. The Chris who had threatened Meagher later got drunk and stabbed a man named Spencer. Chris was court-martialed and acquitted. Leforge's own captain quit in disgust, and so did most of the men in that company. Deserters simply scattered.

After the first lot melted away, a second bunch of militiamen were recruited and enlisted for four months. They built barracks and some other buildings at present Livingston. The Montana Volunteers numbered between 150 and 250 men, and they didn't fight any Indians. All they really accomplished was the death of three Indians, two shot and one hanged, all for stealing horses. Cleaning out these dangerous hostiles cost close to $375,000 per hostile.

But this cost accounting was in the future when Thomas Francis Meagher rode into Fort Benton on July 1, 1867, with a few of his Volunteer officers, to take delivery of the promised muskets that were coming upriver by steamboat. His lucky star did seem to be shining again. Governor Smith was back, had just arrived at Fort Benton, so Meagher was no longer Acting Governor, but he had his Volunteers (and he loved to command troops), and the government had grudgingly shipped 130 muskets. Furthermore, his wife was coming upriver after a visit of almost half a year to her father in New York.

Meagher had been ailing for a week with "summer complaint." He spent part of the day—the last day of his life—in the back room of a trading post and drank three glasses of blackberry wine as medicine. Two men who knew him well enough to be surprised that he wasn't taking anything stronger noted that he turned down many invitations to have a drink. One of these men was Wilbur Fisk Sanders, who noticed that he was nervous and concluded later that he was deranged.

John T. Doran, pilot of the *G. A. Thompson*, who invited him to noon dinner on board, also noted that he was nervous and jumpy. Meagher exclaimed, "Johnny, they threaten my life in that town! As I passed I heard some men say, 'There he goes!' Are you armed?" Doran showed him two pistols. Meagher gave them back.

About half past nine, Doran put the agitated Meagher to bed in his own stateroom on the *G. A. Thompson* and promised to return. Shortly thereafter a sentry saw someone in white underwear moving near the "temporary accommodation place" of the vessel and, to save the distinguished guest embarrassment, turned his back. Then he heard a shout and a splash. He whirled and yelled "Man overboard!"

Men ran, shouted, threw out ropes, searched, but Thomas Francis Meagher was seen no more. Mrs. Meagher arrived a few days later and waited pitifully for two months, hoping that someone would report finding his body. Then she went back home to her father. To this day, nobody knows whether Meagher fell, jumped, or was pushed.

CHAPTER 10

The Long, Long Trip Upriver

Wilbur Fisk Sanders' family could afford to travel, and they could have the best in transportation. The best, when they went to Bannack in 1863, was a well-fitted wagon train plodding across the Plains and through the mountains of Idaho. When they went home to Ohio for a visit in February of 1866, the best way to go was by sleigh and coach to Atchison, Kansas, and then by train.

Coach travel was not easy, but Harriet Sanders was happily surprised at how good her two little boys were. The family left their home in Virginia City on February 21, and except for a brief stop in Salt Lake City, they traveled night and day, sleeping on the floor in blankets and fur robes. They took the train at Atchison on March 14.

Returning to Montana, slightly more than a year later, was a different matter. This time Mrs. Sanders' mother was along, as well as a nephew, Eddie. Because her mother was in the party, the family traveled this time the easy way, by Missouri River steamboat—but how appallingly slow and tedious it was! [41]

They boarded the *Abeona* at St. Joe, Missouri, April 24. The next day was Harriet Sanders' thirty-third birthday. On April 30 they reached Omaha, went up town, and did some shopping. Then Colonel Sanders bade them good-by and went back to St. Joe by train and thence to Montana the fast way, by coach. He had been away from his business affairs long enough.

River travel was exasperating, even to the placid Mrs. Sanders.

The paddle wheel broke and the boat waited for repairs. There were races, with steamboats sometimes sideswiping. On May 5, Mrs. Sanders noted in her journal that they had gone 100 miles in five days. They passed one boat on a sand bar, another with a burst steampipe, then three more aground at Bonhomme Island. The *Abeona* cruised cautiously on the other side of the island, where the river was six inches deeper, but it took all one day for the men to pull the boat three times its own length over sand bars. The *Abeona* got into a fine four feet of water—and then ran out of wood for the boiler, so the men went ashore to get some.

The average steamboat burned about thirty cords of cottonwood in twenty-four hours of travel. Below Fort Randall there were wood yards aplenty, but above that place they were scarce. The hardy men who dared cut firewood for sale to hungry steamboats could get $8 a cord for it—if they lived. In 1868 alone, seven of these wood hawks were killed by Indians between Fort Benton and the downriver settlements.

On May 13, Harriet Sanders wrote: "We passed the Yankton Agency at ten this A.M. and Fort Randall at five P.M. Mailed a despatch to Mr. Sanders. Any number of Indians all along the bank today and Indian graves in the air." Next day the boat tied up most of the day because of wind and made only ten miles.

On the fifteenth, Mrs. Sanders mentioned, not for the first time, that "we are making very poor time" and commented wistfully that "Mr. Sanders is in Virginia City tonight I think." (He wasn't. He didn't get there until May 31, but he made it several weeks before his family did.)

Day after day there were delays because of sand bars, broken rudders, a burnt-through boiler. Delays were maddening, because high water was required if a boat were to reach Fort Benton, and it might start falling at any moment. The boat was tied up for repairs from May 23 until May 26, when they made twenty-five miles. Two days later there was "Alarm of Indians, they have attacked two boats, and killed one man." With four other boats, the *Abeona* was tied up while the crew tried to find the channel—and the river was falling.

They tied up for fog, for wind, for shallow water, for wood. June 2 they stopped briefly at Fort Rice, which had been attacked by Indians three weeks before. There was much visiting back and forth between boats tied up or boats moving slowly. On June 5 Mrs.

Sanders noted a social call from a party of gentlemen passengers from the *Octavia,* including Green Clay Smith, Governor of Montana, who was on his way back from a trip to Washington.

Now they kept meeting boats that had reached Fort Benton and turned around. The upper Missouri was no lonely road. Traffic on it was tremendous in 1867, the biggest year of steamboating on the upper river. At times that year thirty or forty steamboats were on that river between Fort Benton and the mouth of the Yellowstone.

There were delays—the river bank fell in and broke the *Abeona's* fantail and twenty feet of guard rail; a few days later the boat struck the bank and broke the fantail again. They passed the mouth of the Yellowstone June 13 and Fort Union later that day.

June 15 Mrs. Sanders had a message from her husband, delivered by a friend from a downriver boat. He was coming down; he met her the next day. Now social life was brisk, with much visiting back and forth and group singing in the evening.

On June 24 the *Abeona* stopped for thirteen hours to wood up. All the next day it was stuck on a sand bar. And now comes the first sign of complaint from Harriet Sanders: "All got the blues. Have thrown off every stick of wood that the men cut yesterday from six A.M. to seven P.M." The twenty-sixth they had to stop after a few miles of travel, to wood up and mend the boiler again. Next day they wooded all day. They got twenty loads, all the boat could carry.

On June 30 there was excitement. The men shot at three buffaloes swimming the river and got two of them. The third escaped onto the bank and took after the men on shore, who prudently scattered. "One dropped his gun and climbed a tree in about no time," wrote Mrs. Sanders with a smile. "He was nearly frightened to death."

They were past Cow Island now; there seemed hope of getting home. But there was more trouble: "Reached Bird's Rapids at seven P.M. Tried to rope up. Mr. Sanders and four others were left on the opposite shore. Our boat dashed against the perpendicular wall of rocks on the bank and broke it some and the 'nigger.' I did not go to bed till half past two in the morning, when we got over the rapids and sent a small boat across for the men. They built a large fire last night on the shore." She said not a word about being worried, but why else did she stay up until half past two?

Next day the *Abeona* stopped again to wood up. A deserter from

Camp Cook, fifty miles upriver, arrived in a small boat and came aboard, having changed his mind about trying to go back to the States. It was safer to stay in the Army. At Camp Cook the *Abeona* unloaded eighty tons of freight and Colonel Sanders walked three miles to another boat, the *Gallatin,* so as to reach Fort Benton ahead of his family and engage coach passage for them.

July 1 there was more trouble with the unpredictable river. The crew worked for three hours roping the *Abeona* up Drowned Man's Rapids, and men had to carry wood half a mile. The boilers used up all the fuel in making a mere thirty miles. Next day the boat stopped all day to wood up. This time wood was a full mile away. Some of the steamer hands deserted, starting for Fort Benton on foot with a few crackers for provisions.

Traffic was congested. The *Tacony* and the *Agnes* came up. The *Gallatin* and the *G. A. Thompson* came down. July 3, the *Tacony* passed the *Abeona,* and the *Amaranth* came down. The *Abeona* stopped at a coal yard and took on 150 bushels. "We are sixty miles from Benton," wrote Mrs. Sanders, adding, "Heard that Gen'l T. F. Meagher was drowned at Benton day before yesterday."

July 4—ah, happy day!—the *Abeona* passed the mouth of the Marias River at one in the afternoon and made the other twenty-seven miles to Benton by eleven that night. Here, in the journal as copied by the Sanderses' oldest son James nine years later, he inserted: "Everybody drunk and celebrating in the full sense of the word. Papa delivered the oration during the day."

The Sanders family ignored the revelry. At 11 P.M. they arrived and disembarked; at 2 A.M. they were off and away by coach to Helena. The *Abeona* had been seventy-two days coming from St. Joe, eighty days from St. Louis.

All day July 5 they rode in the coach, which was crowded, "and we are all tired," wrote Harriet Sanders in Spartan understatement. All night they rode, reaching Helena at eight in the morning. They stopped with friends but had little rest. They had callers, because they were important people: two judges, a minister, their wives, and some other friends. That night they were serenaded—a pleasant custom unless one wants to go to bed and get some sleep.

Next day was Sunday, so they went to church. Then Colonel and Mrs. Sanders went calling. At two o'clock next morning they started for Virginia City, 120 miles away, arriving home after twenty-one hours on wheels.

Sunday, July 14, Mrs. Sanders made a final entry in her "Journal of a Trip from Ohio to Montana Ty. in the summer of 1867 via Chicago, St. Joe and the Missouri River, on board Steamer *Abeona*, Ft. Benton and Helena to Virginia City." She wrote: "Slept in our new house last night for the first time. It is on Idaho Street." After the long tedious journey up the Missouri River, having to move from one house to another must have been more pleasurable than moving usually is.

CHAPTER 11

Still Waiting for Good Fortune

Frank Kirkaldie's letters to his wife this year mentioned Indian troubles more frequently than in previous years, but he played down those troubles so that she and the children, reading over and over, would not worry about him. Early in March he reported a new discovery and a stampede to the Salmon River country in Idaho, 260 miles southwest of his place near Deep Creek and 75 miles west of Bannack. He hoped the strike was rich, because needs of the miners there would divert freighters from Salt Lake and leave Montana a better market for his produce.

He was building yet another log house, trying to sell one of the little farms whose sod he had broken. He couldn't write at night, being out of candles. The photographs of his children came. Looking at them time and again, he was disturbed at how much they had changed. But he had been away from them now for three years.

A week later he wrote a longer letter; April 21 was Sunday and he could write in the daytime. The winter had been severe; many cattle had died because the snow was too deep for them to reach grass. He wrote of Indians thus:

> You have doubtless noticed in the papers accounts of Indian massacres at Ft. Phil Kearney & since then at some other military posts

on the Yellowstone or somewhere in that country. I dont like to hear of men being killed but I believe a few such massacres are necessary to *wake up* the authorities at Washington to a just sense of "the situation" in regard to the "Poor Indian." Hitherto they have only considered it necessary to assemble the Indians occasionally and go through a farce of making a treaty with them—at the same time making them liberal presents of fire arms and ammunition—apportioning their gifts in such way—that those Indians who have been most hostile & have committed most murders & depradations shall receive the Lions share—thus furnishing them anew for their murderous work.

It seems evident—& I think is generally believed that the Indians mean mischief the coming season. Where the scene of their operations will be laid or what will be their programme of operations yet remains to be seen. We are told that a large force of soldiers are on their way here [this rumor had been suggested by a Montana newspaper]—and I hope they will be commanded by some man who means business—and who will not stop nor be stopped by Govt. until he has given the Indians a most unmerciful thrashing *for that is the only thing* that will do any good.

I am inclined to believe that the operations of this season will quiet the Indians hereafter for several years—unless the Govt. should fall into its old habit of trying to make peace with them & make treaties etc. The only way to secure a permanent peace with them is to fight it out of them—to continue to punch them until they beg for peace & then grant it to them reluctantly & on the most humiliating terms—for it is only through *fear* of the whites that they will ever be induced to let them alone.

There is some excitement in regard to Indians in this part of the country or rather in the upper Gallatin Valley & some families I heard are leaving—I heard that there was to be a stockade placed around the little town of Bozeman & also around the Grist Mill there. Govt. should establish a military post there as long as any danger exists from Indian depradations.

"Govt." was indeed alert to the Gallatin's need for a fort. The establishment of Fort Ellis was authorized August 27. Two companies of the 13th Infantry soon arrived, and in December several buildings had been completed. A ten-foot stockade enclosed the whole fort when it was finished. Fort Ellis was garrisoned for twenty years.

Kirkaldie wrote this letter three days after John Bozeman was killed. If he had heard this shocking news, he carefully omitted it from his letter home. He did not mention it in any later letter, either.

When Kirkaldie wrote again, May 18, he had been studying the pictures of his family again; he hadn't liked them at first, but now he had concluded that it was reasonable for the children to have changed so much. But his wife looked too solemn, he thought. In this letter he said the Governor had called for volunteers and several companies had been raised and sent to the divide between the Gallatin and the Yellowstone.

Some of Kirkaldie's letters in this year have not survived, or else he wrote home less often than in the past—which doesn't seem likely for that homesick, hopeful man. August 11 he soothed Lizzie about Indians—there wasn't the least apprehension of trouble with them that season—but brooded about something the disagreeable Mrs. Munger (with whom he had come part way to Montana) had said to his wife:

> You say that Mrs. Munger thinks we are too old to think of starting in a new country—I begin to feel too old to think of starting in an old country—and especially one where I have once had a start. I should never expect to get beyond the starting point—and if we have to live from hand to mouth for the rest of our lives I prefer to do it somewhere else than in Illinois. . . . It seems as though every move I have made in the last ten years has been one from bad to worse . . . & if I should abandon this country poor & go back to work by the day for our support it would look like the last term in the decreasing series.

In mid-September he had given up hope of going home that year, but:

> I hope to arrange my affairs so as to go down the river in the spring—or else send for you to come up—Are you willing to come? I do not ask you to come or wish to have you come unless you can come willingly & cheerfully—come prepared for the inevitable inconveniences incident to the country . . . I do not feel like staying here much longer without my family but I could not bear to have them come here against their will—I have inferred from your letters that the idea of coming here was not an agreeable one to you and that you hoped I would abandon it.

Everything was getting better, Kirkaldie assured his Lizzie. He thought the river trip from St. Louis to Benton would be by far the most comfortable way for the family to come. And there was talk of a stage line from Minnesota to Helena. He would, if absolutely necessary, borrow some money to send if payment for his crop was delayed much longer. The interest would cost him 5 per cent *per month*.

October 5 he wrote about his crop—in spite of grasshoppers, he had done very well. On the other hand, prices were very low. His partner had given up, so Kirkaldie had bought out his half interest and would pay $650 for it the next year. No other letter from 1867 survives.

C H A P T E R   12

The Empty Road

There was so much travel on the Bozeman Trail in 1866 that in one day at one place, where the ferry crossed the Big Horn River at Fort C. F. Smith, 300 wagons were lined up waiting for passage.

But in 1867 the situation changed drastically. *No* journals or reminiscences of either emigrants or freighters come to light. The accounts of experience on the Bozeman Trail in 1867 were written by military men or their wives or civilians who worked at the forts. Can it be that *no* emigrant wagons, *no* freighters except those serving the forts, traveled through the Powder River country the summer after the three posts were established to protect them?

Yes, it can be. That road was more dangerous after the forts were built than it had been without them! News of the Fetterman "massacre" rocked the nation. Here were eighty-one soldiers, who were supposed to know how to fight Indians, dead and cut to pieces! What chance would a bunch of civilians have against an enemy like Red Cloud's Sioux? Not much. Better to take some other route if one was determined to go to Montana.

The railroad was still being built; it would not connect across the continent until 1869. Stagecoach travel was fast but expensive, sometimes dangerous, horribly uncomfortable. Steamboats up the Missouri were frequent now; travel was not very risky, not very expensive, either, if passengers were willing to go without the comforts of cabin class. So there were several ways to reach Montana without daring the perils of the Bozeman Trail.

Emigrants avoided the Bozeman Trail after that bloody summer of 1866. Only the hardiest of frontiersmen dared its dangers. One of these was Nelson Story, who brought a train of twelve freight wagons and another herd of cattle—700 head this time—up the trail late in 1867. He arrived in Bozeman December 4.

Story said in a letter to the University of Wyoming (dated August 25, 1920), "No freighting was done on that road to Montana after I came through." Dozens of wagons moved along the road, but they were government-owned or under contract to the government. Story wrote:

> I delivered in the fall of 1867 a train load of potatoes and chopped wheat at C. F. Smith. I & others bought the goods at Smith in July 1868 & part of the goods at Philcarney [*sic*] and took them to Helena, Montana. . . . Trail was not used after 1868 only small parties going to the black hills from Montana.

By building the three forts in 1866 the government defeated the very purpose for which they were built. The Sioux concentrated on keeping whites off the Bozeman Trail, and the Sioux won.

CHAPTER 1

Red Cloud Wins His War

The Great Father in Washington kept coaxing Red Cloud to sign a treaty that would stop the war in the Powder River country. In late fall of 1867 another peace commission showed up at Fort Laramie but found only a few well-disposed Crows there to touch the pen. Red Cloud sent word—patiently or arrogantly, depending on how you look at the matter—that his war against the whites was to defend his people's hunting grounds and that he would stop fighting whenever the garrisons were withdrawn from Fort Phil Kearny and Fort C. F. Smith.

Early in March of 1868 General Grant wrote General Sherman that the forts might as well be closed. So in April peace commissioners went again to Fort Laramie, but Red Cloud did not. Slowly the relinquishment of all three of the Bozeman Trail forts moved forward. They were evacuated early in August—but Red Cloud was in no hurry to sign. His people were on their fall hunt, making meat for winter. On November 4 he arrived with some 125 chiefs and head men. After due ceremony and argument, he signed on November 6. The treaty set up a great reservation:

> Commencing on the east bank of the Missouri River where the 46th parallel of north latitude crosses the same, thence along low water mark down east bank to a point opposite where the northern line of the State of Nebraska strikes the river, thence west across said river, and along the northern line of Nebraska, to the 104th degree of longitude west from Greenwich, thence north on said meridian to a point where the 46th parallel of north latitude intercepts the same, thence due east along said parallel to the place of beginning; and in addition thereto all existing reservations on the east bank of said river shall be and the same is, set apart for the absolute and undisturbed use and occupation of the Indians herein named, and for such other friendly tribes or individual Indians as from time to time they may be willing, with the consent of the United States, to admit among them.

One article after another in the long treaty set forth the fine things that the U. S. government would do for the Indians. It would set up an agency and an agent to look after them; they would be taught to farm and given a cow per family and a pair of good oxen as well as implements and seed if they settled down. For thirty years certain clothing would be provided for each Indian; for four years, limited rations; they would have a doctor, teachers, a carpenter, a miller, an engineer, a boss farmer, blacksmiths.

But they would still have the right to hunt in the unceded Indian territory north of the North Platte River and east of the summits of the Big Horn Mountains. No white person was even to pass through that country without permission of the Indians. This was specified in Article XVI, which included the vital point for which Red Cloud's Sioux had been fighting:

> ... it is further agreed by the United States, that within ninety days after the conclusion of peace with all the bands of the Sioux nation, the military posts now established in the territory, in this article named, shall be abandoned, and that the road leading to them and by them to the settlements in the Territory of Montana shall be closed.

Red Cloud complained later, in his bitter old age, that he had not thoroughly understood the treaty, that it had not been clearly explained to him. The part about abandonment of the forts he understood, of course. But they were not abandoned *after* the conclusion of peace. He saw to it that peace did not come until weeks after the forts were evacuated.

Much had been promised to the Indians who would declare their intention to settle on the great reservation, but they could not have realized that the time would come when all of them would have to do so. They had won the Powder River country for their hunting grounds. Why wouldn't it always provide abundant game? Why couldn't they always live as they had lived, free and on the move, sustained by the bounty of nature, with the reservation for those who wanted to learn to walk the white man's road?

By no means all the Sioux agreed to this treaty anyway. Red Cloud did, and lived to regret it. But some other hostile chiefs, notably Sitting Bull, remained hostile and ignored the white man's blandishments. The Sioux wiped out Lieutenant General George Armstrong Custer and some 225 of his men at the Little Big Horn eight years after the treaty signing. Then they moved across the Medicine Line to Canada, because they could trust the faraway Grandmother in England more than the Great Father in Washington, and they could be sure of justice from the Grandmother's men in red coats but not from the Great Father's men in blue.

Many writers have said that Sitting Bull's people "fled" to Canada. It was a very leisurely flight. The Battle of the Little Big Horn was in June of 1876, and the "fleeing" red men, who could move very fast when they cared to, didn't get to Canada until February of 1877. The end of their freedom was coming, as the red coats warned them. They could live in Canada if they supported themselves, as long as the buffalo ran, but the Grandmother would not feed them. They weren't her children.

The time came in 1881 when, hungry and ragged, they returned to the United States and surrendered, to live on the great reservation, which was gradually whittled away because it was land that the Great Father's white children decided *they* wanted. In December of 1890 Sitting Bull was killed by Indian police. Two weeks later, on December 29, some 300 Sioux men, women, and children were gunned down by the 7th Cavalry in a massacre on Wounded Knee Creek in Dakota Territory, and there was peace at last. The good hunting in the Powder River country was only a memory.

When Red Cloud was about eighty-seven, just before he died in 1909, he said this of the reservation where he lived: "You see this barren waste. We have a little land along the creek that affords good grazing, but we must have some of it for corn and wheat. There are other creeks that have bottoms like this, but most of the land is poor and worthless. Think of it! I, who used to own rich soil in a well-watered country so big that I could not ride through it in a week on my fastest pony, am put down here! Why, I have to go five miles for wood for my fire! Washington took our lands and promised to feed and support us. Now I, who used to control five thousand warriors, must tell Washington when I am hungry! I must beg for what I own. If I beg hard, they put me in the guard house."

CHAPTER 2

The Last Days
of Fort C. F. Smith

There were shortages of various kinds at Fort C. F. Smith—food, for one thing. The commanding officer asked for additional rations because half his men were green troops, who required more food than old soldiers. "In this cold dry climate," he added, "all men require more than would satisfy them farther south."

One day in the spring of 1868 the garrison was alerted and considerably alarmed by the sound of rapid rifle fire from a sentry. It was not the signal for Indians, and nobody was expected from Fort Phil Kearny. Astonishingly, a look through field glasses showed a wagon coming from the *north*. Nothing *ever* came from that direction except Indians. The wagon brought a load of potatoes and onions and even a few pounds of butter from the Gallatin Valley.

Now for baked potatoes instead of desiccated potato cubes! And even butter on them! But alas, potatoes and onions were $15 a bushel, and butter was $2 a pound. The wagon was emptied fast, but nobody got very much of anything. Even so, the price was not exorbitant, everyone agreed, considering the risks involved in getting the load to C. F. Smith through 200 perilous miles.

The hardest thing to do without, in Mrs. Andrew Burt's estimation, was mail. The winter mailman was a Crow Indian named Iron Bull, who had another Crow to help him. Once a month they set out, with the good wishes of the entire garrison, for Fort Phil Kearny, each man riding a stout pony and leading two others to carry mail sacks and provisions. They dared not follow the main trail for fear of Sioux attacks but went their own secret, cautious way.

Everyone at the fort knew what day they should be back with the stored-up riches of mail in the sacks on their ponies. A sentry watched for them, and the garrison listened anxiously to hear his signal that the mailmen were in sight. Women and children flocked out to watch from the south bastion for the first welcome glimpse.

Lieutenant Colonel Bradley, who had asked for leave, got it at the end of March. When he left, Andy Burt took over as post commander and the Burts moved into Bradley's headquarters. A double treat came in the spring when the paymaster accompanied the mail. He spent a day paying off the garrison and left the next morning, but the officers and their wives kept him busy talking in the little time he had to spare. Mrs. Burt wrote: "To see and talk with one who had so recently come from Omaha with the latest news and telling of our friends at the posts below gave us unbounded pleasure."

Another excitement in March was the arrival of Colonel John E. Smith, regimental commander, from Phil Kearny on an inspection trip. He was escorted by a troop of cavalry. He made a "trip of observation" to the Big Horn Canyon and invited the ladies to join the party for a picnic. This was a splendid event for the imprisoned females. They had never seen the spectacular canyon, had only guessed at what kind of country the post hunter traversed when he brought in wild meat. The post couldn't spare men to look after the safety of local sightseers, but when the regimental commander wanted a look and also provided the escort, that was a different matter.

Mrs. Burt and another officer's wife rode in an ambulance with the Burt children, the servant girl Christina, and the lunch, jolting over the rocky trail and enjoying every minute of it. Mrs. Burt's sister Kate rode horseback—sidesaddle, of course. The picnic was wonderful—"a camp kettle of good coffee, cold venison plate, a great pan of army pork and beans." They watched herds of elk and deer grazing on the slopes across the canyon.

A taste of freedom made the ladies hungry for more. On April 16 they listened to the Burts' soldier cook, who told of a beautiful spring near the fort where grew quantities of violets and ferns. He said some of the men went there every day. How could there be any danger? Mrs. Burt and her sister walked through the gate, taking along four-year-old Andrew Gano. The spring was beautiful indeed and they lingered happily—until they heard a gunshot from the fort and men's voices yelling "Indians! Indians!"

Each of the two women grabbed a hand of the little boy. They picked up their skirts and ran literally for dear life. On the way into the fort they met men going out on the double to fight off the raiders, who had tried to stampede the mule herd. One mule was killed by Sioux arrows. After that, the imprisoned ladies never walked more than a few feet outside the stockade.

A great event was the arrival, in that last spring of Fort C. F. Smith's existence, of the wife of First Lieutenant Alexander Wishart with their three children. Mrs. Wishart was fresh from the States, she was full of news of the faraway world back there, she knew what the latest fashions were. One couldn't hope to have such garments, but ah, the delight of finding out what one ought to want!

The hostile Sioux were of course to be feared, but even the friendly Crows were sometimes frightening. One day Mrs. Iron Bull, wife of the esteemed mailman, came to call with an interpreter and her little daughter, Pinahawney. She was dressed for a social call, in a fringed buckskin dress with elaborate trimming of elk teeth and porcupine-quill embroidery. Around her broad middle she wore a broad leather belt that the post blacksmith had decorated with brass tacks that spelled out Iron Bull.

She had several friends outside who wanted a look at the Big White Chief's squaw and her fair-haired sister Kate, the Pale Squaw. They also wanted to look at little Edith because they had never seen a white baby. They looked clean and well scrubbed, so the Big White Chief's anxious squaw let them take turns holding the infant. Their admiration was boundless.

Mrs. Burt had a more disturbing experience one day as she sat sewing while the baby napped. Three Crow men, big men, came soundlessly into the room, said "How!" politely, and sat down on the floor. By frantic signs, and using the few words of Crow that she had picked up, Mrs. Burt told them emphatically to get out, but they ignored her and simply talked among themselves. She refrained from screaming; she grabbed the baby and ran. When she came back with the family's soldier cook, the unwelcome visitors were gone, along with her gold thimble and a jet-and-gold cross that she treasured. After that, sentries were ordered to keep all Indians out unless they had special permission to enter the post.

The latest fashions never reached Fort C. F. Smith, but plenty of gossip did. There were rumors, hard to believe, that all three of the Bozeman Trail forts were to be abandoned. The land that had been fought over was to be given back to the Indians. All the effort, the planning, the hardship and fear and pain, the lives of the men who slept in the little graveyard—had all these been wasted?

The rumors were true. Andy Burt received orders in May to sell the government property that was stored at C. F. Smith. In mid-June he regretted officially in a letter that the property was selling poorly. Buyers coming down from the Gallatin were few. They were afraid of Indians. Besides, money was scarce. Burt explained to headquarters in Omaha that most of the property wasn't worth transporting to the railroad, and buyers could hardly be expected to pay much for articles they would have to pick up "in the heart of an Indian country 300 miles from a settlement or market and that a poor one at this writing." Finally he was ordered to abandon what couldn't be sold or hauled out. The indomitable Nelson Story was one of the very few who dared to buy and freight some of this stuff up to Bozeman.

While the garrison waited for the order that would set the date of departure, Elizabeth Burt conceived the idea of another picnic, this one to celebrate Andrew Gano's fifth birthday, in July. Her husband said the equivalent of "Nonsense, my dear! There's too much danger from Indians on the banks of the Big Horn."

But she had her gentle arguments all prepared. They wouldn't go so far up the canyon this time as they had with Colonel Smith and his armed escort. And couldn't her husband post sentinels to give them warning in time to get safely back to the fort? Even the sentinels would enjoy it; they would share the picnic lunch while watching for danger. It would do everybody good! She won her argument, and the danger-spiced picnic was a fine affair.

The order to abandon came. The regiment would march to Fort D. A. Russell (Cheyenne) and would be informed there of its final destination. Mrs. Burt started packing in a frenzy of excitement. Now even more care had to be taken to prevent the friendly Crows from walking off with anything that was loose. It was easy for an Indian to whisk something under a blanket. Mrs. Burt saw a lordly Crow wearing the jet-and-gold cross that had been taken from her house. He gave it back, unwillingly, when her husband sternly demanded it.

The ladies were ready to climb into the ambulance that would transport them when Kate cried, "My red shawl!" and ran after a woman who had a corner of it hanging out from under her blanket. After a brisk little argument, Kate retrieved her shawl, and the woman went off muttering, "White squaw no good, no good!"

The wagons pulled out, carrying provisions and whatever government property was worth moving, and the troops fell in for the long march. Behind the men came the commanding officer's ambulance accompanied by his two hunting dogs. Major Burt rode horseback. Good little old Susie, the family cow, shod again for a long journey, was in the procession. The Brahma rooster and his harem traveled in their coop, slung on the back of a baggage wagon. A pet elk calf named Monte, short for Montana, rode in the ambulance boot because he refused to budge when he was tied to it and expected to walk.

It is quite possible, of course, to feel stirrings of nostalgia in leaving a place where one never wanted to be in the first place. The outbound command halted on the crest of some hills that looked toward the fort, and there they gazed back for the last time at that doomed and distant outpost, Fort C. F. Smith. Even after the howling, triumphant Sioux set fire to everything that would burn, the adobe walls stood for a long time.

CHAPTER 3

The Last Wagon Train Book

Each wagon train up or down the Bozeman Trail was recorded at each fort it passed, from the time the forts were being hastily established in the summer of '66. Only one Wagon Train Book, of ten handwritten sheets, now survives in the National Archives. This "Train Report," kept at Fort Phil Kearny, is a record of the trail's last gasp in 1868.

No emigrant trains at all are listed. There is only one train of civilian freight wagons. All the rest moved along that road only to take personnel and equipment away from the doomed forts. That one civilian train left Fort Laramie July 6, arrived at Phil Kearny

July 20, and departed for C. F. Smith July 23. The adjutant who kept the record in his neat, elegant penmanship wrote: "Civilian Outfit—Reshaw on Private Account." Joseph Reshaw (one of the Richard family) is listed as one of nineteen drivers. The wagon master is shown as John Porie. He was J. B. Pourier, known as Big Bat.

There were 15 wagons, 164 cattle, 7 horses, 2 mules, only 15 guns for 20 men, and 500 rounds of ammunition. Even without enough guns to go round, this train was better equipped than some of the others in that last summer of the Bozeman Trail. They were a rag-tag-and-bobtail lot, hustled up from anywhere. Most of them came from Fort D. A. Russell, and their announced destination, when they headed down again, was "the East." The Army was moving out.

Few trains had as many firearms as men, and some of the firearms were no good. One train of thirty wagons and three ambulances had 39 men along, 24 Spencer carbines, and 7 Springfield muskets, with plenty of ammunition, 1300 rounds. But none of this was for the Springfields, and five of the guns were listed as unserviceable. This train turned around at Phil Kearny and headed back south accompanied by two companies of the 27th Infantry, so the shortage of firearms among the drivers didn't matter any more.

Some trains were so short of ammunition that more had to be issued before they could move on. Twenty-eight men with 21 muskets were listed as "Ammunition played out—Issued 840 rounds of musket cartridges for use of this train." There was ammunition to spare now. This wasn't 1866 with a shortage that didn't even permit target practice. And the ammunition could not be left behind for the Sioux.

Some of these wagons may have used up their ammunition in fighting their way up the Montana Road, but others were poorly equipped to begin with. A train of 20 wagons had 13 drivers, 13 "worthless guns," and no ammunition at all. Attached to it were 6 men, not teamsters, with 6 guns and a total of only 35 rounds.

All except the lone civilian outfit are listed as either contract trains or transportation trains. The latter belonged to the Army. The contract trains were hired. In most cases the departure date is carefully listed, but when the last two trains left, it didn't matter any more. The adjutant packed up his records, including the last Wagon Train Book, and went with them.

The Army was finished on the Bozeman Trail. The road and the forts and the Powder River country were left for the Sioux's exultation. The post cemeteries, the scattered graves along the road, the fear and endurance and suffering and horror were left in the memories of those who had lived to tell the story.

CHAPTER 4

The Patience of Frank Kirkaldie

John Bozeman's trail, opened in 1863 and closed in 1868, but used by emigrants for only the first four of those six years, and Jim Bridger's safer but tougher trail, used for only two years, went back to the wilderness. Their purpose had been accomplished. They had brought emigrants to the treasures of the gold fields and the great spaces that would become cattle, sheep, and grain ranches and a few cities.

Frank Kirkaldie had come to Montana in 1864, the second year of the migration to Montana. In 1868 he was still seeking his fortune. He was desperate when he wrote his wife a very long letter on the fifth of January, 1868. Because her letters to him do not survive, Lizzie remains a shadowy figure to us, long-suffering, mutinous, utterly dependent, unable to change her situation, unwilling to endure it. Under pressure from relatives, she had marshaled her reasons why he should give up in Montana. Anxiously and patiently, with his hurt apparent, he answered them.

Back home there was nothing for him but day wages. On his farm near Deep Creek there was hope that he could do better. He had sent $800 home since he started in this new country and hoped to send at least that much in the spring of '68. He was going to stay. He wrote:

> I do not *insist* upon your coming, but you may be assured that it is pretty hard for me to look forward for some years to come, & think that I am to live alone, or at least away from my family.... Do not ask me to "consider" any longer. I hope you will send me your final answer as soon as may be after you receive this.

On March 1 he wrote with a heavy heart; he couldn't send money to bring his family out this spring. The flour market was very poor. He did not, however, have to part with money to pay his former partner for his share of the farm; instead, he had taken another partner who paid that amount. He still had a bachelor's life to look forward to, while his wife remained a widow, "but it will not always be so," he promised. "Although often deferred hope is not dead within me."

And so his letters went—the crops he was planting, the depressed state of the flour market, love to the children. He was out of debt—unless something unforeseen went wrong. He had an English couple with two little girls living in his cabin temporarily; he and his partner slept in the granary. Mr. Slee worked for him and Mrs. Slee kept house. It was so pleasant that it made him homesick. "I have not been used to living like a white man for the last four years," he remarked.

In August he was delighted with the news that little Frank had worked to earn enough money to take himself and his sister Fanny to a show. "I think that so much energy & perseverance in a boy of his age are worthy of much praise," the fond father wrote.

> I am glad—my boy! that you possess those qualities—they are necessary to success in any undertaking—whatever enterprise you engage in—go at it with a will—determined not to give up until your purpose is accomplished—and if the cause is a good one and you continue to persevere without faltering—you will be almost sure to succeed—sooner or later.

So he wrote, and so he hoped. This faith that perseverance led to success must have been about all that Frank Kirkaldie himself had to sustain him. He was making his house bigger for the family he would welcome so jubilantly at some time in the future. He had dismantled his cabin near Diamond and hauled the logs to Deep Creek. The house there would have two big rooms.

But he was still looking for a better farm, in spite of his glowing reports on this year's crop. Was that the reason it took him five years to raise enough money to bring his family from Illinois? He always saw greener pastures somewhere else.

He kept expanding. In November he regretted that he couldn't send any money because he had bought two yoke of fine young cattle. But he was jubilant that Grant and Colfax had been elected.

Communication had become remarkably fast since Kirkaldie came to Montana. By midnight of Election Day, the general result of the election back in America was known in Helena.

Whereupon, the little brass field piece was brought out and the surrounding hills & mountains trembled repeatedly under its outspoken language and sleep was said to be out of the question there any more that night.

And the next Monday morning after election—less than a week —the Helenaites were reading in their daily papers—extracts from London & Paris newspapers—commenting on the result of the Presidential election in the United States! Who says we are out of the world? . . . The U.P.R.R. [Union Pacific Railroad] lays 7½ miles of track in one day—wonders are becoming so common that we will soon cease to wonder at anything I think.

Travel was fast, too. The stage from Helena usually reached the end of the railroad in four and a half days. Kirkaldie did not say where that was in November of 1868; it was probably Corinne, Utah. The transcontinental railroad was connected the year after he wrote.

With considerable satisfaction he mentioned that "some of the old Rebs" from the Southern states were in trouble since the land survey. Any man who wanted to take up land under homesteading or pre-emption laws had to swear that he had never taken up arms against the United States or aided or abetted the Rebellion. He didn't pity them much; they shouldn't have been rebels. But we, from the safe distance of more than a century, can pity the defeated who had come to make a new life in the wilderness and were caught in the cruel vise of the Ironclad Oath.

In December, Kirkaldie had some more money to send home— $100 in paper currency, which he had to enclose in an envelope with a letter because there was no other way to send it. And once more he was thinking of moving. Deep Creek was fine for farming, but Helena would be a better place for his family. He was a man of some property now. He owned seven yoke of cattle and two wagons. He hired men to work for him sometimes. He was hoping to return to Illinois by February of 1869, or to send for Lizzie to come up the Missouri or perhaps by rail via Salt Lake.

But two weeks later he resolved to move again. He had bought a piece of ground two miles from Helena and a town lot on Rodney

Street. Helena, only four years old, had three free schools and an academy. Kirkaldie was going to make a big change, from grain and vegetables to small fruit; nobody was raising that near Helena. He asked Lizzie to find plants for strawberries, currants, raspberries, blackberries. His new farm had cost $1,400, so he couldn't go to Illinois after all. But sometime. . . .

After
1868

CHAPTER 1

The Bodies of the Slain

In the fall of 1888, a young fellow of twenty, J. F. Kirkpatrick, heard that the bodies in the Phil Kearny cemetery, one hundred and eleven of them, were being removed to Fort McKinney at Buffalo, Wyoming. He leaped on his horse and rode over to the cemetery, seven miles from his family's ranch on Prairie Dog Creek. Elsa Spear Byron of Sheridan interviewed him in 1935 and included gruesome details in her *Bozeman Trail Scrapbook*.

When he arrived they were just opening Lt. Bingham's grave. The box around the coffin was rotted but the tin coffin was intact and as the screws were rusted out, they lifted the top right off. There was a silk handkerchief across the face. The features were very distinct, his head had been scalped and a piece of blue lined white paper was pasted over the top of the skull. He was dressed in full evening dress with white shirt and black cravat. While they were all gasping at the sight, it began to dissolve to dust right before their eyes. Mr. K. said he was so scared that he was ready to dissolve too.

When they opened the long trench where seventy-six bodies from the Fetterman Massacre were buried, the top tier was nothing but a pile of bones. The government had furnished small wooden boxes (for removing the remains) so the men would shovel out a skull and a few bones for each box. The next tier was in better shape and the bottom tier was well preserved, enough so they could see how terribly the men had been mutilated. These bodies had many stone and metal arrow heads in them and all were scalped but the hair remaining had grown to 8 to 10 feet in length. [This is nonsense. Did they see the long roots of vegetation?] It was matted and the field mice had nests all through it. Mr. K. took three of the metal arrow heads out of one body. The soldiers in the trench had been buried when the temperature was below zero in Dec. 1866.

One of the ranchers who was present wanted a long metal arrow head which had the red-headed bugler's hair stuck to it, but the soldier who had it would not give it up. That night the rancher won the arrow in a poker game!

CHAPTER 2

What Happened to Some of Them

JOHN WHITE

John White "and party"—the party being Charlie Reville and William Still—discovered gold at Grasshopper Creek on July 28, 1863. The discovery was fabulous, but the discoverers, who came from obscurity, returned to obscurity. Something is known, however, about the death of White. He did not live long, and he died poor.

He was prospecting with some other men in the winter of 1863–1864 near the head of Big Boulder Creek. White and Rudolph Dorsett started on horseback for Deer Lodge to replenish their provisions. They came upon two men camped—one of them was Charles Kelly—snowed in, with nothing to eat but the meat of a horse they had killed. White and Dorsett fed the destitute men, took them to Virginia City, got them clothing, and arranged for free meals in a restaurant. This was a fatal kindness.

White and Dorsett went prospecting again. A little later Dorsett learned that Kelly had stolen a horse and a mule from another man. He and White, angry that a man they had rescued turned out to be a scoundrel, set out to catch him. Ten days later, friends in Virginia City learned that Kelly had been seen in Deer Lodge with Dorsett's horse, revolver, and rifle.

Rudolph Dorsett's brother James organized a search party. They came upon some friends camped in the brush, horrified at a discovery they had just made: the body of John White with his saddle covering his face, and Rudolph Dorsett's body with an overcoat thrown over it. Apparently they had captured Kelly and tied him up, but he worked himself loose and killed both of them as they were building a campfire.

Two friends of the murdered men found Dorsett's saddle in the possession of an Indian near Hell Gate and took it away from him. Forty miles farther on, they reclaimed his horse, which Kelly had traded off. Continuing west, they learned that Kelly had been seen heading for Lewiston, Idaho, two weeks earlier. The avengers pursued. One of them, named Coburn, stayed in Lewiston to keep watch; the other, Thompson, forged on to Walla Walla, Washington, where he found Kelly's name on a hotel register. He followed to Portland, Oregon, only to learn that the murderer had sailed for San Francisco. Thompson telegraphed the chief of police there to watch for Kelly and took ship himself. But Kelly was gone, and Thompson never caught him.

The estate of John White, who had opened up riches with his pick and pan, was probated April 29, 1864. No money or property of value was found with his body. He had two horses worth about $75 each and a mining claim worth $100. That was the total of his worldly goods. A man could find great riches without having much of it stick to his fingers.

THE ALDER GULCH DISCOVERERS

The discoverers of Alder Gulch were of one mind—jubilant—about the riches they found, but they split four to two about how to divide things up. George Orr was not one of them; he had stayed in Deer Lodge with a promise to grubstake the others when they came back broke.

The day after the miners who rushed to Alder organized their mining district there, Barney Hughes set out for Deer Lodge. He went to tell Orr that the rest of them were giving him a full and equal share in the claims they had staked. Mike Sweeney and Harry Rodgers didn't like this idea one bit. When Henry Edgar wrote his story of the great discovery, in 1897, he said that Orr's "being given this caused Sweeney and Rodgers to separate from the rest of the party."

What about Lew Simmons, who had stayed with the Crows? Didn't he deserve a share, much more than Orr did? He had been the interpreter, the pacifier, during those terrible hours when the prospectors were in danger of death. He and the rash Bill Fairweather, who impressed the Crows by obviously not giving a damn about either Indians or rattlesnakes, got equal credit for saving the day. But Henry Edgar made no mention of holding a share in the rich gold strike for Lew Simmons. In fact, Edgar did not mention him again after they left him in the Crow camp.

Some of the discoverers did not profit much by their brief glory. A dyed-in-the-wool prospector lives for the delight of the search, and no matter what he finds he goes searching again. He dies in obscurity.

Bill Fairweather, bold and wild-eyed in a portrait that survives, was twenty-seven at the time of the great discovery. Gold was fine to have; having was better than not having; but he enjoyed literally throwing it away. He used to ride down Virginia City's main street, roaring and laughing with other hilarious drunks (one of them was Joseph Albert Slade), tossing out nuggets just for the fun of watching the children and the Chinese laborers squabble to snatch them up.

Fairweather abandoned his Alder Gulch claims and prospected for a time in Alaska. Then he came back to the gulch that had made him famous, and there he died after thirty-nine fun-filled years. He drank himself to death. His funeral was the first service held in Virginia City's new Grace Episcopal Church. The man who had had riches in his grasp was buried at public expense.

His grave is in Virginia City's "respectable" cemetery. The other one, known as Boot Hill, holds thirteen road agents, all hanged by the Vigilantes, and a perfectly decent family named Dalton whose relatives, if they had any, simply never moved them up the hill away from bad company.

Fairweather's grave is surrounded by a plain metal railing and is marked with a metal historical sign:

Bill Fairweather
Discoverer of
Alder Gulch
Died Aug. 25, 1875

There is, in addition, a weathered wooden marker that may once have said the same thing.

There was a bunch of artificial flowers on the grave when I looked at it on September 1, 1968. Bill Fairweather has relatives, descended from a sister, in a nearby town. And here is an odd thing: I remembered vividly, from a visit a few years earlier, that his grave had a big gray granite stone on it, and I drove up there on purpose to see what the inscription was. But there is no stone and there never was one. Memory plays tricks. It's no wonder that memoirs written by old men who fought Indians along the Bozeman Trail when they were young are sometimes wildly inaccurate.

Thomas Cover was the only one of the discoverers who went on to riches. He also went on to a terrible death under mysterious circumstances. He had been a witness to the violent death of John M. Bozeman at the hands of renegade Blackfeet Indians, but there was no witness to his own passing in 1884.

By that time he was wealthy. He lived in Riverside, California, a town that, with two other men, he had helped to establish. He owned large orange groves there. Cover had a wife and two daughters, and his brother Perry also lived in Riverside.

Tom Cover was a solid citizen who had used his share of the discovery prudently to build a good life and a comfortable fortune. But gold still lured him. An old miner staggered into town one day, and just before he died he told Tom Cover that he had discovered the Peg Leg Mine. Everybody knew stories about that fabulous lost gold mine. There was a curse on it, the Indians said. Only one man at a time could know where it was, and he must not touch the gold. Sometime the Great Emperor of the Aztecs would return to claim it and distribute its wealth. Then nobody would need to work and there would be no more hunger, no more unhappiness. All men would live in peace.

The old miner, dying, told Tom Cover that he had learned the location of the mine from an Indian who was dying of a horrible disease because he had defied the curse. He had taken some of the gold. The old miner had found the Peg Leg Mine and he, too, had picked up some of the free gold that lay in it. (It was named for a sailor with a wooden leg; he had died, too.)

Tom Cover had struck it rich in '63. Fortune might repeat. He and a friend named William Russell set out with a buggy and a team to find the Peg Leg Mine. At the edge of a desert in southern California they separated. Russell would drive the team around—a journey that would take about six hours. Cover would walk across, and they would meet at an appointed place.

But Cover never got there. Russell returned to Riverside and organized a search party, but they never found Tom Cover. Mrs. Cover finally sold the orange groves. The daughters grew up. And in 1901, seventeen years after Tom Cover disappeared, a government survey party found whitened human bones, partly covered with drifting sands, in the desert.

One of the finger bones was encircled by a Masonic ring. In the ring was engraved the name Thos. Cover. The men of the survey party gathered up the bones and the ring and took them to Mrs. Cover, who had not known all those years whether she was wife or widow.

The spelling of Cover's last name has long been a matter of dispute. One man who mentioned him in his journal spelled it Couvier; perhaps it was pronounced Coover. It was spelled Coover by several men who knew him in Montana. Coover is a perfectly good name; there are Coovers in Montana now. But Tom's name was spelled Cover as engraved in the ring that identified his skeleton.

FIRST GOVERNOR OF MONTANA

The life of Sidney Edgerton reads like a story by Horatio Alger. He didn't go from rags to riches, but he rose very far indeed above rags. He was born in Cazenovia, New York, in 1818, one of six children. His father died when Sidney was six months old. His mother did sewing and weaving to support her hungry brood. Sidney left home when he was *eight years old.*

When his daughter, Martha Edgerton Plassman, wrote a biographical sketch of him, she didn't say how he lived after that, but he always liked to read and he became a schoolteacher. He moved to Akron, Ohio, when he was twenty-six and studied law under the Hon. Rufus P. Spaulding for two years. Then he opened his own law practice. He married Mary Wright of Tallmadge, Ohio, in 1849.

Seven years later he was a delegate to the first national convention of the Republican Party, in Pittsburgh. He was elected to Congress in 1858 and 1860. When President Lincoln appointed him chief justice of the new Territory of Idaho in 1863, he went overland by ox train in the company of his family with relatives and friends.

As the first Governor of Montana, he left Bannack in September of 1865 to go back to Washington and use his influence to promote his Territory; he and some friends had been paying the expenses of government themselves, since no tax money was coming in. Another reason for his journey back east, his daughter said, was that he wanted to put his older children in school. Governor Edgerton went well provided with proof of Montana's riches: in his valise and quilted into his overcoat lining he carried nuggets of beautiful gold to dazzle Congress with.

But Edgerton left Montana without getting an official leave of absence. The reasons he gave for leaving, when he arrived in Washington, were not sufficient, in the opinion of Secretary of State William H. Seward. He "resigned" and President Andrew Johnson appointed Green Clay Smith, a Kentucky Democrat, to succeed him.

Although one of Montana's original nine counties was named for Edgerton, none bears his name now. The fourth territorial legislature changed the name to Lewis and Clark. There wasn't even a fight about it. The name-change bill was introduced in the House by J. W. Rhodes, member from Edgerton County, and passed without a dissenting vote. Only one member of the Legislative Council voted No. Governor Smith approved the bill December 20, 1867, and Edgerton's name was wiped off the map.

The reason for this near-unanimity was political. Montana's supreme court judges had ruled that the acts of Meagher's "extraordinary" legislative session of 1865–1866 were null and void. Democrats were furious. Edgerton's nephew, Wilbur Fisk Sanders, went to Washington to lobby for the nullification. Then Democrats were even madder, and the whole Democratic slate was elected in September of '66.

Edgerton wasn't around any more, but the territorial legislature was able to take some vengeance on the judges and Sanders by changing the name of Edgerton County. There is still a county named for Sanders, however. Sidney Edgerton died July 19, 1900.

WILBUR FISK SANDERS

Wilbur Fisk Sanders, born in April of 1834 in Leon, New York, was admitted to the bar at twenty-two and practiced law for the rest of his life. Early in the War of the Rebellion he held the rank of first lieutenant while serving as acting assistant adjutant general on the staff of General James W. Forsyth. For most of his life he was known as Colonel Sanders, but this was simply because he was respected.

[331]

Sanders resigned his commission because of poor health and took his family west in 1863 when his uncle, Sidney Edgerton, went out to Idaho Territory.

Sanders was respected even by men who detested him—and there were plenty of them. He was a fighter from way back, an eloquent speaker, and always involved in politics. He first came to the attention of his fellow new-come Montanans when he refused to defend George Ives on a charge of murder, and instead volunteered to act for the prosecution. During the tense hours after the trial, friends of the late George Ives tried to lure Sanders behind a building where they could kill him. He fired a shot—accidentally, he *said* —from a pistol in his pocket and set his overcoat on fire, but he succeeded in discouraging the assassins.

Three times during territorial days Sanders was a Republican candidate for delegate to Congress. He was defeated every time. But he was one of Montana's first two senators after statehood.

Sanders knew he was making history. He was president of the Montana Historical Society for thirty years. A county was named for him just before he died in 1905.

A bronze statue of Wilbur Fisk Sanders in the Montana capitol bears the legend, "Men do your duty," the usual order to Vigilantes to pull the drop out from under the feet of a man who was being hanged.

John Owen

What became of that hardy traveler, Major John Owen, who was in Jim Bridger's second wagon train in 1864? His end was worse than that good, hard-working man deserved. His mind began to fail when he was in his fifties. Father L. Palladino attributed this to the fact that he was a drinking man. As his mind clouded, his business at Fort Owen began to fall apart. He was a Mason, and the Grand Master of the lodge took him to St. John's Hospital in Helena. He spent months there in 1873. The Governor had contracted with the Sisters of Charity to look after deranged persons, including John Owen.

When he was fifty-eight, Father Palladino baptized him "conditionally and privately, his mind being defective." He was baptized in a lucid interval, the priest noted. The date was February 15, 1877. Very soon thereafter Owen made his last long earthly journey, to Philadelphia, where he had relatives. W. E. Bass, president of Montana's tenth legislative assembly, took him there because he could no longer travel alone. John Owen lived twelve years more.

JIM BRIDGER

The friends of his youth called him Old Gabe. They were about all gone when he was a guide on the trail he broke through the Big Horn Basin in competition with John Bozeman's Trail up Powder River, and when he was a scout for the U.S. Army. Jim Bridger had become a legend in his own time, and he was addressed respectfully as "Major" by wide-eyed pilgrims who had heard great tales about him.

He was a paragon among guides—he was never wrong about the way to go, he never got anybody lost, and the Indians never surprised him. Where you didn't see ary sign of them, he warned, there they were the thickest. He had lived with Indians and had adopted some Indian customs that bewildered the emigrants and Army men whose guide he was. He didn't live by the clock or even by the sun. If he felt sleepy in camp in the middle of the afternoon, he rolled up in his blanket and went to sleep. Then after everyone else had turned in, he woke up, built a fire, roasted meat for a meal, and chanted like an Indian the rest of the night.

His first wife was a Flathead, his second a Ute. She died in childbirth. There is a story, maybe true, about how he kept the baby alive, while riding hard to the nearest place where a woman could be found to care for it. When the baby needed feeding, Bridger simply shot another buffalo cow and gave the child the milk from her udder. His third wife was a Snake girl.

Because he had a large goiter, some Indians identified him as Big Neck. His keen sight failed as his years mounted, and the eyes that had seen half a continent when it was all frontier grew dim. He died at seventy-seven, blind, in 1881.

NELSON STORY

Nelson Story entered the pages of history with a line or two in *Five Years a Dragoon*, by Percival G. Lowe, who, on the way to Utah with supplies for U.S. troops in September, 1858, left two of his mule-team drivers sick in the hospital at Fort Laramie. One was named Mike Flood; the other was Nelson Story, "a friendless youth of twenty."

As has been related, Story made a stake in the Montana mines a few years later and in 1866 drove a herd of Texas longhorns up the Bozeman Trail in defiance of the whole Sioux nation and the U.S. Army. He ran a store in Bozeman, had a ranch in the Gallatin Valley, built an empire of cattle and horses. In 1892 he sold 13,000 head of blooded cattle and went to Los Angeles for the winter. He built that city's first skyscraper, the Story Building. He was eighty-eight when he died in 1926.

Nelson Story I founded a fortune and a dynasty. A son, a grandson, and a great-grandson bore his name. Nelson Story IV, called Fourthie, was born in 1922. Fourthie joined the Montana National Guard when he was a year under age. Both he and his father, who held the rank of colonel, went to war in the Pacific.

Fourthie fractured an ankle in jumping from a weapons carrier in southern Australia. When his outfit moved north, he went absent from the hospital and, with a heavy cast on his leg, bummed his way *1,500 miles* to join them. The shade of Nelson Story I must have chuckled. This young spriggins had the same attitude toward authority that he did. Fourthie was a corporal then; he had been busted from sergeant but was on his way up again.

After the battles of Sananandar and Buna, both father and son returned to Australia, Colonel Story to a hospital and Fourthie to Officer Candidate School. The colonel was shipped back to the United States just one week too soon—he did not have the pleasure of pinning a second lieutenant's bars on his son's shoulders.

Fourthie was killed in action in New Guinea on August 6, 1944. In his memory his parents built the beautiful Soldiers' Chapel in the Gallatin Valley, fifty miles south of Bozeman and two miles north of the border of Yellowstone National Park.

FRANKLIN KIRKALDIE

In January of 1869 Frank Kirkaldie was full of plans for his new place near Helena, busy figuring out how his family should come and what they should bring. He was full of hope but he dared not feel certain. He had been disappointed too often. The best way for the family to come, he sometimes thought, was by boat to Fort Benton. Early May would be soon enough to start. The earliest boats to start upriver often didn't make the best time.

An act to remove the territorial capital from Virginia City to Helena had passed both branches of the Legislature and would now be voted on by the people. (The capital did move to booming Helena and, in spite of shenanigans involving bribery later on when the Territory became a state, it is still there.)

When he wrote January 24 he was still uncertain about the best route for his family. The stage would be faster than the river, but more expensive and more fatiguing. Now he had learned that express on his cuttings and roots, fast though it was, would cost a dollar a pound. Maybe Lizzie could bring these as baggage if she came upriver.

Still dreaming happily of the reunion with her and the children, he wrote February 1 (still from his place near Deep Creek) that the best way to come was by railroad to the end of the line or into the Salt Lake Valley, and he would meet her there with a team and wagon. The rail trip would take three days; the wagon trip on to Helena he could make in fifteen to twenty days. The rail fare he thought would be about $75 a ticket, and she should be able to bring the four children for two fares, a total of $225. He had traded two yoke of cattle for a span of horses and harness for the journey to bring his loved ones up from the railroad.

"Tell Nelly I could read her letter very well," he said. She was one of the twins; they had been less than a year old when he saw them last, and now Nelly was writing a letter! (Or had she, perhaps, scribbled something that she just thought was a letter for Papa?)

He wrote again February 14 from his new place near Helena. Wells, Fargo stages were expected to run from there to the end of the railroad in sixty-six hours. He believed he could cover that distance with team and wagon in fifteen days. Now the time was drawing near. February 26 he urged that Lizzie bring clothing, beds, and bedding; crockery could be packed and shipped.

Frank had several hundred dollars due him from his former partner, he wrote March 15, and hoped to send $800 to Lizzie for travel. "Then you can pay *some* to Mrs. Bartleson & have enough to bring you to the end of the R.R. too." Mrs. Bartleson was, apparently, the woman with whom his family had been staying, and he owed her considerable money after all this time. "If I am not able to pay her *all* before you come—I think I shall be able to do so sometime during the present season—as soon as I have time to convert what grain & other property I have to spare into money—and I feel assured that after her kindness in waiting *so long*—she will still be lenient and extend the time a little longer if by that means I can again be united to my family from which I have so long been exiled."

More details follow about what to bring: their books, Lizzie's sewing machine, a good clothes wringer, beds (but not bedsteads or chairs or tables), and bedding. Everything else that he couldn't make they could get in Helena. His last letter was dated March 30, 1869. Once more he was disappointed; he couldn't raise as much money as he had expected, because merchants were hoarding their dust to send down the river by steamer. Money was tight and markets dull. But he could send five or six hundred dollars. Lizzie should start by train about May 4 or 5; he would leave April 20 to meet her.

He had dug the cellar and the well, laid sills on the foundation, and had logs all ready to build their house. He had bought two cows and arranged to buy chickens. They would have their own milk, butter, eggs, pork, lard, flour, and potatoes. In a postscript dated April 3, he added more details about what to bring. He would leave for the railroad in three weeks.

He did meet his family, at Corinne, Utah. After five long years, he hardly knew his own children. Bringing them home from Corinne took three weeks of travel. They reached Helena June 6 and moved into the unfinished log house two miles from town. The Kirkaldies' last child, Robert, was born February 8, 1871.

The family moved twice more but things didn't go right so both times they came back. In 1882 they moved again, this time to a ranch near present Augusta. Frank Kirkaldie died of a stroke ten years later. About 1905 his widow sold the home ranch and the cattle and moved to Great Falls. She died in 1933, just six months short of one hundred years of age.

Lizzie saved his letters; then his daughter Nellie did. Her daughter-in-law, Mrs. Irene Askew Gray, presented them with biographical material to Montana State University, Bozeman.

THE CARRINGTONS

While Frances Grummond was visiting a sister in Cincinnati in 1868 she read Margaret Carrington's book, *Absaraka, Home of the Crows,* which was based on the journal Margaret had kept. Mrs. Grummond learned that Henry Carrington was Professor of Military Science at Wabash College in Crawfordsville, Indiana.

Two years later Frances Grummond saw a newspaper report of the death of a Mrs. Carrington and wrote to find out whether it was Margaret, whose sisterly love and compassion she remembered vividly. It was indeed. As a result of the correspondence that followed between Mrs. Grummond and Henry Carrington, they were married in 1871. He retired from active service with the rank of brigadier general.

In July of 1908, General Carrington and his wife Frances returned to the scene of drama and heartbreak and horror. They traveled by Pullman, instead of mule train, to Sheridan, Wyoming, a town and a state that had not existed forty-two years earlier. Wyoming was celebrating its fortieth anniversary as a territory and its eighteenth anniversary as a state. More than four hundred towns had sprung up in Wyoming. The returning couple saw new sights —fields of grain, mailboxes in front of farmhouses—and heard old sounds: bands playing and cannon firing, for General Carrington was entitled to a salute of eleven guns.

By automobile they revisited Massacre Hill, where Fetterman and his eighty men had died. The few old soldiers in the party picked wild flowers to decorate a monument there. The bodies had long ago been moved to the National Cemetery at the Custer battlefield. At the monument, on July 3, General Carrington delivered a memorial address. He was still bitter, for the world remembered him, when it thought of him at all, as the officer responsible for the Fetterman disaster. Now he had a chance to vindicate himself publicly before at least a small audience. He had been on the defensive before government and the military ever since he sent his telegrams about the Fetterman slaughter in December of 1866.

If those telegrams, he said, "had been treated with decent respect by the aged Department Commander, General Philip St. George Cooke, their solemn dignity of demand for reinforcements would have commanded respect, instead of being used as a scapegoat to falsify the true record."

A commission of nine men, representing both the military and civilians, had met at his house at Fort McPherson for thirty consecutive days. (He was still on crutches from the injury caused by his defective revolver.) He was completely cleared. The commission had remarked, "The difficulty, in a nutshell, was that the commanding officer of the district was furnished no more troops or supplies for this state of war than had been provided and furnished for him for a state of profound peace."

Then President Andrew Johnson, who had so recently declared that the Indians had signed a peace treaty, ordered a strictly military court to find out who, if anyone, should be punished for the Fetterman tragedy. This court cleared Carrington, too. But the commission's findings had been suppressed *for twenty years* in the cellar of the Interior Department until Congress demanded for a third time that they be published. They were published at last in 1887.

On the spot at old Phil Kearny where the flag of the United States was unfurled in October, 1866, another flag with a few more stars was raised in 1908 by the same man, William Daley. There were more ceremonies on July 4. S. S. Peters, another of Carrington's veterans, made a speech. William Murphy told his story.

General Carrington published several editions of his first wife's book even after her death, always trying to clear his reputation. Frances wrote a book, too, *Army Life on the Plains,* published in 1910. (The title page makes it "My Army Life and the Fort Phil. Kearney Massacre.") She included the story of their visit to the Powder River country.

There were no hostile Indians any more to dispute the blood-soaked ground along the Bozeman Trail. A Sheridan newspaper prophesied, "The time ought to come before many years, and will come, if the present policy is carried out, when the Indians will have the same rights and duties as other Americans, and will live as they do."

Rights and duties they have, but most of the descendants of the Indians who fought for the Powder River country live on reservations, and not so well as other Americans.

Footnotes

1. Later someone realized that the creek had already been named almost sixty years before by the Lewis and Clark Expedition. It had been called Willard's Creek for expedition member Alexander Willard. The miners would willingly have given up "Grasshopper" in favor of the original name, because a certain reverence was owed to that historic band of adventurers, but there was in the community a man named J. S. Willard who made them so mad that they wouldn't give him the satisfaction of being able to boast that the stream was named for *him*.

2. A rocker is a wooden cradle in which dirt and water are rocked back and forth. The gold sinks to the bottom as the waste material washes away.

3. There is an old fool-catcher question: "Which is heavier, a pound of lead or a pound of feathers?" There is no difference, of course; avoirdupois weight is used for both.

But which is heavier, an ounce of lead or an ounce of gold? Now things get complicated. With precious metals, troy weight is used. Sixteen avoirdupois ounces equal one avoirdupois pound, but it takes only twelve troy ounces to make a troy pound. The only weight that is the same in the two systems is the smallest one, the grain, which Henry VIII set up for England, based on a grain of wheat: 480 grains make a troy ounce; 437½ grains make an avoirdupois ounce.

So a little arithmetic brings out the peculiar fact that although a troy ounce of gold is heavier than an avoirdupois ounce of lead or feathers, when we get into pounds it's the other way round. A troy pound weighs 5,760 grains, but an avoirdupois pound weighs 7,000 grains, and grains don't vary.

4. Colors are bits of gold, from mere specks up to larger sizes, that show in the crease in a gold pan.

5. "Mountain fever," common in the frontier West, was a serious affliction. It may have been typhoid or malaria or Rocky Mountain spotted fever. James Stuart was a doctor of sorts, but he called it mountain fever like everyone else.

6. A sluice is a long trough, about a foot deep and 15 to 20 inches wide, placed on supports to regulate the flow of water. Sections taper at the lower end so that any number can be fitted together. The trough has a false bottom, perforated and fitted with cross slats, or riffles, to catch the gold. One man stands at the upper end, shoveling in gravel. A second throws out the rocks with a steel fork, and a third shovels away the tailings, the waste. Only the gold and heavy black sand remain after washing. "Cleanup" was usually once a week; water was turned aside so the gold could be scraped off the bottom.

"He couldn't make the riffle," slang still used in Montana after more than a hundred years, means he failed. Another placer-mining term still in use is "pan out," usually in the negative: "His hopes didn't pan out." That means the same thing: he couldn't make the riffle.

7. In 1876, when the Montana Historical Society published Volume I of its *Contributions,* the names or fragments of names of 374 men were remembered and listed as having been at Bannack that first winter, and 34 females were recorded. By 1876 many of the men had only a past and no future. Several had earned final footnotes identifying them as "killed by Indians" or "murdered by road agents," and six of those early comers qualified for "hung by Vigilantes."

Daniel S. Tuttle, Episcopal bishop who came to Montana in 1867, wrote years later that in the winter of 1862–1863 there were 37 men and 2 women in or near Fort Benton, up north and east on the Missouri River. In Missoula County, west of the Continental Divide, there were 69 men and 8 women. The total population of the wilderness that became Montana Territory he estimated as 604 men and 65 women. There were also thousands of Indians, of course, but nobody counted them.

8. Another way to spell it in English is Absaraka. There is a mountain range in Montana named Absaroka, too.

9. These three belonged to "the fraternity," Henry Edgar wrote later. This may have been the Masonic Lodge or it may have been the Union League. Both were well represented on the frontier. Members of either could trust one another—an important matter among men whose very lives sometimes depended on being suspicious of strangers' intentions.

10. Neither Stuart nor Hauser, in narrating the horrors of this affair, mentioned the death of Watkins, but neither mentioned his regaining consciousness. He had been shot in the head. It must be assumed that the party buried him with Bostwick before leaving.

11. Some definitions: A *nugget* is a piece of gold big enough to make a gold pan ring when dropped into it. Small, flat nuggets like scales are *flake gold.* Larger pieces are *scads.* "Scads" is still in colloquial use by persons who don't dream that the word has any connection with gold. Nowadays scads means simply lots—like jillions.

12. This Stinking Water, in Montana, is now the Ruby River. The water does not stink. It does not turn up any rubies, either, but some garnets have been found there. At least one stream in Wyoming was also called the Stinking Water; it is now the Shoshone River.

13. A young traveler named Sam Clemens, who became famous as Mark Twain, had breakfast with Slade one morning at a station on the stage line and told about it in *Roughing It.* He described Slade as "the most gentlemanly appearing, quiet and affable officer we had yet found along the road in the Overland Company's service."

When there was only one cup of coffee left, Slade insisted that Clemens drink it, but "I was afraid," the traveler wrote, "that he had not killed anybody that morning and might be needing diversion." Clemens did drink the coffee, "But it gave me no comfort, for I could not feel sure that he would not feel sorry presently and proceed to kill me to distract his thoughts from his loss."

14. Perhaps Bozeman assumed that, because staff officers at military posts had authority to perform the marriage ceremony in emergencies, he did too. No doubt he carried out his self-assigned task at least as well as a certain officer at Fort Kearny, Nebraska, who undertook it for the first time. Another officer held a tallow candle to light the Book of Common Prayer and pointed out the appropriate sections. The officiating officer got through a prayer with proper solemnity but, in the candle's flickering light, missed the next section

and astonished those gathered together by intoning, "Whereas, it has pleased Almighty God to remove our beloved brother. . . ."

15. When Reconstruction began, and United States government was restored painfully in the states that had seceded, no man could take office until he swore not only to support and defend the Constitution of the United States but also that he had never voluntarily borne arms against the United States, had never voluntarily given "aid, countenance, counsel or encouragement" to persons in rebellion, and had never exercised or attempted to exercise the functions of any office under the Confederacy. Virtually no man in the South who was competent to hold local office and respected enough to be chosen for it could subscribe to this "Ironclad Oath." It was simply too harsh.

16. Langford had come out in '62 as second assistant to Captain James L. Fisk, leader of the Northern Overland Expedition, from St. Paul. Before long, Langford—a man of integrity and considerable stubbornness—was in bad with almost everybody. When three murderers were tried in Bannack, Langford alienated his friends, the respectable element, by insisting on a jury trial as more likely to serve the ends of justice than a haphazard miners' court, in which everybody had a vote. Then, as a member of the twelve-man jury, he was the only juror who dared to vote "Guilty"—and that made the roughs hate him. The murderers went free.

17. Punishment had to be practical and swift. A man couldn't be kept in jail where there was no jail. If his crime did not warrant either hanging or banishment, what could be done to him? In the fall of 1863, in a camp in Bivin's Gulch near Alder, a miners' court heard a case in which A charged B with stealing a horse. B, who felt he had no chance to get a fair deal, stacked the deck by bringing in two friends who volunteered to serve on the jury. The verdict was that the defendant should beat the stuffing out of the plaintiff, with the jury standing by to see that nobody interfered while the sentence was carried out.

18. Of all the men the Vigilantes executed, George Ives was the only one who had a public trial. Most of the others had a chance to talk back, but with nobody present except Vigilantes and other road agents who were about to be hanged.

19. Some of the men in the gold camps had a gruesome interest in corpses. One who especially hated Jack Gallagher dug him up enough to get his head out of the grave. Then he boiled the meat off it and kept the skull around. It is said to be somewhere in Virginia City yet.

Years after the five-men hanging in Virginia City on January 14, some of the aged ex-Vigilantes got into an argument about which road agent was buried where in the row of graves on barren Cemetery Hill. The identifying markers were long gone by then. One man claimed that he knew, because he helped bury them. "Club Foot George is right *there*," he maintained. So they dug right there and found George Lane, identified by his crippled foot. The brownish bones, still in the fragment of a sock, are the pride of one of Virginia City's two museums to this day.

20. James M. Ashley, who defended the name Montana and won his argument, in 1867 instigated the plot to impeach President Andrew Johnson. Johnson's supporters won by a single vote.

When U. S. Grant became President, Ashley had his choice of several political plums. He chose to be territorial governor of Montana. While the family lived in Helena, his son Jim, fifteen, spent a terrible winter alone in the mountains and barely lived through it. Governor Ashley paid two trappers to look after the boy in the wilderness, but they deserted him, leaving him blankets, some flour and salt, ammunition for his rifle, and his dog. The boy lived on game. He killed two mountain lions and used their hides to keep warm. He and his dog fought off mountain rats that swarmed into the cabin.

His mother, when she found out where he had gone, raged at his father, who sent out men with supplies for the boy, but they never showed up. In early spring Governor Ashley himself went out with a relief expedition and found the boy almost starved. It would appear that Ashley was sometimes lacking in good judgment.

21. If Latin is more suitable than Spanish for a northern territory's name, then Montana's first legislative session should have made the territory's motto *Aureum argentumque.* But it is *Oro y plata,* Spanish for gold and silver. Colonel Sanders disapproved of the thought behind the words. When he spoke at the dedication of the state's capitol building in 1902, he said bitterly that he thought the motto was in poor taste because it "casts a reproach upon our people as if the jingle of gold and silver was the only music they could appreciate."

But Montana's motto is not a warlike threat like Virginia's "Thus ever to tyrants" or Massachusetts' "By the sword she seeks peace under liberty," both elegant in Latin. It is an honest, exuberant boast, inviting the world to "Look what we've got!"

22. David Weaver, who was in Captain Coffinbury's train, behind Townsend's, said Townsend's guides were Michael Boulier and John Richards. These names make more sense; Boulier sounded like Boyer, Gogeor doesn't sound like anything, but you could find a Richards, or Reshaw, behind every rock.

23. If you want to know precisely where this occurred, you are at liberty to figure it out from the following description, given to a newspaper writer by David Weaver years later:

> On July 22, 1864, the Coffinbury train reached the Powder River at the junction of what is now known as Sand Creek but was known then as Dry Creek. [Old maps show more than one Dry Creek. The new ones I have do not show Sand Creek.] The train crossed the [Powder] river, followed up the north bank for about six miles, or to the junction of the South Fork of the Powder River with the westerly fork, the latter consisting of the union, a few miles still further westward, of the north fork and the middle fork; and the train went into corral here just a little above the junction of the south fork. [None of these forks are identified on my 1871 map, which probably isn't accurate anyway. The place may have been near Crazy Woman Crossing.]

24. Several sources make the flat statement that in 1865 Montana had a population of 120,000, but none of them say where that figure came from. Apparently it came from someone's imagination or a misprint. Even in the spring of 1866, N. P. Langford, Federal revenue agent, estimated the total at only 18,000. He based this on the number of men who voted (6,230), the yield of the gold mines, and how much it cost to live.

25. Galvanized Yankees, also known as "whitewashed rebs," were former Confederate prisoners who, discouraged and hungry, signed up in the U.S. Army for service on the frontier in order to get out of the Yankee prison camps. Officially they were U.S. Volunteers.

26. Long delays in the movement of mail in 1864 and 1865 were caused by Indian scares along the Overland Stage route, and some were due to sheer carelessness. Drivers or stock tenders, reloading mail when two or three Concord coaches were waiting together, sometimes tossed the sacks into the wrong vehicle. Mail bound for California and Montana would be returned to Atchison, Kansas, and eastbound pouches would go back to Salt Lake and the Pacific Coast.

For six weeks in the summer of 1864, no westbound mail moved at all because hostile Indians had control of the roads. No stages traveled over a distance of 340 miles.

Frank A. Root said in the *Overland Stage to California* that 109 sacks of mail, two or three tons, piled up at the station at Latham, Colorado. They were stacked for breastworks in case the men had to defend the station against Indian attack.

27. On some maps of Wyoming, Forts Connor and Reno are shown with separate dots. An official-looking painted road sign in the area showed "Ft Reno 8 mi" and "Ft. Conner [*sic*] 6 mi" when I photographed it in 1969. But they never were separate places, two miles apart. Fort Connor was simply the old name for Fort Reno. The order changing the name arrived there soon after New Year's of 1866.

28. Captain H. E. Palmer, who had been with Connor's expedition in 1865, wrote about his part in it twenty years later and said of Lake De Smet:

> The lake is strongly impregnated with alkali, in fact so strong that an egg or potato will not sink if thrown into the water; large red bluffs are to be seen on both sides, and underneath the lake is an immense coal vein. Not many miles from this lake is a flowing oil well. A scheme might be inaugurated to tunnel under this lake, pump the oil into the lake, set the tunnel on fire and boil the whole body of alkali water and oil into soap.

It hasn't been done yet, but the world needs men who think big.

29. When Carrington first came and there was still a possibility that Fort Reno would be abandoned, the new fort was called Fort Reno and the old one became Reno Station. The old post had too many supplies to move, however, so it was not abandoned. Its name reverted to Fort Reno and the next one up the trail was named Fort Philip Kearny.

This one was never called simply Fort Kearny. It needed a fuller name to distinguish it from older establishments in Nebraska. Fort Philip Kearny, named for a brilliant cavalry general in the Civil War, was called Fort Phil. Kearny (with a careful period after the abbreviation) informally and even in military records.

Nebraska had "old" Fort Kearny, established in 1847 as a blockhouse on the Missouri River and named for Stephen Watts Kearny. It was abandoned when "new" Fort Kearny was built on the Platte River in 1848.

All these Kearnys were properly spelled with only one *e*, but most people, including Army officers, spelled the name Kearney. Present Kearney, Nebraska, is still spelled that way.

30. Communication between picket posts and forts was vital. At Phil Kearny, signals came from a platform on Pilot Knob with an entrenchment behind it for use in case pickets were attacked. Flag signals were used here. If wagons were seen on the Bozeman Trail, going either way, the picket started his flag at the ground, raised it 90 degrees to the zenith, then swung it back to

the ground and furled it back over the heads of the soldiers there. If Indians were sighted, the flag started from the ground on one side and whirled over to the other side, then back. Sentries (but they were "sentinels" in 1866) in the fort kept constant watch.

In other spots, a man on horseback signaled by the way he rode (in circles, for instance) and the direction he pointed his horse.

31. A howitzer was a small cannon. A mountain howitzer was a twelve-pounder with wheels; it weighed a little over one hundred pounds and could be pulled by one mule or dismantled and carried on two pack mules. It used a powder bag and a spherical shell with fuze up front or spherical case shot. It didn't even require a shell; it could shoot pebbles. The barrel was thirty-four to thirty-eight inches long.

32. Even at little one-company posts along the Oregon Trail the post commander (a lieutenant or a captain) had considerable authority over civilians who passed by. There were squabbles between bullwhackers and wagon bosses, for example. The post commander sat in judgment, decided who was right and how to settle the dispute. If a wagon boss got so disagreeable that one of his men quit and then he refused to pay the man off, the post commander could order payment to be made then and there—and put the wagon boss in the guardhouse if he refused.

Of if a bullwhacker was in the wrong, he could be consigned to the guard-house for ten days or so. By the time he got out, the train of freight wagons was far away, and how the quarrelsome driver looked after himself until he got to some other place was his own problem.

If an emigrant—and some of them were very unruly—was judged guilty of stealing a saddle, some harness, a sack of feed, or anything else from another emigrant, the post commander simply took enough of the defendant's goods to pay back the plaintiff.

Some commanders even enforced the payment of gambling debts if the debt could be proved.

33. "Massacre" depends on one's point of view. If everybody on your side is killed, it's a dirty shame and a massacre, but by dictionary definition *massacre* denotes wholesale and promiscuous slaughter, especially of those who can make little or no resistance. Fetterman's men were well able to resist, and did resist as long as they lasted. So did George Armstrong Custer's men nine and a half years later at the Battle of the Little Big Horn. But when Custer's old out-fit avenged that defeat by killing some 300 desperate Sioux, including women and children, at Wounded Knee Creek in 1890, that really *was* a massacre although it is usually called the Battle of Wounded Knee.

34. The Indians themselves disagreed about this years later when they had been defeated for the last time and some of those who had been present were willing to talk.

35. John Guthrie, who helped load the bodies after the massacre, wrote:

We walked on top of their internals and did not know it in the high grass. Picked them up, that is their internals, did not know the soldier they belonged to, so you see the cavalry man got an infantry man's gutts and an infantry man got a cavalry man's gutts.

Guthrie said that wolves, hyenas (!), and coyotes hung around but did not touch the bodies that were out all night. Some people thought wild animals didn't like white men because there was too much salt in the meat.

FOOTNOTES

Colonel Carrington, in a long report he prepared January 3, listed these mutilations:

> Eyes torn out and laid on the rocks; noses cut off; ears cut off; chins hewn off; teeth chopped out; joints of fingers; brains taken out and placed on rocks with other members of the body; entrails taken out and exposed; hands cut off; feet cut off; arms taken out from sockets; private parts severed and indecently placed on the person; eyes, ears, mouth and arms penetrated with spear-heads, sticks and arrows; ribs slashed to separation with knives; skulls severed in every form, from chin to crown; muscles of calves, thighs, stomach, breast, back, arms, and cheek taken out; punctures upon every sensitive part of the body, even to the sole of the feet and palms of the hand. All this does not approximate the whole truth.

In addition to the horror of the deaths of all these men there was the nightmare of their suffering, for many of these mutilations were performed on *living* men. Post Surgeon S. M. Horton said that not more than six were killed by gunfire. Hundreds of arrows, removed from the naked bodies, had obviously been shot into them after they were stripped.

36. "Union man" in this context has nothing to do with labor unions. Langford means he was loyal to the United States during the War of the Rebellion.

37. Thomas Dimsdale's *The Vigilantes of Montana* had been published by this time. Langford himself wrote *Vigilante Days and Ways*, published in 1890.

38. Wild onions had been an effective frontier remedy for scurvy for decades. In April of 1834, Prince Maximilian of Wied-Neuwied was close to death at Fort Clark on the upper Missouri River, extremely weak, with a high fever, one leg badly swollen. A Negro cook at the fort diagnosed scurvy and sent a bunch of Indian children out to gather wild onions. Prince Maximilian ate quantities of them, boiled, and felt better within a few hours.

The surgeon at a small one-company post on the Oregon Trail invented a successful anti-scorbutic that worked wonders with his sick men: "hands" of prickly pear cactus with the thorns scraped off were cut up and boiled with sugar. This mess tasted better when they called it applesauce.

39. This Max Littman was a remarkable man. He was a green emigrant from Germany, twenty-one years old, when he enlisted in March of 1866. He knew no English at all, but in seven months he made sergeant. He had a comrade write down the commands, and he memorized them. He did his fighting in the wagon-box corral flat on his belly behind a barrel half full of salt, with ox yokes piled on top. He said the men could not have held out another half hour, because of heat, exhaustion, and smoke.

40. Private Frederic Claus said that someone warned Lieutenant Jenness to get into one of the wagon boxes for shelter, but he replied that he knew how to fight Indians as well as anyone. Just then a fatal bullet took him in the head.

41. Steamboat travel was also expensive for cabin class. In 1866 cabin passengers paid $300 each. Mrs. Sanders did not mention the cost in 1867.

Bibliography

Alderson, W. W., "Gold Camp Tubers," *Montana, The Magazine of Western History*, vol. III, no. 4, Autumn, 1953.

Alter, J. Cecil, *Jim Bridger*. Norman: University of Oklahoma Press, 1962.

Atchison, William Emory, "Excerpts from the Personal Diary of the Late William Emory Atchison in 1864," mimeographed, published by J. E. Haynes and Charles H. Ramsdell, Yellowstone National Park Museum.

Athearn, Robert G., *Thomas Francis Meagher: An Irish Revolutionary in America*. Boulder: University of Colorado Press, 1949.

Bancroft, Hubert Howe, *History of Washington, Idaho and Montana*. San Francisco: The History Company, 1890.

Barsness, Larry, *Gold Camp*. New York: Hastings House, 1963.

Birney, Hoffman, *Vigilantes*. Philadelphia: The Penn Publishing Company, 1929.

Bozeman Courier, Bozeman, Montana, May 25, 1901: "The Mystery Cleared Up: The Remains of Thomas Cover Completely Identified. . . ."

Bratt, John, *Trails of Yesterday*. Lincoln: University Publishing Co., 1921.

Brier, Warren J., *The Frightful Punishment*. Missoula: The University of Montana Press, 1969.

Brosnan, Cornelius James, *History of the State of Idaho*. New York: Scribner's, 1926.

Brown, D. Alexander, *The Galvanized Yankees*. Urbana: University of Illinois Press, 1963.

Brown, Dee, *Fort Phil Kearny, An American Saga*. New York: G. P. Putnam's Sons, New York, 1962.

Brown, Jesse, "The Freighter in Early Days," *Annals of Wyoming*, vol. 19, no. 2, July, 1947.

Burgess, Perry, The Diary of, "From Illinois to Montana in 1866," Robert Athearn, ed., *Pacific Northwest Quarterly*, vol. 41, no. 1, January, 1950.

Burlingame, Merrill G., "John M. Bozeman, Montana Trailmarker," *Mississippi Valley Historical Review*, vol. XXVII, no. 4, March, 1941.

Burnett, F. G., "History of the Western Division of the Powder River Expedition," *Annals of Wyoming*, vol. 8, no. 3, January, 1932.

Byron, Elsa Spear, *Bozeman Trail Scrapbook*. Published by the author, Mills Co., Sheridan, Wyoming, 1967.

Carrington, Frances C., *Army Life on the Plains* (title page: "My Army Life and the Fort Phil. Kearney Massacre"). Philadelphia: J. B. Lippincott Company, 1910.

Carrington, Mrs. Margaret I., *Absaraka, Home of the Crows,* reprint ed. by Milo Milton Quaife. Chicago: The Lakeside Press, 1950.

Cavanagh, Michael, *Memoirs of Gen. Thomas Meagher.* Worcester, Mass.: The Messenger Press, 1892.

Chittenden, H. M., *History of Early Steamboat Navigation on the Missouri River.* New York: F. P. Harper, 1903.

Clark, Barzilla W., *Bonneville in the Making.* Published by the author, Idaho Falls, 1941.

Collister, Oscar, "Life of Oscar Collister, Wyoming Pioneer," as told to Mrs. Charles Ellis, *Annals of Wyoming,* vol. 7, no. 1, July, 1930, and no. 2, October, 1930.

Coutant, C. G., *History of Wyoming from the Earliest Known Discoveries.* Laramie: Chaplin, Spafford & Mathison, 1899.

Cox, Samuel S., *Three Decades of Federal Legislation.* Providence: J. A. and R. A. Reid, 1888.

Creigh, Thomas Alfred, Diary of, "From Nebraska City to Montana 1866," *Nebraska History,* vol. 29, no. 3, September, 1948.

Dailey, Benjamin, Diary July 26–September 9, 1866. Manuscript file, Montana State University, Bozeman.

David, Robert Beebe, *Finn Burnett, Frontiersman.* Glendale, California: The Arthur H. Clark Company, 1937.

Dickson, Arthur Jerome, ed., *Covered Wagon Days,* Journals of Albert Jerome Dickson. Cleveland: The Arthur H. Clark Company, 1929.

Dimsdale, Thos. J., *The Vigilantes of Montana,* Fourth Edition, ed. by A. J. Noyes. Helena: State Publishing Co. No date.

Drago, Harry Sinclair, *The Steamboaters.* New York: Dodd, Mead & Company, 1967.

Edgar, Henry, "Journal of Henry Edgar—1863," *Contributions to the Historical Society of Montana,* vol. 3, 1900.

Fletcher, Mrs. Ellen (Nellie), letters to relatives in Cuba, N.Y., April, 1866–1870. Manuscript file, Montana State University, Bozeman.

Fox, George W., "George W. Fox Diary," *Annals of Wyoming,* vol. 8, no. 3, January, 1932.

Ghent, W. J., *The Road to Oregon.* New York: Longmans, Green & Co., 1929.

Grant, Bruce, *American Forts Yesterday and Today.* New York: E. P. Dutton & Co., 1965.

Great Western Indian Fights, Potomac Corral of The Westerners. Lincoln: University of Nebraska Press, 1960.

Hafen, LeRoy R. and Ann W., *Powder River Campaigns and Sawyers Expedition of 1865.* Glendale, California: A. H. Clark Co., 1961.

Hafen, LeRoy R., and Francis Marion Young, *Fort Laramie and the Pageant of the West, 1834–1890.* Glendale, California: The Arthur H. Clark Company, 1938.

Hamilton, James McClellan, *From Wilderness to Statehood, A History of Montana.* Portland, Ore.: Binfords & Mort, 1957.

BIBLIOGRAPHY

Hanson, J. M., *Conquest of the Missouri*. Chicago: A. C. McClurg and Co., 1909.

Hebard, Grace Raymond, and E. A. Brininstool, *The Bozeman Trail*, 2 vols. Cleveland: The Arthur H. Clark Company, 1922.

Henry, Ralph C., *Our Land Montana*. Helena: State Publishing Co., 1962.

Herndon, Sarah Raymond, *Days on the Road: Crossing the Plains in 1865*. New York: Burr Printing House, 1902.

Hewitt, Edward Ringwood, *Those Were the Days*. New York: Duell, Sloan and Pearce, 1943.

Holman, A. M., "A Fifteen Day Fight on Tongue River, 1865," *Wyoming Annals*, vol. 10, no. 2, April, 1938.

—— and C. R. Marks, *Pioneering in the Northwest*. Sioux City: Deitch & Lamar Co., 1924.

Homsher, Lola M., ed., *South Pass, 1868, James Chisholm's Journal of the Wyoming Gold Rush*. Lincoln: University of Nebraska Press, 1960.

Hosmer, J. Allen, *A Trip to the States, By the Way of the Yellowstone and Missouri, Virginia City, Mon.* [sic] *Ter.* Beaverhead News Print, 1867. Reprint in Montana State University Sources of Northwest History, no. 17.

Howard, Helen Addison, *Northwest Trail Blazers*. Caldwell, Idaho: The Caxton Printers, Ltd., 1963.

Hyde, George E., *Life of George Bent*. Norman: University of Oklahoma Press, 1968.

——, *Red Cloud's Folk*. Norman: University of Oklahoma Press, 1937.

Irvin, George W. II, "Overland to Montana with John Bozeman," *The Holiday Miner*, Butte City, Jan. 1, 1888.

Jackson, W. Turrentine, *Wagon Roads West*. Berkeley: University of California Press, 1952.

Johnson, Dorothy M., "Flour Famine in Alder Gulch," *Montana, The Magazine of Western History*, Winter, 1957.

——, "Life with the Sanders Family in the 1870's," *Montana, The Magazine of Western History*, Winter, 1962.

——, "Slow Boat to Benton," *Montana, The Magazine of Western History*, Winter, 1961.

——, *Some Went West*. New York: Dodd, Mead & Company, 1965.

Kalispell Times, November 5, 1931, "Captain Townsend Was Victor in Battle of Powder River on Bozeman Trail in 1863."

Kirkaldie, Franklin Luther, The Letters of, May 1, 1864–March 30, 1869, manuscript file, Montana State University, Bozeman.

Kirkpatrick, James, "A Reminiscence of John Bozeman," Historical Reprints, Sources of Northwest History, no. 7, 1929, Montana State University, Missoula.

——, "First Organized Attempt to Open the Bozeman Cut-Off . . . ," *Powell County Post*, October 1, 1920.

Koch, Peter, "Bozeman, Gallatin Valley and Bozeman Pass," *Contributions to the Montana Historical Society*, vol. II, 1896.

Langford, Nathaniel Pitt, *Vigilante Days and Ways*. Missoula: Montana State University Press, 1957.

———, letter to J. W. Taylor, Commissioner Internal Revenue Service, mimeographed, May 20, 1866.

[Leeson, Michael A.], *History of Montana, 1739–1885*. Chicago: Warner, Beers & Co., 1885.

Leforge, Thomas H., *Memoirs of a White Crow Indian*, as told to Thomas B. Marquis. New York: The Century Co., 1928.

Lewis, William S., "The Camel Pack Trains in the Mining Camps of the West," *Washington Historical Quarterly*, vol. XIX, October, 1928.

Lockwood, James D., *Life and Adventures of a Drummer Boy*. Albany: John Skinner, 1893.

Lowe, Percival G., *Five Years a Dragoon ('49 to '54)*. Norman: University of Oklahoma Press, 1965 reprint.

McClure, A. K., *Three Thousand Miles Through the Rocky Mountains*. Philadelphia: J. B. Lippincott & Co., 1869.

Marcy, Randolph B., *The Prairie Traveler*. New York: Harper & Brothers, 1859. Reprinted by Filler and Ochs, no place stated.

Mattes, Merrill J., *Indians, Infants and Infantry*. Denver: The Old West Publishing Company, 1960.

Meredith, Mrs. Emily R., letter from, dated Bannock City, Idaho, April 30, 1863. Historical Reprints, Sources of Northwest History, no. 24, 1929, Montana State University, Missoula.

Miller, Joaquin, *An Illustrated History of the State of Montana*. Chicago: The Lewis Publishing Co., 1894.

Montana Almanac, 1959–60. Missoula: Montana State University Press, 1958.

Montana Post, Virginia City. Various issues.

Moore, Bishop John M., *The Long Road to Methodist Union*. Nashville: The Methodist Publishing House, 1943.

Murray, Robert A., *The Army on the Powder River*. Bellevue, Nebraska: The Old Army Press, 1969.

———, "The Hazen Inspections of 1866," *Montana, The Magazine of Western History*, vol. XVIII, no. 1, January, 1968.

———, *Military Posts in the Powder River Country of Wyoming, 1865–1894*. Lincoln: University of Nebraska Press, 1968.

Murphy, William, "The Forgotten Battalion," *Annals of Wyoming*, vol. 7, no. 2, October, 1930, and no. 3, January, 1931.

Nadeau, Remi, *Fort Laramie and the Sioux Indians*. Englewood Cliffs, New Jersey: Prentice-Hall, Inc., 1967.

Noyes, Alva J., *The Story of Ajax: Life in the Big Hole Basin*. New York: Buffalo-Head Press, New York, 1966, reprint.

Oberholtzer, Ellis Paxson, *A History of the United States Since the Civil War*, vol. 1, 1865–1868. New York: The Macmillan Company, 1917.

Official Records, War of the Rebellion, series I, vol. XLVIII, Part II. Washington, D.C.

BIBLIOGRAPHY

Olson, James C., *Red Cloud and the Sioux Problem*. Lincoln: University of Nebraska Press, 1965.

O'Neil, Elizabeth E., "A Story of Pioneer Days," manuscript file, Montana State University, Bozeman.

Ostrander, Alson B., *An Army Boy of the Sixties*. Chicago: World Book Company, 1924.

———, *The Bozeman Trail Forts Under General Philip St. George Cooke in 1866*. Privately published. Casper, Wyoming: Commercial Printing Co., 1932.

Ovitt, Mable, *Golden Treasure*. Caldwell: Caxton Printers, 1952.

Owen, John, *The Journals and Letters of Major John Owen, Pioneer of the Northwest, 1850–1871*, ed. by Seymour Dunbar, 2 vols. New York: Edward Eberstadt, 1927.

Pace, Dick, *Golden Gulch*. Published by the author, Virginia City, Montana, 1962.

Pemberton, Judge W. Y., "Changing Name of Edgerton County," *The Missoulian*, Missoula, April 23, 1916.

Plassman, Martha Edgerton: "Biographical Sketch of Hon. Sidney Edgerton, First Territorial Governor," *Contributions to the Historical Society of Montana*, vol. 3, 1900.

Progressive Men of the State of Montana [no author]. Chicago: A. W. Bowen & Co., 1901.

Rickey, Don Jr., *Forty Miles a Day on Beans and Hay*. Norman: University of Oklahoma Press, 1963.

Rolle, Andrew F., *The Road to Virginia City*. Norman: University of Oklahoma Press, 1960.

Ronan, Margaret, "Memoirs of a Frontierswoman [Mollie Sheehan]," unpublished master's thesis, University of Montana, Missoula, 1932.

Ronan, Peter, "Discovery of Alder Gulch," *Contributions to the Historical Society of Montana*, vol. 3, 1900.

Root, Frank A., and William Elsey Connelley, *The Overland Stage to California*. Topeka: published by the authors, 1901. Reprinted by Long's College Book Co., Columbus, Ohio: 1950.

Ryan, William, "The Bozeman Trail to Virginia City," *Annals of Wyoming*, vol. 19, no. 2, July, 1947.

Sanders, Harriet Peck Fenn, manuscript journals in the private collection of William Bertsche, Jr., Great Falls, Montana.

Sanders, James U., manuscript journals in the private collection of William Bertsche, Jr., Great Falls, Montana.

Sanders, Wilbur Edgerton, "Montana—Organization, Name and Naming," *Contributions to the Historical Society of Montana*, vol. 7, 1910.

Schaefer, Jack, *Heroes Without Glory*. Boston: Houghton Mifflin Company, 1965.

Spear, Elsa, *Fort Phil Kearny, Dakota Territory, 1866–1868*. Published by the author. Sheridan, Wyoming: Quick Printing Co., 1939.

Sprague, Marshall, *A Gallery of Dudes*. Boston: Brown and Company, 1966.

Stanley, E. J., *Life of L. B. Stateler*. Nashville: Publishing House of the M. E. Church, South, 1916.

Stanley, Henry N., *My Early Travels and Adventures in America and Asia*, vol. I. New York: Charles Scribner's Sons, 1895.

Stewart, Edgar I., *Custer's Luck*. Norman: University of Oklahoma Press, 1955.

Stone, Arthur L., *Following Old Trails*. Missoula: M. J. Elrod, 1913.

Story, Nelson, letter dated August 25, 1920, to the University of Wyoming; in the Grace Raymond Hebard Collection.

Stout, Tom, *Montana, Its Story and Biography*. Chicago: The American Historical Society, 1921.

Stuart, Granville, *Forty Years on the Frontier*, ed. by Paul C. Phillips, 2 vols. in one. Glendale, California: The Arthur H. Clark Company, 1957.

——, "A Memoir of the Life of James Stuart," *Contributions to the Historical Society of Montana*, vol. 1, 1876.

——, "Montana As It Is," Historical Reprints, Sources of Northwest History, no. 16, 1929, Montana State University, Missoula.

Stuart, James, "The Yellowstone Expedition of 1863," *Contributions to the Historical Society of Montana*, vol. 1, 1876.

Switzer, M. A., "Reminiscences of a Trip Over the Bozeman Trail in 1865," manuscript file, Montana State University, Bozeman.

Thane, James L., Jr., "Thomas Francis Meagher: 'The Acting One,'" unpublished master's thesis, University of Montana, Missoula, 1967.

Toponce, Alexander, *Life and Adventures of Alexander Toponce*. Ogden, Utah: published by Katie Toponce, 1923.

Vaughn, J. W., *Indian Fights: New Facts on Seven Encounters*. Norman: University of Oklahoma Press, 1966.

Wagon Train Report, Month of June, 1868, through July 17; Post Hqs. Records, Fort Phil Kearny, Wyoming, from Provost Record Book; National Archives Record Group 393.

Walker, Henry Pickering, *The Wagonmasters*. Norman: University of Oklahoma Press, 1966.

Walker, Tacetta B., *Stories of Early Days in Wyoming*. Casper, Wyoming: Prairie Publishing Company, 1936.

Ware, Captain Eugene F., *The Indian War of 1864*. Lincoln: University of Nebraska Press, 1960.

Weaver, David B., "Captain Townsend's Battle on the Powder River," *Contributions to the Historical Society of Montana*, vol. 8, 1917.

——, "Early Days in Emigrant Gulch," *Contributions to the Historical Society of Montana*, vol. 7, 1910.

Weisel, George F., ed., *Men and Trade on the Northwest Frontier*, Montana State University Studies, vol. 2, Montana State University Press, 1955.

Wellman, Paul I., *Death on Horseback: Seventy Years of War for the American West*. Philadelphia: J. B. Lippincott Company, 1947.

White, Helen McCann, ed., *Ho! for the Gold Fields: Northern Overland Wagon Trains of the 1860's*. St. Paul: Minnesota Historical Society, 1966.

BIBLIOGRAPHY

White, Thomas Edward, "Cornelius Hedges: Uncommon Hero of the Common Life," unpublished master's thesis, Montana State College, Bozeman, 1963.

Wolle, Muriel V. S., *Montana Pay Dirt*. Denver: Sage Books, 1963.

Word, Samuel, "Diary of Colonel Samuel Word," *Contributions to the Historical Society of Montana*, vol. 8, 1917.

Young, Will H., "Journals of Travel of Will H. Young, 1865," *Annals of Wyoming*, vol. 7, no. 2, October, 1930.

Index

INDEX

INDEX

INDEX

About the Author

DOROTHY M. JOHNSON *began to write her first story at age six, but after a couple of sentences retired for some years in order to learn spelling and other aspects of the craft. Two years after graduation from the University of Montana, where she wrote for the campus literary magazine,* Frontier, *she sold a Western story to* The Saturday Evening Post. Time *once remarked that she "looks as if she may have just talked to the ladies at the opening of a church bazaar" but that she "writes with authentic familiarity about the men who opened the American West.... Her characters are primitive and romantic, as they probably were in real life, and she has a surprising quality of humor." In addition to dozens of magazine stories and articles, Miss Johnson is also the author of* The Hanging Tree *and a biography of* Sitting Bull.